Discover
Costa Rica

Experience the best of Costa Rica

This edition written and researched by

Wendy Yanagihara,
Gregor Clark, Mara Vorhees

Contents

Contents

Discover Costa Rica

In Focus

Survival Guide

This is Costa Rica

If you have long sought a piece of tropical paradise, take a deep breath: you've found it. The perfect balance of adrenaline-charged adventure destination and unplugged tropical getaway, Costa Rica is a land of dormant volcanoes, desolate beaches and dense jungle. The canopies rustle with riotous troupes of white-faced monkeys, hillsides echo with the squawk of scarlet macaws and the trees along the trail are overburdened with the day's lunch of ripe star fruit. It might seem like a wondrous tropical fantasy land, but this is Costa Rica.

Adventure is as abundant as the tropical fruit here.
Learn to surf in warm water and hike above the clouds; rush down white-water rivers and then hoist yourself up to a zip line to sail over jungle canopies. Sound good? That's only the beginning. Costa Rica is the preeminent eco- and adventure-tourism capital of Central America.

Costa Rica walks the walk when it comes to being green.
Its government has managed to protect more than 25% of this rich land as national conservation zones. With an estimated 5% of the planet's biodiversity in a compact landmass the size of West Virginia, this verdant, vibrant landscape naturally attracts birders, hikers, and eco-conscious seekers of all types. Even visitors without preexisting interest in avian life or hiking can't help but be enticed by the promise of glimpsing an iridescent-green quetzal, or finding that local waterfall and swimming hole at the end of a trail.

Then there are the people.
Costa Ricans, or Ticos as they call themselves, are largely proud of their little slice of paradise. They welcome guests into the easygoing rhythms of *pura vida* – the pure life – that is as much a catchy motto as it is an enduring mantra.

> ❝
> It might seem like a wondrous tropical fantasy land, but this is Costa Rica.
> ❞

Green thorntail
GLENN BARTLEY/GETTY IMAGES ©

Costa Rica

NICARAGUA

Lago de Nicaragua

Sapoá
Peñas Blancas
San Carlos
La Cruz
Santa Cecilia
Los Chiles
San José
Upala
Caño Negro
Río Frío
Llanura de Guatusos
Río San Juan

Parque Nacional Santa Rosa
21

Cordillera de Guanacaste
Volcán Rincón de la Vieja (1895m)
Río Liberia
Volcán Santa María (1916m)
San Rafael de Guatuso
Nuevo Arenal
Río Arenal
Muelle de San Carlos
Pital
Puerto Viejo de Sarapiquí
15
Boca Tapada
Llanura de San Carlos
Río San Carlos
Río Toro

Golfo de Papagayo

El Coco
LIBERIA
Bagaces
Laguna de Arenal
Tilarán
Volcán La Fortuna (1633m) Arenal
2
Jabillos
San Miguel

Parque Nacional Marino Las Baulas De Guanacaste
18
Huacas
Filadelfia
Bebedero
Cañas
Santa Elena
Monteverde
Cordillera de Tilarán
1
Ciudad Quesada (San Carlos)
Zarcero
Parque Nacional Volcán Poás
Volcán Poás (2704m)
Cordillera Central
13

Tamarindo
11
Playa Tamarindo
Santa Cruz
Puerto Humo
Corralillo
Nicoya
Puente La Amistad
16
Miramar
San Ramón
ALAJUELA
HEREDIA
8
SAN JOSÉ

Paraíso
Río Tempisque
Interamericana
Río Barranca
Esparza
San Mateo
Ciudad Colón
San Ignacio de Acosta
San Marcos de Tarrazú

Nosara
23
Hojancha
Carmona
Ferry
PUNTARENAS
Santiago de Puriscal
Río Tárcoles

Sámara
19
Bejuco
Playa Naranjo
Paquera
Golfo de Nicoya
Parque Nacional Carara
25
Valle de Parrita

Península de Nicoya

Tambor
Playa Santa Teresa
Mal País
9
Montezuma
4
Jacó
Parrita

Quepos
3
Savegre
Parque Nacional Manuel Antonio

Isla del Coco (300km; See inset)

PACIFIC OCEAN

85°W
86°W
84°W
11°N
10°N
9°N

Inset

87°04'W
87°02'W
5°34'N
5°32'N
5°30'N

0 — 4 km
0 — 2 miles

Isla del Coco
Cerro Iglesias (634m)

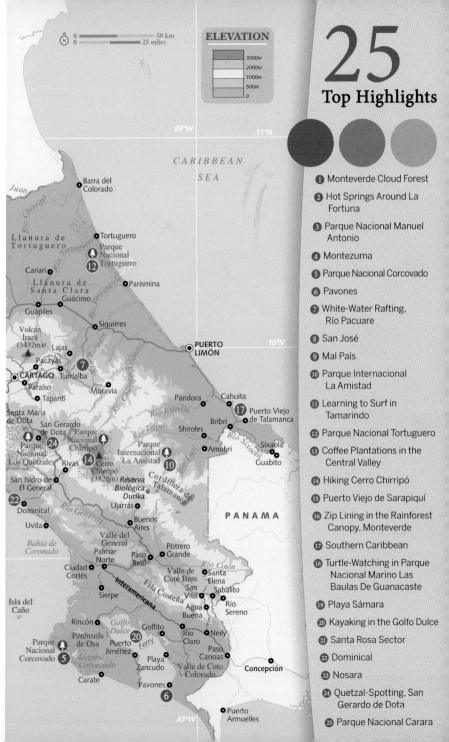

ELEVATION

3000m
2000m
1000m
500m
0

25
Top Highlights

25 Costa Rica's Top Highlights

Monteverde Cloud Forest

A pristine expanse of virginal forest, Monteverde Cloud Forest (p180) owes much of its impressive natural beauty to Quaker expats, who left the US in the 1950s to protest the Korean War and helped foster conservationist principles with Ticos of the region. But as fascinating as the history is, the real romance of Monteverde is in nature itself: a mysterious Neverland dripping with mist, dangling with mossy vines, sprouting with ferns and bromeliads, gushing with creeks and blooming with life.

2

Hot Springs Around La Fortuna

Though the molten night views of Volcán Arenal are no more, the area's tectonic activity continues to keep the hot springs hot around the base of this slumbering giant. Around La Fortuna, you are a short drive away from several hot springs, some of which are free and can be found by asking any local. Others are a bit more luxurious – dip your toes into the romantic Eco-Termales (p152), for starters.

Parque Nacional Manuel Antonio

Although droves of visitors pack Parque Nacional Manuel Antonio (p261) – the country's most popular (and smallest) national park – it remains an absolute gem. Capuchin monkeys scurry across its idyllic beaches, brown pelicans dive-bomb its clear waters and sloths watch over its accessible trails. It's a perfect place to introduce youngsters to the wonders of the rainforest. There's not much by way of privacy, but it's so lovely that you won't mind sharing.

Three-toed sloth at Parque Nacional Manuel Antonio

The Best...
Idyllic Sunsets

MANUEL ANTONIO
Perched high on a hilltop, the restaurants en route to Manuel Antonio offer an ideal sundowner. (p261)

TORTUGUERO VILLAGE
Sip an ice-cold *cerveza* (beer) and nod along to reggae beats. (p116)

PLAYA TAMARINDO
Sail on the deep-blue Pacific and watch the sun dip below the jagged coastline. (p218)

CERRO CHIRRIPÓ
Bundle up and take in the wild, wind-swept panoramic views from the Crestones Base Lodge atop Costa Rica's highest point. (p304)

The Best...
National Parks

PARQUE NACIONAL CORCOVADO
An untamed rainforest adventure and loads of wildlife await brave souls who make the trek. (p294)

MONTEVERDE CLOUD FOREST
Cloud forests straddle both sides of the Continental Divide. (p180)

PARQUE NACIONAL MANUEL ANTONIO
An excellent day at the beach with monkeys and easy hiking for the whole family. (p261)

PARQUE NACIONAL LOS QUETZALES
A cool mountain home to the elusive bird of paradise. (p308)

PARQUE NACIONAL TORTUGUERO
Sea turtles and caimans complement the Caribbean environs. (p123)

Montezuma

4

If you enjoy rubbing shoulders with neo-Rastas and yoga freaks or have always wanted to spin fire, study Spanish or lounge on sugar-white coves, find your way to Montezuma (p230). Strolling this intoxicating town and rugged coastline, you're never far from the rhythm of the sea. From here you'll have easy access to the famed Cabo Blanco reserve and can take the tremendous hike to a triple-tiered waterfall. And when your stomach growls, the town has some of the best restaurants in the country.

Parque Nacional Corcovado

5

Muddy, muggy and intense, the vast, largely untouched rainforest of Parque Nacional Corcovado (p294) is anything but a walk in the park. Here, travelers with a flexible agenda and a sturdy pair of boots thrust themselves into the unknown and come out the other side with the story of a lifetime. You'll find the country's best wildlife-watching and the most desolate beaches along Corcovado's seldom-trodden trails.

Pavones

Pavones (p299) is the end of the road for surfers on the Pacific trail, a lovely little place in the remote south-west corner of the country. Those willing to make the trip while away their visit swaying on hammocks and taking on one of the longest left-hand surf breaks in the world. Add to the equation a suite of clean, basic *cabinas*, a number of rushing streams and hills that are dotted with wild tropical fruit trees, and it's a difficult place to leave.

White-Water Rafting, Río Pacuare

So many rivers, so little time. But the dedicated adrenaline junkie could easily cover some heart-pounding river miles in the span of a few days in this compact country. For those without the drive to do them all, try Pacuare or Sarapiquí. Stretches of smooth water allow rafters to take in the luscious jungle scenery surrounding these river gorges. (p100)

San José

The heart of Tico culture and identity lives in San José (p60). While not the most attractive capital in Central America, it does have some graceful neoclassical and Spanish-colonial architecture, leafy neighborhoods, museums housing pre-Columbian jade and gold, nightlife that goes on until dawn and some of the most sophisticated restaurants in the country. Street art adds unexpected pops of color and public discourse to the cityscape. Metropolitan Cathedral in San José

The Best...
Adrenaline Rushes

LA FORTUNA
Costa Rica's center for adventure sports, from bungee jumping to zip lining. (p153)

TURRIALBA
Home to the fiercest white water that Costa Rica has on tap. (p100)

PARQUE NACIONAL CORCOVADO
Ford rivers en route to the Sirena Ranger Station to seek a sighting of the elusive jaguar. (p294)

LA VIRGEN
Head to this northern destination if kayaking floats your boat. (p197)

NOSARA
Fly along on the world's longest zip-line canopy tour. (p224)

Mal País

In the rugged little surf town of Mal País (p235), the sea is alive with marine wildlife and the waves are near-ideal shape, color and temperature. The hills are lush and the coastline long – both dotted with stylish boutique sleeps. And though the road in is still rutted, ending in an authentic Tico fishing hamlet where you can feel sort of like a castaway, you can still score a dinner worthy of royalty.

The Best...
Tropical Beaches

MONTEZUMA
Sprawl out on white sand in a hidden cove to take in sunset on the Nicoya Peninsula. (p230)

MARINO BALLENA
Scan for whales on your own deserted piece of paradise. (p270)

MANZANILLO
Swaying palms and golden sand make this the Caribbean coast's most scenic stretch of water. (p138)

MAL PAÍS
Backed by lush tropical jungle, raging surf crashes in each direction. (p235)

PLAYA CONCHAL
Crushed shells and turquoise water. (p215)

10 Parque Internacional La Amistad

Ready to rough it? Try a visit to the edge of the 'friendship' park (p312), an enormous sprawl of protected land shared by Costa Rica and Panama. Thoroughly off the beaten path, this is where the most adventurous travelers go to visit indigenous mountain villages and find utter solitude. It's no simple stroll (most trips here are multiday guided expeditions) but the rewards are on the same colossal scale as the park itself.

Learning to Surf in Tamarindo

While seasoned surfers head to the Caribbean's Salsa Brava or the legendarily long left-hand break of Pavones, novices and total newbies can also find beginner-friendly beach breaks and plenty of surfing instructors elsewhere in Costa Rica. One of the most accessible places to learn is in the Nicoya Peninsula's town of Tamarindo (p218), which is also loaded with good restaurants and lively nightlife.

11

Parque Nacional Tortuguero

Canoeing the canals of Parque Nacional Tortuguero (p123) is a boat-borne safari, where thick jungle meets the water and you can get up close with shy caimans, herons, monkeys and sloths. In the right season, under cover of darkness, watch the awesome, millennia-old ritual of turtles building nests and laying their eggs on the black-sand beaches. Sandwiched between extravagantly green wetlands and the wild Caribbean Sea, this is among the premier places in Costa Rica to watch wildlife.

Coffee Plantations in the Central Valley

Take a country drive on the scenic, curvy Central Valley back roads, where the hillsides are a patchwork of varied agriculture and coffee shrubbery. If you're curious about that magical brew, tour one of the coffee plantations and learn about how Costa Rica's golden bean goes from plant to cup. One of the best places for a tour is Café Britt Finca (p95) in Barva.

Hiking Cerro Chirripó

The view from the rugged peak of Cerro Chirripó (p304), Costa Rica's highest summit – of windswept rocks and icy lakes – may not resemble the Costa Rica of the postcards, but the two-day hike above the clouds is one of the country's most satisfying excursions. A pre-dawn expedition rewards hardy hikers with a chance to catch the fiery sunrise and a panoramic view of both the Caribbean and the Pacific from 3820m above. Parque Nacional Chirripó

The Best...
Bird- & Wildlife-Watching

WILSON BOTANICAL GARDEN
Very popular among birdwatchers, who keep an eye out for some rare high-altitude species. (p310)

PARQUE NACIONAL CORCOVADO
The elusive jaguar makes its home here, but you are more likely to see scarlet macaws. (p294)

PARQUE NACIONAL LOS QUETZALES
This park is named for its banner attraction, the Resplendent Quetzal. (p308)

TORTUGUERO
Birds, turtles, monkeys, sloths and much more are all common at this wildlife-rich park. (p123)

The Best...
Off the Beaten Path Spots

ZANCUDO
Find excellent surf, quaint bungalows and a bit of tranquility in the far south. (p299)

PARQUE NACIONAL VOLCÁN TENORIO
Ample hiking trails, a bright-blue waterfall and little more than a few scattered footprints. (p192)

RESERVA INDÍGENA BORUCA
Difficult to access, but worth the trip if you want insight into the country's pre-Columbian past. (p309)

PUNTA MONA
Extremely remote, but the lodge is home to an amazing ongoing experiment in sustainable living. (p140)

Puerto Viejo de Sarapiquí

Sarapiquí rose to fame as a principal port in the nefarious old days of United Fruit dominance, before it meandered into agricultural anonymity, only to be reborn as a paddler's mecca thanks to the frothing serpentine mocha magic of its namesake river. These days it's still a paddling paradise, and it's also dotted with fantastic ecolodges and private forest preserves that will educate you about pre-Columbian life, get you into that steaming, looming, muddy jungle and introduce you to local wildlife up close. (p199) Above right: Aracari perched on a bunch of bananas; Left: Río Sarapiquí

(ABOVE) MLORENZPHOTOGRAPHY/GETTY IMAGES ©; (LEFT) JOHN COLETTI/GETTY IMAGES ©

Zip Lining in the Rainforest Canopy, Monteverde

The wild-eyed happiness of a canopy tour is self-evident. Few things are more joyful than clipping into a high-speed cable, laced above and through the seething jungle canopy. This is where kids become little daredevils and adults become kids. Invented in Monteverde (p173), zip-lining outfits quickly multiplied, cropping up in all corners of Costa Rica.

16

Southern Caribbean

17

By day, lounge in a hammock, cruise by bike to snorkel off uncrowded beaches, hike to waterfall-fed pools and visit the remote indigenous territories of the Bribrí and Kèköldi. By night, dip into zesty Caribbean cooking and sway to reggaetón at open-air bars cooled by ocean breezes. Puerto Viejo de Talamanca (p134), an outpost of this unique mix of Afro-Caribbean, Tico and indigenous culture, is the perfect, laid-back home base for such adventures. Beachside shop in Puerto Viejo de Talamanca

Turtle-Watching in Parque Nacional Marino Las Baulas De Guanacaste

World-class parks, long-standing dedication to environmental protection and mind-boggling biodiversity enable the country to harbor scores of rare and endangered species. And no matter where you travel, the branches overhead are alive with sloths, monkeys and toucans. But one of Costa Rica's most magical wildlife experiences is watching nesting sea turtles. Parque Nacional Marino Las Baulas De Guanacaste (p216) is the best place to see nesting leatherbacks, the world's largest sea turtles.

The Best...
Ecolodges

LUNA LODGE
Remote and luxurious, this far-flung ecolodge on the Osa borders Parque Nacional Corcovado. (p294)

CELESTE MOUNTAIN LODGE
Sustainable practices meets contemporary style, in the shadow of Volcán Tenorio. (p192)

SELVA VERDE LODGE
This former *finca* (farm) is now an elegant lodge that protects more than 500 acres of rainforest. (p199)

ARENAS DEL MAR
This architectural stunner near Manuel Antonio has private Jacuzzis overlooking the coast. (p259)

LAPA RÍOS
A living classroom where sustainability meets eco-luxury. (p294)

Playa Sámara

Some expat residents call Playa Sámara (p227) the black hole of happiness, which has something to do with that crescent of sand spanning two rocky headlands, the opportunity to learn to surf, stand-up paddle, surf cast or fly above migrating whales in an ultra-light, and the plethora of nearby all-natural beaches and coves. All of it is easy to access on foot or via public transportation, which is why it's becoming so popular with families who enjoy Sámara's palpable ease and tranquility.

JONATHAN GREGSON/LONELY PLANET ©

The Best...
Chill-Out Spots

SAN GERARDO DE DOTA
Fresh mountain air, trout fishing and chilly nights complement excellent high-altitude bird-watching. (p306)

CAHUITA
A low-key beach destination which moves to its own relaxed Caribbean rhythm. (p127)

NOSARA
A magical collection of remote wilderness, beaches and raging surf. (p223)

UVITA
This quiet community at the edge of a quiet marine park is a perfect place to unplug. (p269)

20 Kayaking in the Golfo Dulce

Getting out in Golfo Dulce (p295) (the 'sweet gulf') brings paddlers in contact with the abundant marine life in the bay – here dolphins play, whales breach and sparkling schools of tropical fish whiz by. Leaving the open water and navigating the maze of mangrove channels is another world completely, offering a chance to glide silently past herons, crested caracaras, snakes and sloths.

ZUMA/ALAMY ©

Santa Rosa Sector

Among the oldest and largest protected areas in Costa Rica, the sprawling 386-sq-km Área de Conservación Guanacaste protects the largest remaining stand of tropical dry forest in Central America. Almost all the worthy diversions can be found in a vast area known as the Santa Rosa Sector (p193). Biologists and naturalists come for its stunning biological diversity, and way-out hiking trails.

Green-barred woodpecker, Parque Nacional Santa Rosa

Dominical

A permanently chilled-out beach town where time slows to a crawl, Dominical (p265) has a way of forestalling your future plans. But when the surf is crashing and the sun is blazing, few travelers seem to really care. This is an excellent place to learn how to surf, hang out with international surf bums and enjoy some locally caught seafood. Bonus: its location is perfect for visiting a handful of the country's national parks.

Nosara

Nosara (p223) is a cocktail of international surf culture, jungled microclimes and yoga bliss, where three stunning beaches are stitched together by a network of swerving, rutted earth roads that meander over coastal hills. Visitors can stay in the alluring surf enclave of Playa Guiones – where there are some fabulous restaurants and a drop-dead gorgeous beach – or in Playa Pelada, which is as romantic as it is rugged and removed. Playa Pelada

The Best...
Surf Breaks

DOMINICAL
The central Pacific's hub for surfers offers excellent lessons by day and party scene by night. (p265)

PLAYAS AVELLANAS & NEGRA
This is home to the on-screen surf epic, *Endless Summer II*. (p221)

PAVONES
This ramshackle slice of paradise boasts one of the world's longest left-hand breaks. (p299)

PUERTO VIEJO DE TALAMANCA
Centered on Salsa Brava, one of the country's gnarliest breaks. (p134)

MAL PAÍS & SANTA TERESA
Huge swaths of prime beachfront are shaped by a variety of breaks. (p235)

Quetzal-Spotting, San Gerardo de Dota

Once considered divine by pre-Columbian cultures of Central America, the resplendent quetzal was sought after for its long, iridescent-green tail feathers, which adorned the headdresses of royalty. This striking, jewel-toned bird remains a coveted find in modern times, but now as a bucket-list sighting for bird-watchers. Quetzals are commonly sighted in San Gerardo de Dota (p306), especially during its breeding season in April and May.

The Best...
Family-Friendly Spots

MONTEVERDE
A host of outdoor activities and fun will keep kids entertained in the cloud forest. (p168)

RÍO SARAPIQUÍ
Home to the best Class I and Class II floats that are good for kids and wildlife-watching. (p197)

PARQUE NACIONAL MANUEL ANTONIO
Highly accessible, kid-friendly trails full of a wondrous assortment of animals. (p261)

JACÓ
A kid's paradise: body boarding, canopy tours, horseback riding, and family-friendly hotels with pools. (p250)

GLENN BARTLEY/GETTY IMAGES ©

25

Parque Nacional Carara

Carara (p250) is where two of Costa Rica's most wildlife-rich climate zones collide in an explosion of color, sound and life, and one of the best places in the country outside of the remote Península de Osa to spot the country's iconic macaws. The best part is that this park requires minimal effort: just off the Interamericana, Carara's trail heads are just a few steps from the parking lot and easy for all abilities. Scarlet macaws

Costa Rica's
Top Itineraries

San José to Monteverde
5 DAYS
Northern Highlights

This classic route will take you through the capital and into the mountains, passing bubbling volcanoes, hot springs and tranquil cloud forests.

NICARAGUA

CARIBBEAN SEA

LA FORTUNA & VOLCÁN ARENAL

MONTEVERDE & SANTA ELENA ❸ ❷

❶ SAN JOSÉ

PACIFIC OCEAN

❶ San José (p60)

Costa Rica's sprawling capital can be a shock to the senses, but there is plenty to do here. Start with a trip to the bustling Mercado Central where you can bargain-hunt for anything from coffee to mangoes. If you need respite from the crowds and heat, head to the Museo de Jade to admire centuries-old pre-Columbian jade carvings. Architecture and culture buffs shouldn't miss the Teatro Nacional, a stunning colonial construction that is the heart of San José's theater scene.

SAN JOSÉ ➲ LA FORTUNA
🚗 **3.5 hours** Along the Interamericana, via Alajuela. 🚌 **Four hours** Buses leave three times daily, via San Ramón.

❷ La Fortuna & Volcán Arenal (p152)

On the flanks of Volcán Arenal, tourist-friendly La Fortuna is a world away from the hustle and bustle of San José. Your first destination is the brooding Volcán Arenal. Ample daylight allows long hikes through the surrounding forests, while at night you can enjoy a brilliant star display. If the weather isn't cooperating, wait it out in one of the town's luxurious hot springs, which are an attractive enough draw on their own.

LA FORTUNA ➲ MONTEVERDE
🚌 **Six to eight hours** via Tilarán. 🛥 **Three hours** via boat across Laguna de Arenal, followed by a shuttle to Santa Elena.

❸ Monteverde & Santa Elena (p168)

The peaceful, artsy town of Santa Elena comprises cute cafes, eclectic restaurants, specialized wildlife museums, interesting art galleries and delicious ice cream. But the main attraction is Reserva Biológica Bosque Nuboso Monteverde, where you can search for the elusive quetzal and other beautiful birds. The nearby Reserva Santa Elena and the Children's Eternal Rainforest offer misty cloud-forest experiences.

Monteverde Cloud Forest (p168)
JERRY DRIENDL/GETTY IMAGES ©

5 DAYS

Volcán Irazú to Volcán Poás
The Mystical Central Valley

This circuit is about sleeping volcanoes, strong coffee and the spiritual core of the country. Since most tourists head to the beaches, you'll enjoy markets and squares without the crowds.

PARQUE NACIONAL VOLCÁN POÁS
5
PARQUE NACIONAL VOLCÁN IRAZÚ
1
San José
2 TURRIALBA
CARTAGO
4
3 VALLE DE OROSI

PACIFIC OCEAN

① Parque Nacional Volcán Irazú (p97)

This trip begins with the biggest and baddest volcano in Costa Rica, Irazú, whose indigenous name aptly translates to 'thunder-point.' Climb to its beautifully barren volcanic landscape early, on a clear day – you'll spy the waters of the Pacific and the Caribbean on the distant horizons.

VOLCÁN IRAZÚ ➲ TURRIALBA

🚗 **1.5 hours** Much of the trip is navigated along twisting mountain roads. Follow Rte 230 to Rte 10. 🚌 **6.5 hours** via Cartago.

② Turrialba (p99)

Just down the mountain is Turrialba, an excellent hub for two very different destinations. First is Monumento Nacional Arqueológico Guayabo, the country's only significant archaeological site, where visitors marvel at petroglyphs and a system of aqueducts. Then, raft the white water of the Río Pacuare, one of the country's best white-water runs, in one of Central America's most breathtaking river gorges.

TURRIALBA ➲ VALLE DE OROSI

🚗 **One hour** Retrace Rte 10 east and go south on Rte 224. 🚌 **Two hours** via Cartago.

③ Valle de Orosi (p97)

Swing south into the heart of the Valle de Orosi, where pastoral villages dot the endless rolling hills. The caffeinated 60km loop through terraced hills harbor a perfect combination of the country's two most notable economic treasures: tourism and coffee. To see the valley's untamed side, navigate to Parque Nacional Tapantí-Macizo Cerro de la Muerte, a wild and rugged piece of country run through with hundreds of rivers and aflutter with rare high-altitude birds.

VALLE DE OROSI ➲ CARTAGO

🚗 **30 minutes** Travel Rte 224 to Rte 10 west to Cartago city center. 🚌 **40 minutes**.

④ Cartago (p95)

Stretch your legs with a stroll around the country's grandest colonial temple, the Basílica de Nuestra Señora de Los Ángeles, in Cartago, a brilliantly white beacon among the utilitarian concrete structures of this otherwise unexciting city.

CARTAGO ➲ VOLCÁN POÁS

🚗 **1.5 hours** Follow the Interamericana to Alajuela, then north to Rte 120. 🚌 **2.5 hours**, departing every 15 minutes for San José, then from San José via Alajuela at 8:30am.

⑤ Parque Nacional Volcán Poás (p88)

Bookend this itinerary with a morning visit to Volcán Poás, another easily accessed set of mist-shrouded crater lakes in the Central Highlands.

Volcán Poás (p88)

KRYSSIA CAMPOS/GETTY IMAGES ©

Tamarindo to Parque Nacional Corcovado
Pacific Explorer

Take in the Península de Nicoya for Costa Rica's banner attractions, then cruise south along the central Pacific coast for beach towns, and scenic national parks where wilderness and wildlife abound.

NICARAGUA

CARIBBEAN SEA

TAMARINDO ①

Puntarenas
Paquera

MAL PAÍS ②

QUEPOS & ③
MANUEL ANTONIO ④

DOMINICAL

PANAMA

PARQUE NACIONAL
CORCOVADO ⑥ ⑤ PUERTO JIMÉNEZ

PACIFIC
OCEAN

1 Tamarindo (p218)

Kick things off with a party in Tamarindo, Nicoya's famous tourist draw, packed with resorts, sunny beaches, sophisticated dining and thumping club scene. The waves of Playa Grande are tame, but if you're in Costa Rica for a surf safari they're a perfect warm-up.

TAMARINDO ➡ MAL PAÍS

🚗 **Five hours** Follow the Pacific shore on Rte 160. 🚌 **10 to 12 hours**, via Puntarenas with ferry connection.

2 Mal País (p235)

With wildlife, bigger waves, untouched nature and top restaurants, Mal País is worth every minute of the long journey. Limber up in the morning with yoga, catch some surf in the afternoon and tuck into sophisticated plates of Latin American fusion cuisine at night. The 'Bad Country' is not so bad at all.

MAL PAÍS ➡ QUEPOS

🚗 **Four hours** Drive up the coast to get the car ferry at Paquera, then follow coastal highways. 🚌 ⛴ **Four to five hours** Includes a transfer after the Paquera–Puntarenas ferry.

3 Quepos & Manuel Antonio (p254)

Continuing south along the Pacific coast, the road leads to Quepos, a tiny Tico town bordering the chart-topping Parque Nacional Manuel Antonio. Here, monkeys descend from the treetops to frolic (and filch picnic goodies) along the palm-fringed coastline.

QUEPOS ➡ DOMINICAL

🚗 **45 minutes** Travel along Hwy 34, the Costañera Sur. 🚌 **Two to three hours**.

4 Dominical (p265)

If you haven't had enough of the postcard-perfect Pacific coast, head south to Dominical to catch more waves, soak up more rays and delay your return home. You may get stuck in this terminally chilled-out beach town where time passes to the rhythm of the crashing surf.

DOMINICAL ➡ PUERTO JIMÉNEZ

🚗 **2.5 hours** Travel along Hwy 34, the Costañera Sur, which joins the Interamericana (Hwy 2) at Palmar Norte. Then take Rte 245. 🚌 **Six hours** Via San Isidro or Palmar Norte.

5 Puerto Jiménez (p289)

Further down the peninsula is the official gateway to Corcovado, Puerto Jiménez. Kayak around the mangroves or take in the charm of this tiny town as you stock up on supplies for the big adventure ahead.

PUERTO JIMÉNEZ ➡ PARQUE NACIONAL CORCOVADO

🚗 **2.5 hours** 4WD essential. 🚌 **Three hours** *Colectivos* (shared truck taxis) leave twice daily.

6 Parque Nacional Corcovado (p294)

The undisputed highlight of the Península de Osa is Parque Nacional Corcovado, one of the country's top wildlife-watching spots. Day hikes are spectacular, but it's worth spending a few days forging deeper into the park – guides enhance the experience a hundredfold.

Mal País (p235)

10 DAYS

Turrialba to Tortuguero
Mountain White Water & Caribbean Escape

Spanish gives way to English, and Latin beats change to Caribbean vibes as you explore the 'other Costa Rica'. Some of the more remote coastal villages are only accessible by boat.

NICARAGUA

CARIBBEAN SEA

5 TORTUGUERO

Moín

1 TURRIALBA

CAHUITA **2**
PUERTO VIEJO DE TALAMANCA **3** **4**
MANZANILLO

PACIFIC OCEAN

PANAMA

① Turrialba (p99)

Before you float in the turquoise waters of the Caribbean, why not squeal gleefully down Central America's best white water? Adventurers go crazy for the super-scenic, jungle-lined rapids of the Río Pacuare.

TURRIALBA ➡ CAHUITA

🚗 **2.5 hours** Follow Hwy 10 to Hwy 32 to the coast, then take Hwy 36 along the coast. 🚌 **4.5 hours** Six daily buses connect through Siquirres and Limón.

② Cahuita (p127)

Continue to the coast down to Cahuita, capital of Afro-Caribbean culture and gateway to Parque Nacional Cahuita. Along these white-sand beaches, you can watch in fascination as hungry mammals dash out of the jungle to snack on scurrying crabs. Around town, get your fill of this mellow little village where the air is thick with reggae music and the scent of coconut rice.

CAHUITA ➡ PUERTO VIEJO DE TALAMANCA

🚗 **20 minutes** Take coastal Hwy 36. 🚌 **30 minutes to one hour** Direct buses leave five times daily.

③ Puerto Viejo de Talamanca (p134)

It's just a quick bus or taxi ride south to Puerto Viejo de Talamanca, the Caribbean coast's center for surfing, nightlife and Rasta culture. Fronting the beach is Salsa Brava, an epic surf break that first put the town on the map. Serious surfers take note: this is Costa Rica's biggest wave. Even if you're not a proficient short-boarder, you can easily spend a few days here bar-hopping.

PUERTO VIEJO DE TALAMANCA ➡ MANZANILLO

🚗 **20 minutes**. 🚲 **One hour**.

④ Manzanillo (p138)

After sampling the surf and late-night partying, rent a bike and ride to nearby Manzanillo. This is the end of the line, where you can snorkel, kayak and take a hike in the Refugio Nacional de Vida Silvestre Gandoca-Manzanillo. The refuge has protected Manzanillo from developers and helped it maintain its allure as an off-the-beaten-track destination, despite the newly paved road.

MANZANILLO ➡ TORTUGUERO

🚌 ⛴ **2.5 hours** Connect to water taxis in Puerto Viejo and transfer in Moín.

⑤ Tortuguero (p116)

For the adventurous, head north to grab a boat from Moín and travel the canal-lined coast to the village of Tortuguero, where you can watch nesting green and leatherback turtles. You can also arrange a canoe trip through the mangrove-lined canals of Parque Nacional Tortuguero, Costa Rica's mini-Amazon.

Beachside forest, Manzanillo (p138)

2 WEEKS

The Costa Rica Circuit
The Whole Enchilada

This two-week trip around Costa Rica includes all the bells and whistles – volcanoes, waterfalls, surf towns and high mountain hikes.

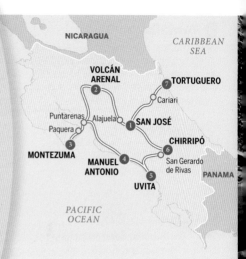

---

① San José (p60)

Since you'll most certainly fly in to San José, make the most of it. Get into the groove of Latin American life by exploring the city's museums and leafy historic barrios, its international cuisine and its live-music scene. The country's best sights lie outside the city's borders, but you'd be remiss to not spend an afternoon hanging out in Chepe.

SAN JOSÉ ◯ VOLCÁN ARENAL

🚗 **3.5 hours** Along the Interamericana, via Alajuela. 🚌 **3.5 hours** Buses leave three times daily, via San Ramón.

---

② Volcán Arenal (p158)

On a two-week itinerary, you can take your time and spend a relaxed few days hiking Volcán Arenal, soaking in the nearby hot springs and taking a side trip to La Catarata de Fortuna, a jungle waterfall. Once you've had your fill, come down off the mountain and travel across Laguna de Arenal.

VOLCÁN ARENAL ◯ MONTEZUMA

🚗 **Four hours** Via Hwy 18 and Hwy 21. 🚌 ⛴ **Six hours** Bus to Puntarenas, take the ferry to Paquera and another short bus ride north.

---

③ Montezuma (p230)

Mingle with backpackers, ecotourists and surf bums in this far-flung alternative beach-town. It has great beaches, scenic waterfalls and a terminally laid-back ethos. The nearby Isla Cabo Blanco is an excellent side trip.

MONTEZUMA ◯ MANUEL ANTONIO

🚗 ⛴ **Three hours** Via the Paquera–Puntarenas ferry and coastal highway. 🚌 ⛴ **Eight hours** Paquera–Puntarenas ferry, then bus transfer in Quepos.

---

④ Manuel Antonio (p261)

Sure, this is no secret destination – the place is loaded with visitors – but how can you blame the crowd when it is so beautiful? A place of swaying palms, playful monkeys, sparkling blue water and great bird watching: this is Costa Rica at its best.

MANUEL ANTONIO ◯ UVITA

🚗 **One hour** South on the Costanera Sur. 🚌 **1.5 hours** South along the coast.

Waterfall, Uvita (p269)
CYRIELLE BEAUBOIS/GETTY IMAGES ©

CHIRRIPÓ ➡ TORTUGUERO

🚗 **4.5 hours** Drive via the Interamericana back to San José, then to Cariari where the rest of the journey is by boat. 🚌 ⛴ **24 hours** Bus and overnight in San José, then bus to Cariari and boat to Tortuguero.

7 Tortuguero (p123)

Sweep down navigable rainforest canals and into one of the country's most iconic parks for the final stop. 'Central America's Amazon' is a memorable way to end a visit of breathtaking biodiversity. Even the river trip taking you to Tortuguero is a wildlife-watching adventure in itself, on which you're likely to spot sunning crocodiles, roseate spoonbills, iguanas, sloths and monkeys.

TORTUGUERO ➡ SAN JOSÉ

⛴ 🚌 **Seven hours** Boat and bus to Cariari, then bus to San José, change in Guápiles.

5 Uvita (p269)

Connected to the rest of the world via the Costanera Sur several years back, Uvita is coming alive as a central Pacific destination in its own right. Its waters beckon kayakers and snorkelers, while the long, deserted beaches in Parque Nacional Marino Ballena offer solitude for sunbathing.

UVITA ➡ CHIRRIPÓ

🚗 **One hour** North on Costanera Sur, then Rte 243 to San Isidro, then mountain road to San Gerardo de Rivas. 🚌 **Three hours** Change buses in San Isidro.

6 Chirripó (p304)

Tired of life at the beach? Adjust your altitude by getting high on Chirripó, one of the highest peaks in Central America and the highest in Costa Rica. It's well worth the slow road up to the base town of San Gerardo de Rivas, and the cool climate is a refreshing shock. A two-day excursion atop the mountain presents hikers with an adventure wholly different from Costa Rica's coastal charms, culminating with a once-in-a-lifetime sunrise.

Costa Rica Month by Month

Top Events

 Las Fiestas de Palmares,
January

 Feria de la Mascarada,
March

 Día de Juan Santamaría,
April

 Independence Day,
September

 Día de los Muertos,
November

 January

Every calendar year opens with a rush of visitors, as North American and domestic tourists flood beach towns to celebrate. January weather is ideal, with dry days and only occasional afternoon showers.

✪ Fiesta de la Santa Cruz

Held in Santa Cruz in the second week of January, this festival centers on a rodeo and bullfights. It also includes the requisite religious procession, music, dances and a beauty pageant.

✪ Jungle Jam

The biggest musical event to hit Jacó, the Jungle Jam stretches over several days and multiple venues outside of the main event, which is set in the lush tropical jungle just outside of town. Held in mid-January.

✪ Las Fiestas de Palmares

Ten days of beer drinking, horse shows and other carnival events take over the tiny town of Palmares in the second half of the month. There's also a running of the bulls. (www.fiestaspalmares.com)

February

February is the perfect month to visit, with ideal weather and no holiday surcharges. The skies above the Nicoya are particularly clear, and it is the peak of turtle-nesting season.

✪ Best Fest

A young music festival that showcases up-and-coming Tico bands as well as others from elsewhere in Latin America and North America, Best Fest comes to Uvita in early February. (www.thebestfestival.com)

(left) Parade, Liberia
S.B. NACE/GETTY IMAGES ©

42

Fiestas de La Fortuna

This big annual bash features two weeks of Tico-rules bullfights (the bull isn't harmed), colorful carnival rides, greasy food, craft stands and unusual gambling devices. It's free, except for the beer. Held in La Fortuna in mid-February.

 Envision Festival

Held in Uvita in late February, this is a festival with a consciousness-raising, transformational bent, bringing together fire dancers and performance artists of all stripes, yoga, music and spiritual workshops. (www.envisionfestival.com)

 Fiesta Cívica de Liberia

A beauty pageant and a carnival atmosphere enliven Liberia at the end of February.

March

Excellent weather continues through the early part of March, though prices shoot up at the end of the month if it corresponds with Semana Santa, the week leading up to Easter, and North American spring break.

 Día del Boyero

A colorful parade, held in Escazú on the second Sunday in March, honors oxcart drivers and includes a blessing of the animals.

 Feria de la Mascarada

During the Feria de la Mascarada, people don massive colorful masks (some of which weigh up to 20kg) and gather to dance and parade around the town square of Barva; it's usually held during the last week of March.

 Festival Imperial

A crowd of 30,000 music fans fills the La Guácima outdoor venue in Alajuela for the country's biggest rock festival. Performers recently included TV on the Radio, Skrillex, Björk, LMFAO and the Flaming Lips. Loosely scheduled every two years in March or April.

April

Easter and the preceding week, Semana Santa, can fall early in April, which makes beaches crowded and prices spike. Nicoya and Guanacaste are very dry and hot, with very little rain.

 Día de Juan Santamaría

Commemorating Costa Rica's national hero, who died in battle against American colonist William Walker's troops in 1856, this week-long celebration includes parades, concerts and dances. The most festive celebrations take place on April 11 in Alajuela, Santamaría's proud hometown.

 FIA (Festival Internacional de las Artes)

This multidisciplinary arts festival descends upon venues all across San José during the first half of April. The festival has been running since 1989. (www.festivaldelasartes.go.cr in Spanish)

May

Wetter weather patterns begin to sweep across the country in May, which begins the country's low season and discounted prices. Good bargains and reasonably good weather make it an excellent season for budget travel.

 Día de San Isidro Labrador

An opportunity to taste the bounty of the surrounding region (wherever you are in Costa Rica, but particularly in any town or village called San Isidro), this is one of the nation's largest agricultural fairs. It takes place on May 15.

Fiesta de la Virgen del Mar

Held in Puntarenas and Playa del Coco, this party involves colorful, brightly lit regattas and boat parades. It's held on the Saturday closest to 16 July.

Día de Guanacaste

Celebrates the annexation of Guanacaste from Nicaragua. There's also a rodeo in Santa Cruz. It takes place on July 25.

August

The middle of the rainy season doesn't mean that mornings aren't bright and sunny. Travelers who don't mind some rain will find great hotel and tour deals, and surfers will find storm-generated swells.

La Virgen de los Ángeles

The patron saint of Costa Rica is celebrated with an important religious procession from San José to Cartago on August 2.

September

The Osa peninsula gets utterly soaked during September, which is in the heart of the rainy season and what Ticos refer to as the *temporales del Pacífico* – the cheapest time of year to visit the Pacific side.

Costa Rican Independence Day

Independence Day is a fun party throughout Costa Rica. The center of the action is the relay race that passes a 'Freedom Torch' from Guatemala to Costa Rica. The torch arrives at Cartago on the evening of the 14th, when the nation breaks into the national anthem.

June

The Pacific Coast gets fairly wet during June, though this makes for good surfing swells. The beginning of the so-called green season, this time of year has lots of discounted rates.

Costa Rica Film Festival

The arts come to the southern Península de Nicoya with this film fest in Montezuma. (www.costaricafilmfestival.com)

Día de San Pedro & San Pablo

Celebrations with religious processions are held in villages of the same names on June 29.

July

July is mostly wet, particularly on the Caribbean coast, but the month also occasionally enjoys a brief dry period that Ticos call *veranillo,* or summer.

October

Many roads become impassable as rivers swell and rain continues to fall in one of the wettest months in Costa Rica. Many of the lodges and tour operators are closed.

Día de la Raza

Columbus' historic landing on Isla Uvita has traditionally inspired a small carnival in Puerto Limón on October 12, with street parades, live music and dancing.

 # November

The weather can go either way in November. Access to Corcovado national park is very difficult after several continuous months of rain.

Día de los Muertos

Families visit graveyards and have religious parades in honor of the dead – a lovely and picturesque festival. It takes place on November 2.

 # December

Although the beginning of the month is a great time to visit, with clearer skies and less-crowded sights, things really ramp up toward Christmas, when travelers need to make reservations well in advance.

Las Fiestas de Zapote

If you're around San José between Christmas and New Year's Eve, this week-long celebration of all things Costa Rican (namely, rodeos, cowboys, carnival rides, fried food and booze) annually draws tens of thousands of Ticos to the bullring in the suburb of Zapote.

Fiesta de los Diablitos

Men wear carved wooden devil masks and burlap sacks and, after roaming from house to house for free booze, re-enact the fight between the indigenous people and the Spanish. The festival is held in Boruca from December 30 to January 2 and in Curré from February 5 to February 8.

Far left: Rodeo **Left:** Woman in traditional Guanacaste dress

What's New

For this new edition of Discover Costa Rica, our authors hunted down the fresh, the transformed, the hot and the happening. Here are a few of our favorites. For up-to-the-minute recommendations, see lonelyplanet.com/costa-rica.

1 COSTA RICA CRAFT *CERVEZA*

Artisanal beers are gaining momentum in Costa Rica, a development that doubtless will thrill visiting beer aficionados. Over the last several years, craft breweries have popped up in various hot spots, bringing creative *birras* (beers) to palates thirsting for something more complex than the ubiquitous Imperial. Imagine sipping a locally brewed pineapple Hefeweizen or cacao stout at sunset – it brings a hoppy tear to our eye.

2 RÍO PERDIDO

A unique new resort on 600 acres of private reserve, Río Perdido is an out-of-the-way retreat, complete with canopy tour through unusual dwarf forest and thermal-spring-fed river. (p187)

3 MUSEO DE JADE

Housing its spectacular collection of pre-Columbian jade and gold artifacts, this museum will move to new purpose-built digs across from the Museo Nacional in late 2014. (p60)

4 BIG FOREST HIKE

Fit hikers can now do a two-day trek from Monteverde to Arenal through this iconic land of cloud forest and highland rivers.

5 CINCO CEIBAS

This huge, new private reserve in the Valle de Sarapiquí features Costa Rica's longest boardwalk through the jungle and offers activities such as horseback riding, kayaking and yoga. (p195)

6 BEST FEST

Adding to the festival scene on the central Pacific coast, Best Fest brings international music to the Costa Ballena in early February. (www.thebestfestival.com)

7 JUNGLE JAM

This ever-growing Jacó music festival draws headliners such as Slightly Stoopid and features live music that rocks the main jungle venue to local spots in town.

8 EL SÓTANO

A fun, artsy nightspot in San José, this restored mansion has a very cool, intimate basement jazz club, plus a second stage upstairs where other live bands play. (p68)

9 CARTAGO COMMUTER TRAIN

Weekday train service from San Jose's century-old Estación del Atlántico resumed in 2013. It's a convenient and fun way to travel between the two cities.

Get Inspired

Books

Costa Rica: A Traveler's Literary Companion (ed Barbara Ras) A fine collection of 26 short stories by modern Costa Rican writers.

Tropical Nature: Life and Death in the Rain Forests of Central and South America (Adrian Forsyth and Ken Miyata) Easy-to-digest natural-history essays on rainforest phenomena, by two biologists.

Travelers' Tales Central America (eds Larry Habegger and Natanya Pearlman) Essays from writers including Paul Theroux.

Films

El Regreso (*The Return*) Featuring a realistic, contemporary plot, the first Tico film to earn international acclaim.

Agua Fría de Mar (*Cold Ocean Water*) This social commentary unfolds at a paradisical Pacific beach; the film won several international awards.

El Cielo Rojo (*The Red Sky*) A comedic coming-of-age story of young Ticos on the cusp of adulthood in contemporary Costa Rica.

Music

Various Artists, Sí San José (2011) A collaboration between a WFMU engineer and nine of Costa Rica's indie rock acts.

Chavela Vargas, Coleccion Original RCA (1946) Long out of print, this 2011 reissue of Costa Rican–born singer features hauntingly beautiful folk ballads.

Malpaís, Un Día Lejano (2009) Costa Rica's innovative and now-defunct rock band mixes calypso, jazz and Latin American balladry.

Websites

Costa Rica Tourism Board (www.visitcostarica.com) Official website of the Instituto Costarricense de Turismo (ICT).

Anywhere Costa Rica (www.anywherecostarica.com) Great, detailed destination information for pre-trip planning.

Guías Costa Rica (www.guiascostarica.com) Links that connect you to everything you'd ever need to know – from entertainment to health to government websites.

Short on time?

This list will give you an instant insight into Costa Rica.

Read Dr Skutch weaves his philosophies into beautiful descriptions of flora and fauna in *Naturalist in Costa Rica*, an enchanting memoir and natural history guide.

Watch Surfers Pat O'Connell and Robert 'Wingnut' Weaver ride Costa Rica's magical waves in *Endless Summer II*.

Listen *Calypsos: Afro-Limonese Music From Costa Rica* (Various) is a raucous collection which captured the heart of Costa Rico's Afro-Caribbean folk scene.

Log on For English-language news and current local events, the Tico Times (www.ticotimes.net) is an invaluable resource.

Surfers at sunset
COREY RICH/GETTY IMAGES ©

Need to Know

Currency

Colones (₡) and US Dollars ($)

Language

English is spoken in tourist areas and along the Caribbean coast, but Spanish prevails elsewhere.

Visas

No visa is required of citizens of the US, Canada, many Western European countries, Australia and New Zealand.

Money

ATMs widely available; machines dispense both colones and US dollars. Visa and Mastercard widely accepted, others less so.

Cell Phones

Local, prepaid SIM cards can be installed in your cell phone; make sure the phone is unlocked before leaving your home country.

Wi-Fi

Although speeds are slow, wi-fi is increasingly common at restaurants and many accommodations.

Internet Access

Almost all hostels, hotels and B&Bs throughout the country provide a common internet terminal for their guests, usually for free or a nominal fee.

For more information, see Survival Guide (p349)

When to Go

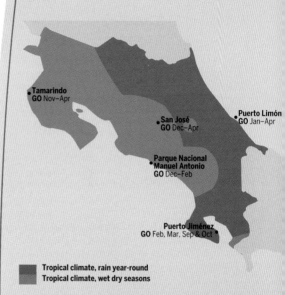

Tamarindo
GO Nov–Apr

San José
GO Dec–Apr

Puerto Limón
GO Jan–Apr

Parque Nacional
Manuel Antonio
GO Dec–Feb

Puerto Jiménez
GO Feb, Mar, Sep & Oct

▓ Tropical climate, rain year-round
▓ Tropical climate, wet dry seasons

High Season
(Dec–Apr)

○ The 'dry' season still sees rain, but beach towns fill with domestic tourists.

○ Semana Santa (week before Easter), Christmas and New Year have the highest rates for accommodations and services.

Shoulder
(May–Jul, Nov)

○ Rain picks up and the stream of tourists tapers off.

○ Roads are muddy, making off-the-beaten-track travel challenging.

Low Season
(Aug–Oct)

○ Rain is heaviest, but brings swells to the Pacific and the best surfing conditions.

○ Rural roads can be impassable due to river crossings.

○ Accommodations prices drop significantly.

Advance Planning

○ **Two months before** Reserve accommodations in advance if traveling during Semana Santa or the Christmas holidays.

○ **One month before** Book car rental online so you can pick up your car at the airport and make the most of your time.

Daily Costs

Budget less than US$40

○ Dorm beds: US$8–US$15

○ Eat at ubiquitous *sodas* (lunch counters) and shop at local markets, self-cater: US$3–$7

○ Park entrance fees: US$5–$15

○ Travel via local bus: less than US$25 to nearly anywhere within the country

Midrange US$40–$100

○ Basic room with private bathroom: US$20–$50

○ Eat at restaurants geared toward travelers: US$5–$12

○ Travel via efficient first-class bus companies such as Interbus: from US$39

Top End more than US$100 a day

○ Luxurious beachside lodges and boutique hotels: from US$80

○ Dine at international restaurants: from US$15

○ Hire guides for wildlife-watching excursions: from US$25

○ Rent a 4WD for local travel: from US$70 daily

Exchange Rates

Australia	A$1	₡504
Canada	C$1	₡500
Europe	€1	₡744
Japan	¥100	₡536
Mexico	MXN10	₡423
New Zealand	NZ$1	₡467
UK	£1	₡919
US	US$1	₡545

For current exchange rates see www.xe.com.

What to Bring

○ **Insect repellent** DEET-containing repellents are most effective, especially for large-scale jungle adventures.

○ **Refillable water bottle** Tap water is safe to drink, and a refillable bottle helps diminish your environmental impact.

○ **Spanish phrasebook** Learning a little of the local lingo makes all the difference.

○ **Proper footwear** Bring along a pair of waterproof sandals and sturdy hiking shoes.

Arriving in Costa Rica

○ **Aeropuerto Internacional Juan Santamaria**

Bus US$0.75; Alajuela–San José buses run frequently and will drop you anywhere along Paseo Colón.

Taxis US$20–$30; depart from an official stand; 20 minutes to one hour to San José.

Rental Car Many rental-car agencies have desks in the airport.

Getting Around

○ **Air** Domestic airlines and private charters can help you squeeze the most into your travels.

○ **Bus** Depending on your desired level of comfort, choose from air-conditioned private shuttles and more economical local coaches.

○ **Car** Renting a car is the best way to explore Costa Rica at your own pace, though a 4WD is necessary for all but the most heavily touristed areas.

○ **Taxi** In San José as well as in rural areas, a taxi is worth the cash if you don't have time to waste.

Sleeping

○ **B&Bs** Midrange to top-end affairs typically run by North American and European expats.

○ **Hostels** Good-value accommodations with the needs of the modern backpacker in mind.

○ **Hotels** Highly variable in range, including everything from budget crash pads to lavish five-star resorts.

Be Forewarned

○ **Climate** Tropical sun along the coasts, frequent precipitation in the rainforests and evening chills at high altitude – be prepared with the proper attire.

○ **Rental Car Fees** Mandatory national insurance is a hidden cost of car rental and can double the rate quoted online.

○ **Petty Theft** *Never* leave anything (valuable or not) in your vehicle or unattended on the beach. Don't leave valuables unsecured in your hotel room.

San José

San José's more peaceful attractions lie within its seeming maelstrom. The city's reputation may have preceded it and colored your first glance, but give Chepe (as San José is affectionately known) a chance, and it will quickly reveal its charms. Walk around its historic neighborhoods and the sounds of honking horns and thumping reggaetón fade to the background as you admire the colonial mansions that have been converted into contemporary art galleries, and the islands of small city parks amid the busy urban streets.

Colorfully arresting murals and graffiti tell contemporary tales of the city, while hipster buskers or the odd juggling unicyclist pop up on the most unexpected corners. And in the city's museums of gold, jade and national history, lie all the layers of indigenous heritage, colonial past and great minds that made Costa Rica the environmental champion and military-free country we love today.

Milkman, San José
ERIC L. WHEATER/GETTY IMAGES ©

Arched doorway leads to a San José street

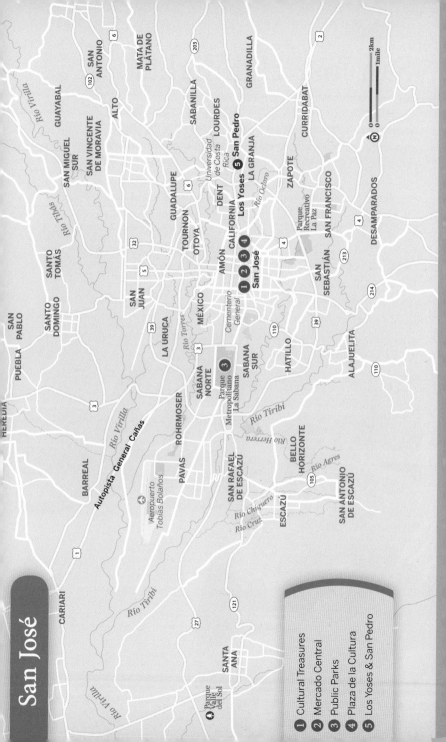

San José

Río Virilla
Río Tibás

GUAYABAL
SAN MIGUEL SUR
SAN VINCENTE DE MORAVIA
SAN ANTONIO
ALTO
MATA DE PLÁTANO
SAN ANTONIO

102

6

203

SABANILLA
LOURDES
SABANILLA
GRANADILLA

PUEBLA
HEREDIA
SAN PABLO
SANTO DOMINGO
SANTO TOMÁS

SAN JUAN

GUADALUPE
TOURNÓN
OTOYA
AMÓN
DENT
CALIFORNIA
Universidad de Costa Rica
LOURDES
LLA
LA GRANJA
San Pedro
Los Yoses
CURRIDABAT

6

32

5

39

MÉXICO
LA URUCA
Río Torres
Cementerio General

5 San Pedro

ZAPOTE
SAN FRANCISCO
DESAMPARADOS

4

213

BARREAL

Río Virilla
Autopista General Cañas

ROHRMOSER
PAVAS
Aeropuerto Tobías Bolaños

SABANA NORTE
SABANA SUR
Parque Metropolitano La Sabana

3

110

SAN SEBASTIÁN
HATILLO

39

214

110

3

1 2 3 4 San José

Parque Recreativo La Paz

4

CARIARI

Río Tiribí

SANTA ANA

Parque Valle del Sol

27

121

SAN RAFAEL DE ESCAZÚ

Río Chiquero
Río Cruz

ESCAZÚ
SAN ANTONIO DE ESCAZÚ

Río Tiribí
Río Herrera
BELLO HORIZONTE
Río Agres

105

ALAJUELITA

1

3

5

2

① Cultural Treasures
② Mercado Central
③ Public Parks
④ Plaza de la Cultura
⑤ Los Yoses & San Pedro

2km
1mile

0
0

N

San José Highlights

Cultural Treasures

Peer into the cultural heart of Costa Rica in San José's excellent museums – ponder ancient, pre-Columbian gold frogs, stunning jade carvings and Costa Rican avant-garde art in the museums that showcase these works. Up-and-coming art, music and theater are most vibrant here in the capital. But to get a real feel for the country's cultural consciousness, start with the Museo Nacional de Costa Rica (p61). Gran Nicoya ceramics, Museo Nacional de Costa Ric (p61)

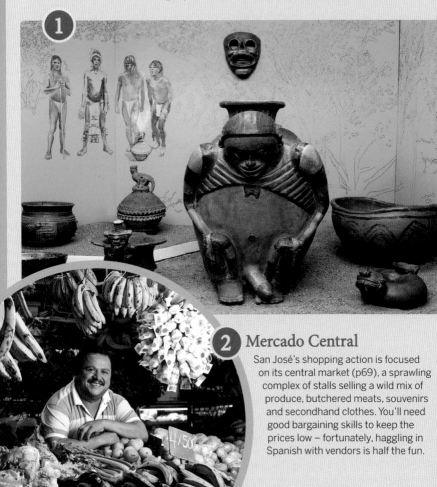

1

2 ## Mercado Central

San José's shopping action is focused on its central market (p69), a sprawling complex of stalls selling a wild mix of produce, butchered meats, souvenirs and secondhand clothes. You'll need good bargaining skills to keep the prices low – fortunately, haggling in Spanish with vendors is half the fun.

Public Parks

3

San José may lack tree-lined promenades, but fortunately there's no shortage of leafy green parks throughout the city center. One of the capital's best escapes is Parque Metropolitano La Sabana (p64), a perfect oasis for a traffic-free run or a relaxed family picnic by the lake. Within the park there's also a free Costa Rican art museum and the recently revamped national stadium.

Parque Metropolitano La Sabana (p64)

4

Plaza de la Cultura

Both the spiritual and the physical heart of the city, the Plaza de la Cultura (p64) is little more than a slab of concrete in the middle of downtown. But for the residents of San José, this is the city's greatest public space for gathering with friends and family, and people-watching while indulging in an ice-cream cone.

5

Los Yoses & San Pedro

Two more San José suburbs that definitely merit a visit are Los Yoses and San Pedro (p72), each with its own distinct character. Los Yoses is prim and proper, while the university district of San Pedro has noticeably more bohemian leanings.

55

San José's Best...

Splurges

Hotel Grano de Oro Ensconce yourself in an early-20th-century 'Tropical Victorian' mansion complete with period furniture. (p65)

Park Café Michelin-starred chef Richard Neat presents sublime dishes in singular, romantic environs. (p66)

Shopping

Mercado Central A traditional Latin American shopping extravaganza makes for fun and chaotic browsing. (p69)

Galería Namu A fair-trade gallery showcasing excellent examples of indigenous artwork. Proceeds go directly to indigenous artists. (p69)

Biesanz Woodworks No need to worry about the origin of the pieces here, this artisan shop is arguably the country's best woodcrafting studio. (p75)

Entertainment

Teatro Nacional Catch a high-culture performance in the city's most historic theater. (p61)

Jazz Café This intimate club is a buzzing nightspot unmatched for its calendar of live jazz, folk and rock performances. (p74)

Centro Comercial El Pueblo A complex of dozens of bars and clubs. Don't show up early: the action gets started well after midnight. (p68)

Need to Know

Eats

○ **La Esquina de Buenos Aires** Crisp linens, candles and old tango enliven Costa Rica's finest steakhouse. (p67)

○ **Sofía Restaurante Mediterráneo** Authentic Mediterranean cuisine, occasionally accompanied by cultural events and entertainment. (p73)

○ **Café Mundo** Occupying a superb location in a vintage mansion, the terrace is terribly romantic for a bite of Italian. (p66)

○ **Café de los Deseos** Sip a smoothie or glass of wine with the artsy kids in this colorfully eclectic cafe. (p66)

Left: Spices for sale at a market
Above: Dining room, Hotel Grano de Oro (p65)

San José Walking Tour

Get to know the heart of Costa Rica's capital with this short stroll through the compact city center, roaming its museums, parks and markets. From a macro perspective, San José may intimidate a bit; but on a micro scale, an intimate walk makes Chepe feel easily relatable.

WALK FACTS

- **Start** Museo de Jade
- **End** Mercado Central
- **Distance** 2.5km
- **Duration** Four hours

1 Museo de Jade

With the world's largest collection of precious jade, this museum's multicultural and well-preserved relics warrant an hour's worth of exploration. Jade was the most valuable trading commodity among pre-Columbian cultures, and Costa Rica's location at the center of Central America has resulted in an excellent collection (p60).

2 Parque Nacional

After taking in the museum, wander through the shaded Parque Nacional, where lovers stroll and old men talk politics under the watchful statues of Latin American cultural and political heroes.

3 Museo de Arte y Diseño Contemporáneo

Although the historic National Liquor Factory was once housed here, these days the strongest stuff the building holds is the contemporary works of Costa Rican, Central American and South American artists (p61).

4 Galería Namu

If you're not planning on a deep exploration of Costa Rica's indigenous areas, stop at this fair-trade gallery and boutique (p69) for fine examples of Boruca masks, baskets, Ngöbe (Guaymí) dolls and carvings.

⑤ Parque Morazán

Although this park (p61) has a bit of an unsavory history as the turf of prostitutes, it's inching away from its seedy past and offers shaded benches that are perfect for a midwalk rest. At the park's center is the Templo de Música, a concrete bandstand that is the unofficial symbol of San José.

⑥ Plaza de la Cultura

Clowns, sidewalk vendors and lots of foot traffic make this plaza (p64) buzz with life. Sitting here savoring an ice-cream cone makes for excellent people-watching as suits, shoppers and dolled-up working girls whisk by.

⑦ Teatro Nacional

Beethoven and Calderón de la Barca (a 17-century Spanish dramatist) peek out from the bold, gracefully columned neoclassical facade of this iconic landmark (p61). If you catch it during opening hours, peek inside the lavish marble lobby, making sure not to miss the painting *Alegoría al café y el banano*, an idyllic canvas portraying coffee and banana harvests. The painting came from Italy, and the image once graced a Costa Rican bank note.

⑧ Mercado Central

If all the walking has worked up your appetite, sniff around in the Mercado Central (p69), the exciting, chaotic, sometimes overwhelming hub of the city's commercial life. You can pick up just about anything here (bananas by the kilo, imported trinkets by the truckful), but before you start browsing, belly up to one of the popular *sodas* for cheap, fresh, delicious home cooking.

San José In...

ONE DAY

Get a glimpse of Costa Rican culture by following the walking tour. Instead of heading to the Mercado Central, stroll back to Barrio Amón for lunch on the terrace of **Kalú Café & Food Shop** (p67). Afterwards, browse the shops and small galleries of historic Barrio Amón. End your day with an Argentinean dinner at **La Esquina de Buenos Aires** (p67).

TWO DAYS

Start at the **Museo Nacional de Costa Rica** (p61), then explore the Mercado Artesanal (p68) for handicrafts. Head northwest to **Parque España** (p64) to check out the notable nearby architecture. Next, head northwest to the **Mercado Central** (p69) to shop for Costa Rican coffee, cigars and cheap eats. In the evening, venture east to Los Yoses and San Pedro, where you'll find some of San José's best eateries and bars, and end with live music at the **Jazz Café** (p74).

Marketplace in San José
ALFONSE PAGANO/GETTY IMAGES ©

Discover San José

At a Glance

○ **San José** Costa Rica's capital might not wow you at first blush, but there's plenty to love beneath the surface.

○ **Los Yoses** (p72) Modernist structures, historic inns and chilled-out eateries.

○ **San Pedro** (p72) A bohemian atmosphere and cool local shops, near the University of Costa Rica (UCR).

○ **Escazú** (p74) This trendy neighborhood is complete with boutiques, fine dining and expat presence.

San José street mural
JONATHAN GREGSON/LONELY PLANET ©

SAN JOSÉ

POP OVER 1.5 MILLION (GREATER METRO AREA)

San José is small and best explored on foot, joining locals along teeming sidewalks and pedestrian boulevards that lead to vintage theaters, crowded cafes, tree-shaded parks and some of the finest museums in Central America.

◎ Sights

Museo de Oro Precolombino y Numismática   Museum

(Map p66; ☎2243-4221; www.museosdelbanco-central.org; Plaza de la Cultura, Avs Central & 2 btwn Calles 3 & 5; adult/student/child US$11/8/free; ◷9:15am-5pm) This three-in-one museum houses an extensive collection of Costa Rica's most priceless pieces of pre-Columbian gold and other artifacts, including historical currency and some contemporary regional art. The museum, housed underneath the Plaza de la Cultura, is owned by the Banco Central and its architecture brings to mind all the warmth and comfort of a bank vault. Security is tight; visitors must leave bags at the door.

Museo de Jade   Museum

(Map p66; ☎2287-6034; www.ins-cr.com; Plaza de la Democracia; adult/child US$9/free; ◷8:30am-3:30pm Mon-Fri, 10am-2pm Sat) Reopened in its brand-new home in mid-2014, this museum houses the world's largest collection of American jade (pronounced 'ha-day' in Spanish). The ample new exhibition space allows the public greater access to the museum's varied collection of nearly 7000 finely crafted, well-conserved pieces, from translucent jade carvings depicting fertility goddesses, shamans, frogs and snakes to incredible ceramics (some reflecting Mayan influences), including a highly unusual ceramic head displaying a row of serrated teeth.

Teatro Nacional   Notable Building

(Map p66; ☎2010-1100; www.teatronacional. go.cr; Av 2 btwn Calles 3 & 5; admission US$7; ⏱9am-6pm Jan-Apr, to 4pm Mon-Sat May-Dec) On the southern side of the Plaza de la Cultura resides the Teatro Nacional, San José's most revered public building. Constructed in 1897, it features a columned neoclassical facade that is flanked by statues of Beethoven and famous 17th-century Spanish dramatist Calderón de la Barca. The lavish marble lobby and auditorium are lined with paintings depicting various facets of 19th-century life. If you're looking to rest your feet, there's also an excellent onsite **cafe** (Map p66; ☎2010-1119; www.almadecafe.net; Teatro Nacional; mains US$5-10; ⏱9am-7pm Mon-Sat, to 6pm Sun).

Museo Nacional de Costa Rica   Museum

(Map p62; ☎2257-1433; www.museocostarica. go.cr; Calle 17 btwn Avs Central & 2; adult/child US$8/4; ⏱8:30am-4:30pm Tue-Sat, 9am-4:30pm Sun) Entered via a beautiful glassed-in atrium housing an exotic butterfly garden, this museum provides a quick survey of Costa Rican history. Exhibits of pre-Columbian pieces from ongoing digs, as well as artifacts from the colony and the early republic are all housed inside the old Bellavista Fortress, which served historically as the army headquarters and saw fierce fighting (hence the pockmarks) in the 1948 civil war.

Museo de Arte y Diseño Contemporáneo   Museum

(Map p66; ☎2257-7202; www.madc.cr; cnr Av 3 & Calle 15; admission US$3, Mon free; ⏱9:30am-5pm Mon-Sat) Commonly referred to as MADC, the Contemporary Art & Design Museum is housed in the historic National Liquor Factory building, which dates from 1856. The largest and most important contemporary-art museum in the region, MADC is focused on showing the works of contemporary Costa Rican, Central American and South American artists and occasionally features temporary exhibits devoted to interior design, fashion and graphic art.

Parque Morazán   Park

(Map p66; Avs 3 & 5 btwn Calles 5 & 9) To the southwest of the Parque España is Parque Morazán, named for Francisco Morazán, the 19th-century general who attempted to unite the Central American nations under a single flag. Once a notorious center of prostitution, the park is now beautifully illuminated in the evenings. At its center is the **Templo de Música** (Music

Museo Nacional de Costa Rica

San José

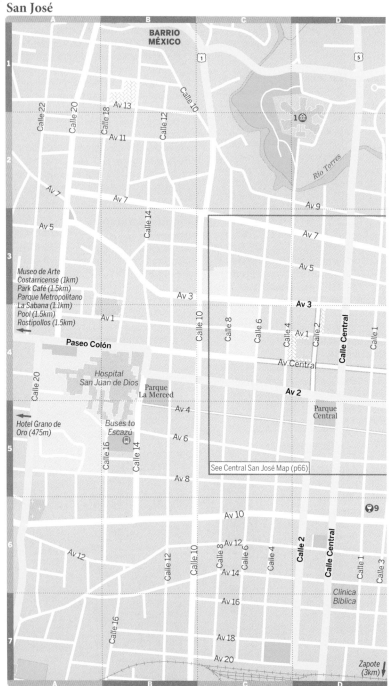

See Central San José Map (p66)

BARRIO MÉXICO

Calle 22
Calle 20
Calle 18
Av 13
Av 11
Calle 10
Calle 12
Río Torres

Av 7
Av 7
Calle 14

Av 5

Museo de Arte
Costarricense (1km)
Park Café (1.5km)
Parque Metropolitano
La Sabana (1.1km)
Pool (1.5km)
Rostipollos (1.5km)

Av 3
Av 9
Av 7
Av 5
Av 3
Av 1
Av Central
Av 2

Av 1
Calle 10
Calle 8
Calle 6
Calle 4
Calle 2
Calle Central
Calle 1

Paseo Colón

Hospital
San Juan de Dios

Parque
La Merced

Parque
Central

Calle 20

Hotel Grano de
Oro (475m)

Buses to
Escazú

Av 4

Av 6

Calle 16
Calle 14

Av 8

Av 10

Av 12
Av 12
Av 14

Calle 12
Calle 10
Calle 8
Calle 6
Calle 4
Calle 2
Calle Central
Calle 1
Calle 3

Av 12

Av 16

Clínica
Bíblica

Calle 16

Av 18

Av 20

Zapote
(3km)

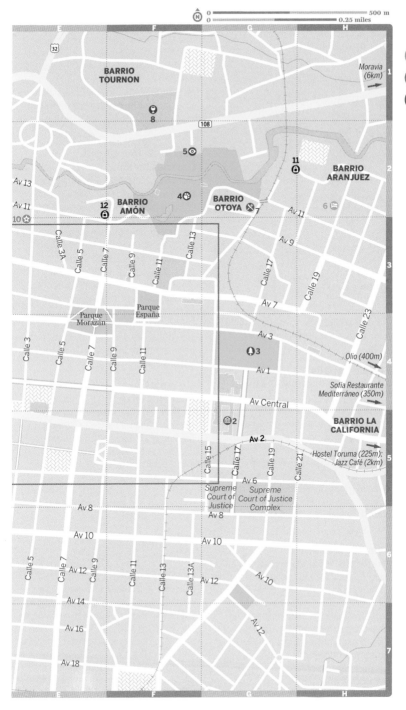

0   500 m
0   0.25 miles

Moravia
(6km)

BARRIO
TOURNON

32

108

8

5

11

BARRIO
ARANJUEZ

Av 13

4

BARRIO
OTOYA 7

Av 11

6

Av 11

Av 9

12   BARRIO
AMÓN

10

Calle 3A
Calle 5
Calle 7
Calle 9
Calle 11
Calle 13

Calle 17

Calle 19

Calle 23

Av 7

Parque
España

Av 3

Parque
Morazán

Olio (400m)

Calle 3
Calle 5
Calle 7
Calle 9
Calle 11

3

Av 1

Sofía Restaurante
Mediterráneo (350m)

Av Central

2

BARRIO LA
CALIFORNIA

Calle 15
Calle 17
Calle 19
Calle 21

Av 2

Hostel Toruma (225m);
Jazz Café (2km)

Av 6

Supreme
Court of
Justice

Supreme
Court of Justice
Complex

Av 8

Av 8

Av 10

Av 10

Calle 5
Calle 7
Calle 9

Av 12

Calle 11

Calle 13

Calle 13A

Av 12

Av 10

Av 14

Av 16

Av 12

Av 18

San José

◎ Sights

Temple; Map p66), a concrete bandstand that serves as an unofficial symbol of San José.

Parque España   Park

(Map p66; Avs 3 & 7 btwn Calles 9 & 11) Surrounded by heavy traffic, Parque España may be small, but it becomes a riot of birdsong every day at sunset when the local avian population comes in to roost. In addition to being a good spot for a shady break, the park is home to an ornate statue of Christopher Columbus that was given to the people of Costa Rica in 2002 by his descendants, commemorating the quincentennial of the explorer's landing in Puerto Limón.

Plaza de la Cultura   Plaza

(Map p66; Avs Central & 2 btwn Calles 3 & 5) For many Ticos, Costa Rica begins here. This architecturally unremarkable concrete plaza in the heart of downtown is usually packed with locals slurping ice-cream cones and admiring the wide gamut of San José street life: juggling clowns, itinerant vendors and cruising teenagers. It is perhaps one of the safest spots in the city since there's a police tower stationed at one corner.

Parque Metropolitano La Sabana   Park

Once the site of San José's main airport, this 72-hectare green space at the west end of Paseo Colón is home to a museum, a lagoon and various sports facilities – most notably Costa Rica's national soccer stadium. During the day, the park's paths make a relaxing place for a stroll, a jog or a picnic.

Museo de los Niños & Galería Nacional   Museum

(Map p62; ☑ 2258-4929; www.museocr.org; Calle 4, north of Av 9; adult/child US$2.60/2; ◎ 8am-4:30pm Tue-Fri, 9:30am-5pm Sat & Sun; ⌖) If you were wondering how to get your young kids interested in art and science, this unusual museum – actually two museums in one – is an excellent place to start. Housed in an old penitentiary built in 1909, it is part children's museum and part art gallery. Small children will love the hands-on exhibits related to science, geography and natural history, while grown-ups will enjoy the unusual juxtaposition of contemporary art in abandoned prison cells.

Museo de Arte Costarricense   Museum

(☑ 2256-1281; www.musarco.go.cr; east entrance of Parque La Sabana; ◎ 9am-4pm Tue-Sun; ⌖) At the eastern entrance to the Parque La Sabana is the Museo de Arte Costarricense, in a Spanish-style structure that served as San José's main airport terminal until 1955. The newly remodeled museum features regional art and other exhibits.

🛏 Sleeping

Hostel Pangea   Hostel $

(Map p66; ☑ 2221-1992; www.hostelpangea. com; Av 7 btwn Calles 3 & 3A, Barrio Amón; dm US$14, d with/without bathroom US$45/34, ste from US$55; P @ 🛜 🏊) This industrial-strength, Tico-owned hostel – 25 dorms and 25 private rooms – has been a popular 20-something backpacker hangout for years. It's not difficult to see why: it's smack in the middle of the city and comes stocked with a pool, a rooftop restaurant-lounge with stellar views, and a combination bar–movie theater. Needless to say, it's a party spot.

Hotel Aranjuez
Hotel $$

(Map p62; ☎2256-1825; www.hotelaranjuez.com; Calle 19 btwn Avs 11 & 13; incl breakfast s US$37-52, d US$52-67, s/d without bathroom US$27/36; [P][@][🛜]) This rambling hotel in Barrio Aranjuez consists of five nicely maintained vintage homes that have been strung together with a labyrinth of gardens and connecting walkways. The 36 spotless rooms come in various configurations, all with lockboxes and cable TV. The hotel's best attribute, however, is the lush garden patio, where a legendary breakfast buffet is served every morning.

Hotel Grano de Oro
Boutique Hotel $$$

(☎2255-3322; www.hotelgranodeoro.com; Calle 30 btwn Avs 2 & 4; d US$170-289, f/garden/vista-del-oro ste US$300/345/515; [P][😋][@][🛜]) It's easy to see why honeymooners love it here. Built around a sprawling early-20th-century Victorian mansion, this elegant inn has 39 demure 'Tropical Victorian' rooms furnished with wrought-iron beds and rich brocade linens. A few rooms even boast private courtyards with gurgling fountains, while the public areas sparkle with fresh tropical flowers and polished-wood accents.

Hotel Don Carlos
Hotel $$$

(Map p66; ☎2221-6707; www.doncarloshotel.com; Calle 9 btwn Avs 7 & 9; incl breakfast s US$85-96, d $96-107; [P][@][🛜][💦]) Built around an early-20th-century house that once belonged to President Tomás Guardia, this welcoming Barrio Amón inn exudes a slightly campy colonial-era vibe. Thirty-three rooms are nestled around a faux-pre-Columbian sculpture garden with a sundeck, jacuzzi and small kiddie-depth pool. All rooms have cable TV, lockbox and hair dryer; upstairs units are generally nicer than the mustier ones downstairs.

Local Knowledge

Tico Art & Culture in San José

RECOMMENDATIONS FROM MARIA AMALIA, FORMER MARKETING DIRECTOR FOR THE COSTA RICA TOURISM BOARD (INSTITUTO COSTARRICENSE DE TURISMO; ICT)

1 TEATRO NACIONAL
The stately national theater (p61) is a late-19th-century neoclassical architectural masterpiece. It houses a series of lavish paintings that provide visual commentary on Costa Rica's rural heritage. The theater hosts music performances and other major events.

2 MUSEO DE ORO PRECOLOMBINO Y NUMISMÁTICA
This three-in-one museum (p60) showcases a collection of pre-Columbian gold containing hand-tooled ornaments dating back to AD 400. The second part of the museum details the history of Costa Rican currency, while another features a changing selection of temporary exhibitions.

3 MUSEO DE JADE
The world's largest collection of jade (p60) has display cases full of elaborate carvings depicting everything from frogs and serpents to shamans and fertility goddesses. The craftsmanship is superb, and the pieces are in a fine state of conservation.

4 MUSEO NACIONAL DE COSTA RICA
Costa Rica's most significant historical museum (p61) holds a collection of metates (grinding stones), an excellent gold collection and an exhibit dedicated to Nobel Peace Prize winner Óscar Arias.

5 MUSEO DE ARTE Y DISEÑO CONTEMPORÁNEO
There's no better place to get a sense of the nation's artistic and cultural past, present and future than this collection of works (p61) by contemporary Costa Rican and Latin American artists.

Eating

Café de los Deseos   Cafe $

(Map p62; ☎2222-0496; www.facebook.com/
Cafedelosdeseos; Calle 15 btwn Avs 9 & 11; mains
US$5-12; ⏱2-10pm Tue-Sat) Abuzz with artsy
young bohemians, this cozy, colorful
Barrio Otoya cafe makes a romantic
spot for drinks (from wine to cocktails to
smoothies), *bocas* (handmade tortillas
with Turrialba cheese, salads, teriyaki
chicken, individual pizzas), and tempting
desserts. Walls are hung with the work of
local artists and rooms are adorned with
hand-painted tables, beaded curtains and
branches entwined with fairy lights.

Café Mundo   Italian $$

(Map p66; ☎2222-6190; cnr Av 9 & Calle 15;
mains US$8-36; ⏱11am-10:30pm Mon-Thu,
11am-11:30pm Fri, 5pm-midnight Sat; ☞)
Location. Location. Location. This long-
time Italian cafe and expat favorite has
it. Set on a sprawling terrace in a vintage
Barrio Otoya mansion, it's a perfect spot
to enjoy a glass of wine and good (if not
earth-shattering) pizzas and pastas within sight of a splashing outdoor fountain.
At lunchtime on weekdays, don't miss the
good-value *plato del día* (US$8).

Park Café   European $$$

(☎2290-6324; parkcafecostarica.blogspot.
com; tapas US$6-15; ⏱5:30-9:30pm Tue-Sat)
At this felicitous fusion of antique shop
and French restaurant, Michelin-starred
chef Richard Neat offers an exquisite
dégustation menu featuring smaller
sampling plates (Spanish tapas–style) and
a carefully curated wine list. The romantic,

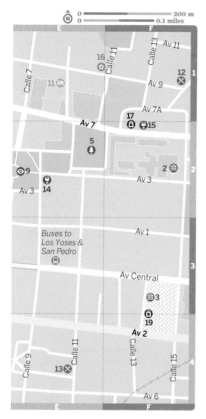

Central San José

candlelit courtyard is eclectically decorated with Asian antiques imported by Neat's partner, Louise French. It's near Parque La Sabana's northeast corner (100m north of Rostipollos restaurant).

La Esquina de Buenos Aires
Argentine $$$

(Map p66; ☑2223-1909; laesquinadebuenosaires.com; cnr Calle 11 & Av 4; mains US$15-29; ⊙11:30am-3pm & 6-10:30pm Mon-Thu, 12:30-11pm Fri & Sat, noon-10pm Sun; ☑) Spanish-tile floors, white linens and the sound of old tangos evoke the atmospheric bistros of San Telmo, as does the menu, featuring grilled Argentine cuts of steak, house-made *empanadas* and an extensive selection of fresh pastas in exquisite sauces. The excellent South American–centric wine list, attentive service and flickering candlelight make this an ideal place for a date. Reservations recommended.

Kalú Café & Food Shop
International $$$

(Map p62; ☑2221-2081; www.kalu.co.cr; cnr Calle 7 & Av 11; mains US$15-21; ⊙noon-7pm Mon & Tue, noon-10pm Wed-Fri, 8am-10pm Sat; ☑) Sharing a sleek space with **Kiosco SJO** (☑2258-1829; www.kioscosjo.com; cnr Av 11 & Calle 7; ⊙11am-6pm Mon, 11am-9:30pm Tue-Sat) in Barrio Amón, chef Camille Ratton's exceptional back-patio cafe serves a global fusion menu of soups, salads, sandwiches, pastas and unconventional delights such as the fish taco trio filled with mango-glazed salmon, red curry prawns and macadamia-crusted tuna. Don't miss the mind-meltingly delicious cheesecake, served with fresh strawberries stewed in balsamic.

♥ If You Like… Markets

If you like the Mercado Central, we think you'll like these other markets in San José:

1 MERCADO BORBÓN
(Map p66; cnr Av 3 & Calle 8) Adjacent to the Mercado Central, the Borbón is more focused on fresh produce.

2 MERCADO ARTESANAL
(Crafts Market; Map p66; Plaza de la Democracia, Avs Central & 2 btwn Calles 13 & 15; ⊗9am-6pm) This tourist-oriented open-air market sells typical handicrafts and souvenirs.

3 FERIA VERDE DE ARANJUEZ
(Map p62; www.feriaverde.org; ⊗7am-noon Sat) Organic coffee, artisanal chocolate, tropical-fruit popsicles, fresh produce, baked goods, leather, jewelry and more in the park at the north end of Barrio Aranjuez, Saturdays.

4 ESCAZÚ FARMERS MARKETS
Saturday market is held along Av 2, just south of the park in Escazú Centro. An organic farmers market happens on Wednesday, 1km south of Paco, across from the Red Cross building.

🍷 Drinking & Entertainment

Stiefel
Pub
(Map p66; www.facebook.com/StiefelPub; ⊗6pm-1am Mon-Sat) A dozen-plus Costa Rican microbrews on tap and an appealing setting in a historical building create a convivial buzz at this recently opened pub half a block from Plaza España. Grab a pint of Pelona or Maldita Vida, Praying Nun or Japi Ending; better yet, order a flight of four miniature sampler glasses and try 'em all!

El Morazán
Bar
(Map p66; ☎2256-5110; www.facebook.com/barmorazan; cnr Calle 9 & Av 3; cocktails US$5-7; ⊗5pm-2am Mon-Sat) Facing Parque Morazán, this exposed-brick, Spanish tile–clad space dates back to 1904.

Throughout its long life it has hosted all manner of historical figures (including Che Guevara, according to one account). It is a popular hangout among Chepe's young artsy set. In addition to beer, there is a full menu of classic cocktails and snacks. On some nights, there is live music.

La Avispa
Gay & Lesbian
(Map p62; ☎2223-5343; www.laavispa.com; Calle 1 btwn Avs 8 & 10; ⊗8pm-1am Thu, 8pm-3am Fri & Sat, 5pm-3am Sun) A gay establishment that has been in operation for more than three decades, La Avispa (the Wasp) has a bar, pool tables and a boisterous dance floor that's been recommended by travelers. There are lesbian nights once or twice a month (including the last Friday of every month).

Centro Comercial El Pueblo
Bar, Club
(Map p62; ☎2221-9434; ⊗hours vary) This Mediterranean-style outdoor mall in Barrio Tournon is a warren of bars, clubs and music venues. The proximity of one place to the next makes it ideal for a pub crawl and there's stringent security (though wee hours can get a bit unruly). Things get going around 9pm and can go as late as 7am. Best of all, there's no cover charge midweek.

El Sótano
Live Music
(Map p62; ☎2221-2302; www.facebook.com/sotanocr; cnr Calle 3 & Av 11; ⊗8pm-2am) One of Chepe's most atmospheric new nightspots, Sótano is named for its cellar jazz club, where people crowd in for frequent performances including intimate Tuesday jam sessions; upstairs, a cluster of elegant high-ceilinged rooms in the same mansion have been converted to a gallery space, stage and dance floor where an

eclectic mix of groups play regular live gigs.

🔒 Shopping

Galería Namu
Handicrafts

(Map p66; 📞2256-3412, in USA 800-616-4322; www.galerianamu.com; Av 7 btwn Calles 5 & 7; ⏰9am-6:30pm Mon-Sat year-round, plus 1-4pm Sun Dec-Apr) This fair-trade gallery brings together artwork and cultural objects from a diverse population of regional ethnicities, including Boruca masks, finely woven Wounaan baskets, Guaymí dolls, Bribrí canoes, Chorotega ceramics, traditional Huetar reed mats, and contemporary urban and Afro-Caribbean crafts. It can also help arrange visits to remote indigenous territories in different parts of Costa Rica.

Kiosco SJO
Arts & Crafts

(Map p62; 📞2258-1829; www.kioscosjo.com; cnr Av 11 & Calle 7; ⏰noon-7pm Mon & Tue, noon-8pm Wed-Fri, 10am-8pm Sat) With a focus on sustainable design by Latin American artisans, this sleek shop in Barrio Amón stocks handmade jewelry, hand-tooled leather boots and bags, original photography, artisanal chocolates, fashion and contemporary home decor by established regional designers. It's pricey, but rest assured that everything you find here will be of exceptional quality.

eÑe
Arts & Crafts

(Map p66; 📞2222-7681; laesquina13y7@gmail.com; cnr Av 7 & Calle 13; ⏰10am-6:30pm Mon-Sat) This hip little design shop across from Casa Amarilla sells all manner of pieces crafted by Costa Rican designers and artists, including clothing, jewelry, handbags, picture frames, zines and works of graphic art.

Barrio Bird Walking Tours

The knowledgeable and engaging Stacey Corrales shows visitors San José's famous and not-so-famous sights on the Barrio Bird Walking Tours (www.toursanjosecostarica.com), providing history and insights on the city's architecture, murals and urban art. Specialized tours also cater to gourmands, photographers and bar-crawlers.

Mercado Central
Market

(Map p66; Avs Central & 1 btwn Calles 6 & 8; ⏰6am-6pm Mon-Sat) This is the best and cheapest place in the city to buy just about anything, from hammocks (*Hecho en Nicaragua*) to *pura vida* T-shirts (made in China) to a vast assortment of forgettable

Shopping, San José
ALFONSE PAGANO/GETTY IMAGES ©

Below: sculpture in the lobby of the Teatro Nacional; **Right:** Teatro Nacional (p61)

(BELOW) RICHARD CUMMINS/GETTY IMAGES ©; (RIGHT) MATTHEW D WHITE/GETTY IMAGES ©

knickknacks. For something decidedly more Costa Rican, export-quality coffee beans and cigars can be bought here at a fraction of the price you'll pay in tourist shops.

ℹ️ Information

Canatur (Cámara Nacional de Turismo; ☎2234-6222, 2440-1676; www.canatur.org; Aeropuerto Internacional Juan Santamaría; ⏰7am-10pm)

Instituo Costarricense de Turismo (☎2222-1090; www.visitcostarica.com; Edificio de las Academias, Av Central btwn Calles 1 & 3; ⏰9am-5pm Mon-Fri)

Hospital CIMA (☎2208-1000; www.hospitalcima.com; Los Laureles)

ℹ️ Getting There & Away

San José is the country's transportation hub, and it's likely that you'll pass through. If you're only in town for a couple of days, most travel will be on foot.

Car

Don't rent a car if you're not leaving San José. The traffic is heavy, the streets narrow and the meter-deep curbside gutters make parking nerve-wracking. In addition, break-ins are frequent. If you are renting a car, note that there is a surcharge for renting cars at Aeropuerto Internacional Juan Santamaría.

Air

Two airports serve San José. There is an international departure tax of US$29 when leaving the country. Aeropuerto Internacional Juan Santamaría handles all international flights and NatureAir domestic flights in its main terminal. Domestic flights on Sansa depart from the Sansa terminal.

In the San José suburb of Pavas, Aeropuerto Tobías Bolaños services private charter flights.

Airports & Airlines

All international flights leave from Juan Santamaría (SJO) airport outside Alajuela.

Aeropuerto Internacional Juan Santamaría (☎2437-2400; fly2sanjose.com) Handles all

international flights and NatureAir domestic flights in its main terminal. Domestic flights on Sansa depart from the Sansa terminal.

Aeropuerto Tobías Bolaños (☎2232-2820) In the San José suburb of Pavas; services private charter flights.

Bus

Bus transportation in San José can be bewildering. There is no public bus system, no central terminal, and schedules and prices change regularly. Download a useful but not always up-to-date PDF copy from the ICT website.

To Northwestern Costa Rica

Buses to **La Fortuna** (US$5, four hours) depart from Terminal San Carlos at 7am, 10:45am and 2:30pm.

Buses to **Monteverde/Santa Elena** (US$5.60, 4½ hours) depart from Terminal San Carlos at 6:30am and 2:30pm. Book ahead as this bus fills quickly.

To Península de Nicoya

Buses to **Montezuma** and **Mal País** (US$13, six hours) depart from Terminal Coca-Cola at 6am, 8am, 10am, noon, 2pm, 4pm and 6pm.

Empresas Alfarohas buses to **Nicoya** (US$7.80, five hours) depart at 6:30am, 10am, 1pm, 3pm and 5pm. It also runs buses to **Playa Nosara** (US$9.60, six hours, depart at 6am) and **Playa Tamarindo** (US$11.30, five hours, depart at 11:30am and 3:30pm).

To the Caribbean Coast

Empresarios Guapileños (Gran Terminal del Caribe) has buses to **Cariari** (US$3.35, 2½ hours) for transfer to **Tortuguero**, which depart at 6:10am, 9am, 10:30am, 1pm, 3pm, 4:30pm, 6pm and 7pm.

Autotransportes Caribeños (Gran Terminal del Caribe) runs buses to **Puerto Limón** (US$6.30, three hours) every 30 minutes from 5am to 7pm.

Autotransportes Mepe (Gran Terminal del Caribe) runs to **Puerto Viejo de Talamanca** (US$10.85, 4½ hours), leaving at 6am, 10am, noon, 2pm and 4pm.

To the Central Pacific Coast & Southern Costa Rica

Transportes Morales (Terminal Coca-Cola) goes to **Dominical** and **Uvita** (US$5, seven hours) at 6am and 3pm.

San José for Kids

If you're in Costa Rica for a day with your kids, the Museo de los Niños (p64) is a sure hit for children who just can't keep their hands off the exhibits. Young nature-lovers will enjoy getting up close and personal with butterflies at the **Spirogyra Jardín de Mariposas** (Map p62; ☎2222-2937; www.butterflygardencr.com; Barrio Amón; adult/child US$7/5; ⏲8am-4pm;; ☒to El Pueblo) or checking out the exotic animals at the **Parque Zoológico Nacional Simón Bolívar** (Map p62; ☎2233-6701; www.fundazoo.org; Av 11 btwn Calles 7 & 9; adult/child US$5/3.50; ⏲8am-3:30pm Mon-Fri, 9am-4:30pm Sat & Sun).

Transportes Jacó (Terminal Coca-Cola) runs buses to **Jacó** (US$4.75, three hours), departing at 7:30am, 10:30am, 1pm, 3:30pm and 6:30pm.

Blanco Lobo runs to **Puerto Jiménez** (US$15, eight hours) at 8am and noon. This bus fills up quickly in high season, so book tickets in advance.

Shuttle Buses

Grayline (☎2220-2126; www.graylinecostarica.com; $33-89) and Interbus (☎2283-5573; www.interbusonline.com; US$37-57) shuttle passengers in air-conditioned minivans from San José to a long list of popular destinations around Costa Rica. They are more expensive than the standard bus service, but they offer door-to-door service and can get you there faster.

San José Cultural Centers

Various foreign institutions host film nights, art exhibits, theater, live music and academic conferences. Call ahead in January and February, when these spots tend to have limited hours.

Alianza Francesa (☎2222-2283; www.afsj.net; cnr Calle 5 & Av 7) Has French classes, a small library and rotating art exhibits in a historic Barrio Amón home.

Centro Cultural de España (☎2257-2919; www.ccecr.org; Rotonda del Farolito, Barrio Escalante) Offers a full roster of events, an audiovisual center and lending library.

Centro de Cine (Map p66; ☎2223-0610, 2223-2127; www.centrodecine.go.cr; cnr Calle 11 & Av 9) This film center holds festivals, lectures and events in outside venues.

AROUND SAN JOSÉ

Over the years, San José's urban sprawl has crawled up the hillsides, blurring the lines between the heart of the city and its surrounding villages. The region now has a little bit of everything, from crowded slums to stylish residential neighborhoods. A few hundred meters east of downtown San José are the contiguous neighborhoods of Los Yoses and San Pedro, home to a number of embassies and the most prestigious university in the country, the Universidad de Costa RIca (UCR). To the west, about 7km away, is Escazú, where Americanized housing developments sit alongside old Tico homesteads.

Los Yoses & San Pedro

These two side-by-side neighborhoods may lie in close proximity to each other, but their characters are totally unique. Los Yoses is a charming residential district, dotted with modernist structures, historic inns and chilled-out eateries. San Pedro, on the other hand, houses the university district, and is brimming with bars, clubs and student activity.

Sleeping & Eating

Hostel Toruma
Hostel $

(📞info 2234 8186; www.hosteltoruma. com; Av Central btwn Calles 29 & 33; dm/s/d US$12/35/45; 🅿 @ 🛜 ⚧; 🚇 San Pedro, taxi) Overlooking Av Central from a small hill, this graceful neoclassical home once belonged to José Figueres, the Costa Rican president who abolished the army and granted women the right to vote. In late 2009 the hotel completed a top-to-bottom makeover that preserved the Spanish-tile floors and left the facade's decorative friezes sparkling. While the Toruma contains four dormitories, it feels much more like an inn, with 17 large private rooms, each of which is equipped with a modern bathroom, a sofa, wi-fi and a flat-screen TV. Upstairs, an internet lounge is dotted with bean bags; downstairs, a small poolside restaurant serves breakfast, light snacks and beer. It's a mellow spot, popular with chilled-out solo travelers, couples and young families – and one of the best budget deals in San José.

Olio
Mediterranean $$

(📞2281-0541; www.facebook.com/ Restaurante.olio; cnr Calle 33 & Av 3; tapas from US$5, dishes US$10-20; ⊙noon-midnight Mon-Fri, from 6pm Sat; 🍴) This cozy, Mediterranean-flavored gastropub in a century-old brick building in Barrio Escalante serves a long list of tempting tapas, including divine stuffed mushrooms (*hongos madrileños*), goat-cheese croquettes, house-made pastas and garlic shrimp. The entic-

ing drinks list includes homemade sangría and a decent selection of beers and wines. It's a romantic spot for a date, with imaginative, conversation-worthy quirks of decor and beautiful patrons.

Sofía Restaurante Mediterráneo
Mediterranean $$

(📞2224-5050; www.sofiamediterraneo.com; cnr Calle 33 & Av 1; mains US$8-22; ⊙noon-11pm Tue-Sat, to 5pm Sun; 🍴) This hidden Barrio Escalante gem serves a superb mix of authentic Mediterranean specialties, including house-made hummus, dolmas, tortellini, grilled lamb and a rotating selection of daily specials, accompanied by sweet, delicate baklava for dessert. The restaurant doubles as a community cultural center where Turkish owner Mehmet Onuralp hosts occasional theme dinners featuring musicians, chefs and speakers from around the Mediterranean.

Chorreadas (savory corn pancakes)
DREAMPICTURES/SHANNON FAULK/GETTY IMAGES ©

Entertainment

Jazz Café
Live Music

(☎2253-8933; www.jazzcafecostarica.com; Av Central; cover US$6-10; ⏰6pm-2am Mon-Sat) This San Pedro venue is *the* destination in San José for live music, with a different band every night. Countless performers have taken to the stage here, including legendary Cuban bandleader Chucho Valdés and Colombian pop star Juanes. Its sister club in **Escazú** (☎2288-4740; **north side of Autopista Próspero Fernández;** ⏰**from 7pm**) features a similar mix of local and international bands. Variable cover charges start around US$5.

Escazú

You can find an unusual juxtaposition of gringo expats, moneyed aristocrats and old-world Tico village life in this sprawling suburb that climbs a steep hillside overlooking San José and Heredia.

Sleeping & Eating

Costa Verde Inn
Inn $$

(☎2228-4080, in USA 800-773-5013; www.costaverdeinn.com; s/d/tr incl breakfast $60/70/80, d apt from $90; P@🛜🏊) This homey stone inn is surrounded by gardens that contain a hot tub, a mosaic-tile swimming pool, a BBQ area and a sundeck with wi-fi. Fourteen rooms of various sizes have king-size beds, comfy rocking chairs and folk-art accents. Five apartments come with fully equipped kitchen. A generous Tico breakfast is served on the outdoor terrace. Weekly rates are available.

Posada El Quijote
B&B $$

(☎2289-8401; www.quijote.cr; Calle del Llano; **d standard/superior/deluxe/studio apt incl breakfast US$85/95/105/115;** P🍽❄🛜) This Spanish-style hillside *posada* in Bello Horizonte rates as one of the area's top B&Bs. Homey standard rooms have wood floors, throw rugs, cable TV and hot-water bathrooms; superior and deluxe units have a patio or a private terrace. Guests are invited to take a nip at the honor bar, then soak up sweeping Central Valley views on the patio.

La Casona de Laly
Costa Rican $

(☎2288-5807; cnr Av 26 & Calle 132; bocas $2-5, mains $6-15; ⏰11am-midnight Mon-Sat, to 6pm Sun) At the heart of Escazú Centro, this much-loved restaurant-tavern specializes in country-style Tico fare. Locals and expats alike pack the joint for cheap, lip-smacking *bocas,* ice-cold beers and a soundtrack of merengue accompanied by the cackling of the owner's pet birds, who inhabit the cages along the restaurant's west wall. Don't miss the delicious *dados de queso* (fried cheese cubes).

San José skyline
JOHN COLETTI/GETTY IMAGES ©

Buena Tierra

Organic **$**

(☎2288-0342; www.facebook.com/CafeOr-
ganicoBuenaTierra; cnr Calle 134 & Av 34; mains
US$6-8; ⊙9am-5:30pm Mon-Fri, to 2pm Sat;
⚡) With tree-trunk tabletops and huge
windows letting in fresh breezes, this
cute, friendly cafe in Escazú Centro is a
good place to detox. Only organic fruits,
vegetables, rice and beans are used, while
batidos (fruit shakes) are made with your
choice of water, milk, goat's milk, yogurt
or almond milk. The cafe also organizes
a Wednesday-morning organic farmers
market.

 Shopping

Biesanz Woodworks

Arts & Crafts

(☎2289-4337; www.biesanz.com; ⊙8am-5pm
Mon-Fri, 9am-3pm Sat) Located in the hills of
Bello Horizonte in Escazú, the workshop
of Biesanz Woodworks can be difficult to
find, but the effort will be well worth it.
This shop is one of the finest woodcrafting
studios in the nation, run by celebrated
artisan Barry Biesanz. His bowls and other
decorative containers are exquisite and
take their inspiration from pre-Columbian
techniques, in which the natural lines
and forms of the wood determine the
shape and size of the bowl. The pieces are
expensive (from US$85 for a palm-size
bowl), but they are unique – and so deli-
cately crafted that they wouldn't be out of
place in a museum.

ⓘ Getting There & Around

Frequent buses between San José and Escazú
cost about US$0.75 and take about 25 minutes.
All depart San José from east of the Coca-Cola
Terminal or south of the Hospital San Juan de
Dios. They take several routes via San Rafael.

Central Valley

Costa Rica's soul sprang from the Central Valley's coffee-cultivated hillsides. This is not only the geographical center of the country, it is its cultural and spiritual core. It is here that the Spanish first settled, and here that coffee built a prosperous nation. In this mountainous region of nooks and crannies, entertainment consists of hanging out in a bustling mountain town, and watching folks gather for market days and church. That doesn't mean, however, that there is nothing to do. You can ride raging rapids, visit the country's oldest colonial church, look for trogons in mist-shrouded forests and hike myriad volcanoes. So take your time. When you explore the Central Valley, you'll not only witness great beauty, but also see the landscape that gave Costa Rica its character.

Sarchí's signature geometric designs (p90)
LATITUDESTOCK · BILL BACHMANN/GETTY IMAGES ©

Central Valley

La Virgen

Florencia

Aguas Zarcas

Venecia

Rio Cuarto

Ciudad Quesada (San Carlos)

Colonia del Toro

San Miguel

Volcán Platanar (2183m)

El Sucre

Laguna Hule

Parque Nacional Juan Castro Blanco

Cariblanco

Río Toro

Río Sarapiquí

Volcán Porvenir (2267m)

Bajos del Toro

10°15'N

Parque Nacional Volcán Poás

Volcán Poás (2704m)

Parque Nacio Braulio Carr

Los Angeles Cloud Forest Adventure Park

Zarcero

Poasito

Vara Blanca

Volcán Barva (2906m)

Concepción

Río Barranca

Alajuela

Reserva Forestal Grecia

Fraijanes

120

Sacramento

126

San Ramón

Naranjo

4 Sarchí

Paso Llano

Monte de la Cruz

141

Palmares

1

Grecia

San Pedro de Poás

130

San José la Mont

Puente de Piedra

World of Snakes

3 El Casti

Zona Protectora Río Grande

Rosario

La Argentina

Las Cataratas de Los Chorros

Santa Bárbara

Barva

San

135

Rincón de Salas

The ARA Project

San Joaquín de Flores

San Rafa

ALAJUELA

3 HERED

Atenas

La Garita

Juan Santamaria International Airport

San Antonio

Santo Domingo

Túrrucares

La Guácima

Butterfly Farm

Tobías Bolaños

3

San Juan de Tiba

Río Virilla

27

Pavas

7

SAN JO

Ciudad Colón

Santa Ana

Escazú

Alajuelita

1 Rafting in Turrialba

2 Monumento Nacional Arqueológico Guayabo

3 Barva

4 Sarchí

5 Volcán Irazú

Reserva Indígena Quitirrisí

Aserri

Santiago de Puriscal

Tarba

San Ignacio de Acosta

San Gabriel

San José

Río Candelaria

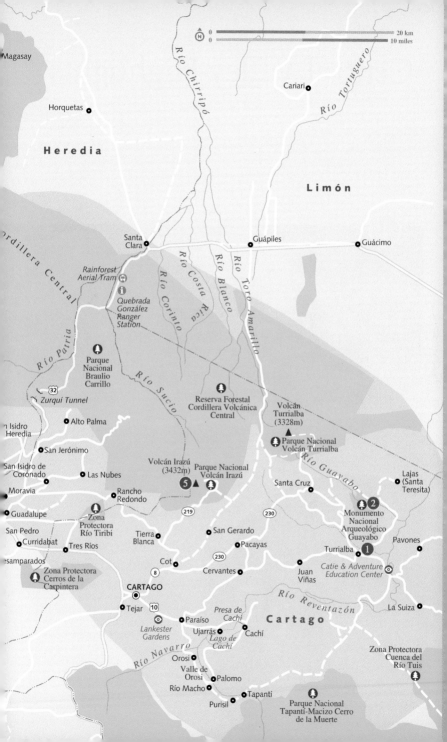

Central Valley Highlights

Rafting in Turrialba

A beautiful town in Costa Rica's Central Valley, Turrialba (p99) serves as a jumping-off point to excellent white-water rafting. With big mountains and a long rainy season, Turrialba's nearby rivers offer a range of intensity, making trips suitable for any comfort level.

White-water rafting, Río Pacuare (p100)

1

2 ### Monumento Nacional Arqueológico Guayabo

Walking along the aqueducts and seeing the mysterious petroglyphs at Costa Rica's largest archaeological site offers a peek into the past. While now only the modest remains of a pre-Columbian city, Guayabo (p102) was once inhabited by more than 20,000 sophisticated urban dwellers.

Barva

3

Lying on the edge of the city of Heredia, the historic colonial town of Barva (p94) was first settled in 1561 by the Spanish conquistadors. More relevant to modern interests, Barva is also the home of the most famous coffee roaster in Costa Rica, Café Britt Finca (p95). Coffee fruits

Sarchí

4

Sarchí (p90) is the birthplace of the *carreta* (painted oxcart). Beyond these colorful symbols of the Costa Rican working class, this tiny town in the Central Valley is also home to dozens of woodworking studios that fashion richly hued hardwoods into elaborate handicrafts. Colourful wheel of a *carreta*, Sarchí

Volcán Irazú

5

The roof of the Central Valley is this 3432m-tall active volcano (p97), which in the country's brief history has unleashed its liquid fury more than 15 times. These days things have temporarily quietened down, and on clear days, views from the summit open out to both the Pacific Ocean and the Caribbean Sea.

Central Valley's Best...

Historical Sites

○ **Museo Juan Santamaría** Visit this historic jail to learn about Costa Rica's famous drummer boy. (p86)

○ **El Fortín** The remains of a Spanish fortress is the symbol of Heredia. (p92)

○ **Basílica de Nuestra Señora de Los Ángeles** The country's most celebrated religious monument. (p96)

○ **Monumento Nacional Arqueológico Guayabo** Costa Rica's most prominent pre-Columbian site. (p102)

Splurges

○ **Xandari Resort Hotel & Spa** Luxuriate in a quiet refuge before catching your flight home. (p88)

○ **Casa Turire** An exceedingly elegant throwback to the colonial era. (p101)

○ **Hotel Chalet Tirol** Treat yourself to a bit of surprising Alpine gingerbread quaintness. (p92)

Photo Ops

○ **Volcán Irazú** On a clear day, the summit affords a killer panorama of both coasts. (p97)

○ **Palmares** Tens of thousands head here for one of the biggest parties in the country. (p91)

○ **Lower Pacuare** Home to some of Central America's most scenic rafting. (p100)

Need to Know

Eats & Drinks

○ **Xandari** A place where the views are as impressive as the organic menu. (p89)

○ **FInca Rosa Blanca** This picturesque hillside inn's restaurant serves locally focused, creative dishes. (p95)

○ **La Casona del Maíz** Specializing in regional corn-based dishes and superb Tico country cooking. (p89)

○ **Café Britt Finca** The best spot for a freshly brewed cup of shade-grown coffee. (p95)

ADVANCE PLANNING

○ **One month before** Book car rental for collection from Aeropuerto Internacional Juan Santamaría.

○ **Two weeks before** Check the Tico Times (www.ticotimes.net) for upcoming festivals in the region and book hotels.

○ **One week before** Book rafting trips.

GETTING AROUND

○ **Air** Alajuela – not San José – is actually the closest city to the international airport.

○ **Bus** Intercity bus connections are fast and frequent.

○ **Car** Winding mountain roads offer expansive views over the valley, making this the best way to get around the region.

○ **Walk** All of the major cities in the region are safe to walk around by day, and are generally safe at night.

BE FOREWARNED

○ **Signage** Roads in the Central Valley are poorly signed, so it's best to bring along a good road map when setting out; better yet, rent a GPS unit with your car.

○ **Flat tire scam** A scam involving flat tires on rental cars has plagued travelers to Aeropuerto Internacional Juan Santamaría for years. If your rental gets a flat immediately upon leaving the airport, be very wary of accepting 'help' from a good Samaritan. Most rental companies advise that you drive (on the flat tire) to the nearest gas station for help.

○ **Car break-ins** This area is generally very safe, but there are regular reports of car break-ins. As anywhere in the country, never leave anything valuable in your car.

Left: Basílica de Nuestra Señora de Los Ángeles (p96) **Above:** Río Pacuare (p100)

UDY BELLAH/GETTY IMAGES ©; (ABOVE) KEVIN SCHAFER/GETTY IMAGES ©

Central Valley Itineraries

A romp to the white water and glorious valley vistas of the Central Valley and highlands is thrilling unto itself, and a perfect way to fill a few days at the beginning or end of a trip.

3 DAYS

TURRIALBA TO PARQUE NACIONAL VOLCÁN TURRIALBA

THE TURRIALBA CIRCUIT

If your time is limited, hop on a bus to Turrialba, the perfect base for getting an exhilarating, quick taste of what the region has to offer: white water, pre-Columbian history and scenic countryside drives. Furthermore, if your travels started in San José, you need only hop on a quick bus to Turrialba, and then use the town as a base for exploring a couple of the Central Valley's top highlights.

After getting your bearings in ❶ **Turrialba** (p99), arrange a white-water rafting trip with any of the town's recommended operators. Depending on the time of year and your skill level, your next destination will be one of the stretches along the ❷ **Ríos Reventazón**

& Pacuare (p100). Day trips can take in a good sampling of rapids, though you can always extend your time out on the water with an overnight rafting trip. When you're ready to dial things down a notch, the ❸ **Monumento Nacional Arqueológico Guayabo** (p102) provides a rich cultural perspective on the pre-Columbian inhabitants of the area. If you can squeeze in a misty horseback ride on the slopes of rarely visited Volcán Turrialba, make the trek up to ❹ **Volcán Turrialba Lodge** (p103).

5 DAYS
CITY HOPPING IN THE CENTRAL VALLEY

Costa Rica's beaches and rainforests may garner most of the spotlight, but to truly understand the country, you need to understand its people. As the vast majority of Ticos live in the cities of the Central Valley, spending a few days here will acquaint you with the true pulse of the nation.

As the closest city to the airport, **Alajuela** (p86) provides a soft landing for bleary-eyed travelers, but it's also home to an attractive park that invites long bouts of people-watching.

Home to a large university, **②Heredia** (p92) bustles with activity, and has a few storied buildings that retell Costa Rica's

history as a Spanish colony. Today it is an elegant alternative to the nearby capital.

The *original* capital and long-time rival of San José (especially on the soccer field!), **③Cartago** (p95) is centered on one of the most impressive basilicas in Central America.

Finally, though it's not much more than an oversized town in comparison to the big three, **④Turrialba** (p99) offers up some bucolic charm as well as stunning natural surrounds.

View of the mountains from Turrialba
SWISH PHOTOGRAPHY/GETTY IMAGES ©

85

Discover
Central Valley

ALAJUELA

POP 43,000

Alajuela is by no means a tourist 'destination.' Much of the architecture is unremarkable, the streets are often jammed and there isn't a lot to see here. But it's an inherently Costa Rican city and, in its more relaxed moments, it reveals itself as such, with families having leisurely Sunday lunches and teenagers stealing kisses in the park. It's also a good base for exploring the countryside to the north.

◉ Sights

Parque Central   Park

(Avs Central & 1 btwn Calles Central & 2) The shady Parque Central is a pleasant place to relax beneath the mango trees, or people-watch in the evenings.

Museo Juan Santamaría   Museum

(☎ 2441-4775; Av 1 btwn Calles Central & 2; ⊙ 10am-5pm Tue-Sun) **FREE** Situated in a century-old structure that has served as both a jail and an armory, this museum chronicles Costa Rican history from early European settlement through the 19th century, with special emphasis on the life and history of Juan Santamaría and the pivotal mid-1850s battles of Santa Rosa, Sardinal and Rivas. Exhibits include videos, vintage maps, paintings and historical artifacts related to the conflict that ultimately safeguarded Costa Rica's independence.

Cathedral   Church

(Calle Central btwn Avs Central & 1) To the east of Parque Central is the 19th-century cathedral, which suffered severe damage in

Alajuela Cathedral
TRAVELIB PRIME/ALAMY ©

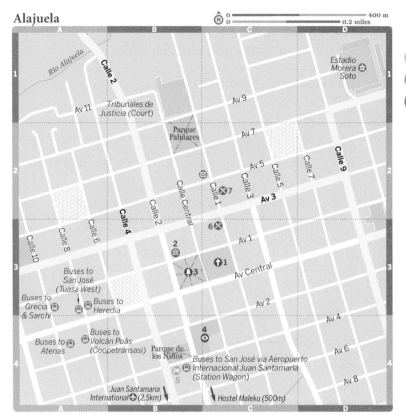

the 1991 earthquake. The hemispherical cupola is unusually constructed of sheets of red corrugated metal. Two presidents are buried here.

Parque Juan Santamaría Plaza
(Calle 2 btwn Avs 2 & 4) Two blocks south of Parque Central, this plaza features a statue of the hero in action, flanked by cannons. Across the way, the **Parque de los Niños** has a more park-like scene going, complete with playground equipment, chattering toddlers and canoodling teenagers.

 Sleeping

Hostel Maleku Hostel $
(☎2430-4304; www.malekuhostel.com; incl breakfast dm US$15, s/d without bathroom US$25/38; @ 🛜) This super-friendly,

family-run backpackers' abode has five spick-and-span rooms tucked into a vintage home between the airport and downtown Alajuela (opposite Hospital San Rafael). There's a communal kitchen, plus free storage for items brought from home that you don't need while in Costa

Detour:
Parque Nacional Volcán Poás

Just 37km north of Alajuela by a winding and scenic road is the most heavily trafficked national park in Costa Rica. And for those who want to peer into an active volcano – without the hardship of hiking one – it's ideal. The centerpiece is, of course, Volcán Poás (2740m), which had its last blowout in 1953. This event formed the eerie and enormous crater, which is 1.3km across and 300m deep – and offers the wonderful opportunity to watch the bubbling, steaming cauldron belch sulfurous mud and water hundreds of meters into the air. There are two other craters as well, one of which contains a sapphire-blue lake ringed by high-altitude forest.

The main crater at Poás continues to be active to varying degrees. In fact, the park was briefly closed in 1989 after a minor eruption sent volcanic ash spouting more than 1km into the air, and lesser activity closed the park intermittently in 1995. In recent years, however, Poás has posed no imminent threat, thought scientists still monitor it closely.

In the meantime, the most common issue for visitors is the veil of clouds that gather around the mountain at about 10am (even in dry season). Even if the day looks clear, get to the park as early as possible or you won't see much.

Rica (winter coats, bike boxes). Free airport drop-off service is available hourly between 5am and 5pm.

Alajuela Backpackers Boutique Hostel
Hotel $

(☎ 2441-7149; www.alajuelabackpackers.com; cnr Av 4 & Calle 4; dm/r/ste US$17/55/70; ❄@🛜) This four-story place with cookie-cutter rooms may feel a tad institutional at first glance, but dig deeper and you'll discover some big pluses: free shuttles to and from the airport, air-conditioned dorms and doubles with en-suite bathrooms and a super-cool 4th-floor bar terrace where you can sip beers while watching planes take off in the distance.

Trapp Family Lodge
Inn $$

(☎ 2431-0776; www.trappfam.com; incl breakfast r US$99, additional person US$20, child 3-11yr US$15; P@🛜🏊) The most attractive option you'll find so close to the airport landing strip, this hacienda-style country inn houses eight terra-cotta–tiled rooms with comfortable beds. The

best units have balconies overlooking the inviting turquoise pool and verdant garden laced with bougainvillea and fig trees. Despite its rural feel, it's only 2km from the international airport; free airport transfers are provided.

Xandari Resort Hotel & Spa
Hotel $$$

(☎ 2443-2020, in USA 866-363-3212; www.xandari.com; d villa US$299-418, q villa US$622; P❄🛜🏊) ✈ With spectacular bird's-eye views of the Central Valley, this romantic spot is the fanciful creation of a Californian architect–designer couple. Spacious individual villas, tastefully but playfully decorated in vibrant tropical colors and hand-woven textiles, include garden-view shower and sitting area. The grounds offer 4km of trails, five waterfalls, three pools, two Jacuzzis, a spa and an organic-foods restaurant. Find directions on the website.

Eating

Jalapeños Central   Mexican $
(☎2430-4027; Calle 1 btwn Avs 3 & 5; mains US$4-8; ☉11:30am-9pm Mon-Sat, to 8pm Sun)
Run by an animated Colombian-American from New York City, this popular Tex-Mex spot will introduce some much-needed spice into your diet. You'll also find Tico specialties, spit-roasted chicken and New York–style cheesecake.

Coffee Dreams Café   Cafe $
(☎2430-3970; cnr Calle 1 & Av 3; mains US$5-9; ☉7:30am-9pm Mon-Sat, 9am-7pm Sun; 🍴)
For breakfast, *bocas* (appetizers) and a variety of *típico* (traditional Costa Rican) dishes, this centrally located cafe is a reliably good place to dine or enjoy a coffee accompanied by one of its rich desserts.

La Casona del Maíz   Costa Rican $
(☎2433-5363; mains US$4-16; ☉7am-9pm)
About 14km west of Alajuela, La Casona del Maíz is usually jam-packed with families enjoying the spectacular Tico country cooking. The menu is heavy on the grilled meats and corn dishes, though there are veggie *casados* (set meals) as well. The *chorreadas* (savory pancakes) are excellent, but don't leave without sampling the tasty corn soup, studded with sweet, fresh kernels, or the falling-off-the-bone pork ribs (*costillas de cerdo*). Divine.

Xandari   International $$$
(☎2443-2020; www.xandari.com; Xandari Resort Hotel & Spa; mains US$9-24; ☉7am-10pm; 🍴) 🌿 If you want to impress a date, you can't go wrong at this elegant restaurant with incredible views. The menu is a mix of Costa Rican and international, with plenty of vegetarian options. The restaurant utilizes the resort's homegrown organic produce, supplemented by locally grown organic produce whenever possible – making for tasty *and* feel-good gourmet meals.

Getting There & Away

Taxis (around US$7) go to Juan Santamaría International Airport from central Alajuela.

There is no central bus terminal; instead, a number of small terminals and bus stops dot the southwestern part of the city. Buses go to the following destinations from Calle 8 between Avs Central and 1:

Heredia (Tuasa East) US$1.05, 30 minutes, departs every 15 minutes from 4am to 10pm.

San José via Juan Santamaría International Airport (Station Wagon); US$1.10, 45 minutes, departs every 10 minutes from 4am to 11:30pm.

San José (Tuasa West) US$1.10, 45 minutes, departs every 10 minutes from 5am to 11pm.

Sarchí US$0.75, 30 minutes, departs half-hourly from 5am to 10pm.

Volcán Poás (Coopetransasi) round-trip US$4.65, 1½ hours each way, departs 9am, returns at 2:30pm.

Volcán Poás
OLIVER J DAVIS PHOTOGRAPHY/GETTY IMAGES ©

Detour:
Los Ángeles Cloud Forest Adventure Park

This private **reserve** (2289-6569; per person US$20-45; 8am-4pm), 18km north of San Ramón, is centered on a lodge and dairy ranch that was once owned by ex-president Rodrigo Carazo. Some 800 hectares of primary and secondary forest have a short boardwalk and 11km of foot trails that lead to towering waterfalls and misty cloud forest vistas. The appeal of this cloud forest (which is actually adjacent to the reserve at Monteverde) is that it is comparatively untouristed, which means you will have a good chance of observing wildlife (jaguars and ocelots have been spotted), and the bird-watching is fantastic.

Bilingual naturalist guides are available to lead hikes (per person US$30) and guided horseback-riding trips (per hour US$20). Alternatively, you can zip along the tree tops on the reserve's obligatory canopy tour (per person US$45).

A taxi to the reserve and hotel costs about US$15 from San Ramón, and the turnoff is well signed from the Interamericana.

SARCHÍ

POP 12,300

Welcome to Costa Rica's most famous crafts center, where artisans produce the ornately painted oxcarts and leather-and-wood furnishings for which the Central Valley is known. You'll know you've arrived because just about everything is covered in the signature geometric designs – even city hall. Yes, it's a tourist trap, but it's a pretty one.

Sarchí is divided by the Río Trojas into Sarchí Norte and Sarchí Sur, and is rather spread out, straggling for several kilometers along the main road from Grecia to Naranjo. It's easiest to explore by private car.

In Sarchí Norte, you'll find the heart of the village, including a twin-towered **church**, some restaurants and *pulperías* (corner stores), and what is purported to be the **world's largest oxcart** (photo op!).

Eating

Don Felipe　　Costa Rican **$$**
(2454-4374, 8816-8212; Sarchí Sur; mains US$8-18; 9am-5pm Tue-Sun) One of the most popular spots for a lunch break is this family restaurant adjacent to the Fá-brica de Carretas Joaquín Chavarrí. Steak is the specialty here, but it also serves up a full range of *típico* cuisine.

Super Mariscos　　Seafood **$$**
(2454-4330; mains US$9-24; 11am-10pm; P) At a low-lying bend in the road in Sarchí Sur, 1km southeast of the plaza, Super Mariscos serves up good *ceviche* (seafood marinated in lemon or lime juice, garlic and seasonings), rice dishes and seafood galore, as well as pasta and a few beef dishes. Everything comes with a side of fries and a smidgen of salad.

 Shopping

Most travelers come to Sarchí for one thing only: *carretas,* the elaborate, color-fully painted oxcarts that are the unofficial souvenir of Costa Rica – and official symbol of the Costa Rican worker – or the super-comfortable leather-and-wood rocking chairs you'll see gracing terraces across Costa Rica.

Workshops are usually open from 8am to 4pm daily, accept credit cards and US dollars and can arrange international shipping for you. Following is a list of the most respected and popular spots, though with more than 200 vendors, it pays to shop around as prices and quality vary.

Coopearsa
Handicrafts

(☎ 2454-4196, 2454-4050; www.coopearsa. com; 200m west of soccer field, Sarchí Norte) In Sarchí Norte, 200m west of the soccer field, is this kitsch-filled paradise of *carretas,* woodwork and painted feathers.

Fábrica de Carretas Eloy Alfaro
Handicrafts

(☎ 2454-4131; Sarchí Norte) Just west of the town center (100m north of the Palí supermarket); produced the massive oxcart in Sarchí's main plaza.

Fábrica de Carretas Joaquín Chaverri
Handicrafts

(☎ 2454-4411; Sarchí Sur) Sarchí's oldest and best-known factory, 1.5km southeast of the plaza; watch artisans doing their meticulous work in the small studio in the back.

❶ Getting There & Away

Buses arrive and depart from Sarchí Norte.

Alajuela US$1.65, 1¼ hours, departs half-hourly from 5am to 10pm.

Grecia US$1, 20 minutes, departs half-hourly from 5am to 8:30pm.

San José US$2.25, 1½ hours, three direct buses daily; otherwise make connections in Grecia.

PALMARES

Palmares's claim to fame is the annual **Las Fiestas de Palmares**, a 10-day beer-soaked extravaganza that takes place in mid-January and features carnival rides, a *tope* (horse parade), fireworks, bands, exotic dancers, fried food, *guaro* (the local firewater made from sugarcane), tents and some 10,000 people. It is one of the biggest events in the country and is covered widely on national TV. For the other 355 days of the year, Palmares is a tumbleweed town, where life is centered on the ornate stained-glass **church** in the beautifully tree-shaded central plaza.

Buses run continuously from San José to Palmares throughout the festival. For information on the musical lineup, visit www.fiestaspalmares.com.

If you're driving, the road from Sarchí continues west to Naranjo, where it divides – head south for 13km to reach Palmares. It is well signed.

Brightly painted *carretas* (oxcarts)

RICHARD CUMMINS/GETTY IMAGES ©

HEREDIA

POP 123,600

During the 19th century, La Ciudad de las Flores (the City of the Flowers) was home to a *cafetalero* (coffee grower) aristocracy that made its fortune exporting Costa Rica's premium blend. Today the historic center retains some of this well-bred air, with a leafy main square, and low-lying buildings reflecting Spanish-colonial architectural style.

Sights

Iglesia de la Inmaculada Concepción
Church

Built in 1797, this striking white church facing wide, pleasant **Parque Central** is still in use. The church's thick-walled, squat construction is attractive in a Volkswagen Beetle sort of way. The solid shape has withstood the earthquakes that have damaged or destroyed almost all the other buildings in Costa Rica that date from this time.

El Fortín
Tower

This tower, constructed in 1876 by order of Heredia's provincial governor, is the official symbol of Heredia. It was declared a national historic monument in 1974, but because of its fragile state, it remains closed to the public.

Casa de la Cultura
Museum

(☎2261-4485; cnr Calle Central & Av Central; ⏰hours vary) **FREE** Occupying a privileged position on the corner of the plaza just above the church, this low-lying Spanish structure dates back to the late 18th century. It served at one point as the residence of President Alfredo González Flores, who governed from 1913 to 1917. It is beautifully maintained and now houses permanent historical displays as well as rotating art exhibits.

INBioparque
Gardens

(☎2507-8107; www.inbioparque.com/en; Santo Domingo; adult/student/child US$25/19/15, separate serpentarium admission adult/child US$3/2; ⏰9am-3pm Fri, 9am-4pm Sat & Sun; ♿) 🍃 At this excellent, wheelchair-accessible botanical garden, run by the non-profit National Biodiversity Institute (INBio), visitors can admire native plants and animals in miniature versions of the country's various life zones. Other attractions include farm animals, a butterfly garden, a serpentarium and a model sustainable home. Children's theater and multi-media shows run throughout the day. It's 4km south of Heredia; see the website for directions.

🛏 Sleeping

Hotel Chalet Tirol
Inn $$$

(☎2267-6222; www. hotelchaleltirol.com; d/ste US$98/138; 🅿🛜🐾) Northeast of Heredia (3km north of Castillo Country Club), this

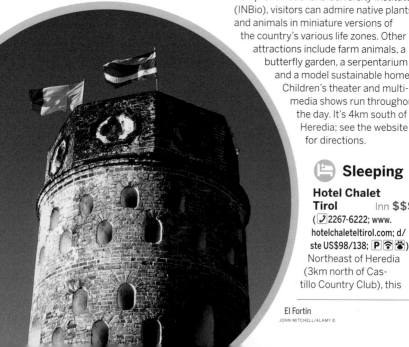

El Fortín
JOHN MITCHELL/ALAMY ©

Heredia

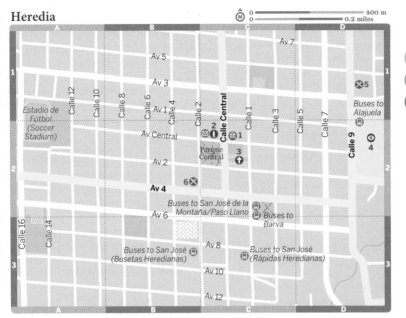

charming hotel channels the gingerbread quaintness of the Alps. (It once served as a backdrop for a German beer advert.) The 25 suites and chalets have cable TV, room service and a gorgeous mountain setting; some also have Jacuzzis, fireplaces or wheelchair-accessible facilities. The in-house restaurant hosts live music on weekends.

Hotel Bougainvillea Hotel $$$
(☎2244-1414; www.hb.co.cr; Santo Domingo; d incl breakfast US$123-152; P ⊜ @ ⊛ ☀) Set on 4 hectares about 6km outside of town, this efficient hotel is surrounded by an expansive, well-manicured garden dotted with old-growth trees, stunning flowers and plenty of statuary. Eighty-two crisp, whitewashed rooms have balconies with views of mountains or city, and several private trails wind by the swimming pool and tennis courts, through forest and orchards. Credit cards accepted.

Heredia

⦿ Sights
1 Casa de la Cultura...............................C2
2 El Fortín..C2
3 Iglesia de la Inmaculada
   Concepción.......................................C2
4 Universidad Nacional D2

⊗ Eating
5 Cowboy Steakhouse D1
6 Espigas B2

Eating

Espigas Costa Rican $
(☎2237-3275; cnr Av 2 & Calle 2; meals US$7-8; ⊙7am-9pm) One of the only eateries open on Sunday, Espigas is the go-to cafe for traditional *casados* and breakfasts, with views of the main plaza diagonally across the street. Order sit-down meals at the counter, stop by the front window to pick up fresh *batidos* (fruit shakes) or pop in for a look at the tantalizing pastry case.

If You Like...
Flora & Fauna

If you like the natural wonders of flora and fauna at INBioparque, we think you'll like these other glimpses into the astounding nature of the Central Valley.

1 WORLD OF SNAKES

(☏2494-3700; www.theworldofsnakes.com; adult/child US$11/6; ☻8am-4pm) Grecia's premiere attraction is a well-run breeding center focused on supporting endangered snake populations. It's a slithering delight for families.

2 ZOO AVE

(☏2433-8989; www.zooavecostarica.org; La Garita; adult/child US$11/5; ☻9am-5pm; P⛟) This well-designed animal park shelters more than 115 species of birds, all four species of Costa Rican monkey, wild cats, reptiles and other native critters, many of which are rescues. Though technically a zoo, it is also an important animal breeding center that aims to reintroduce native species into the wild; admission fees fund wildlife rescue, rehabilitation, release and conservation programs.

3 LANKESTER GARDENS

(☏2511-7939; www.jbl.ucr.ac.cr; adult/student US$7.50/5; ☻8:30am-4:30pm) The University of Costa Rica runs this exceptional garden, a tranquil 11-hectare spot, with more than 1100 orchids. There is also a Japanese garden, as well as areas full of bromeliads, palms, heliconias and other tropical plants. Find it 5km west of Paraíso on the road to Cartago.

Cowboy Steakhouse Steakhouse $$
(☏2237-8719; Calle 9 btwn Avs 3 & 5; dishes US$7-18; ☻5-11pm Mon-Sat) This yellow-and-red joint with two bars has patio seating and the best beef cuts in town. As the title suggests, steak is the focal point, making it a meat-lover's must. But the hearty salads and extensive list of *bocas* are worth a nibble as well.

ⓘ Getting There & Away

Buses go to the following destinations:

Alajuela US$1.05, 45 minutes, departs every 15 minutes from 5am to 10pm.

Barva US$0.55, 15 minutes, departs half-hourly from 5:15am to 11:30pm.

San José (Busetas Heredianas) US$1.05, 20 minutes, departs every 10 minutes from 5am to 11pm.

San José (Rápidas Heredianas) US$0.85, 20 minutes, departs every 15 minutes from 4:40am to 11pm. Best option if you're transferring to a Caribbean-bound bus, as it drops you near San José's Terminal Caribeña.

San José de la Montaña/Paso Llano for Volcán Barva (Transportes del Norte; ☏2266-0019; www.transportesdelnorteltda.com); US$1.40, one hour, departs at 5:25am and 6:25am Monday to Friday, 6:40am Saturday, 6:45am Sunday.

BARVA
POP 5000

Just 2.5km north of Heredia, the historic town of Barva dates back to 1561 and has been declared a national monument. The town center is dotted with low-lying 19th-century buildings and is centered on the towering **Iglesia San Bartolomé**, which was constructed in 1893. Surrounded by picturesque mountains, it oozes colonial charm.

◉ Sights & Activities

Museo de Cultura Popular Museum
(☏2260-1619; Santa Lucía; ☻8am-4pm Mon-Fri, 10am-5pm Sun) FREE Housed in a restored 19th-century farmhouse 1.5km southeast of Barva and 3km north of Heredia, this tiny museum surrounded by well-labeled gardens is run by the Universidad Nacional. Visitors can tour rooms full of antique furniture, textiles, ceramics and other period pieces. On Sunday the onsite restaurant, La Fonda, serves *casados* (US$8) on its pleasant open-air terrace.

Café Britt Finca
Guided Tour

(☎ 2277-1600; www.coffeetour.com; adult with/without lunch US$37/22, student US$32/17; ⏰ tours 11am year-round, plus 3pm seasonally;) Costa Rica's most famous coffee roaster offers a 90-minute bilingual tour of its plantation that includes coffee tasting, a video presentation and a hokey stage play about the history of coffee (small kids will likely dig it). More in-depth tours are available, as are packages including transport from San José; reserve ahead. Drivers won't be able to miss the *many* signs between Heredia and Barva.

🛏 Sleeping & Eating

Finca Rosa Blanca
Inn $$$

(☎ 2269-9392, in USA 305-395-3042; www.fincarosablanca.com; Santa Bárbara; d incl breakfast US$305-540; P @ 🛜 🐾) 🌿 Set amid a stunning hillside coffee plantation 6km northwest of Barva, this honeymoon-ready, Gaudí-esque confection of suites and villas is cloaked in fruit trees that shade private trails. Thirteen sparkling white adobe rooms with wood-beam ceilings and private balconies are lavishly appointed; one tops a tower with 360-degree views, reached by a winding staircase made from a tree trunk.

Shower in an artificial waterfall, take a moonlit dip in the pool, have an organic citrus-coffee bath soak at the spa – or, better yet, dip into a very romantic dinner at the hotel's recommended restaurant, which serves locally focused dishes, such as mountain trout with sweet-corn ragout. Credit cards accepted.

ℹ Getting There & Around

Half-hourly buses travel between Heredia and Barva (US$0.55, 15 minutes), picking up and dropping off in front of Barva's church.

CARTAGO

POP 147,900

Following major earthquake damage in the early 20th century, nobody bothered to rebuild Cartago to its former quaint specifications. As in other commercial towns, expect plenty of functional concrete structures. One exception is the bright white **Basílica de Nuestra Señora de los Ángeles**, which is visible from many parts of the city, standing out like a snowcapped mountain above a plain of one-story edifices.

◎ Sights

Las Ruinas de la Parroquia
Ruin

(Iglesia del Convento; Calle 0 btwn Avs 0 & 2) This now-ruined church was built in 1575 as a shrine to St James the Apostle (Santiago, in Spanish), destroyed by the 1841 earthquake, rebuilt a few years later and then destroyed again in the 1910 earthquake. Today only the outer walls remain, but 'the Ruins' are a pleasant spot for hanging out – though legend has it that the ghost of a headless priest wanders the ground on foggy nights.

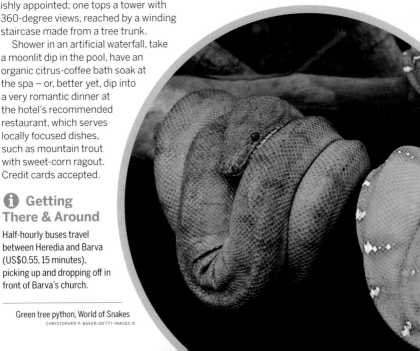

Green tree python, World of Snakes
CHRISTOPHER P. BAKER/GETTY IMAGES ©

MATTHEW D WHITE/GETTY IMAGES ©

 Don't Miss

Basílica de Nuestra Señora de Los Ángeles

Cartago's most important site, and Costa Rica's most venerated religious shrine, this basílica exudes airy Byzantine grace, with fine stained-glass windows, hand-painted interiors and ornate side chapels featuring carved wood altars. Though the structure has changed many times since 1635, when it was first built, its central relic remains unharmed: **La Negrita** (the Black Virgin), a small (less than 1m tall), probably indigenous, representation of the Virgin Mary, found on this spot on August 2, 1635.

NEED TO KNOW
Calle 15 btwn Avs 0 & 1

 Sleeping & Eating

Cartago works well as a day trip from San José or Orosi, as attractive lodging options here are limited. For an atmospheric, authentically local eating experience, pull up a seat at one of the *sodas* inside the Mercado Central, or browse the aisles for fresh produce. You'll also find plenty of bakeries and other eateries along Avs 0 and 1 in the heart of town.

Los Ángeles Lodge   B&B **$$**
(2591-4169, 2551-0957; hotel.los.angeles@ hotmail.com; Av 1 btwn Calles 13 & 15; incl

breakfast s US$35-40, d US$50-65; ❄ ☎) With its balconies overlooking the Plaza de la Basílica, this decent B&B stands out with spacious and comfortable rooms, hot showers and breakfast made to order.

La Puerta del Sol   Costa Rican **$$**
(2551-0615; Av 1 btwn Calles 13 & 15; mains US$8-13; 8am-10pm) Located downstairs from Los Ángeles Lodge and decorated with vintage photos of Cartago, this pleasant restaurant has been around since 1957 and serves myriad Tico specialties along with burgers and sandwiches.

Getting There & Away

Bus

Bus stops to the following destinations are scattered around town.

Orosi (Autotransportes Mata Irola) US$0.70, 40 minutes, departs half-hourly from 5:30am to 10pm Monday to Saturday.

San José (Lumaca) US$0.85, 45 minutes, departs every 15 minutes between 5am and midnight.

Turrialba (Transtusa) US$1.40, 1½ hours, departs every 45 minutes from 6am to 10pm weekdays, less frequently on weekends.

Volcán Irazú US$6, five hours round-trip, departs Cartago around 8:30am, returns around 12:30pm.

PARQUE NACIONAL VOLCÁN IRAZÚ

Looming on the horizon 19km northeast of Cartago, Irazú, which derives its name from the indigenous word *ara-tzu* (thunder-point), is the largest and highest (3432m) active volcano in Costa Rica. In 1723 the Spanish governor of the area, Diego de la Haya Fernández, watched helplessly as the volcano unleashed its destruction on the city of Cartago (one of the craters is named in his honor). Since the 18th century, 15 major eruptions have been recorded.

One of the most memorable occurred in March of 1963, welcoming visiting US President John F Kennedy with a rain of volcanic ash that blanketed most of the Central Valley (it piled up to a depth of more than 0.5m). In 1994 Irazú unexpectedly belched a cloud of sulfurous gas, though it quickly quietened down. At the time of research, the volcano was slumbering peacefully, aside from a few hissing fumaroles.

The national park was established in 1955 to protect 23 sq km around the base of the volcano. The summit is a bare landscape of volcanic-ash craters. The principal crater is 1050m in diameter and 300m deep; the adjacent Diego de la Haya Crater is 1000m in diameter, 80m deep and contains a small lake.

Getting There & Away

The only public transportation to Irazú (US$9) departs from San José at 8am and arrives at the summit around 10am. The bus departs from Irazú at 12:30pm.

VALLE DE OROSI

This straight-out-of-a-storybook river valley is famous for its mountain vistas, hot springs, a lake formed by a hydroelectric facility, a truly wild national park and coffee – lots and lots of coffee. A well-paved 32km scenic loop winds through a landscape of rolling hills terraced with shade-grown coffee plantations and expansive valleys dotted with pastoral villages. If you're lucky enough to have a rental car (or a good bicycle), you're in for a treat, though it's still possible to navigate most of the loop via public buses.

The loop road starts 8km southeast of Cartago in Paraíso, then heads south to Orosi. At this point you can either continue south into Parque Nacional Tapantí-Macizo Cerro de la Muerte or loop back to Paraíso via Ujarrás.

Sleeping & Eating

Orosi Lodge   Inn **$$**
(☎2533-3578; www.orosilodge.com; d/tr US$66/77, d/tr/q chalet US$107/124/141; 🅿🛜) This quiet haven, run by a friendly German couple, has six bright rooms with wood-beam ceilings, tile floors, minibar, coffeemaker and free organic coffee. Most face a lovely garden courtyard with a fountain, and one is wheelchair-accessible. Delicious, wholesome breakfasts cost US$8 at the colorfully decorated onsite cafe with scenic balcony seating.

Next door is a two-story, three-bedroom chalet that sleeps up to five, with its own parking spot and private entrance, a kitchen and comfy sitting area downstairs and a master suite and deck upstairs offering incredible views of volcanoes Irazú and Turrialba. Across the street there's also a *casita* sleeping up to four.

Left: Banded peacock butterfly; **Right:** Parque Nacional Tapantí-Macizo Cerro de la Muerte

(LEFT) MATTHEW D WHITE/GETTY IMAGES ©; (RIGHT) KONRAD WOTHE/GETTY IMAGES ©

Hotel Quelitales   Bungalow $$$

(☎ 2577-2222; www.hotelquelitales.com; d US$160-185; 🛜) This idyllically sited collection of six contemporary-chic bungalows features spacious rooms with wood floors, ultra-comfy mattresses, indoor and outdoor showers, private decks (some with waterfall views) and large canvases depicting the hummingbirds, ladybugs, toucans and other critters for whom the cabins are named. The onsite restaurant (open to non-guests on weekends only) serves trout and other Tico specialties.

Restaurante Coto   Costa Rican $$

(☎ 2533-3032; mains US$7-15; ⏱ 8am-9pm) Established in 1952, this family-run eatery on the north side of the park dishes out good *típico* food in a wood-beamed dining room with open-air seating. It's a great place to enjoy mountain views and the goings-on about town.

PARQUE NACIONAL TAPANTÍ-MACIZO CERRO DE LA MUERTE

Protecting the lush northern slopes of the Cordillera de Talamanca, this 580-sq-km **national park (adult/child 6-12yr US$10/1; ⏱ 8am-4pm; ♿)** is the wettest in Costa Rica, receiving an average of 7000mm of precipitation per year. Known simply as Tapantí, the park protects wild and mossy country that's fed by literally hundreds of rivers. Waterfalls abound, vegetation is thick and the wildlife is prolific, though not always easy to see because of the rugged terrain. In 2000 the park was expanded to include the infamous Cerro de la Muerte (Mountain of Death), a precipitous peak that marks the highest point on the Interamericana and the northernmost extent of *páramo,* a highland shrub and tussock-grass habitat – most commonly found in the Andes – that shelters a variety of rare bird species.

There is an **information center** (☎2200-0090; ⊙8am-4pm) near the park entrance where you can pick up a simple park map to a couple of trails leading to various attractions. The 'dry' season (January to April) is generally considered the best time to visit.

❶ Getting There & Away

With your own car, you can drive the 11km from Orosi to the park entrance; about halfway along, near the town of Purisil, the route becomes a bumpy gravel road (4WD recommended).

TURRIALBA

POP 31,100

When the railway shut down in 1991, commerce slowed down, but Turrialba nonetheless remained a regional agricultural center, where local coffee planters could bring their crops to market. And with tourism on the rise in the 1990s, this modest mountain town soon became known as the gateway to some of the best white-water rafting

on the planet. By the early 2000s, Turrialba was a hotbed of international rafters looking for Class-V thrills. For now, the Río Pacuare runs on, but its future is uncertain.

◉ Sights

Catie Gardens

(Centro Agronómico Tropical de Investigación | Center for Tropical Agronomy Research & Education; ☎2556-2700; www.catie.ac.cr; adult/student/youth US$10/8/6, guided tours US$25-50; ⊙7am-4pm Mon-Fri, 8am-4pm Sat & Sun) Catie's sprawling grounds, 2km east of Turrialba, encompass 1000 hectares dedicated to tropical agricultural research and education. Agronomists from all over the world recognize this as one of the most important centers in the tropics. You need to make reservations for one of several guided tours through laboratories, greenhouses, a seed bank, experimental plots and one of the most extensive libraries of tropical-agriculture literature in the world. Alternatively, pick up a map and take a self-guided walk.

White-Water Rafting in the Central Valley

The Turrialba area is a major center for white-water rafting. Traditionally the two most popular rafting rivers have been the **Río Reventazón** and the **Río Pacuare**, but the former has been dramatically impacted by a series of hydroelectric projects, including a huge 305-megawatt dam currently under construction.

As a result, most organized expeditions from Turrialba now head for the **Río Pacuare**, which arguably offers the most scenic rafting in Central America. The river plunges down the Caribbean slope through a series of spectacular canyons clothed in virgin rainforest, through runs named for their fury and separated by calm stretches that enable you to stare at near-vertical green walls towering hundreds of meters above.

○ **Lower Pacuare** With Class II–IV rapids, this is the more accessible run: 28km through rocky gorges, past an indigenous village and untamed jungle.

○ **Upper Pacuare** Classified as Class III–IV, but a few sections can go to Class V, depending on conditions. It's about a two-hour drive to the put-in, after which you'll have the prettiest jungle cruise on earth all to yourself.

The Pacuare can be run year-round, though June to October are considered the best months. The highest water is from October to December, when the river runs fast with huge waves. March and April are when the river is at its lowest, though it is still challenging.

Tours

Plenty of local operators offer either kayaking or rafting in the area. **Costa Rica Ríos** (☎ 2556-8664, in USA & Canada 888-434-0776; www.costaricarios.com) offers week-long rafting and kayak trips that must be booked in advance. Other operators include **Locos** (☎ 2556-6035, in USA 707-703-5935; www.whiteh2o.com), **Explornatura** (☎ 2556-0111, in USA & Canada 866-571-2443; www.explornatura.com; Av 4 btwn Calles 2 & 4) and **Tico's River Adventures** (☎ 2556-1231; www.ticoriver.com).

Sleeping & Eating

Casa de Lis Hostel Hostel $
(☎ 2556-4933; www.hostelcasadelis.com; Av Central near Calle 2; dm US$10, s/d/tr/q US$36/40/45/50, without bathroom US$20/25/35/40; ☎) Hands down Turrialba's best value, this sweet, centrally located six-room place (expanding to 10 rooms at research time) is a traveler's dream come true. Spotless dorms and doubles with comfy mattresses and individual reading lamps are complemented by a fully equipped kitchen, volcano-view roof terrace, pretty back garden, fantastic information displays and a distinctly friendly atmosphere. Breakfasts (US$6) and laundry service (per load US$8) are available.

Hotel Interamericano Hotel $
(☎ 2556-0142; www.hotelinteramericano.com; Av 1 near Calle 1; s/d/tr/q US$27/37/50/65, without bathroom US$12/22/33/44; P ☎)
On the south side of the old train tracks is this basic 21-room hotel, traditionally regarded by rafters as *the* meeting place in Turrialba. The eclectic collection of rather tired-looking rooms includes some with private bathrooms, some without and many that combine bunks with regular beds. Upstairs units are brighter and more welcoming; it's worth comparing before committing.

Turrialtico Lodge
Lodge $$

(☎2538-1111; www.turrialtico.com; d incl
breakfast US$58-75; P 🛜) Commanding
dramatic, sweeping views of the Río
Reventazón valley, this Tico-run lodge in
an old farmhouse 9km east of Turrialba
(off the highway to Siquirres) offers 19
attractive, polished-wood-panel rooms
decorated with local artwork. Rooms
in the reception building share a large
terrace and sitting area, and a pleasant
open-air restaurant (mains US$4 to
US$18) serves up country cooking.

Casa Turire
Luxury Hotel $$$

(☎2531-1111; www.hotelcasaturire.com;
d standard/ste/master ste incl breakfast
US$160/250/400, additional person US$25-
35, child under 6yr free; P ❄ @ 🛜 ☂) 🎋
This elegant three-story plantation
inn has 16 graceful, well-appointed
rooms with high ceilings, wood floors
and wrought-iron beds; a massive
master suite comes with a Jacuzzi
and excellent views of the coffee and
macadamia-nut plantations in the
distance. Adding icing to the cake are
spa services, a restaurant and bar,
horseback riding, bird-watching and
kayaking on the onsite lake.

Restaurant Betico Mata
Barbecue $

(☎2556-8640; Hwy 10; gallos US$1.80,
mains US$5-9; ⏲11am-midnight, until later
Sat & Sun) This carnivore's paradise at
the south end of town specializes in
gallos (open-face tacos on corn tortillas) piled with succulent, fresh-grilled
meats including beef, chicken, sausage
and pork, all soaked in the special
house marinade. All go smashingly well
with an ice-cold beer. A street-facing
counter makes it easy to park and grab a
snack if you're driving through town.

Rafting in Turrialba

RECOMMENDATIONS FROM
DANIEL BUSTOS ARAYA, RIVER
GUIDE FOR EXPLORNATURA

1 RÍO REVENTAZÓN FOR BEGINNERS
The Río Reventazón is divided into four
sections between the dam and the takeout point
in Siquirres. Las Máquinas (Power House) is a
Class II–III float that's perfect for families, while
Florida, the final and most popular segment, is a
scenic Class III with a little more white water to
keep things interesting.

2 LOWER PACUARE
Not to be outdone by its top competitor,
the Río Pacuare is divided into lower and upper
stretches, both of which are home to an excellent
variety of white-water runs. The Class III–IV
Lower Pacuare is the more accessible bit: 28km
through rocky gorges and isolated canyons, past
an indigenous village, untamed jungle and lots
of wildlife curious as to what the screaming is all
about.

3 UPPER PACUARE
The upper reaches of the Río Pacuare are
also classified as Class III–IV, but there are a
few sections that can go to Class V depending
on conditions. It's about a two-hour drive to the
put-in, so you need a bit more time to access this
remote stretch. It's most definitely worth the trip
though, especially since you'll be able to paddle
alongside the area's densest jungles.

4 RÍO REVENTAZÓN FOR THRILL-SEEKERS
If you've gone white-water rafting before, or
you're confident in your physical prowess and
quick reflexes, you might want to consider
some of the more advanced runs on the Río
Reventazón.

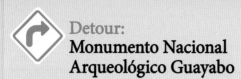

Detour:
Monumento Nacional Arqueológico Guayabo

Nestled into a patch of stunning hillside forest 19km northeast of Turrialba is the largest and most important archaeological site in the country. Guayabo (p102) is composed of the remains of a pre-Columbian city that was thought to have peaked at some point in AD 800, when it was inhabited by as many as 20,000 people. Today visitors can examine the remains of old petroglyphs, residential mounds, an old roadway and an impressive aqueduct system – built with rocks that were hauled in from the Río Reventazón along a cobbled, 8km road. Amazingly, the cisterns still work and (theoretically) potable water remains available onsite.

The settlement, which may have been occupied as early as 1000 BC, was mysteriously abandoned by AD 1400 and Spanish explorers left no record of ever having found the ruins. For centuries, the city lay largely untouched under the cover of the area's thick highland forest. But in 1968, archaeologist Carlos Aguilar Piedra of the University of Costa Rica began systematic excavations of Guayabo, finding polychromatic pottery and gold artifacts that are now exhibited at San José's Museo Nacional.

In 1973, as the site's importance became evident, Guayabo was declared a national monument, with further protections set forth in 1980. The site occupies 232 hectares, most of which remains unexcavated. It's a small place, so don't go expecting Mayan pyramids.

By car, head north out of Turrialba and make a right after the metal bridge. The road is well signed from there, and all but the last 3km is paved; 4WD is recommended, though not required, for the final rough section.

Buses from Turrialba (US$0.95, one hour) depart at 6:20am, 11:15am, 3:10pm and 5:30pm Monday through Saturday and at 9am and 3pm on Sunday. Buses return from Guayabo to Turrialba at 7am, 12:30pm and 4pm daily. You can also take a taxi from Turrialba (about US$25 round trip, with one hour to explore the park).

ℹ Getting There & Away

A modern bus terminal is located on the western edge of town off Hwy 10.

San José via Paraíso and Cartago US$2.80, 1¾ hours, departs hourly from 5am to 6:30pm.

Siquirres, for transfer to Puerto Limón US$2.30, 1½ hours, departs every 60 to 90 minutes from 6am to 6pm.

PARQUE NACIONAL VOLCÁN TURRIALBA

This rarely visited active volcano (3328m) was named Torre Alba (White Tower) by early Spanish settlers, who observed plumes of smoke pouring from its summit.

Turrialba was declared a national park in 1955, and protects a 2km radius around the volcano. Below the summit, the park consists of mountain rainforest and cloud forest, dripping with moisture and mosses, full of ferns, bromeliads and even stands of bamboo. Although small, these protected habitats shelter 84 species of bird and 11 species of mammal.

Turrialba's last major eruption was in 1866, but a century and a half later, the slumbering giant has begun showing sustained signs of life. Since 2010 it has regularly been belching forth quantities of sulfuric gas and ash, damaging the road to the summit, killing off trees and other vegetation and displacing small farming communities from the volcano's western slopes.

At the time of research visitors were only being allowed to climb as far as the park entrance gate, 3km below the summit; the park itself remained closed, pending completion of road repairs and construction of a protective bunker at the summit. For up-to-the-minute details on the volcano's status, contact **park headquarters** (☏ 8704-2432, 2557-6262; pnvolcanturrialba@gmail.com; ☺ 8am-3:30pm). At research time it was anticipated that,

when the park does reopen, entrance fees will be higher than at other national parks, as all visitors will need to be accompanied by an official guide.

In the meantime, a good way to experience some of Turrialba's magic up close is via a guided horseback excursion along the volcano's western flanks, offered by **Volcán Turrialba Lodge** (☏ 2273-4335; www.volcanturrialbalodge.com; per person incl breakfast US$45).

Caribbean Coast

The Caribbean coast's distinct flavor represents another culture altogether. While the sunny climate and easy accessibility of the Pacific have paved the way (literally) for development on that rich coast, the Caribbean side has languished in comparison. The same rain-drenched malarial wildness that thwarted the first 16th-century Spaniards has isolated this region for centuries. Thus, its culture – influenced by indigenous peoples and West Indian immigrants – blended slowly and organically to create this unique region of Costa Rica. It still takes a little more effort to travel here to see the nesting turtles of Tortuguero or dive the reefs of Manzanillo, but the Caribbean flavor is well worth a taste.

Ecolodge, Puerto Viejo de Talamanca (p134)
BRIAN BAILEY/GETTY IMAGES ©

Caribbean Coast

1 Parque Nacional Tortuguero
2 Puerto Viejo de Talamanca
3 Cahuita
4 Manzanillo
5 Salsa Brava

20 miles
40 km

CARIBBEAN SEA

NICARAGUA

San Juan de Nicaragua (Greytown)

Barra del Colorado

Río San Juan

Heredia

Río Chirripó

Río Colorado

Refugio Nacional de Vida Silvestre Barra del Colorado

Intercoastal Waterway

Llanura de Tortuguero

Tortuguero

Cuatro Esquinas Ranger Station

Canales de Tortuguero

Parque Nacional Tortuguero

La Pavona

Parque Nacional Tortuguero

Río Tortuguero

Río Suerte

Río Chirri

247

Cañari

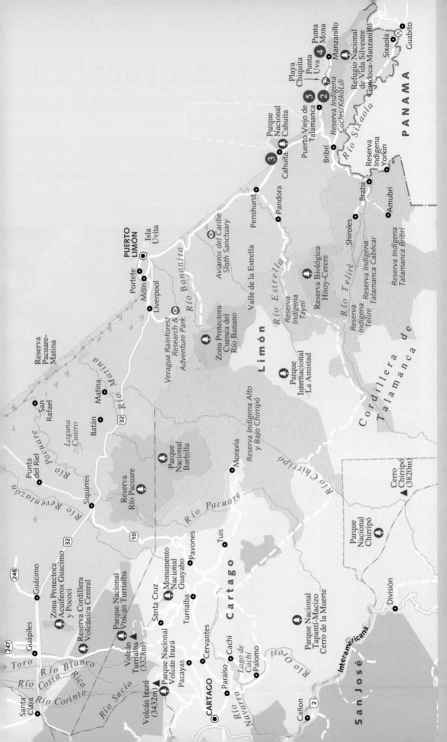

Caribbean Coast Highlights

Parque Nacional Tortuguero

Navigating Tortuguero's (p123) largely impenetrable jungles and expansive marshlands means quietly canoeing down narrow waterways. The motivation? Phenomenal wildlife-watching, with caimans, unique birds, rare river otters and troups of leaf-rustling monkeys.

Puerto Viejo de Talamanca

Without a doubt, Puerto Viejo (p134) is the cultural heart of the Caribbean coast. A loud and proud bastion of Rastafarianism, Puerto Viejo lures countless visitors with Jamaican-influenced music and munchies. When you're not jamming to reggae beats or stuffing yourself with jerk chicken, kick back on a blissful stretch of sand while sipping a fresh coconut.

Cahuita

3

Not nearly as developed as Puerto Viejo de Talamanca, Cahuita (p127) is just the way the locals like it. Indeed, Cahuita offers a measure of salt-of-the-earth authenticity missing from its brasher neighbor, not to mention that it's also the jumping-off point for the stunning national park of the same name. Crab-eating raccoon, Parque Nacional Cahuita (p131)

4

Manzanillo

Manzanillo (p138) has the most positive vibe of any place in the region. Roots, reef and rainforest round out one little community. No matter where you're from, you can make friends immediately. Everything's within walking, swimming or paddling distance. The town lives up to its slogan: in Manzanillo the least you can get is the best.

5

Salsa Brava

This truly legendary wave has been chewing up and spitting out surfers for generations. Just off the coast of Puerto Viejo, Salsa Brava (p136) is named for the heaped helping of 'spicy sauce' it serves up on the sharp, shallow reef, continually collecting its debt of fun in broken skin, boards and bones.

The Caribbean Coast's Best...

Journeys

o **Parque Nacional Tortuguero** A waterborne safari is arguably the best journey in the Caribbean. (p123)

o **Manzanillo** Cycling down the coast from Puerto Viejo lets you take it all in mindfully. (p138)

o **Sloth Sanctuary of Costa Rica** Mini river tours and close encounters with insanely adorable baby sloths. (p131)

o **Parque Nacional Cahuita** A leisurely walk through this coastal park reveals sloths in trees, birds flitting and feeding, and wild Caribbean beauty. (p131)

Splurges

o **Tortuga Lodge & Gardens** Explore acres of private gardens in this serene Tortuguero hideaway. (p119)

o **Cashew Hill Jungle Cottages** A secluded spot set far back from the Puerto Viejo scene. (p136)

o **Congo Bongo** Bed down in the middle of a reclaimed cacao plantation. (p139)

o **Playa Negra Guesthouse** This garden oasis lies opposite a stretch of black-sand beach. (p129)

Vistas

o **Parque Nacional Tortuguero** Panoramic views of incredible nature surround your tiny canoe. (p123)

o **Parque Nacional Cahuita** Watch the sunrise over Caribbean shores. (p131)

o **Salsa Brava** If you don't have the skills to surf it, watching those that do is a thrill. (p136)

o **Refugio Nacional de Vida Silvestre Gandoca-Manzanillo** Hike out here for isolated, sweeping ocean views. (p140)

Need to Know

Eats

○ **Sobre Las Olas** Seafood, seaside, with a relaxed, romantic ambience. (p130)

○ **Stashu's con Fusion** Tuck into a heady fusion of Caribbean, Indian, Mexican and Thai flavors. (p137)

○ **Selvin's Restaurant** The chicken caribeño is a perfect blend of Caribbean flavors. (p138)

○ **La Pecora Nera** Candlelight and Italian dishes make this a romantic, upscale treat. (p138)

Above left: Butterfly, Manzanillo; **Above right:** Parque Nacional Tortuguero (p123)
(ABOVE LEFT) FERRAN VEGA VALLRIBERA/GETTY IMAGES ©;
(ABOVE RIGHT) BRIAN BAILEY/GETTY IMAGES ©

RESOURCES

○ **Tortuguero Information** (www. tortugueroinfo.com) Current travel info and directory for Tortuguero Village and the national park.

○ **Cahuita.CR** (www. cahuita.cr) Useful details on Cahuita accommodations, eateries, and more.

○ **Puerto Viejo Satellite** (www.puertoviejosatellite. com) Local listings, area map, and local news.

GETTING AROUND

○ **Bicycle** Cycling from Puerto Viejo to Manzanillo is the best way to travel, allowing you to stop for monkey sightings, beach picnics and smoothies.

○ **Boat** The only way to access Parque Nacional Tortuguero.

○ **Bus** The Caribbean coast is well serviced by buses, alleviating the need for a rental car.

○ **Walk** Any of the region's beaches invite long sessions of beachcombing.

BE FOREWARNED

○ **Crime** Puerto Limón is generally safe for foreigners, but it can be a little sketchy after dark. Don't roam alone at night and stay aware of your surroundings at all times.

○ **Riptides** Riptides are a concern at some Caribbean beaches, so pay attention to local advisories.

ADVANCE PLANNING

○ **One month before** Make reservations if you plan to stay at an all-inclusive lodge in Tortuguero; lodges generally offer packages that include transfers to and from San José.

○ **Two weeks before** Visiting remote Parque Nacional Tortuguero is hard to do on a whim; work out transportation logistics if you plan to arrive independently, especially if your time is limited.

Caribbean Coast Itineraries

While most visitors head directly for Pacific waves, the Caribbean allows for an entirely different cultural perspective. The highlights are strung along calm waters, making for a lazy, relaxing coastal trip.

PUERTO VIEJO DE TALAMANCA TO THE PANAMA BORDER

PUERTO VIEJO & AROUND

3 DAYS

If you can only spare a few days on the Caribbean side, your first stop should be ❶ **Puerto Viejo de Talamanca** (p134). The region's most developed beach town will not only give you a good taste of Afro-Caribbean culture but also serves as a convenient base for nearby attractions and has a rocking party scene. Direct buses from San José take only a few hours' travel time. Serious surfers will want to prove their prowess at Salsa Brava, while the less experienced can head down the coast to the more forgiving breaks of Playa Cocles. In the evening you'll find the Caribbean groove in the excellent regional cuisine and the rhythm of reggae.

If you have extra energy to burn off, rent a bike and head along the 13km road past gorgeous palm-lined beaches to the idyllic community of ❷ **Manzanillo** (p138)for some snorkeling, diving or kayaking. Finally, end this dreamy trip by searching for animals in the ❸ **Refugio Nacional de Vida Silvestre Gandoca-Manzanillo**, (p140) which stretches all the way to the Panamanian border.

5 DAYS

PUERTO LIMÓN TO PARQUE NACIONAL TORTUGUERO

EXPLORING TORTUGUERO

With a bit more time and an adventurous streak, consider forgoing Caribbean comforts and tackling the region's wildest national park. From spying on sea turtles to canoeing past caimans and crocodiles, Tortuguero is rightly regarded as the Amazon in miniature and a must-see for die-hard naturalists.

Although you won't want to linger, start in the port city of ❶ **Puerto Limón** (p114), where you can ponder the complicated history of the Caribbean's largest city before heading to the docks in nearby ❷ **Moín** (p116) for the real start of your journey. By boat, you'll travel the canal-laced coast to the remote village of ❸ **Tortuguero** (p116). Although the strong Afro-Caribbean roots and hordes of sea turtles make it a destination in its own right, your journey continues into the jungles and mangroves of the surrounding ❹ **Parque Nacional Tortuguero** (p123). Prime territory for excellent viewing of nesting sea turtles, frogs and amphibians galore, this wilderness is a world away from the airbrushed beach towns further down the coast.

Refugio Nacional de Vida Silvestre Gandoca-Manzanillo (p140)

KRYSSIA CAMPOS/GETTY IMAGES ©

113

Discover
Caribbean Coast

PUERTO LIMÓN

POP 61,100

The biggest city on Costa Rica's Caribbean coast, the birthplace of United Fruit and capital of Limón Province, this hardworking port city sits removed from the rest of the country.

A historical lack of political and financial support from the federal government means that Limón has not aged particularly gracefully. Despite its shortcomings, however, Limón is safer for visitors than San José–dwelling Ticos (Costa Ricans) would have you believe, with its welcoming Afro-Caribbean charms and traditions.

◉ Sights

Parque Vargas   Park

The city's waterfront centerpiece won't ever win best in show, but its decrepit bandstand, paths and greenery are surprisingly appealing, all shaded by palms and facing the docks.

Playa Bonita   Beach

Playa Bonita, 4km northwest of town on the Limón–Moín bus route, offers sandy stretches of seashore and good swimming. Surfers come for Bonita's point/reef break, which makes for a powerful (and sometimes dangerous) left. Experienced surfers might also want to hit the punishing reef break at Isla Uvita, the wild green rock 1km offshore.

Heron, Parque Nacional Tortuguero (p123)
HOLGER LEUE/GETTY IMAGES ©

Puerto Limón

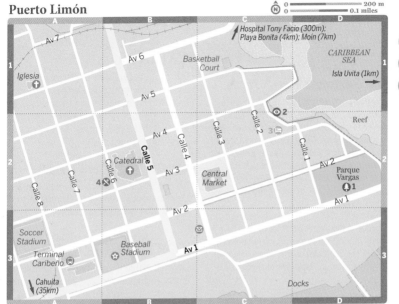

🛏 Sleeping & Eating

Park Hotel
Hotel $$

(☏ 2798-0555; www.parkhotellimon.com; Av 3 btwn Calles 1 & 2; s/d standard US$55/74, superior US$64/90, deluxe US$77/103; P ❄ @ 🛜) Downtown Limón's most attractive hotel has 32 rooms in a faded yellow building that faces the ocean. Tiled rooms are tidy and sport clean bathrooms with hot water; superior and deluxe units come with ocean views and balconies. The hotel also houses the swankiest restaurant in the town center.

Caribbean Kalisi Coffee Shop
Caribbean $

(☏ 2758-3249; Calle 6 btwn Avs 3 & 4; mains from US$5; ⏱ 7am-8pm Mon-Fri, 8am-7:30pm Sat, 8am-5pm Sun) Belly up to the cafeteria-style counter at this friendly family spot and cobble together a plate of coconut rice, red beans and whatever Caribbean meat and veggie dishes are cooking today. Also recommended in the mornings

for its affordable à la carte breakfasts and excellent *café con leche* (coffee with milk).

ℹ Getting There & Away

Boats to and from San José, Moín, Guápiles and Siquirres arrive at **Terminal Caribeño** (Av 2 btwn Calles 7 & 8) on the west side of the baseball stadium.

Moín, for boats to Tortuguero (Tracasa; US$0.60, 20 minutes) depart hourly from 5:30am to 6:30pm.

San José (Autotransportes Caribeños; US$6.30, three hours) depart every 30 minutes from 5am to 7pm.

MOÍN

Just 8km northwest of Puerto Limón, this is the town's main transportation dock, where you can catch a boat to Parismina or Tortuguero.

Getting There & Away

The journey by boat from Moín to Tortuguero can take anywhere from three to five hours, depending on how often the boat stops to observe wildlife (many tours also stop for lunch). Indeed, it is worth taking your time. As you wind through these jungle canals, you're likely to spot howler monkeys, crocodiles, two- and three-toed sloths and an amazing array of wading birds, including roseate spoonbills.

The route is most often used by tourist boats, and if the canal becomes blocked by water hyacinths or logjams, it might be closed altogether. Schedules exist in theory only and change frequently, depending on demand.

Bus

Tracasa buses to Moín from Puerto Limón (US$0.60, 20 minutes) depart from Terminal Caribeño hourly from 5:30am to 6:30pm (less frequently on Saturday and Sunday). Get off the bus before it goes over the bridge. If driving, leave your car in a guarded lot in Limón.

CARIARI

Due north of Guápiles, Cariari is a blue-collar, rough-around-the-edges banana town. Most travelers make their way quickly through here, en route to Tortuguero. If that's you, Cariari is your last opportunity to get cash.

Getting There & Away

Buses to San José (US$3.35, two hours) depart from the *estación nueva* (new station) at 7:30am, 9am, 11:30am, 1pm, 3pm and 5:30pm.

TORTUGUERO VILLAGE

Located within the confines of Parque Nacional Tortuguero (p123), accessible only by air or water, this bustling little village with strong Afro-Caribbean roots is best known for attracting hordes of sea turtles (the name Tortuguero means 'turtle place') – and the hordes of tourists who want to see them. While the peak turtle season is in July and August, the park and village have begun to attract travelers year-round. Even in October, when the turtles have pretty much returned to the sea, caravans of families and adventure travelers arrive to go on jungle hikes and to canoe the area's lush canals.

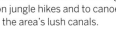 Activities

VOLUNTEERING

Sea Turtle Conservancy
Volunteering
(formerly Caribbean Conservation Corporation; ☎2709-8091, in USA 352-373-6441; www.conserveturtles.org; museum admission US$2) About

Tortuguero Village
JOE LASKY/GETTY IMAGES ©

200m north of the village, Tortuguero's original turtle-conservation organization operates a research station, visitor center and museum. Exhibits focus on all things turtle-related, including a 20-minute video about the history of local turtle conservation.

Canadian Organization for Tropical Education & Rainforest Conservation
Volunteering

(COTERC; ☎2709-8052; www.coterc.org) This not-for-profit organization operates the Estación Biológica Caño Palma, 7km north of Tortuguero village. This small biological research station runs a volunteer program in which visitors can assist with upkeep of the station and ongoing research projects, including sea-turtle and bird monitoring and plant-diversity inventories. Call ahead to arrange a visit.

BOATING & CANOEING

Non-motorized boat transport obviously offers the best chance of spotting wildlife while exploring the surrounding waterways. Numerous area businesses rent kayaks and canoes and offer boat tours.

HIKING

Hikers can follow the self-guided El Gavilán Land Trail (adjacent to Cuatro Esquinas ranger station), parallel to the beach on the well-worn coastal trail north from the village to the airport, or walk the beach during daylight hours. Other hiking opportunities exist in and around the park but require the services of a guide. Inquire at the agencies listed under Tours. Note: night hiking in the national park is not allowed.

Tours

Guides have posted signs all over town advertising their services for canal tours and turtle walks. The two most dependable and convenient places to arrange tours are at local hotels and at the official **Asociación de Guías de Tortuguero** (☎2767-0836; www.asoprotur.com) kiosk by the boat landing. Rates at the time of research were US$20 per person for a

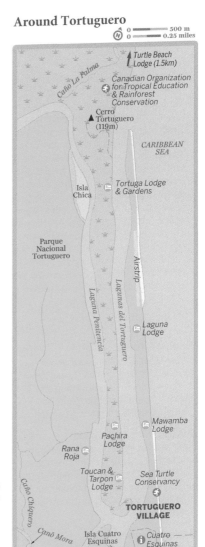

Around Tortuguero

two-hour turtle tour (possibly increasing to US$25 in 2014), and US$20 to US$35 for a two- to three-hour boat tour.

Detour:
Reserva Biológica Hitoy-Cerere

One of Costa Rica's most rugged and rarely visited reserves, **Hitoy-Cerere** (☎2795-3170; admission US$6; ⏱8am-4pm) is only about 60km south of Puerto Limón. The 99-sq-km reserve sits on the edge of the Cordillera de Talamanca, characterized by varying altitudes, evergreen forests and rushing rivers. This may be one of the wettest reserves in the parks system, inundated with 4000mm to 6000mm of rain annually.

Naturally, wildlife is abundant. The most commonly sighted mammals include gray four-eyed opossums, tayras (a type of weasel), and howler and capuchin monkeys. There are plenty of ornithological delights as well (with more than 230 avian species), including keel-billed toucans, spectacled owls, green kingfishers and the ubiquitous Montezuma oropendola, whose massive nests dangle from the trees like twiggy pendulums. The moisture, in the meantime, keeps the place hopping with various species of poison-dart frog.

The reserve is surrounded by some of the country's most remote indigenous reserves, which you can visit with a local guide.

Although there is a ranger station with bathrooms at the reserve entrance, there are no other facilities nearby. A 9km trail leads south to a waterfall, but it is steep, slippery and poorly maintained. Jungle boots are recommended.

Tinamon Tours   Tour
(☎8842-6561, 2709-8004; www.tinamontours. de) Trained zoologist and 20-year Tortuguero resident Barbara Hartung offers hiking, canoe, cultural and turtle tours in German, English, French or Spanish.

Castor Hunter Thomas   Tour
(☎8870-8634; http://castorhunter.blogspot. com; Soda Doña María) Excellent local guide and 40-year Tortuguero resident who has led hikes, turtle tours and canoe tours for over 20 years. Contact Castor at Soda Doña María.

Ballard Excursions   Tour
(www.tortugerovillage.com/ballardexcursions) Ross Ballard, a Canadian with deep local roots, leads 3½-hour walking tours focusing on the biology and ecology of the species-rich rainforest at the foot of Cerro Tortuguero, the region's tallest hill.

Don Chico Tours   Tour
(☎2709-8033) Long-time local guide Chico offers both hiking and canoe tours; look for his sign just beyond Miss Miriam's res-

taurant (towards the beach on the north side of the soccer field).

Sleeping

TORTUGUERO VILLAGE

In addition to places listed below, the village has a number of basic *cabinas* (cabins) charging US$18 and up for a double room.

Princesa del Mar   Cabina $
(☎2709-8131; albertovr2206@hotmail.com; r per person US$10, incl breakfast US$15; 🛜🍴) This oceanfront spot offers excellent value for budget travelers. A clapboard structure with 22 basic wood-and-concrete rooms faces an open garden with two pools (one for children), and there's an onsite restaurant with ocean views serving Caribbean-Tico cuisine. It's 50m east of the Guardia Rural post on main street, or about 100m up the beach from the soccer field.

Casa Marbella
B&B $$

(☎ 2709-8011, 8833-0827; http://casamarbella.
tripod.com; incl breakfast s US$35-60, d US$40-
65, extra person US$10; @ 🛜) In the heart of
the village, with a spacious and delight-
ful canal-side deck, this B&B owned by
naturalist Daryl Loth is easily Tortugue-
ro's most appealing in-town option. Ten
simple, well-lit rooms come with ceiling
fans, super clean bathrooms and hearty
breakfasts served overlooking the water.

Hotel Miss Junie
Cabina $$

(☎ 2709-8102; www.iguanaverdetours.com;
incl breakfast s/d standard US$45/50, superior
US$55/65; 🛜) Tortuguero's longest-estab-
lished lodging, Miss Junie's place is set on
spacious, palm-shaded grounds strewn
with hammocks and wooden armchairs.
Spotless, wood-paneled rooms in a nicely
kept tropical plantation-style building are
tastefully decorated with wood accents
and bright bedspreads. Upstairs rooms
share a breezy balcony overlooking the
canal. It's at the northern end of the
town's main street.

NORTH OF THE VILLAGE

Most of the lodges north and west of
the village cater to high-end travelers on
package deals, though most will accept
walk-ins (er, boat-ins) if they aren't full.
Rates typically include all meals,
boat and walking tours and transport to/from San José.

Toucan & Tarpon Lodge
Cabinas $

(☎ 8524-1804; www.
toucanandtarpon.com;
s/d/tr/q incl breakfast
US$30/40/45/50) Just
across the river from
Tortuguero village, this
place was opened in
late 2013 by Canadian
expatriates Jeff and
Sue. Three simple
cabinas with solar
electricity and Gua-
temalan textiles sleep

between two and four. Other amenities
include delicious homemade breakfasts,
a communal kitchen with a well-stocked
spice cabinet, free canoe use and excellent wildlife-spotting (monkeys, sloths,
toucans) in the surrounding trees.

Rana Roja
Lodge $$

(☎ 2223-1926, 2709-8260; www.tortuguero-
ranaroja.com; r/cabins per person incl breakfast
US$40/45, r/cabins per person incl 3 meals
US$60; @ 🛜 ⛱) This Tico-run spot is one of
Tortuguero's best values, especially for solo
travelers. Twelve immaculate rooms and
five cabins with private terraces and rock-
ers are connected by elevated walkways; all
have tile floors, hot showers and awesome
jungle views. Free kayaks are available
onsite and guests can make use of the pool
at the adjacent Evergreen Lodge.

Tortuga Lodge & Gardens
Lodge $$$

(☎ 2521-6099, 2257-0766; www.tortugalodge.
com; r US$138-238, 2-night package per adult/
child US$548/348; 🛜 ⛱) This elegant lodge,
operated by Costa Rica Expeditions, is

Montezuma oropendola

set amid 20 serene hectares of private gardens, directly across the canal from Tortuguero's airstrip. The 27 demure rooms channel a 19th-century safari vibe, with creamy linens, handmade textiles, vintage photos and broad terraces that invite lounging. The grounds come equipped with private trails and a riverside pool, bar and restaurant.

Laguna Lodge   Lodge $$$

(📞 2272-4943, in USA 888-259-5615; www.lagunatortuguero.com; 2-night package per adult/child US$299/150; 🛜 🏊) This expansive lodge, liberally decorated with gorgeous mosaic art and trim, has 110 graceful rooms with high ceilings and wide decks lined with Sarchí-made leather rocking chairs. It also has a restaurant, two bars (canal-side and poolside), a massage room, a soccer pitch and a Gaudí-esque reception area.

Pachira Lodge   Lodge $$$

(📞 2257-2242, 2256-6340; www.pachiral-odge.com; 2-night package per adult/child US$299/150; 🛜 🏊) A sprawling compound set on five landscaped hectares of land, this 88-room hotel with turtle-shaped pool is a popular family spot. Pristine, brightly painted clapboard bungalows with shared terraces house blocks of rooms that sleep up to four. Cribs and children's beds are available.

Mawamba Lodge   Lodge $$$

(📞 2293-8181, 2709-8181; www.mawamba.com; 2-night package per adult/child US$299/150; 🛜 🏊) With pool tables, foosball, a mosaic swimming pool, and butterfly and frog gardens, this lodge sits between the canal and Tortuguero's main turtle nesting beach, within walking distance of town. Simple, wood-paneled rooms have firm beds, good fans and spacious bathrooms with hot water. All are fronted by wide verandas with hammocks and rocking chairs.

Eating

Taylor's Place   Caribbean $

(mains US$7-10; ⏱ 6-8:30pm) Low-key atmosphere and high-quality cooking come together beautifully at this backstreet eatery southwest of the soccer field. The inviting garden setting, with chirping insects, and picnic benches spread under colorful paper lanterns, is rivaled only by

Parque Nacional Braulio Carrillo

Detour:
Parque Nacional Braulio Carrillo

Enter this under-explored national park and you will have an idea of what Costa Rica looked like prior to the 1950s, when 75% of the country's surface area was still covered in forest: steep hills cloaked in impossibly tall trees are interrupted only by cascading rivers and canyons. It has extraordinary biodiversity due to the range of altitudes, from steamy 2906m cloud forest alongside Volcán Barva to lush, humid lowlands on the Caribbean slope. Its most incredible feature, however, is that this massive park is only 30 minutes north of San José.

Founded in the 1970s, Braulio Carrillo's creation was the result of a unique compromise between conservationists and developers. At the time, the government had announced a plan to build a new highway that would connect the capital to Puerto Limón. Back then, San José's only link to its most important port was via a crumbling railway or a slow rural road through Cartago and Turrialba. The only feasible route for the new thoroughfare was along a low pass between the Barva and Irazú volcanoes – an area covered in primary forest. Conservationists were deeply worried about putting a road (and any attendant development) in an area that served as San José's watershed. So a plan was hatched: the road would be built, but the 475 sq km of land to either side of it would be set aside as a national park. Thus, in 1978, Parque Nacional Braulio Carrillo was born.

friendly chef Ray Taylor's culinary artistry. House specialties include beef in tamarind sauce, grilled fish in garlic sauce, and fruit drinks both alcoholic and otherwise.

Miss Miriam's Caribbean $
(mains US$9.50; ☺8am-9pm) This little place on the north side of the soccer field dishes out flavorful local food, including pork chops, fish and well-spiced Caribbean chicken.

Miss Junie's Caribbean $$
(☏2709-8029; mains US$13-20; ☺7-9am, noon-2pm & 6-9pm) Over the years, Tortuguero's best-known eatery has grown from a personal kitchen to a full-blown restaurant. Prices have climbed accordingly, but the menu remains true to its roots: chicken, fish and whole lobster cooked in flavorful Caribbean sauces, with coconut rice and beans. It's at the northern end of the main street.

Wild Ginger Fusion $$
(☏2709-8240; www.wildgingercr.com; mains US$8-26; ☺noon-9pm) Run by a Tico-Californian couple, this low-lit spot near the beach north of town specializes in fusion cuisine incorporating fresh local ingredients, such as lobster mango *ceviche* (seafood marinated in lemon or lime juice, garlic and seasonings), Caribbean beef stew and passionfruit crème brûlée. It's 150m north of the elementary school.

❶ Getting There & Away

Air
The small airstrip is 4km north of Tortuguero village. **Nature Air** (☏2299-6000; www.natureair.com) has early-morning flights daily to/from San José and twice weekly to La Fortuna. Charter flights land regularly here as well.

Bus & Boat
The classic public-transit route to Tortuguero is by bus from San José to Cariari to La Pavona, then by boat from La Pavona to Tortuguero. Alternatively, Tortuguero is accessible by private boat from Moín, near Puerto Limón on the Caribbean coast.

121

Below: Red-eyed tree frog, Parque Nacional Tortuguero; **Right:** Boat cruise along a canal, Parque Nacional Tortuguero

(BELOW) MARTIN VAN LOKVEN/ NIS/ MINDEN PICTURES/GETTY IMAGES ©;
(RIGHT) HOLGER LEUE/GETTY IMAGES ©

From San José via Cariari

From San José, take the 6:10am, 9am or 10:30am bus to Cariari (three hours) from Gran Terminal del Caribe. In Cariari, you will arrive at a bus station at the south end of town (known as the *estación nueva*). From here, walk or take a taxi 500m north to the *estación vieja* (old station), otherwise referred to as the Terminal Caribeño.

Here you can catch a local Coopetraca bus (US$2.20, 6am, 9am, 11:30am and 3pm) to La Pavona, where you'll transfer onto the boat (US$3.20 to US$4) to Tortuguero.

On the return trip, boats leave Tortuguero for La Pavona daily at 5:30am, 9am, 11am and 2:45pm, connecting with Cariari-bound buses at the La Pavona dock.

From Moín

Moín–Tortuguero is primarily a tourist route. While there isn't a scheduled service, boats do ply these canals frequently. When running, boats typically depart at 10am in either direction, charging US$30 to US$40 for the three- to five-hour trip. With advance notice, these same boats can stop in Parismina (one way from either Tortuguero or

Moín US$25). Bear in mind that it may take 24 to 48 hours to secure transportation – especially in the low season. For onward transportation beyond Moín, catch a local bus (US$0.60, 20 minutes) to Puerto Limón's bus terminal.

Tropical Wind (📞 8327-0317, 2798-6059) and **Viajes Bananero** (📞 2709-8005; per person 1-way US$35) are two Tortuguero-based agencies that make the run regularly. Alternatively, you can make arrangements with companies operating out of Puerto Limón.

Shuttle Services

If you prefer to leave the planning to someone else, convenient shuttle services can whisk you to Tortuguero from San José, Arenal-La Fortuna or the southern Caribbean coast in just a few hours. Shuttle companies typically offer minivan service to La Pavona or Moín, where waiting boats take you the rest of the way to Tortuguero. This is a relatively inexpensive, hassle-free option, as you only have to buy a single ticket, and guides help you negotiate the van-to-boat transfer.

Jungle Tom Safaris (📞 2221-7878; www. jungletomsafaris.com) Offers one-way shuttles

between Tortuguero and San José (US$17), Cahuita (US$39), Puerto Viejo (US$39) and Arenal-La Fortuna (US$55), as well as all-inclusive day trips (US$99), overnight packages (from US$120) and two-night packages (from US$152).

Caribe Shuttle (☎8849-7600, 2750-0626; http://caribeshuttle.com/from-tortuguero) Shuttles from Puerto Viejo (US$65) and Arenal-La Fortuna (US$55).

Riverboat Francesca Nature Tours (☎2226-0986; www.tortuguerocanals.com) Shuttles from San José to Tortuguero via Moín (US$75, including lunch) as well as package deals including accommodation.

Exploradores Outdoors (☎2222-6262; www.exploradoresoutdoors.com) More expensive package deals that include transport from San José, Puerto Viejo or Arenal-La Fortuna, a mid-journey Río Pacuare rafting trip, and accommodations in Tortuguero.

PARQUE NACIONAL TORTUGUERO

'Humid' is the driest word that could truthfully be used to describe Tortuguero, a 311-sq-km coastal park that serves as the most important breeding ground of the green sea turtle. With annual rainfall of up to 6000mm in the northern part of the park, it is one of the wettest areas in the country. In addition, the protected area extends into the Caribbean Sea, covering about 5200 sq km of marine habitat. In other words, plan on spending quality time in a boat.

The famed **Canales de Tortuguero** are the introduction to this park. Created to connect a series of lagoons and meandering rivers in 1974, this engineering marvel allowed inland navigation between Puerto Limón and coastal villages in something sturdier than a dugout canoe. Regular flights service the village of Tortuguero – but if

123

Park Admission Fees

A separate park admission fee is charged for each day you visit the national park. If you're planning multiple activities within the park, you can save a few colones by concentrating them in a single day; for example, if you go out on a boat tour in the early morning, then hike the El Gavilán Land Trail that same afternoon, you'll only pay the park admission fee once.

you fly, you'll be missing half the fun. The leisurely taxi-boat ride, through banana plantations and wild jungle, is equal parts recreation and transportation.

Most visitors come to watch sea turtles lay eggs on the wild beaches. The area attracts four of the world's eight species of sea turtle, making it a crucial habitat for these massive reptiles. It will come as little surprise, then, that these hatching grounds gave birth to the sea-

turtle-conservation movement. The Caribbean Conservation Corporation, the first program of its kind in the world, has continuously monitored turtle populations here since 1955. Today, green sea turtles are increasing in numbers along this coast, but the leatherback, hawksbill and loggerhead are in decline.

The area, however, is more than just turtles: Tortuguero teems with wildlife. You'll find sloths and howler monkeys in the treetops, tiny frogs and green iguanas scurrying among buttress roots, and mighty tarpons and endangered manatees swimming in the waters.

Activities

TURTLE-WATCHING

Most female turtles share a nesting instinct that drives them to return to the beach of their birth, or natal beach, in order to lay their eggs. (Only the leatherback returns to a more general region, instead of a specific beach.) During their lifetimes, they will usually nest every two to three years and, depending on the species, may come ashore to lay eggs 10 times in one season. Often, a turtle's ability to success-

Turtle, Parque Nacional Tortuguero

S.B. NACE/GETTY IMAGES ©

fully reproduce depends on the ecological health of this original habitat.

The female turtle digs a perfect cylindrical cavity in the sand using her flippers, and then lays 80 to 120 eggs. She diligently covers the nest with sand to protect the eggs, and she may even create a false nest in another location in an attempt to confuse predators. She then makes her way back to sea – after which the eggs are on their own. Incubation ranges from 45 to 70 days, after which hatchlings – no bigger than the size of your palm – break out of their shells using a caruncle, a temporary tooth. They crawl to the ocean in small groups, moving as quickly as possible to avoid dehydration and predators. Once they reach the surf, they must swim for at least 24 hours to get to deeper water, away from land-based predators.

Because of the sensitive nature of the habitat and the critically endangered status of some species, tours to see this activity are highly regulated. By law, tours can only take place between 8am and midnight. Some guides will offer tours after midnight; these are illegal.

Visitors should wear closed-toe shoes and rain gear. Tours cost US$20 (a flat rate established by the village; at the time of research, there was talk of raising this to US$25 in 2014). Nesting season runs from March to October, with July and August being prime time.

OTHER WILDLIFE-WATCHING

More than 300 bird species, both resident and migratory, have been recorded in Tortuguero – a bird-watchers' paradise. Due to the wet habitat, the park is especially rich in waders, including egrets, jacanas, 14 different types of heron, as well as species such as kingfishers, toucans and the great curassow (a type of jungle peacock known locally as the *pavón*). The great green macaw is a highlight, most common from December to April, when the almond trees are fruiting. In September and October, look for flocks of migratory species such as eastern kingbird,

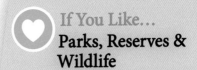

If You Like…
Parks, Reserves & Wildlife

If you like Parque Nacional Tortuguero, we think you'll like these other parks, reserves and wildlife centers around the Caribbean coast:

1 VERAGUA RAINFOREST RESEARCH & ADVENTURE PARK
(☎2296-5056; www.veraguarainforest.com; adult with/without zip-line tour US$99/66, child with/without zip-line tour US$75/55; 👶) In Las Brisas de Veragua, you'll find elevated walkways in the jungle and maintained trails, as well as attractions such as an aerial tram, a reptile vivarium, an insectarium and hummingbird and butterfly gardens.

2 TREE OF LIFE
(Map p128; ☎2755-0014, 8610-0490; www.treeoflifecostarica.com; adult/child US$12/6, guided tour US$15-20; ⏰9am-3pm Tue-Sun Nov–mid-Apr, daily tour 11am Jul & Aug, closed mid-Apr–Jun & Sep-Oct) This wildlife center and botanical garden 3km northwest of Cahuita rescues and rehabilitates animals while also promoting conservation through education.

3 JAGUAR CENTRO DE RESCATE
(☎2750-0710; www.jaguarrescue.com; adult/child under 10yr US$15/free; ⏰tours 9:30am & 11:30am Mon-Sat; 👶) Named in honor of its original resident, this well-run wildlife-rescue center in Playa Chiquita now focuses mostly on other animals, including raptors, sloths and monkeys. Founded by Spanish zoologist Encar and her partner, Sandro, an Italian herpetologist, the center rehabilitates orphaned, injured and rescued animals for reintroduction into the wild whenever possible.

barn swallows and purple martins. The Sea Turtle Conservancy (p116) conducts a biannual monitoring program, in which volunteers can help scientists take inventory of local and migratory species.

Certain species of mammal are particularly evident in Tortuguero, especially mantled howler monkeys, the Central American spider monkey and white-faced capuchin. With good binoculars and a guide, you can usually see both two- and three-toed sloths. In addition, normally shy neotropical river otters are reasonably habituated to boats.

BOATING

Four aquatic trails wind their way through Parque Nacional Tortuguero, inviting water-borne exploration. **Río Tortuguero** acts as the entrance way to the network of trails. This wide, beautiful river is often covered with water lilies and frequented by aquatic birds such as herons, kingfishers and an-hingas – the latter of which is known as the snakebird for the way its slim, winding neck pokes out of the water when it swims.

Caño Chiquero and **Canŏ Mora** are two narrower waterways with good wildlife-spotting opportunities. According to park regulation, only kayaks, canoes and silent electric boats are allowed in these areas (a rule that is constantly violated by many area tour companies and lodges). Caño Chiquero is thick with vegetation, especially red guácimo trees and epiphytes. Black turtles and green iguanas like to hang out here. Caño Mora is about 3km long but only 10m wide, so it feels as if it's straight out of *The Jungle Book*. **Caño Harold** is actually an artificially constructed canal, but that doesn't stop the creatures – such as Jesus Christ lizards and caimans – from inhabiting its tranquil waters.

Canoe rental and boat tours are available in Tortuguero village.

HIKING

Behind Cuatro Esquinas station, **El Gavilán Land Trail** is the only public trail through the park that is on solid ground. Visitors can hike the muddy, 2km out-and-back trail that traverses the tropical humid forest and parallels a stretch of beach. Green parrots and several species of monkey are commonly sighted here. The short trail is well marked. Rubber boots are required (for rent at hotels and near the park entrance).

ⓘ Information

Park headquarters is at **Cuatro Esquinas** (☎2709-8086; park admission US$10; ⊙6-7am, 7:30am-noon & 1-4pm), just south of Tortuguero village. This is a helpful ranger station, with maps and info.

Jalova Station (⊙6am-6pm) is on the canal at the south entrance to the national park. Tour boats from Moín often stop here for a picnic; you will find a short nature trail, bathroom, drinking water and rudimentary camping facilities that may or may not be open (and may or may not be flooded).

ⓘ Getting There & Away

The park is a short walk south of the village of Tortuguero (the most common entry point).

Cahuita
BARRETT & MACKAY/GETTY IMAGES ©

CAHUITA

POP 8300

Even as tourism has mushroomed on Costa Rica's southern coast, Cahuita has managed to hold onto its laid-back Caribbean vibe. The roads are made of dirt, many of the older houses rest on stilts and chatty neighbors still converse in Mekatelyu (a creole spoken by Costa Ricans of West Indian origin). A graceful black-sand beach and a chilled-out demeanor hint at a not-so-distant past, when the area was little more than a string of cacao farms.

Cahuita proudly claims the area's first permanent Afro-Caribbean settler: a turtle fisherman named William Smith, who moved his family to Punta Cahuita in 1828. Now his descendants, along with those of so many other West Indian immigrants, run the backyard eateries and brightly painted bungalows that hug this idyllic stretch of coast.

Situated on a pleasant point, the town itself has a waterfront but no beach. For that, most folks make the five-minute jaunt up the coast to Playa Negra or southeast into neighboring Parque Nacional Cahuita.

◉ Sights & Activities

Playa Negra   Beach

At the northwest end of Cahuita, Playa Negra is a long, black-sand beach flying the *bandera azul ecológica,* a flag that indicates the beach is kept to the highest ecological standards. This is undoubtedly Cahuita's top spot for swimming and is never crowded. When the swells are big, this place also has an excellent beach break for beginners.

🛏 Sleeping

There are two general areas to stay in Cahuita: the town center (which can be a little noisy) or north of town along Playa Negra.

TOWN CENTER

Alby Lodge   Bungalow $$

(☎2755-0031; www.albylodge.com; d/tr/q US$60/65/70; 🅿🛜) This fine German-run

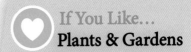

If You Like...
Plants & Gardens

If you like exploring the medicinal and nutritional plants of the region so abundant in Parque Nacional Tortuguero, we think you'll like these other places along the coast:

ECOFINCA ANDAR
(☎2272-1024; www.andarcr.org; 1-day admission US$14, per person homestay incl meals US$17; 🅿) North of Guápiles, 3km northeast of the village of Santa Rosa, is this ecological farm, an impressive educational facility that shows how plants are cultivated for medicinal purposes and used as sources of renewable energy.

FINCA LA ISLA
(☎8886-8530, 2750-0046; self-guided/ guided tour US$6/12; ⊙10am-4pm Fri-Mon) West of Puerto Viejo, this farm and botanical garden has been producing organic pepper, cacao, tropical fruits and ornamental plants for over a decade. Birds and wildlife abound, including sloths, poison-dart frogs and toucans. Informative guided tours (minimum three people) include admission, fruit tasting and a glass of fresh juice; alternatively, buy a booklet (US$1) and take a self-guided tour.

ATEC
(Asociación Talamanqueña de Ecoturismo y Conservación; Map p135; ☎2750-0398; www. ateccr.org; ⊙8am-8pm) This highly reputable not-for-profit organization promotes sustainable tourism by working with local guides and supporting local communities. Activities include hiking, bird-watching, courses in Caribbean cooking and trips to indigenous territories and local farms. Note that 24-hour notice is required for some tours.

lodge on the edge of Parque Nacional Tortuguero has spacious landscaped grounds that attract howler monkeys and birds. Four raised bungalows (two sleeping three people, two sleeping four) are spread out, allowing for plenty of privacy. High ceilings, mosquito nets and driftwood details make for pleasant jungle decor. A common *rancho* (thatched

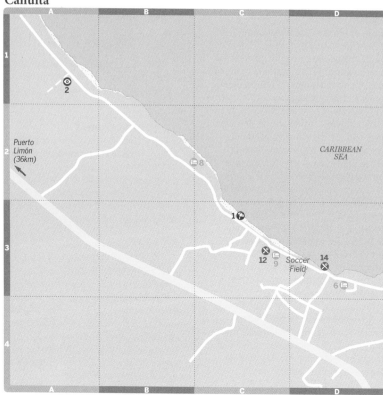

gazebo) has excellent communal kitchen facilities.

Kelly Creek Hotel   Cabina $$
(☎2755-0007; www.hotelkellycreek.com; s/d US$50/60, extra person US$10; [P] [?]) At this place just outside Tortuguero's entrance, you may be serenaded by the dulcet squawks of the resident parrot; draw closer and find four graceful natural wood *cabinas* with high ceilings, cream-colored linens and mosquito nets. Local artwork adorns the reception area, and the onsite restaurant (open from 6pm) serves paella with advance notice (US$16 per person, minimum two people).

Bungalows Aché   Bungalow $$
(☎2755-0119; www.bungalowsache.com; bungalow s US$45, d US$50-55; [P] [?]) In Nigeria,

Aché means 'Amen,' and you'll likely say the same thing when you see these three spotless polished-wood bungalows nestled into a grassy yard bordering the national park. Each octagonal unit comes with a lockbox, minifridge, kettle and small private deck with hammock. A three-bedroom vacation house (doubles US$70, up to seven people US$120) is available 1km inland.

Ciudad Perdida   Bungalow $$$
(☎2755-0303; www.ciudad perdidaecolodge.com; d standard/superior incl breakfast US$106/127, q US$212; [P] [✳] [?])
🍃 In a shady, peaceful spot bordering the national park but only a five-minute walk from Cahuita's town center, this eco-conscious lodge offers cute one- and two-room, candy-colored wood bungalows

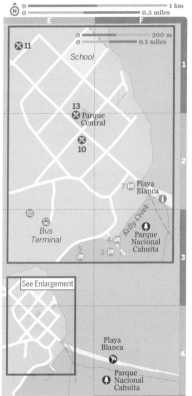

Cahuita

tucked into the well-manicured garden dotted with fan palms.

La Piscina Natural Cabina $$
(📞2755-0146; piscinanatural@cahuita.cr; d/tr US$45/60; P 🛜 🏊) Run by Cahuita native Walter and former Colorado schooteacher Patty, this chilled-out gem of a spot near Playa Negra's northern end is a self-proclaimed 'Caribbean Paradise'. The rooms, which share access to a huge kitchen and open-air lounge, are comfortable enough, but what really make this place special are the lush grounds, gorgeous waterfront and stunning, rock-fringed natural ocean-water pool.

El Encanto B&B B&B $$
(📞2755-0113; www.elencantocahuita.com; incl breakfast s/d US$75/85, d studio/ste US$105/200, extra person US$25; P 🛜 🏊) This pleasant French-and-Spanish-owned B&B, only about 200m northwest of downtown Cahuita, is set in landscaped grounds dotted with easy chairs and hammocks. Demure bungalows have high ceilings, tile floors and firm beds draped in colorful textiles. The studio and a brand-new upstairs apartment both have fully equipped kitchens.

surrounded by landscaped gardens. All include hammocks, ceiling fans, refrigerators and safe boxes. One house has a Jacuzzi, three have kitchens and all have cable TV.

PLAYA NEGRA

Playa Negra Guesthouse Bungalow $$
(📞2755-0127; www.playanegra.cr; s/d US$70/85, cottages US$110-160; P 🛜 🏊) Managed by a delightful Québecois couple, this meticulously maintained place offers three charming rooms in a Caribbean-style plantation house, complemented by three kitchen-equipped storybook cottages. Tropical accents include colorful mosaics in the bathrooms and cozy wicker lounge furniture on the private verandas. A lovely pool, honor bar and barbecue area are

Eating

TOWN CENTER

Cafe Chocolatte 100% Natural
Bakery, International **$**

(dishes US$4-9; ⏱6:30am-3pm) Greet the morning with a cup o' joe and a warm cinnamon roll, or unwind in the afternoon with a refreshing *jugo* (jugo). Breakfast offerings include French toast and waffles, while the lunch menu revolves around salad, spaghetti, baked potatoes and rice dishes. Hearty sandwiches on homemade wholegrain bread are perfect for beach picnics at the national park.

Pizzeria CahuITA
Pizza **$$**

(☎2755-0179; pizzas US$5-12; ⏱4-10pm Mon-Wed, noon-10pm Fri-Sun) As the red-white-and-green color scheme implies, the ITA here stands for Italy, motherland of the two expatriate families who opened this excellent, unpretentious pizzeria in 2013. Grab a seat at the aluminum tables on the cement back patio and enjoy a surf and insect serenade while you wait for your thin-crusted beauty to emerge from the wood-fired oven.

Restaurant La Fé
Seafood **$$**

(dishes US$7-16; ⏱7am-11pm) Chef and owner Walter, a Cahuita native, serves up tall tales and tasty meals at this reasonably priced spot. There's a laundry list of Tico and Caribbean items, but the main draw is anything doused in the restaurant's spicy-delicious coconut sauce.

PLAYA NEGRA

Reggae Restaurant
Caribbean **$**

(mains US$6-10; ⏱noon-10pm) Exuding a friendly, laid-back vibe, this *soda* (lunch counter) serves sandwiches and Caribbean-style *casados* (set meals) on a wooden deck hung with green, red and yellow lampshades in the heart of Playa Negra. Reggae music and waves crashing on the beach across the street enhance the chilled-out atmosphere.

Sobre Las Olas
Seafood **$$**

(Map p128; ☎2755-0109; pastas US$12-15, mains US$12-25; ⏱noon-10pm Wed-Mon; ✈) Garlic shrimp, seafood pasta, or fresh grilled fish of the day come accompanied by crashing waves and sparkling blue Caribbean vistas at this sweet spot owned by a lively Tico-Italian couple. Cahuita's top option for romantic waterfront dining, it's only a 400m walk northwest of Cahuita, on the road to Playa Negra. Save room for the delicious *tiramisù*.

ⓘ Getting There & Away

All public buses arrive and depart at the bus terminal about 200m southwest of Parque Central.

Sixaola US$3.95; two hours; departs hourly from 6am to 7pm, passing through Bribrí en route.

Pargo rojo (whole red snapper) with rice
JONATHAN GREGSON/LONELY PLANET ©

SUZI ESZTERHAS/GETTY IMAGES ©

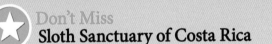

Don't Miss
Sloth Sanctuary of Costa Rica

About 10km northwest of Cahuita, the Arroyo family runs this private 88-hectare wildlife sanctuary (formerly known as Aviarios del Caribe) dedicated to caring for injured and orphaned sloths. Visitors can observe these unique animals up close on group or private tours. (Irrefutable fact: there is nothing cuter than a baby sloth.) Though many of the reserve's rehabilitated sloths lack the skills to return to the wild, the Arroyos have successfully released more than 100 of them back into area forests.

NEED TO KNOW

formerly Aviarios del Caribe; ☑2750-0775; www.slothsanctuary.com; 2hr group tour adult/child 5-11yr US$25/15, private half-day tour per person US$150; ☺8am-2pm Tue-Sun

Puerto Limón US$2.40; 1½ hours; departs half-hourly from 6am to 9pm.

Puerto Viejo de Talamanca/Manzanillo US$1.50/2.40; 30 minutes/one hour; departs roughly every two hours between 7:15am and 7:15pm.

San José US$9.35; four hours; departs 7am, 8am, 9:30am, 11:30am and 4:30pm.

Getting Around

The best way to get around Cahuita – especially if you're staying out along Playa Negra – is by bicycle. Several places around town rent bikes, including Mister Big J's in Cahuita and Centro Turístico Brigitte in Playa Negra.

PARQUE NACIONAL CAHUITA

This small but beautiful park – just 10 sq km – is one of the more frequently visited national parks in Costa Rica. The reasons are simple: the nearby town of Cahuita provides attractive accommodations and

JOHN COLETTI/GETTY IMAGES ©

⭐ Don't Miss
Cacao Trails

Halfway between Cahuita and Puerto Viejo de Talamanca in Hone Creek, this botanical garden and chocolate museum has a couple of small museums devoted to indigenous and Afro-Caribbean culture, a lush garden bursting with bromeliads and heliconias, as well as an onsite chocolate factory where cacao is processed in traditional ways. Two-hour tours include a visit to all of these spots, plus a hike to a nearby organic farm. Additional expeditions allow for further exploration by canoe on the adjacent Río Carbón. Any bus between Cahuita and Puerto Viejo can drop you at the entrance. This is a great outing for kids.

NEED TO KNOW

📞 2756-8186; www.cacaotrails.com; Hone Creek; guided tour US$25, incl canoe trip & lunch US$47; 🕐 7am-4pm; 👪

easy access; more importantly, the white-sand beaches, coral reef and coastal rainforest are bursting with wildlife.

Declared a national park in 1978, Cahuita is meteorologically typical of the entire coast (very humid), which results in dense tropical foliage, as well as coconut palms and sea grapes. The area includes the swampy **Punta Cahuita**, which juts into the sea between two stretches of sandy beach. Often flooded, the point is covered with cativo and mango trees and is a popular hangout for birds such as green ibis, yellow-crowned night heron, boat-billed heron and the rare green-and-rufous kingfisher.

Red land and fiddler crab live along the beaches, attracting mammals such as crab-eating raccoon and white-nosed coati. White-faced capuchin, southern opossum and three-toed sloth also live in these parts. The mammal you are most likely to see (and hear) is the mantled howler monkey, which makes its bellowing presence known. The coral reef represents another rich ecosystem that abounds with life.

Activities

HIKING

An easily navigable 8km **coastal trail** leads through the jungle from Kelly Creek to Puerto Vargas. At times the trail follows the beach; at other times hikers are 100m or so away from the sand. At the end of the first beach, Playa Blanca, hikers must ford the dark Río Perezoso, or 'Sloth River,' which bisects Punta Cahuita. Inquire about conditions before you set out: under normal conditions, this river is easy enough to wade across, but during periods of heavy rain it can become impassable since it serves as the discharge for the swamp that covers the point.

The trail continues around Punta Cahuita to the long stretch of Playa Vargas. It ends at the southern tip of the reef, where it meets up with a road leading to the Puerto Vargas ranger station.

SWIMMING

Almost immediately upon entering Parque Nacional Cahuita, you'll see the 2km-long **Playa Blanca** stretching along a gently curving bay to the east. The first 500m of beach may be unsafe for swimming, but beyond that, waves are generally gentle. (Look for green flags marking safe swimming spots.) The rocky Punta Cahuita headland separates this beach from the next one, **Playa Vargas**.

SNORKELING

Parque Nacional Cahuita contains one of the last living coral reefs in Costa Rica. While the reef represents some of the area's best snorkeling, it has incurred damage over the years from earthquakes and tourism-related activities. In an attempt to protect the reef from further damage, snorkeling is only permitted with a licensed guide. The going rate for one person is about US$25.

You'll find that conditions vary greatly, depending on the weather and other factors. In general, the drier months in the highlands (from February to April) are best for snorkeling on the coast, as less runoff results in less silt in the sea. Conditions are often cloudy at other times.

Eating

Boca Chica   Italian, Costa Rican $
(2755-0415; meals US$8-10; 9am-6pm)
After a long, hot jungle hike, you may think you're hallucinating when you see

Ghost crab
RALONSOPHOTOGRAPHER/GETTY IMAGES ©

this small, whitewashed place at the end of the road. It's not a mirage, just a well-placed bar-restaurant, run by charming Italian expatriate Rodolfo and his Tica wife, Karen. The menu features cold *jugos*, Caribbean specialties, homemade pastas and delicious *platos del día* from noon onwards.

 Getting There & Away

The **Kelly Creek ranger station** (☎2755-0461; admission by donation; ⊙6am-5pm) is convenient to the town of Cahuita, while 3.5km down Hwy 36 takes you to the well-signed **Puerto Vargas ranger station** (☎2755-0302; admission US$10; ⊙8am-4pm Mon-Fri, 7am-5pm Sat & Sun).

PUERTO VIEJO DE TALAMANCA

There was a time when the only travelers to the little seaside settlement once known as Old Harbor were intrepid surfers who padded around the quiet, dusty streets, board under arm, on their way to surf Salsa Brava (p136). That, certainly, is no longer the case. This burgeoning party town is bustling with tourist activity: street vendors ply Rasta trinkets and Bob Marley T-shirts, stylish eateries serve global fusion everything and intentionally rustic bamboo bars pump dancehall and reggaetón. The scene can get downright hedonistic, attracting dedicated revelers who arrive to marinate in ganja and *guaro* (local firewater made with sugarcane).

Despite that reputation, Puerto Viejo nonetheless manages to hold on to an easy charm. Stray a couple of blocks off the main commercial strip and you might find yourself on a sleepy dirt road, savoring a spicy Caribbean stew in the company of local families. Nearby, you'll find rainforest fruit farms set to a soundtrack of cackling birds and croaking frogs, and wide-open beaches where the daily itinerary revolves around surfing and snoozing. So, chill a little. Party a little. Eat a little. You've come to just the right place.

 **Activities**

SURFING

Breaking on the reef that hugs the village is the famed **Salsa Brava**, a shallow break that is also one of the country's most infamous waves. It's a tricky ride – if you lose it, the waves will plow you straight into the reef – and definitely not for beginners.

For a softer landing, try the beach break at **Playa Cocles** – where the waves are almost as impressive and the landing far less damaging. Cocles is about 2km east of town. Conditions are usually best early in the day, before the wind picks up.

SWIMMING

The entire southern Caribbean coast – from Cahuita all the way south to Punta Mona – is lined with unbelievably beautiful beaches. Just northwest of town, **Playa Negra** offers the area's safest swimming.

SNORKELING

The waters from Cahuita to Manzanillo are sheltered by Costa Rica's only two living reef systems, which form a naturally protected sanctuary, home to some 35 species of coral and 400 species of fish, not to mention dolphins, sharks and, occasionally, whales. Generally, underwater visibility is best when the sea is calm.

Just south of **Punta Uva**, in front of the Arrecife Restaurant, is a decent spot for snorkeling, when conditions are calm. The reef at **Manzanillo** is also easily accessible. Most of the dive companies offer snorkeling trips for about US$40 to US$60 per person.

DIVING

Divers in the southern Caribbean will discover upward of 20 dive sites, from the coral gardens in shallow waters to deeper sites with amazing underwater vertical walls. Literally hundreds of species of fish swim around here, including angelfish, parrotfish, triggerfish, shark and different species of jack and snapper.

Puerto Viejo de Talamanca

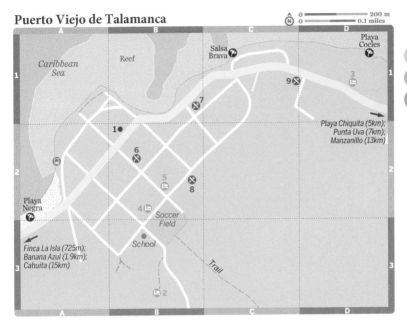

HIKING

There are superb coastal hiking opportunities within 15km of Puerto Viejo in Parque Nacional Cahuita and the Refugio Nacional de Vida Silvestre Gandoca-Manzanillo.

📑 Sleeping

Hotel Pura Vida   Hotel **$**

(☎ 2750-0002; www.hotel-puravida.com; s/d/tr US$34/38/48, without bathroom US$28/32/42; P 🛜) Despite the budget prices, this Chilean-German-run inn opposite the soccer field offers solidly midrange amenities. Ten breezy, immaculate rooms come clad in polished wood, bright linens and ceramic-tile floors; No 6 is especially nice, with views of town from its solar-heated shower. There's a lounge with easy chairs and hammocks, and breakfasts, snacks and chilled beers are available.

Jacaranda Hotel & Jungle Garden   Cabina **$**

(☎ 2750-0069; www.cabinasjacaranda.net; s/d/tr/q from US$30/45/50/55; P 🛜) In a blooming garden intersected by mosaic

Puerto Viejo de Talamanca

⊕ Activities, Courses & Tours
1 ATEC...B2

🛏 Sleeping
2 Cashew Hill Jungle Cottages...............B3
3 Escape Caribeño.................................D1
4 Hotel Pura Vida.................................B2
5 Jacaranda Hotel & Jungle
    Garden...B2

🍴 Eating
6 Bread & Chocolate B2
7 Koki Beach....................................... B1
8 Miss Lidia's Place..............................B2
9 Stashu's con Fusion C1

walkways, this place near the soccer field has 15 simple wood *cabinas* with spotless ceramic-tile floors and murals of flowers, along with a small shared kitchen and patio. Yoga classes are available, the onsite One Love Spa offers massage and bodywork, and there's an organic 'supermarket' (new in 2014) right next door.

Escape Caribeño   Bungalow **$$**

(Map p135; ☎ 2750-0103; www.escapecaribeno.com; s/d/tr garden view US$70/75/85, ocean view US$90/95/105; P ❄ @ 🛜)

135

TROPICALPIX/GETTY IMAGES ©

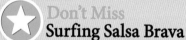

Don't Miss
Surfing Salsa Brava

The biggest break in Costa Rica, for expert surfers only and dangerous even then, Salsa Brava is named for the heaping helping of 'sauce' it serves up on the sharp, shallow reef, continually collecting its debt of fun in broken skin, boards and bones.

One take-off point: newbies waiting around to catch the popular North Peak should keep in mind that there are plenty of people in this town who gave up perks like mom's cooking and Walmart just to surf this wave regularly. Don't get in their way. In a sense, it was Salsa Brava that swept Puerto Viejo into the limelight it enjoys today.

Salsa Brava offers both rights and lefts, although the right is usually faster. Conditions are generally best from December to March, and early in the day before the wind picks up.

Charming Italian owners keep these 14 spick-and-span bungalows with spotless bathrooms, some on the beach side and others in the garden across the road, 500m east of town toward Playa Cocles. More expensive units are in lovely Caribbean-style structures with stained-glass shower stalls, but all have stocked minifridges, cable TV, fans and hammocks. Breakfast (US$5 to US$9 extra) is also available.

Cashew Hill Jungle Cottages
Bungalow **$$$**
(☎ 2750-0001, 2750-0256; www.cashewhill-lodge.co.cr; cottages US$90-150; P 🞀 🞀)
Perched on a lush hillside five minutes from town are seven bright, colorful and comfortable three- to eight-person cottages with full kitchens, loft-style sleeping areas and charming rustic touches. All have private decks or patios stocked with comfy chairs and hammocks, while the two-bedroom Playa Negra cabin offers

exquisite ocean views. A brand-new yoga platform hosts classes twice daily.

Banana Azul
Lodge **$$$**

(☏2750-2035; www.bananaazul.com; incl breakfast d US$104-129, d ste US$164; **P** 🛜 🏊)
Removed from town, this wonderful hotel sits astride a blissfully tranquil black-sand beach. Jungle-chic decor (white linens, mosquito nets, bromeliads in the showers) is complemented by fine ocean vistas from upstairs terraces. Best is the Howler Suite, a corner room with multi-directional views. There's also an onsite restaurant-bar, plus bike and body-board rentals. No children under 16.

Eating

IN TOWN

Bread & Chocolate
Breakfast **$**

(☏2750-0723; cakes US$3, meals US$5-8; 🕐6:30am-6:30pm Wed-Sat, to 2:30pm Sun; 🍴) Ever had a completely homemade PB&J (ie bread, peanut butter *and* jelly all made from scratch)? That and more can be yours at this dream of a gluten-lover's cafe. Coffees are served in individual French presses; mochas come uncon-structed so you have the pleasure of mixing your own homemade chocolate, steamed milk and coffee; and everything else – from the gazpacho to the granola to the bagels – is lovingly and skillfully made in-house.

Stashu's con Fusion
Fusion **$$**

(☏2750-0530; mains US$10-18; 🕐5-10pm Thu-Tue; 🍴) Stroll 250m out of town toward Playa Cocles to this romantic candlelit patio cafe serving up creative fusion cuisine that combines elements of Carib-bean, Indian, Mexican and Thai cooking. Steamed spicy mussels in red-curry sauce and tandoori chicken in coconut are just a couple of standouts. Excellent vegetarian and vegan items round out the menu. Owner and chef Stash Golas is an artist inside the kitchen and out. Do not miss.

Miss Lidia's Place
Caribbean **$$**

(☏2750-0598; dishes US$6-20; 🕐9am-9pm)
A long-standing favorite for classic Caribbean flavors, Miss Lidia's has been around for years, pleasing the palates and satisfying the stomachs of locals and tourists alike. Fruit-and-veggie lovers will appreciate the ice-cold *batidos* (fresh fruit

Puerto Viejo de Talamanca (p134)

shakes) and the delicious assortment of broccoli, green beans, cauliflower, corn-on-the-cob, carrots and mushrooms accompanying most dishes.

Koki Beach   Latin American $$$
(Map p135; 📞2275-0902; www.kokibeach.com; mains US$11-24; ⏰2pm-midnight Wed-Sun; 📶) A high-end favorite for drinks and dinner, this sleek eatery cranks reggae-lite and sports colorful Adirondack chairs that face the ocean from an elevated wooden platform at the east end of town. There's a decent selection of Peruvian-inflected *ceviches,* meat and seafood dishes, but slim pickings for vegetarians.

PUNTA UVA

Selvin's Restaurant   Caribbean $$
(📞2750-0664; mains US$10-18; ⏰8am-8pm Wed-Sun) Selvin is a member of the extensive Brown family, noted for their charm, and his place is considered one of the region's best, specializing in shrimp, lobster, a terrific *rondón* (seafood gumbo) and a succulent chicken *caribeño* (chicken stewed in a spicy Caribbean sauce).

La Pecora Nera   Italian $$$
(📞2750-0490; mains US$12-30; ⏰5pm-late Tue-Sun; 🍴) If you splurge for a single fancy meal during your trip, do it at this romantic eatery run by Tuscan-born Ilario Giannoni. On a lovely, candlelit patio, deftly prepared Italian seafood and pasta dishes are served alongside unusual offerings such as the delicate *carpaccio di carambola:* transparent slices of starfruit topped with shrimp, tomatoes and balsamic vinaigrette.

❶ Getting There & Away

All public buses arrive and depart from the bus stop along the beach road in central Puerto Viejo. The ticket office is diagonally across the street.

Bribrí/Sixaola US$1.50/3.35; 30/90 minutes; departs roughly every hour from 6:30am to 7:30pm.

Cahuita/Puerto Limón US$1.50/3.60; 30/90 minutes; departs roughly every hour from 5:30am to 7:30pm.

Manzanillo US$1.20; 30 minutes; departs every two hours between 6:45am and 6:45pm (less frequently on weekends).

San José US$10.90; five hours; departs 7:30am, 9am, 11am and 4pm daily, plus 1pm Sunday.

❶ Getting Around

A bicycle is a fine way to get around town, and pedaling out to beaches east of Puerto Viejo is one of the highlights of this corner of Costa Rica. You'll find rentals all over town for about US$5 per day.

MANZANILLO

The chill village of Manzanillo has long been off the beaten track, even since the paved road arrived in 2003. This little town remains a vibrant outpost of Afro-Caribbean culture and has also remained pristine,

Manzanillo beach
VILAINECREVETTE/ALAMY ©

thanks to the 1985 establishment of the Refugio Nacional de Vida Silvestre Gandoca-Manzanillo, which includes the village and imposes strict regulations on regional development.

Activities are of a simple nature, *in* nature: hiking, snorkeling and kayaking are king. (As elsewhere, ask about riptides before heading out.) Other than that, you may find the occasional party at the locally renowned Maxi's bar and restaurant at the end of the road (where buses arrive).

Sleeping & Eating

Congo Bongo   Bungalow $$$
(☎ 2759-9016; www.congo-bongo. com; d/tr/q US$165/185/205, per week US$990/1110/1230; 🅿 🛜) About 1km outside Manzanillo towards Punta Uva, these six charming Dutch-owned cottages surrounded by dense forest (formerly a cacao plantation) offer fully equipped kitchens and plenty of living space, including open-air terraces and strategically placed hammocks that are perfect for wildlife-watching. A network of trails leads through the 6 hectares of grounds to the beautiful beach.

Cool & Calm Cafe   Caribbean $$
(☎ 8843-7460; www.coolandcalmcafe. com; mains US$9-18; ⏰ 4-9pm Mon, 11am-9pm Wed-Sun) Directly across from Manzanillo's western beachfront, this front-porch eatery regales visitors with fine Caribbean cooking, from snapper to shrimp, and chicken to lobster, with a few extras like guacamole, tacos and veggie curry thrown in for good measure. Owners Andy and Molly offer Caribbean cooking classes and a 'reef-to-plate' tour where you dive for your own lobster or fish.

Maxi's Restaurant   Caribbean $$
(mains US$9-21, lobster US$23-67; ⏰ noon-9pm; 🎵) Manzanillo's most famous restaurant draws a tourist crowd with large platters of grilled seafood, whole red snappers (*pargo rojo*), steaks and Caribbean-style

1 **JOURNEY TO PUNTA MONA**
One of the best adventures in the Manzanillo area involves following the coastal trail to Punta Mona in the **Refugio Nacional de Vida Silvestre Gandoca-Manzanillo**. On land, seeing the incredible range of biomes will put your legs to the test, or you can rent a kayak and follow the winding coastline.

2 **DOLPHIN-WATCHING**
Several species of dolphin call the Caribbean Sea home, though the most widely known is the Atlantic bottlenose. Their playful and dramatic antics are a highlight of the shallow seas near Manzanillo. Although Costa Rican law prohibits swimming with dolphins, with a knowledgeable local guide you can get up close and personal, watching these amazing creatures from a safe distance.

3 **CORAL REEFS**
Directly in front of town are coral reef formations that are as unique as their evocative names: Sugar, Bloody, Jimmy and Wash a Woman. The easiest way to explore the underwater world is to don a mask, fins and snorkel, and spend a while cruising above the reef and occasionally diving down for a closer look.

4 **SCUBA DIVING**
In addition to the nearby outlying reefs, there are some further-flung dive spots that harbor astonishing varieties of marine life. Even though there are many other more spectacular dive sites in Central America and the Caribbean, it can be a blast. From spiny lobsters hiding in the rocks to enormous pilot whales, the Caribbean Sea is a never-ending showcase of some of the planet's weirdest and most wonderful wildlife.

lobsters (expensive and not necessarily worth it). Despite the somewhat lackadaisical service, the open-air upstairs dining area is a wonderful seaside setting for a meal and a beer with views of the beach and the street below.

❶ Getting There & Away

Buses from Puerto Viejo to Manzanillo (US$1.20, 30 minutes) depart at 6:45am, 7:45am, 9:45am, 11:45am, 1:45pm, 4:45pm and 6:45pm, returning to Puerto Viejo at 7am, 8am, 10am, noon, 2pm, 4pm and 6pm. These buses all continue to Puerto Limón (US$4.90, two hours) for onward transfers. Transportes Mepe also runs one direct bus daily between Manzanillo and San José (US$12, five hours), leaving Manzanillo at 7am and returning from San José at noon.

REFUGIO NACIONAL DE VIDA SILVESTRE GAN-DOCA-MANZANILLO

This little-explored refuge – called Regama for short – protects nearly 70% of the southern Caribbean coast, extending from Manzanillo all the way to the Panamanian border. It encompasses 50 sq km of land plus 44 sq km of marine environment. The peaceful, pristine stretch of sandy white beach is one of the area's main attractions. It's the center of village life in Manzanillo, and stretches for miles in either direction – from Punta Uva in the west to Punta Mona in the east. Offshore, a 5-sq-km coral reef is a teeming habitat for lobsters, sea fans and long-spined urchins.

Other than the village itself, and the surrounding farmland areas (grandfathered when the park was created in 1985), the wildlife refuge is composed largely of rainforest. Cativo trees form the canopy, while there are many heliconia in the undergrowth. A huge, 400-hectare swamp – known as **Pantano Punta Mona** – provides a haven for waterfowl, as well as the country's most extensive collection of holillo palms and sajo trees. Beyond Punta Mona, protecting a natural oyster bank, is the only red-mangrove swamp in Caribbean Costa Rica. In the nearby Río Gandoca estuary there is a spawning ground

Refugio Nacional de Vida Silvestre Gandoca-Manzanillo

for Atlantic tarpon, and caimans and manatees have been sighted here.

The variety of vegetation and the remote location of the refuge attract many tropical birds; sightings of the rare harpy eagle have been recorded here. Other birds to look out for include the red-lored parrot, the red-capped manikin and the chestnut-mandibled toucan, among hundreds of others. The area is also known for incredible raptor migrations, with more than a million birds flying overhead during autumn.

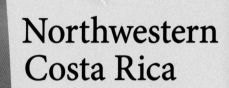

Northwestern Costa Rica

Perfect waves, lush jungles, glowering volcanoes: find it in northwestern Costa Rica. Whether hiking in the shadow of Volcán Arenal, catching a flash of green from a quetzal's wing or riding the perfect barrel at Witch's Rock, the region is heavily traveled for good reason. From blazing, dry beaches of the Guanacaste coast to the mist-shrouded heights of Volcán Miravalles, this is the turf that has long held the banner attractions for Costa Rica's eco-minded adventure travelers.

Beyond the touristed areas lie the northern lowlands, where plantations of bananas, sugarcane and pineapples roll across the humid plains from the Cordillera Central to the Nicaraguan border. This is real-life Costa Rica, where the balance of agricultural commerce and ecological conservation converge to create a contemporary work in green progress.

Volcán Arenal (p158)

Northwestern Costa Rica

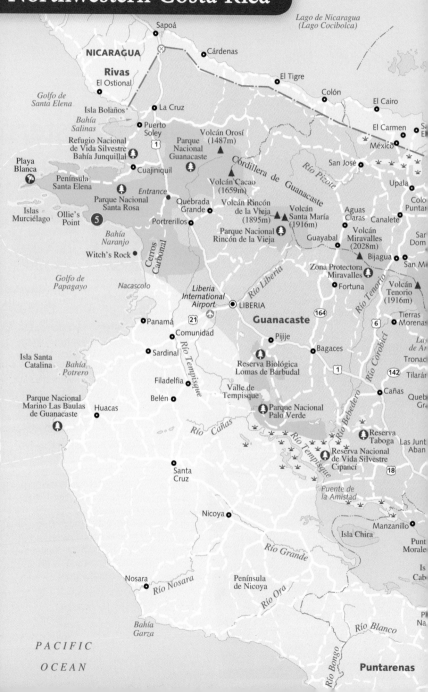

NICARAGUA

Río San Juan

Morrillo

San Carlos

Correa

Los Chiles

Río Frío

Refugio Nacional de Vida Silvestre Caño Negro

ño Negro

Lago Caño Negro

Llanura de Guatusos

Río San Juan

1 Monteverde & Santa Elena

2 Parque Nacional Volcán Arenal

3 Laguna de Arenal

4 La Virgen

5 Santa Rosa Sector

35

Llanura de San Carlos

Río Frío

Reserva Indígena Guatuso

afael atuso

Nacional Tenorio

Alajuela

4

uevo Arenal

42

Unión

Río San Carlos

Laguna Astillero

Río Sarapiquí

Selva Verde Lodge; Chilamate Rainforest Eco Retreat

Volcán Arenal (1633m)

Río Arenal

arque Nacional Volcán Arenal Ranger Station

1 **2** La Fortuna

250

Río Tres Amigos

Río Pital

Heredia

Chilamate

Puerto Viejo de Sarapiquí

La Quinta de Sarapiquí Lodge

Parque Nacional Volcán Arenal

El Castillo

142

Pital

162

La Virgen

Tirimbina Rainforest Center; Centro Neotrópico Sarapiquís

Arenal Observatory Lodge

141

4

4

Reserva Santa Elena

Zona Protectora Arenal-Monteverde

140

Cordillera de Tilarán

Río Balsa

Ciudad Quesada (San Carlos)

126

Zona Protectora La Selva

Sueño Azul Resort

Horquetas

Elena

1

Monteverde

141

San Miguel

4

Reserva Biológica Bosque Nuboso Monteverde

Río Lagarto

Reserva Biológica Alberto Mauel Brenes

Parque Nacional Juan Castro Blanco

Río Toro

Río Sarapiquí

Cordillera Central

Río Patria

Puntarenas

Zarcero

Volcán Poás (2704m)

32

Refugio Nacional de Fauna Silvestre Peñas Blancas

Volcán Barva (2906m)

Río Sucio

Rancho Grande

Miramar

Naranjo

Parque Nacional Braulio Carrillo

1

144

San Ramón

Palmares

Río Poás

Río Barranca

Barranca

San Mateo

ALAJUELA

Juan Sántamaria International Airport

HEREDIA

as

PUNTARENAS

Orotina

Río Virilla

SAN JOSÉ

Zona Protectora Tivives

ia ante a

Golfo de Nicoya

Río Tárcoles

Parque Nacional Carara

Santiago de Puriscal

San Gabriel

Río Candelaria

CARTAGO

Cartago

Tárcoles

sla

Northwestern Costa Rica Highlights

Monteverde & Santa Elena

Monteverde and Santa Elena (p168) are a destination for biologists, and ongoing research has broadened understanding of tropical ecosystems. Monteverde is the more famously known of these popular sister destinations, but both have lodgings, restaurants and activities (like canopy zip lining) for every taste. Zip lining, Monteverde (p173)

1

2 ## Parque Nacional Volcán Arenal

The most obvious reason to visit this park (p158) is Volcán Arenal. Since erupting in 1968, it has been one of the world's most active volcanoes (until recently). The surrounding area is home to jungle hiking, hardened lava flows and waterfalls, and more than 350 species of birds, abundant mammals and fascinating insect life. Hanging bridge, Arenal (p164)

TAN YILMAZ/GETTY IMAGES ©

Laguna de Arenal

3

Make the most of this beautiful region with a road trip around Laguna de Arenal (p163). The vibrant nature on display prompts many to make the comparison to Switzerland. Add to the mix boutique hotels, gourmet restaurants and kite surfing, and you have quite a full itinerary.

IANMCDONNELL/GETTY IMAGES ©

4

La Virgen

Novices and avid kayakers alike trek out to far-flung La Virgen (p196) in the northern lowlands. With a slew of crisscrossing rivers to choose from, the area around La Virgen has the country's most diverse offering of kayaking and rafting runs.

5

Santa Rosa Sector

Lying just south of the Nicaraguan border, this remote sector of Área de Conservación Guanacaste (p193) takes some serious commitment to access. But if you're interested in surfing two legendary breaks – namely Witch's Rock and Ollie's Point – it's most definitely worth the long boat ride out to the country's extreme northwestern corner.

Northwestern Costa Rica's Best…

Splurges

○ **Nayara Hotel, Spa & Gardens** Admire the rainforest from the Jacuzzi. (p157)

○ **Arenal Observatory Lodge** The only lodge within Parque Nacional Volcán Arenal. (p161)

○ **Celeste Mountain Lodge** Relax in sustainable luxury with volcano views. (p192)

○ **Rancho Margot** The self-sufficient farm offers a luxurious connection with the land. (p162)

Vistas

○ **Monteverde & Santa Elena** The cloud forest panoramas are everything you expect them to be: lush, misty and full of wildlife. (p168)

○ **Volcán Arenal** It's hard to top the dramatic sight of this brooding geological monster – impressive even without the lava. (p158)

○ **Laguna de Arenal** Find a Switzerland-like vista in the middle of Central America. (p163)

○ **Cerro Chato** Peer into the crater of Arenal's long dormant partner, which holds a sparkling lake. (p160)

Eats

○ **Restaurant Don Rufino** Eatery blending continental and Tico influences. (p157)

○ **Gingerbread Hotel & Restaurant** Menu changes weekly, ensuring the freshest fare. (p165)

○ **Sofia** Nuevo Latino spot that's transforming the Monteverde restaurant scene. (p177)

○ **Trio** Contemporary fusion cuisine emphasizing local ingredients. (p178)

Need to Know

Activities

○ **Hiking** Monteverde and Santa Elena are within easy walking distance of some of the country's greatest hiking trails. (p172)

○ **Kayaking** Head to La Virgen with oar in hand for excellent river kayaking. (p197)

○ **Surfing** The Santa Rosa Sector is an undisputed surfing mecca, with a variety of breaks for beginners and experts alike. (p193)

○ **Zip Lining** Santa Elena is home to Costa Rica's favorite high-speed jungle zip lines. (p173)

ADVANCE PLANNING

○ **One month before** Book a rental car, as it increases your ability to move around this large and fairly spread-out region. Also make hotel reservations, since this corner of the country is always busy. And although Volcán Arenal is technically still active, lava flows are not expected again anytime soon. Look online to get a sense of what to expect from the mountain.

○ **Two weeks before** Consider booking tours, high-end restaurant reservations or spa appointments in high season.

GETTING AROUND

○ **Air** An increasing number of international flights are touching down at and taking off from Liberia's Aeropuerto Internacional Daniel Oduber Quirós.

○ **Bus** Distances are long, but intercity bus connections are reliable.

○ **Jeep-boat-jeep** This unique transportation combination connects La Fortuna to Monteverde.

○ **Walk** The cloud forests of the northern reaches of this region attract both casual hikers and serious trekkers.

RESOURCES

○ **Arenal Tourism** (www.arenal.net) Familiarize yourself with the area and get general travel info here.

○ **Monteverde Info** (www.monteverdeinfo.com) Another good planning tool to get oriented in the region.

BE FOREWARNED

○ **Signage** Roads in northwestern Costa Rica are poorly signed, so it's best to bring along a good road map (or GPS) before setting out.

○ **Climate** The Arenal and Monteverde are at higher elevations and can get cool and wet; pack accordingly.

ft: Hummingbird; **Above:** Tabacón Hot Springs (p152)

(LEFT) JONATHAN GREGSON/LONELY PLANET ©;
(ABOVE) JOHN COLETTI/GETTY IMAGES ©

Northwestern Costa Rica Itineraries

Even if your time is short, a romp through northwestern Costa Rica will present the country's vivid charms. These two itineraries bring you to the best the region has to offer.

3 DAYS

MONTEVERDE TO RESERVA SANTA ELENA
MONTEVERDE & SANTA ELENA

Northwestern Costa Rica is an enormous region that takes time to access, but by focusing on Monteverde and Santa Elena, three days is just long enough to visit the area's top highlights. You could easily spend a week here and not exhaust the huge number of hiking opportunities, activities, restaurants and galleries.

Base yourself in the adjacent towns of ❶ **Monteverde** and **Santa Elena** (p168), but allow time for coming and leaving as the access roads are largely unpaved and very slowgoing. Make the most of your brief time here by staying busy around the clock – night tours through the Children's Eternal

Forest provide face-to-face encounters with nocturnal wildlife. During daylight hours, a diverse range of hiking awaits at both ❷ **Reserva Biológica Bosque Nuboso Monteverde** (p180) and ❸ **Reserva Santa Elena** (p182), two of the country's most famous protected spaces. By the time you board the flight back home, you'll have seen some of the best the country has to offer.

5 DAYS

LA FORTUNA TO LAGUNA DE ARENAL

LA FORTUNA & AROUND

Monteverde and Santa Elena garner their fair share of the spotlight, but the area around La Fortuna is a close contender when it comes to the country's top attractions. The tiny Tico town of La Fortuna has some of the country's best tourist infrastructures, as well as a remarkable number of luxurious hot-spring resorts and tons of activities. Of course, the main reason you're here is to stand in awe of the Volcán Arenal, one of the world's most active volcanoes. Though the lava no longer flows, the volcano's looming presence still amazes.

Everything centers on **①La Fortuna** (p152) – even if the weather isn't

cooperating and Arenal is shrouded in clouds, you'll still enjoy yourself immensely here. Hedonists can't seem to pry themselves away from Tabacón Hot Springs, while more outdoorsy types can hike to waterfalls or zip line through the forest canopy. If the weather is good, make a beeline to **②Parque Nacional Volcán Arenal** (p158) to hike along hardened lava flows. An added bonus: the roads surrounding the nearby **③Laguna de Arenal** (p163) are perfect for road-tripping.

View of Volcán Arenal (p158)
JONATHAN GREGSON/LONELY PLANET ©

Discover
Northwestern Costa Rica

Heliconia flower
JONATHAN GREGSON/LONELY PLANET ©

LA FORTUNA
& AROUND

First impressions of La Fortuna may be
somewhat lacking, what with all the tourists
and uninspired cinder-block architecture.
But with a little time, this town's charms ap-
pear in the horses grazing in bare lots, spiny
iguanas scrambling through brush and
eternal spring mornings carrying just a kiss
of humidity on their breath. And always,
there's that massive volcano lurking behind
the clouds or sparkling in the sun.

Certainly, the influx of tourism has
altered the face, fame and fortunes of this
former one-horse town. But the longer
you linger, the more you'll appreciate
La Fortuna's underlying, small-town
sabanero (cowboy) feel.

◎ Sights & Activities

Eco-Termales   Hot Spring
(☏ 2479-8484; www.anywherecos-
tarica.com; adult/child US$34/24,
with dinner US$51/38; ☺10am,
1pm & 5pm; 👪) The theme here
is minimalist elegance, and
everything from the natural
circulation systems in the
pools to the soft, mushroom
lighting is understated yet
luxurious. Just 100 visitors per
slot are welcomed at 10am, 1pm
and 5pm, and you must either
phone ahead or book online.

Tabacón Hot Springs   Hot Spring
(☏ 2519-1999; www.tabacon.com; day pass incl
lunch or dinner adult/child US$85/30; ☺10am-
10pm; P) ✿ Some say it's cheesy and some
say it's fun. (We say it's both.) Broad-leaf
palms, rare orchids and other florid tropical blooms part to reveal a 40°C (104°F)
waterfall pouring over a fake cliff, concealing
constructed caves complete with cam-

ouflaged cup holders. Lounged across each well-placed stonelike substance are overheated tourists of various shapes and sizes, relaxing.

La Catarata de la
Fortuna   Waterfall

(admission US$10; ⊙8am-5pm) You can glimpse the sparkling 70m ribbon of clear water that pours through a sheer canyon of dark volcanic rock arrayed in bromeliads and ferns with minimal effort. But it's worth the climb down and out to see it from the jungle floor. Though it's dangerous to dive beneath the thundering falls, a series of perfect swimming holes with spectacular views tiles the canyon in aquamarine. This is also the trailhead for the hike to Cerro Chato (p160).

Springs Resort & Spa   Hot Spring

(☎2401-3313, in USA 954-727-8333; www.thespringscostarica.com; 2-day admission US$50; ⊙8am-10pm; ⊛) If you're looking for a luxurious hot-spring experience, the Springs features 18 free-form pools with various temperatures, volcano views, landscaped gardens, waterfalls and swim-up bars, including a jungle bar with a waterslide. The whole scene is human-made, but it's lovely.

Tours

Aguas Bravas   Rafting, Kayaking

(☎2479-7645; www.costaricaraftingvacation.com; safari float trip US$80, Class III/Class IV trips US$80/95; ⊙7am-7pm) This rafting specialist offers a few options in the area, including a gentle safari float trip on Peñas Blancas, as well as Class III and IV trips. It can also organize hiking, horseback riding and kayaking on Lago Arenal.

Arenal Paraíso Canopy
Tours   Canopy Tour

(☎2479-1100; www.arenalparaiso.com; tours US$45; ⊙8am-5pm) A dozen cables zip across the canyon of the Río Arenal, giving a unique perspective on two waterfalls, as well as the rainforest canopy.

Canoa Aventura   Canoeing

(☎2479-8200; www.canoa-aventura.com; canoe trip US$67, full-day trip to Caño Negro US$113; ⊙6:30am-9:30pm) ⚐ This long-standing family-run company specializes in canoe and float trips led by bilingual naturalist guides. Most are geared toward wildlife- and bird-watching. One popular paddle is the full-day trip to Caño Negro.

Abseiling near La Fortuna

JONATHAN GREGSON/LONELY PLANET ©

La Fortuna

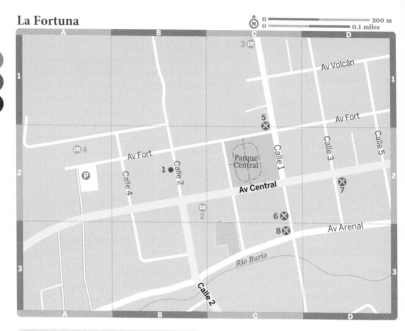

Desafío Adventure Company
Adventure Tour

(Map p154; ☎2479-0020; www.desafiocostarica. com; Calle 2; tours US$65-85; ⏰6:30am-9pm) Desafío has the widest range of river trips in La Fortuna, including paddling trips on the Río Balsa, horse-riding treks to Volcán Arenal, adventure tours rappelling down waterfalls, and mountain-bike expeditions. It can also arrange your transfer to Monteverde by horse, boat or bike.

Ecoglide
Canopy Tour

(Map p156 ☎2479-7120; www.arenalecoglide. com; adult/student & child US$55/45; ⏰7am-4pm; 🚻) Opened in 2008, Ecoglide is the biggest canopy game in town, featuring 13 cables, 15 platforms and a 'Tarzan' swing. The dual-cable safety system provides extra security and peace of mind.

PureTrek Canyoning
Canyoning

(Map p156; ☎866-569-5723, 2479-1313; www. puretrekcanyoning.com; 4hr incl transportation & lunch US$98; ⏰7am-10pm; 🚻) 🍃 The reputable PureTrek leads guided rappels down four waterfalls, one of which is 50m high. Check in at PureTrek headquarters, located in a tree house 6km west of town.

🛏 Sleeping

There are loads of places to stay in town. If you're driving, consider staying on the pastoral road to Cerro Chato, a few kilometers south of town, where several appealing hotels have cropped up, or closed to the volcano in El Castillo.

In the low season rates plummet by as much as 40%.

IN TOWN

Arenal Hostel Resort
Hostel $

(Map p154; ☏2479-9222; www.arenal-hostelresort.com; Av Central; dm/s/d/tr/q US$16/48/58/75/88; P✳@🛜☁) Offering the best of hostel and resort, this welcoming place is arranged around a landscaped garden, complete with hammocks, small pool, party-place bar, and volcano view. All rooms are clean, spacious and air-conditioned, with en suite bathrooms. Service is top notch, if a tad impersonal.

Pay attention: Arenal Hostel Resort and Arenal Backpackers Resort do essentially the same thing, but they are not actually the same place.

La Fortuna Suites
Guesthouse $$

(Map p154; ☏8577-1555; www.lafortunasuites.com; d incl breakfast US$96; P✳🛜) Here's a chance to luxuriate in some high-end amenities at midrange prices. We're talking high-thread-count sheets and memory-foam mattresses, custom-made furniture and flat-screen TVs, gourmet breakfast on the balcony and killer views. Despite all these perks, guests agree that the thing that makes this place special is the hospitality shown by the hosts.

Hotel Arenal Rabfer
Hotel $$

(Map p154; ☏2479-9187; www.arenalrabfer.com; Calle 1; s/d/tr/q incl breakfast US$62/75/87/101; P✳@🛜☁) Arguably the most architecturally appealing of the in town options, with a striking shingled 2nd floor. Set up around a pebbled pool area and shady palm garden, the rooms are spacious with high slanted ceilings and fresh coats of paint. The whole place is immaculate. Located on a quiet side street, two blocks from the action.

OUTSIDE TOWN

Roca Negra del Arenal
Guesthouse $$

(Map p156; ☏2479-9237; www.hotelrocanegradelarenal.com; d/tr/q US$60/70/80, breakfast US$6; P✳🛜☁) Plenty of feathered and furry friends roam the grounds at this gem of a guesthouse, located 2km west of town. Along with the ever-charming owner, they make for quite a welcome party. There are seven spacious rooms, each with stained wood accents, huge tile bathrooms and semi-private terraces facing the garden (complete with rockers).

But what makes this place so special? It's the paradisaical setting. The luscious tiled pool and jacuzzi are surrounded with tropical gardens that are bursting with blooms and buzzing with bees and birds. If you came for R&R in exotic environs, look no further.

Hotel Campo Verde
Bungalow $$

(Map p156; ☏2479-1080; www.hotelcampoverde.com; s/d/tr/q incl breakfast from $US75/90/110/130; P@🛜) An absolutely

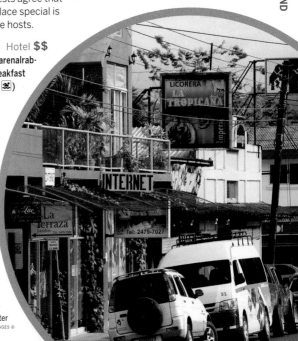

La Fortuna town center
ROB FRANCIS/GETTY IMAGES ©

Around La Fortuna

NORTHWESTERN COSTA RICA LA FORTUNA & AROUND

156

N

0   0
0   0

5 miles | 10 km

Map labels

ALAJUELA

GUANACASTE

La Fortuna

Río Arenal

Laguna de Arenal

Dam

Volcán Arenal ▲ (1633m)

Parque Nacional Volcán Arenal

Cerro Chato (1100m)

Arenal Observatory Lodge

El Castillo

Nuevo Arenal

San Luis

Tronadora

Tilarán

Venado

La Unión

Río Chiquito

Quebrada Grande

Chachagua

Around La Fortuna

darling family-owned property, located 9km west of town. Canary-yellow wooden bungalows have vaulted beamed ceilings, two queen beds, lovely drapes and chandeliers, and a sweet tiled patio blessed with two waiting rockers. Book the wooden bungalows furthest from the road at the foot of the mountain, where the views are unbeatable.

Chachagua Rainforest Hotel
Hotel $$$

(Map p156; ☏2468-1010; www.chachaguarainforesthotel.com; d/bungalows incl breakfast US$236/290; 🅿 🍴 ❄ 🛜 🏊) Situated on a private reserve that abuts the Bosque Eterno de Los Niños, this hotel is a naturalist's dream. Part of the property is a working orchard, cattle ranch and fish farm, while the rest is humid rainforest. Explore it on hiking trails or on horseback. The rooms are nice but arguably overpriced, while the stylish, spacious bungalows are gorgeous as all get-out.

Nayara Hotel, Spa & Gardens
Hotel $$$

(Map p156; ☏2479-1600; www.arenalnayara.com; r/ste incl breakfast US$280/390; 🅿 ❄ @ 🛜 🏊) This intimate and indulgent hotel, 6km west of town, has amassed a slew of awards for its Asian-inspired architecture, minimalist decor and richly romantic setting. The 24 rooms have exquisite furnishings and bedding, rich woods, high-tech gadgetry, an outdoor

shower and a private outdoor Jacuzzi where you can soak up views of Volcán Arenal. Exquisite.

Eating

Rainforest Café
Cafe $

(Map p154; ☏2479-7239; Calle 1 btwn Avs Central & Arenal; mains US$4-6; ⏱7am-8:30pm; 🛜) We know it's bad form to start with dessert, but the irresistible sweets at this popular spot are beautiful to behold and delicious to devour. The savory menu features burritos, *casados* (set meals) and other excellent traditional fare. There's also a full menu of hot and cold coffee, including some tempting specialty drinks (Mono Loco = coffee, banana, milk, chocolate and cinnamon).

There's a dash of urban-coffeehouse atmosphere here. Must be the writing in the milk foam.

Soda Viquez
Soda $

(Map p154; ☏2479-7133; cnr Calle 1 & Av Arenal; mains US$6-10; ⏱7am-10pm) Insanely popular among travelers, this friendly spot takes *tipica* and adds something to it. It has a tasty, saucy steam table but also makes chicken, beef and fish six different ways if you choose to order off the menu. Prices are reasonable, portions ample.

La Cascada
International $$

(Map p154; ☏2479-9145; cnr Av Fort & Calle 1; mains US$6-26; ⏱11am-late) This thatched landmark has been around so long that the *palapa* roof is almost as big an institution as the volcano it mimics. It has a small bar and acquires a drinking crowd at night, but tourists consider it a lunch and dinner option, too. Look for well-prepared roast- and grilled-meat dishes, pastas, sandwiches and a few veggie options. Restaurant Don.

Rufino   International $$$

(Map p154; ☎2479-9997; www.donrufino. com; cnr Av Central & Calle 3; mains US$16-40; ☺11am-11pm) In almost every way, this indoor-outdoor bar and grill is light years ahead of the competition. The highlight of the menu is the grilled meats, which include rib eye, filet, peppercorn tenderloin medallions, and a porterhouse with gorgonzola sauce. If you're cutting back on red meat, look for crab risotto, ginger-glazed grilled tuna, and chicken in coconut curry.

ℹ Getting There & Away

Bus

Most domestic buses stop at the Centro Comercial Adifort. Keep an eye on your bags, particularly on the weekend San José run.

San José (Auto-Transportes San José–San Carlos) US$4.25, 4½ hours, departs 12:45pm and 2:45pm. Alternatively, take a bus to Ciudad Quesada and change to frequent buses to the capital.

Tilarán, with connection to Monteverde (Auto-Transportes Tilarán, departs from the Parque Central) US$2.60, 3½ hours, departs 8am and 4:30pm. To reach Monteverde (US$3.60, six to eight hours), take the early bus to Tilarán, where you'll have to wait a few hours for the onward bus to Santa Elena.

Jeep-Boat-Jeep

The fastest route between Monteverde-Santa Elena and La Fortuna is the sexy-sounding jeep-boat-jeep combo (US$25 to US$40, three hours). The 'jeep' is actually a minivan with the requisite yellow '*turismo*' tattoo. It's still a terrific transportation option and can be arranged through almost any hotel or tour operator in either town. The minivan from La Fortuna takes you to Laguna de Arenal, meeting a boat that crosses the lake, where a 4WD taxi on the other side continues to Monteverde. This is increasingly becoming the primary transportation between La Fortuna and Monteverde as it's incredibly scenic and reasonably priced, and it'll save you half a day of travel over rocky roads.

PARQUE NACIONAL VOLCÁN ARENAL

Arenal was just another dormant volcano surrounded by fertile farmland from about AD 1500 until July 29, 1968, when huge explosions triggered lava flows that destroyed three villages, killing about

Nayara Hotel, Spa & Gardens (p157)

RON NIEBRUGGE/ALAMY ©

Don't Miss
Arenal Observatory Lodge

The Arenal Observatory Lodge was built in 1987 as a private observatory for the Universidad de Costa Rica. Scientists chose to construct this lodge on a macadamia-nut farm on the south side of Volcán Arenal due to its proximity to the volcano – only 2km away – and its relatively safe location on a ridge. Volcanologists from all over the world have since come to study the active volcano, and a seismograph in the hotel continues to operate around the clock.

The lodge offers massages (from US$60), guided hikes and all the usual tours at good prices. It also has an excellent trail network, including the leisurely Waterfall Trail and the challenging-but-worth-it Cerro Chato Trail. You can wander around the macadamia-nut farm or investigate the pine forest that makes up about half of the 347-hectare site. There's also a small museum with exhibits on the history, volcanology and hydrology of Arenal.

NEED TO KNOW

📞 lodge 2479-1070; www.arenalobservatorylodge.com; day pass US$6, museum admission free; P

80 people and 45,000 cattle. The area was evacuated and roads throughout the region were closed. Eventually, the lava subsided to a relatively predictable flow and life got back to normal. Sort of.

Although it occasionally quieted down for a few weeks or even months, Arenal produced menacing ash columns, massive explosions and streams of glowing molten rock almost daily. It all quite abruptly ended in 2010, leaving the alarmed local tourist industry to gasp and spew in its place. Still, any obituary on the Arenal area is premature given the fact that the volcano has retained its picture-perfect conical shape and there is still

159

MARTIN HARRISON/GETTY IMAGES ©

plenty of forest on its lower slopes and in the nearby foothills.

While the molten night views are gone for now (one never knows what lies beneath or beyond), this mighty mountain is still worthy of your time. Clouds may shroud her at any time, but there are excellent trails to explore. And even if it does rain and there is a chill in the air, you are just a short drive away from hot springs.

Activities

Arenal was made a national park in 1995, and it is part of the Área de Conservación Arenal, which protects most of the Cordillera de Tilarán. This area is rugged and varied, and the biodiversity is high; roughly half the species of land-dwelling vertebrates (birds, mammals, reptiles and amphibians) known in Costa Rica can be found here.

Commonly seen mammals include howler monkeys, white-faced capuchins and even anteaters (northern tamandua). Coatis are surprisingly tame, but don't feed them. With more than 400 species, bird life is rich in the park and includes such species as trogons, rufous motmots, fruitcrows and lancebills.

Cerro Chato Trail   Hiking
(www.arenalobservatorylodge.com; Arenal Observatory Lodge; day pass per person $US6)
The ultimate hike in the national park, the Cerro Chato Trail starts at the Arenal Observatory Lodge and meanders through pasture before climbing quite steeply through remnant forest and into patches of virgin growth reaching into misty sky. Eventually the trail crests Cerro Chato, Arenal's dormant partner, and ends in a 1100m-high volcanic lake that is simply stunning. The hike is only 8km round trip, but it will take two to three hours each way.

Waterfall Trail   Hiking
(www.arenalobservatorylodge.com; Arenal Observatory Lodge; day pass per person US$6)
This scenic hike departing from the Arenal Observatory Lodge is an easy, 2km round-trip hike that takes about an hour to complete. The terrain starts out flat then descends into a grotto where you'll find a thundering gusher of a waterfall that's about 12m high. You'll feel the mist long before you see its majesty.

Sendero Los Heliconias
Hiking

From the ranger station (which has trail maps available) you can hike this 1km circular track, which passes by the site of the 1968 lava flow (vegetation here is slowly sprouting back to life). A 1.5km-long path branches off this trail and leads to an overlook.

Sendero Las Coladas
Hiking

This track branches off the Heliconias trail and wraps around the volcano for 2km past the 1993 lava flow before connecting with the **Sendero Los Tucanes**, which extends for another 3km through the tropical rainforest at the base of the volcano. To return to the car-parking area, you will have to turn back. You'll get good views of the summit on the way to the parking lot.

Sendero Los Miradores
Hiking

From the park headquarters (not the ranger station) is the 1.3km Sendero Los Miradores, which leads down to the shores of the volcanic lake, and provides a good angle for volcano viewing.

Old Lava Flow Trail
Hiking

Branching from park headquarters is this interesting and strenuous lower elevation trail. It follows the flow of the massive 1993 eruption, is 4km round trip and takes two hours to complete. If you want to keep hiking, combine it with the 1.8km **El Ceibo Trail**.

Sleeping

Arenal Observatory Lodge
Lodge $$$

(2479-1070, reservations 2290-7011; www.arenalobservatorylodge.com; d/tr/q without bathroom US$97/112/127, with bathroom from US$133/147/176; P @) Set high on the Arenal slopes, this sensational, sprawling lodge is the only accommodation in the national park. Rooms range from La Casona's rustic doubles with shared bathrooms and views from the porch, to plus junior suites, with king-size beds, local art and huge picture windows framing the volcano. Most of the rooms fall somewhere in the middle of this range.

 Information

The **ranger station** (2461-8499; adult/child US$10/1; 8am-4pm) is on the western side of the volcano, and the complex housing includes an information center and parking lot. From here, trails lead 3.4km toward the volcano.

EL CASTILLO

The tiny mountain village of El Castillo is a wonderful alternative to staying in La Fortuna – it's bucolic and reasonably untouristed (although there is a tight expat community), and it has easy access to Parque Nacional Volcán Arenal. It also offers amazing, up-close views of the looming mountain. It's best to have your own wheels out here, as buses don't serve this little enclave.

Sights & Activities

El Castillo-Arenal Butterfly Conservatory
Wildlife Reserve

(2479-1149; www.butterflyconservatory.org; adult/student US$14/10; 8:30am-4:30pm) This is more than just a butterfly conservatory (although it has one of the largest butterfly exhibitions in Costa Rica). Altogether there are six domed habitats, a ranarium, an insect museum, a medicinal herb garden, and an hour's worth of trails through a botanic garden and along the river. The birding is also excellent at this peaceful place.

Arenal EcoZoo
Zoo

(El Serpentario; 2479-1059; www.arenalecozoo.com; adult/child US$16/10; 8am-7pm) Meet 36 of the most dangerous snake species in the world, like Eliza, a 5m-long Burmese python, then handle and milk a venomous snake. The EcoZoo is also home to vibrant frogs, amphibious lizards, spiny iguanas, shy turtles, vengeful scorpions, hairy tarantulas and floating butterflies.

Rancho Adventure Tours
Biking, Kayaking, Horseback Riding

(8302-7318; www.ranchomargot.com; bike rental per day US$15, tours US$45) Rancho

Margot has a good selection of guided tours, including horseback riding on the south side of Lake Arenal, kayaking on Lake Arenal and hiking to Cerro Chato. If you wish to explore the area on your own, you can rent a mountain bike for a day.

Big Forest Hike · Hiking

(☏2479-1747; per person US$130) Offered by the adventurous folks at La Gavilana, this is a two-day round-trip 'extreme hike' between El Castillo and San Gerardo (near Santa Elena). Traversing old-growth forests and raging rivers, hikers overnight at the rustic Rancho Maximo in San Gerardo. Dinner and breakfast are provided, but hikers should bring food and water to sustain them for the hike.

🛏 Sleeping & Eating

Essence Arenal · Hostel $

(☏2479-1131; www.essencearenal.com; d/tr/q from US$43/54/65, d without bathroom US$32, tents US$32; ⏱restaurant 7am-8pm; 🅿@🛜🏊) ⚡ Perched on a 22-hectare hilltop with incredible volcano and lake views, this 'boutique hostel' is the best cheap sleep in the Arenal region. Bed

down in a basic but clean room or a fine hippified tent, done up with plush bedding and wood furnishings. It's an eclectic, positive-energy place, offering group hikes, yoga classes and good vibes.

La Gavilana Herbs & Art · Bakery, Gallery $

(☏2479-1747; www.lagavilana.discoverelcastillo.com; items US$2-6; ⏱8am-5pm Mon-Fri, 9am-2pm Sat) Meet Thomas and Hannah. He's Czech and makes the hot sauce and vinegar; she's American and bakes the cookies and breads. Their place is decked with paintings (by Hannah), while the grounds contain a food forest (by Thomas), filled with medicinal herbs and fruit trees. The whole place is filled with love, beauty and creativity. It's 100m uphill from Essence Arenal hostel.

Nepenthe · B&B $$

(☏8892-5501; www.nepenthe-costarica.com; d incl breakfast US$95; 🅿❄🛜🏊) The highlight of this sweet place is the spectacular infinity pool overlooking the lake. Lodge-like rooms are simple, tiled numbers with colorful artisanal accents, set in a gentle arc of a ranch-style building. There are

El Establo Mountain Resort

hammocks on the patio and its Blue Lagoon spa comes highly recommended.

Hummingbird Nest B&B B&B $$

(Nido del Colibri; ☎2479-1174, 8835-8711; www.hummingbirdnestbb.com; d/tr/q incl breakfast US$85/95/100; P) At the entrance to town, a small path leads up the steep hill to this charming B&B, owned by a former flight attendant and all-round world traveler who found a small slice of paradise to call her own. Her quaint complex has two guest rooms and a garden full of hummingbirds. Soak the night away in a huge outdoor Jacuzzi in the garden. Two-night minimum.

Rancho Margot Resort, Lodge $$$

(☎8302-7318; www.ranchomargot.org; incl meals dm per person US$75, bungalow s/d US$165/245; P🛜🏊) 🍃 Part resort lodge, part organic farm, Rancho Margot is 152 acres of cinematic loveliness, set along the rushing Río Caño Negro and surrounded by rainforested mountains. There are comfortable dorm-style bunkhouse accommodations. If your budget allows, spring for a beautiful teak-furnished bungalow, its deck strung with a hammock and blessed with views of hulking mountains, weeping jungle and a placid lake. Two-night minimum.

LAGUNA DE ARENAL AREA

About 18km west of La Fortuna you'll arrive at a 750m-long causeway across the dam that created Laguna de Arenal – an 88-sq-km lake and the largest in the country. A number of small towns were submerged during its creation, but the lake now supplies valuable water to Guanacaste and produces hydroelectricity for the region. High winds also produce power with the aid of huge steel windmills, though windsurfers and kitesurfers frequently steal a breeze or two.

If You Like…
Secluded Mountain Lodges

If you like staying in secluded mountain lodges such as the Arenal Observatory Lodge (p161), try some of these remote alternatives:

1 EL ESTABLO MOUNTAIN RESORT
(Map p170; ☎2645-5110; www.hotelelestablo.com; d deluxe/ste incl breakfast US$250/325; P😊@🏊) This is a seriously upscale lodge offering open-plan suites that are A-frame lofts with private terraces.

2 LA CAROLINA LODGE
(☎2466-6393; www.lacarolinalodge.com; per person incl meals US$70-90; P) Flanked by a roaring river and tucked into the trees on a volcano slope, this isolated lodge is a gloriously rustic retreat.

3 RIO CELESTE HIDEAWAY
(☎2206-5114; www.riocelestehideaway.com; d incl breakfast US$216-292; P🛜) This elegant retreat has huge, 90-sq-m thatched *casitas* (cottages) with antique furnishings, soaking tubs, outdoor showers and lush landscaped grounds.

If you have your own car (or bicycle), this is one of the premier road trips in Costa Rica. The road is lined with odd and elegant businesses, many run by foreigners who have fallen in love with the place. Strong winds and high elevations give the lake a temperate feel. And the scenic views of lakeside forests and Volcán Arenal are about as romantic as they come.

But things are changing – quickly. Gringo baby boomers, lured to the area by the eternal-spring climate, are snapping up nearly every spot of land with a 'For Sale' sign on it.

Dam to Nuevo Arenal

This beautiful stretch of road is lined on both sides with cloud forest, and there are a number of fantastic accommodations strung along the way.

Sights & Activities

Arenal Hanging Bridges · Forest

(Puentes Cogantes de Arenal; ☎2290-0469; www.hangingbridges.com; adult/student/child US$24/14/free, tours US$36-47; ⏲7:30am-4pm, tours 6am, 9am & 2pm) Unlike the fly-by view you'll get on a zip-line canopy tour, a walk along the hanging bridges allows you to explore the rainforest and canopy from six suspended bridges and 10 traditional bridges at a more natural and peaceful pace. The longest swaying bridge is 97m long and the highest is 25m above the earth. All are accessible from a single 3km trail that winds through a tunnel and skirts a waterfall.

Sleeping

Arenal Lodge · Lodge $$$

(☎2479-1881; www.arenallodge.net; incl breakfast d standard/superior US$102/160, f US$190, junior ste US$198, chalets US$208; P✲🔊☎) Arenal Lodge is at the top of a steep 2.5km ascent, though the entire lodge is awash with views of Arenal and the surrounding cloud forest. Standard rooms are just that, but the spacious junior suites are tiled and have wicker furniture and a picture window or balcony with volcano views. A blue macaw hangs out in the lobby.

Lost Iguana Resort · Resort $$$

(☎2479-1559, 2479-1557; www.lostiguanaresort.com; r/ste incl breakfast US$245/275; P✲@🔊☎) This stylish and splashy tropical resort, just 1.5km from the dam, is set among lush rainforest and rushing streams with glorious volcano views at every turn. Luxurious rooms have private balconies looking out on Arenal, beds made with Egyptian cotton sheets, a terracotta wet bar, and an invaluable sense of peace and privacy. Upgrade to a suite for a Jacuzzi tub or outdoor rain shower.

Unión Area

The following accommodations and restaurants are listed in order of their distance from the Laguna de Arenal dam.

You can't miss **Hotel Los Héroes** (☎2692-8013, 2692-8012; www.pequeniahelvecia.com; incl breakfast d with/without balcony US$65/55, tr/apt US$80/115; P🔊☎), a more than slightly incongruous alpine chalet 13.5km west of the dam. Large, immaculate rooms with wood paneling have hot-water bathrooms; there are also two apartments (each sleeps up to five) with full kitchen, huge bathroom and balcony overlooking the lake. A **narrow-gauge train** (US$10; 11:30am and 1pm) chugs up the hill, bringing guests to the revolving **Rondorama Panoramic Restaurant**, unique in Costa Rica.

About 15.5km west of the dam, **La Mansion Inn Arenal** (☎2692-8018; www.lamansionarenal.com; incl breakfast d US$125-175, ste US$175-195) enjoys amazing lake views from the cottages, pool and restaurant. The large split-level rooms feature king-size beds, private terraces, and mural-painted walls. The fabulous infinity lap pool is surrounded by a relaxing patio and an ornamental garden featuring Chorotega pottery.

About 22km west of the dam, the lovely, laid-back **La Ceiba Tree Lodge** (☎8313-1475, 2692-8050; www.ceibatree-lodge.com; d incl breakfast US$89; P✲🔊) overlooks a magnificent 54m ceiba tree. Seven spacious, Spanish-tiled rooms are hung with original paintings and fronted by Maya-inspired carved doors. Each room has rustic artifacts, polished-wood ceilings and vast views of Laguna de Arenal. The tropical gardens and spacious terrace make this mountaintop spot a tranquil retreat.

Another accommodation option is **Villa Decary** (☎2694-4330, in US or Canada 800-556-0505; www.villadecary.com; r/casitas incl breakfast US$112/160; P✲🔊), an all-around winner, offering epic views and unparalleled hospitality. Elegant, spacious rooms are decorated with bright serape bedspreads and original artwork, boasting balconies with excellent views of the woodland below and the lake beyond. There are larger *casitas* (sleeping four) with kitchenettes. The trails behind the house offer excellent opportunities for birding. It's 24.5km west of the dam and 2km east of Nuevo Arenal.

Make absolutely sure to book dinner reservations at the **Gingerbread Hotel & Restaurant** (8351-7815, 2694-0039; www.gingerbreadarenal.com; mains US$18-32; ⏰5-9pm Tue-Sat, lunch by reservation only), one of the best restaurants in northwestern Costa Rica. Chef Eyal is the larger-than-life, New York–trained, Israeli chef who turns out transcendent meals from the freshest local fare. Favorites include mushrooms smothered in gravy, blackened tuna salad, and enormous, juicy, grass-fed burgers. It's big food that goes down smooth. Cash only.

....

Nuevo Arenal

Although steeped in aging *extranjero cultura* (expat culture), this two-horse town still feels very Tico. Nuevo Arenal is 27km west of the dam, or an hour's drive from La Fortuna. In case you were wondering what happened to old Arenal, it's about 27m below the surface of Laguna de Arenal. In order to create a large enough reservoir for the dam, the Costa Rican government had to make certain, er, sacrifices, which ultimately resulted in the forced relocation of 3500 people. Today, the humble residents of Nuevo Arenal don't seem to be fazed by history, especially since they now own premium lakeside property.

🛏 Sleeping & Eating

Aurora Hotel   Hotel $
(☎2694-4245; r US$24; P@🛜🏊) You'd never know it from the street, but these rooms are rather sweet, spotless, spacious, wood cabin-like constructions with lovely lake views and vaulted beamed ceilings. Located on the east side of the square, it's one of the only budget options on Laguna de Arenal. The attached restaurant does decent pizza.

Tinajas Arenal   Cafe $$
(☎8926-3365; mains US$9-15; ⏰9am-9:30pm; 🛜♿) 🅿 With glorious sunsets and a dock for boat access, this new lakeside retreat

Hanging bridge, near Parque Nacional Volcán Arenal

ALVARO LEIVA/GETTY IMAGES ©

is a hidden gem. The chef – who honed his skills at La Mansion Inn Arenal nearby – has created a menu of traditional favorites and new surprises, using fresh seafood and organic ingredients grown right here. Sample the refreshing cocktail *a la casa*, Limon Hierba (lemonade with mint).

Moya's Place   Cafe, Pizzeria **$$**
(☎ 2694-4001; mains US$6-12; ⊘ 11am-10pm) Murals, masks and other indigenous-inspired art adorn the walls at this friendly cafe. Take your pick from the delicious sandwiches, well-stuffed wraps and burritos, and tasty thin-crust pizza. This place is a sort of local gathering spot, where Ticos and expats alike gather to eat, drink and laugh. The food is good and the beer is cold.

Nuevo Arenal to Tilarán

West and around the lake from Nuevo Arenal, the scenery becomes even more spectacular just as the road gets progressively worse.

🤸 Activities

Some of the world's most consistent winds blow across northwestern Costa Rica, and this consistency attracts riders. Laguna de Arenal is rated one of the best windsurfing spots in the world, and kitesurfers flock here, too, especially from late November to April when **Tico Wind** (☎ 8383-2694, 2692-2002; www.ticowind.com; kitesurf/windsurf per day US$80/84, lessons per hr US$50) sets up camp on the shore. It has state-of-the-art boards and sails, with equipment to suit varied wind conditions. First-timers should consider the 'Get on Board' package (US$120). Beginner kitesurf instruction (US$530) is much more detailed and requires nine hours, but students will graduate IKO certified and ready to ride. The launch is located 15km west of Nuevo Arenal. The entrance is by the big, white chain-link fence with 'ICE' painted on it. Follow the dirt road 1km to the shore.

Laguna de Arenal is now attracting wakeboarders also. Check out **Paradise Adventures Costa Rica**, (☎ 8856-3618, 2479-8159; www.paradise-adventures-costa-rica.com) based in La Fortuna, which offers the latest wakeboarding equipment and package deals.

🛏 Sleeping & Eating

Aqua Inn Spa   B&B **$$**
(☎ 2694-4218; www.aguainnspa.com; d incl breakfast US$80, spa treatments US$60-90; P 🛜 ❄) The sound of the rushing river will lull you to sleep at this intimate B&B on the banks of the rainforest-shaded Río Cote. This gorgeous property is designed for total relaxation and rejuvenation, with a jungle-shaded pool and a private lake trail. Four simple rooms feature

Laguna de Arenal
IMAGEBROKER/ALAMY ©

bold colors and plush linens. Downstairs, the full-service spa does facials, massages and body scrubs.

Minoa Hotel & Microbrewery
Hotel $$

(☎ 2695-5050; www.hotelminoa.com; s/d incl breakfast from US$68/78; ⏰ 11am-9pm; P ✳ ☎ ☲) If you like beer, consider staying at the only hotel (that we're aware of) that has a microbrewery onsite, mixing up the hops and barley to bring you delicious pale ales and nut-brown beers. Drink it while feeling the lake breezes and admiring the views at the top-floor restaurant (the food is also good here).

Mystica Resort
Resort $$$

(☎ 2692-1001; www.mysticacostarica.com; s/d/tr/q incl breakfast US$102/135/152/165; P @ ☎) About 15km west of Nuevo Arenal, this Mediterranean-style retreat has several comfortable, colorful rooms with Spanish-tile floors, woven bedspreads, wooden accents and a wide, inviting front porch with volcano views. If you're not staying here, the restaurant is still a great place to stop for a wood-fired pizza (US$5 to US$14).

Lucky Bug B&B
B&B $$$

(☎ 2694-4515; www.luckybugcr.net; d incl breakfast US$99-129; P ✳ ☎ ☲) Set on a rainforest lagoon, the five blissfully isolated bungalows at the Lucky Bug feature works and decorative details by local artisans. Here are blond-wood floors, wrought-iron butterflies, hand-painted geckos, mosaic washbasins and end tables. Each room is unique and captivating. There's a rainforest trail in the grounds and kayaks for use on the lagoon.

Equus Bar-Restaurant
Restaurant $$

(☎ 8389-2669; mains US$6-14; ⏰ 11am-midnight) Follow your nose to this authentic stone-built tavern, 14.5km west of Nuevo Arenal, where the meat is cooked in an open fire pit, producing decadent, delicious aromas. Take a seat at a wooden-slab picnic table and dig in! A local

favorite, this place has been run by the same family for more than a quarter of a century.

Café y Macadamia
Cafe $$

(☎ 2692-2000; cafeymacadamia@yahoo.com; pastries & coffee US$2-4, mains US$6-13; ⏰ 8am-8pm; P ☎) Pull over for a cup of coffee and maybe an elegant salad or hearty sandwich, but save room for an irresistible dessert. Savor it all along with the spectacular views of Laguna de Arenal. This is your perfect pitstop or sunset vantage point. It's 20.5km west of Nuevo Arenal.

TILARÁN

Near the southwestern end of Laguna de Arenal, the small town of Tilarán has a laid-back, middle-class charm – thanks to its long-running status as a regional ranching center. This tradition is honored on the last weekend in April with a rodeo that's popular with Tico visitors, and on June 13 with a *fiesta de toros* that's dedicated to patron San Antonio.

🛏 Sleeping & Eating

Hotel Guadalupe
Hotel $$

(☎ 2695-5943; www.hotelguadalupe.co.cr; s/d/tr US$36/56/74; P ✳ ☎ ☲) This modern hotel attracts traveling business types, who make themselves at home in simple rooms, dressed up with jewel tones and tiled floors. Service is friendly and efficient. There is a decent restaurant onsite, as well as swimming pool, kiddie pool and hot tub.

La Troja
Restaurant $$

(☎ 2695-4935; mains US$8-12; ⏰ 10am-9pm) This is a popular stop for Ticos and tourists alike, and rightly so. The attractive wooden building has massive windows, offering a lovely vista over Laguna de Arenal. Reliably good Costa Rican fare includes grilled steaks, rotisserie chicken and delicious whole tilapia.

ⓘ Getting There & Away

Tilarán is usually reached by a 24km paved road from the Interamericana at Cañas. The route on to Santa Elena and Monteverde is paved for the first stretch, but then it becomes steep, rocky and rough. A 4WD is recommended, though ordinary cars can get through with care in the dry season

Bus

Buses arrive and depart from the terminal, half a block west of Parque Central.

La Fortuna US$5, 3½ hours, departs 7am and 12:30pm.

Nuevo Arenal US$1, 1¼ hours, departs 12 times daily from 4:30am to 3:30pm.

Puntarenas US$4, two hours, departs 6am and 1pm.

San José US$7, four hours, departs 5am, 7am, 9:30am, 2pm and 5pm.

Santa Elena/Monteverde US$3, 2½ hours, departs 4am and 12:30pm.

MONTEVERDE & SANTA ELENA

Strung between two lovingly preserved cloud forests, this slim corridor of civilization consists of the Tico village of Santa Elena and the Quaker settlement of Monteverde, each with an eponymous cloud-forest reserve. A 1983 feature article in *National Geographic* described this unique landscape and subsequently billed the area as the place to view one of Central America's most famous birds – the resplendent quetzal. Suddenly, hordes of tourists armed with tripods and telephoto lenses started braving Monteverde's notoriously awful access roads, which came as a huge shock to the then-established Quaker community. In an effort to stem the tourist flow, local communities lobbied to stop developers from paving the roads.

It worked – for a while. But the towns grew anyway, attracting tourists as well as new European and North American residents. Eventually, the lobby to spur development bested the lobby to limit development.

The cloud forests around Monteverde and Santa Elena are among Costa Rica's best destinations for everyone from budget backpackers to well-heeled retirees. On a good day, Monteverde is a place where you can be inspired about the possibility of a world in which organic farming and alternative energy sources are the norm. On a bad day, Monteverde can feel like Disneyland in Birkenstocks. Take heart in the fact that the local community continues to fight the good fight to maintain the fragile balance of nature and commerce.

Kayaking, Santa Elena
DREAMPICTURES/GETTY IMAGES ©

Sights

Bat Jungle
Zoo

(📞 2645-7701; www.batjungle.com; adult/child US$12/10; ⏰9am-7:30pm) Learn about echolocation, bat-wing aerodynamics and other amazing flying-mammal facts. The so-called Bat Jungle is small but informative, with good bilingual educational displays and a free-flying bat habitat housing almost 100 bats.

Serpentarium
Zoo

(Herpentario; 📞 2645-6002; adult/student/child US$13/11/8; ⏰9am-8pm) A guide will show you around and introduce you to some 40 species of slithery snakes, plus a fair number of frogs, lizards, turtles and other cold-blooded critters.

Jardín de Orquídeas
Gardens

(Orchid Garden; 📞 2645-5308; www.monteverdeorchidgarden.net; adult/child US$10/free; ⏰8am-5pm) This sweet-smelling garden has shady trails winding past more than 400 types of orchid organized into taxonomic groups. On your guided tour, you'll see such rarities as *Platystele jungermannioides,* the world's smallest orchid. If you have orchids at home, here's your chance to get tips from the experts on how to keep them beautiful and blooming.

Butterfly Garden
Zoo

(Jardín de Mariposas; 📞 2645-5512; www.monteverdebutterflygarden.com; adult/student/child US$15/10/5; ⏰8:30am-4pm) Everything you ever wanted to know about butterflies, with four gardens representing different habitats and home to more than 40 species. Up-close observation cases allow you to witness the butterflies as they emerge from the chrysalis (if your timing is right). Other exhibits feature the industrious leafcutter ant. Explore on your own or take advantage of the knowledgeable naturalist guides.

Local Knowledge

Monteverde & Santa Elena

RECOMMENDATIONS FROM J ANDRÉS VARGAS, DIRECTOR OF EUFORIA EXPEDITIONS

1 RESERVA BIOLÓGICA BOSQUE NUBOSO MONTEVERDE

One of the country's most famous biological reserves (p180), Monteverde is a bird-watching paradise. Although the list of recorded species exceeds 400, the one most visitors want to see is the quetzal. The Maya bird of paradise is most often spotted during the March and April nesting season, but you could get lucky any time. For mammal-watchers, commonly sighted species include coatis, howler monkeys, capuchins, sloths, agoutis and squirrels.

2 MONTEVERDE BACKCOUNTRY TREKKING

Longer, less-developed trails stretch out east across the reserve and down the Peñas Blancas river valley to lowlands north of the Cordillera de Tilarán and into the Bosque Eterno de los Niños (Children's Eternal Forest; p172). If you are strong and have time to spare, these hikes are highly recommended as you'll maximize your chances of spotting wildlife. If you're serious about visiting the backcountry, hire a reliable guide – you'll be entering rugged terrain.

3 RESERVA SANTA ELENA

This community-managed reserve (p182) is slightly higher in elevation than Monteverde. Since some of the forest is secondary growth, there are sunnier places for spotting birds and other animals throughout. This place is moist, and almost all the water comes as fine mist. More than 25% of all the biomass in the forest consists of epiphytes (mosses and lichens), for which this is a humid haven. Ten per cent of species here aren't found in Monteverde, which is largely on the other side of the continental divide.

Monteverde & Santa Elena

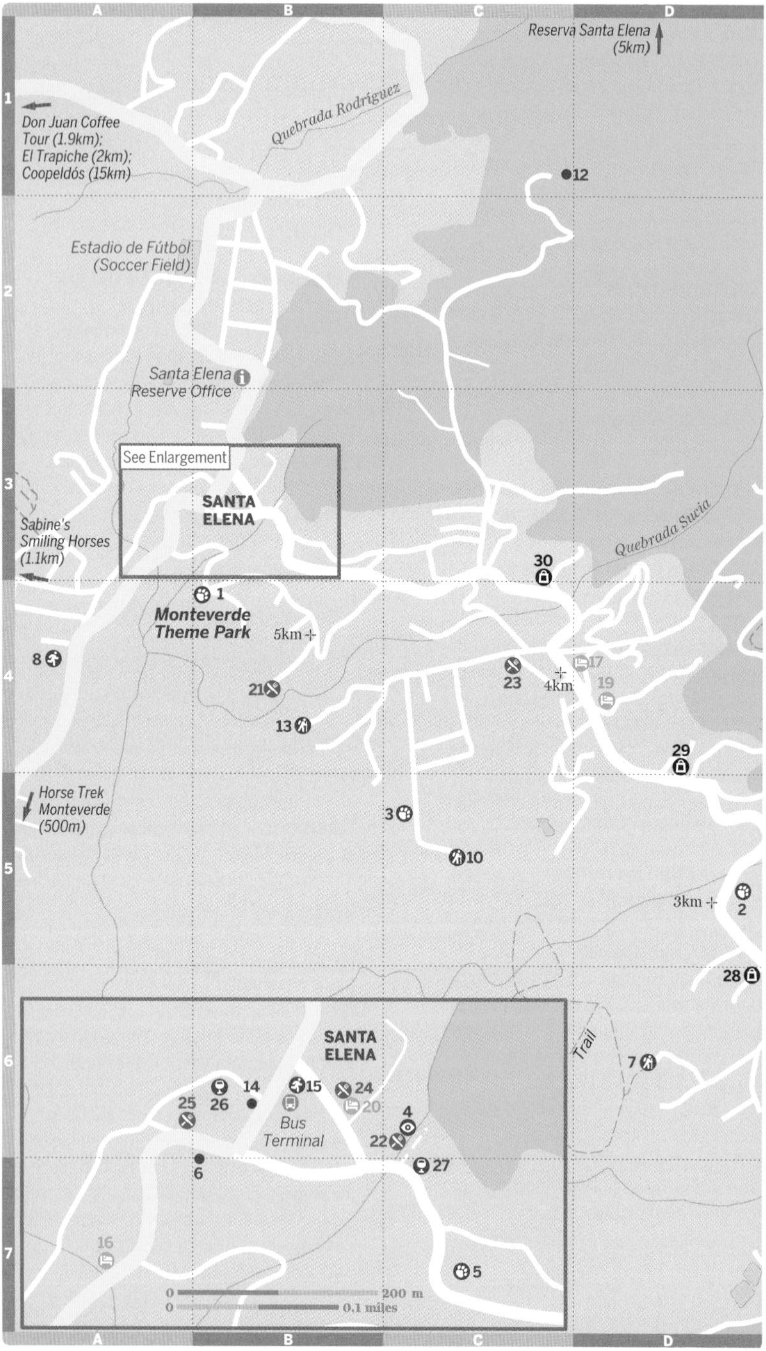

Reserva Santa Elena
(5km)

Quebrada Rodríguez

Don Juan Coffee
Tour (1.9km);
El Trapiche (2km);
Coopeldós (15km)

● 12

Estadio de Fútbol
(Soccer Field)

Santa Elena
Reserve Office

See Enlargement

SANTA
ELENA

Quebrada Sucia

Sabine's
Smiling Horses
(1.1km)

30

⚙ 1
Monteverde
Theme Park   5km ✛

8 ⚙

23 ✖   ✛ 17   19
4km

21 ✖

13 🚶

29

Horse Trek
Monteverde
(500m)

3 ⚙

🚶 10

3km ✛   2

28

7 🚶

Trail

SANTA
ELENA

26   14   15   24
25 ✖   20   4
Bus   22 ✖
Terminal   27
6

16

5

| 0 | | 200 m |
| 0 | | 0.1 miles |

170

Activities

COFFEE PLANTATIONS

Coffee-lovers will be excited to find some of the finest coffee in the world right here. Late April is the best time to see the fields in bloom, while the coffee harvest (done entirely by hand) takes place from December to February. Any time is a good time to see how your favorite beverage makes the transition from ruby-red berry to smooth black brew. Advance reservations are required for all tours, which you can book directly by phone or through many hotels. Most charge about US$30 for adults, including transportation to the *fincas* (farms).

Café Monteverde Coffee Tour

(2645-5901; www.cafemonteverde.com; per person US$15; 7:30am-6pm) Run by the small-scale Cooperative Santa Elena, this highly recommended tour takes visitors to organic *fincas* that are also implementing sustainable growing techniques like composting and biodiesel. Help to pick perfect coffee beans, then head to the *beneficio* (coffee mill) to watch the beans get washed and dried, roasted and packed. The tour includes a taste of the final product.

Coopeldós RL Coffee Tour

(2693-8441; www.coopeldos.com) Coopeldós is a cooperative of 450 small and medium-sized organic coffee growers from the area. You might drink Coopeldós blends back home, as this Fairtrade-certified organization sells to Starbucks, among other clients.

Don Juan Coffee Tour Coffee Tour

(2645-7100; www.donjuancoffeetour.com; adult/child US$30/12; 7am-4:30pm) Don Juan is a more commercial operation offering a three-in-one tour, where you can learn about all of your favorite vices – coffee, chocolate and sugar (OK, maybe not *all* of your favorites, but three of the good ones).

Monteverde & Santa Elena

El Trapiche   Coffee Tour

(☎ 2645-7650; www.eltrapichetour.com; adult/child US$32/12; ⊙10am & 3pm Mon-Sat, 3pm Sun) Visit this family *finca,* where they grow not only coffee but also sugarcane, bananas and plantains. Finish the tour with a cup of coffee or a sample of the area's other famous beverage, *saca de guaro* (sugarcane liquor).

HIKING

The best hiking is at the two cloud-forest reserves bookending the main road, Reserva Biológica Bosque Nuboso Monteverde and Reserva Santa Elena.

Bosque Eterno de los Niños   Hiking

(Children's Eternal Forest, BEN; ☎ 2645-5003; www.acmcr.org; adult/student US$12/6, guided night hike US$20/17, Estación Biológica San Gerardo all-inclusive US$52; ⊙7:30am-5:30pm, night hike 5:30pm) What became of the efforts of a group of school children to save the rainforest? Only this enormous 220-sq-km reserve – the largest private reserve in the country. It is mostly inaccessible to tourists, with the exception of the well-marked 3.5km **Sendero Bajo del Tigre**, which is actually a series of shorter trails. At the entrance there's an educa-tion center for children and a fabulous vista over the reserve.

Santuario Ecológico   Hiking

(Ecological Sanctuary; ☎ 2645-5869; www.santuarioecologico.com; adult/student/child US$10/8/6, guided night tour US$15/12/10; ⊙7am-5:30pm, guided night tours 5:30-7:30pm) Offering hikes of varying lengths, Santuario Ecológico has four loop trails through private property comprising premontane and secondary forest, coffee and banana plantations, and past a couple of waterfalls and lookout points. Coati, agouti and sloth are commonly sighted, as are monkeys, porcupines and other animals. Birders have a good chance of spotting hummingbirds, hawks and toucans as well as high-profile species like the resplendent quetzal and wattled bellbird.

Hidden Valley   Hiking

(Valle Escondido; ☎ 2645-6601; www.monteverdenighttour.com; day pass US$8, guided hike incl lunch US$40, night tour adult/child US$25/15; ⊙7am-4pm, night walk 5:30pm) This trail begins behind Pensión Monteverde Inn and slowly winds its way through a deep canyon into an 11-hectare reserve. During the day, Valle Escondido is quiet and relatively undertouristed, so it's a good

GLENN BARTLEY/GETTY IMAGES ©

 Don't Miss
Monteverde Theme Park

Formerly known as the Ranario, or Frog Pond, this place has recently added a butterfly garden and canopy tour – hence, it's now a theme park. The frogs are still the highlight: about 25 species reside in transparent enclosures lining the winding indoor jungle paths. Sharp-eyed guides lead informative tours in English or Spanish, pointing out frogs, eggs and tadpoles with flashlights. Your ticket entitles you to two visits, so come back in the evening to see the nocturnal species. Combined tickets are available.

NEED TO KNOW
Monteverde Frog Pond; Map p170; ☎2645-6320; per attraction US$13-17, canopy US$35; ⏰9am-8pm

---

trail for birding and wildlife-watching. The two-hour guided night tour is popular, so reserve in advance.

CANOPY TOURS & HANGING BRIDGES

Santa Elena is the site of Costa Rica's first zip lines, today eclipsed in adrenaline by the nearly 100 imitators who have followed, some of which are right here in town. You won't be spotting any quetzals or coatis as you whoosh your way over the canopy, but if you came to Costa Rica to fly, this is the absolute best place to do it. If you want to explore the treetops without the adrenaline rush, several of these outifts also have systems of hanging bridges. Transportation from your lodging is included in the price.

Aventura Canopy Tour
(☎2645-6388; www.monteverdeadventure.com; canopy adult/child US$45/35, bridges US$35/25; ⏰7am-4pm) Aventura has 19 platforms that are spiced up with a Tarzan swing, a

173

Below: Hanging bridge, Monteverde (p173); **Right:** Monteverde Cloud Forest Train

(BELOW) FOCUS_ON_NATURE/GETTY IMAGES ©; (RIGHT) HOLGER LEUE/GETTY IMAGES ©

15m rappel and a Superman zip line that makes you feel as if you really are flying. Aventura's cables and bridges are laced through secondary forest only. It's about 3km north of Santa Elena on the road to the reserve, but there's a booking office in town.

Extremo Canopy Canopy Tour
(☏2645-6058; www.monteverdeextremo. com; canopy US$40, super cable US$30, bungee US$60, tarzan swing US$35; ☉8am-4pm) This outfit doesn't bother with extraneous attractions if all you really want to do is fly down the zip lines. Located in secondary forest, there's a canopy ride, allowing you to fly Superman-style through the air; the highest and most adrenaline-addled Tarzan swing in the area; and a bungee jump. One way or another, you will scream.

Original Canopy Tour Canopy Tour
(☏2291-4465; www.canopytour.com; adult/student/child US$45/35/25; ☉7:30am-4pm) On the grounds of Cloud Forest Lodge, this is the fabled zip-line route that started this adventure–theme park trend. These lines aren't as elaborate as the others, but with 14 platforms, a rappel through the center of an old fig tree and 5km of private trails worth a wander afterward, you can enjoy a piece of history that's far more entertaining than most museums. It's 1km north of town, on the way to Reserva Santa Elena.

Selvatura Canopy Tour
(☏2645-5929; www.selvatura.com; canopy US$45, walkways US$30, each exhibit US$15; ☉7:30am-4pm) One of the bigger games in town, Selvatura has 3km of cables, 18 platforms and one Tarzan swing over a stretch of incredibly beautiful primary cloud forest. In addition to the cables it

has 3km of 'Treetops Walkways', as well as a hummingbird garden, a butterfly garden and an amphibian and reptile exhibition. Selvatura is 6km north of Santa Elena, near the reserve, but there's a booking office in town.

SkyTrek
Canopy Tour

(☎2645-5238; www.skyadventures.travel; Sky-Walk adult/child US$35/22, SkyTrek US$71/45; ☉7:30am-5pm) This seriously fast canopy tour consists of 11 platforms attached to steel towers that are spread out along a road and zoom over swatches of primary forest. We're talking serious speeds of up to 64km/h, which is probably why SkyTrek was the first canopy tour with a real brake system. The SkyWalk is a 2km guided tour over five suspended bridges; a night tour is also available.

TRAMS & TRAINS

SkyTram
Scenic Ride

(☎2645-5238; www.skyadventures.travel; adult/child US$44/28) Owned by SkyTrek, SkyTram is a wheelchair-accessible cable car that floats gently over the cloud forest. On a clear day you can see from the volcanoes in the east to the Pacific in the west. Packages are available if you're also interested in the SkyTrek (canopy tour) and SkyWalk (hanging bridges).

Monteverde Cloud Forest Train
Scenic Ride

(☎2645-5700; adult/child US$50/free; ♿) This charming narrow-gauge train system travels 4 miles through the forest, penetrating one tunnel and crossing four bridges. The scenic railroad offers amazing views of Monteverde and Arenal lake and volcano. This is a great option for families with young children who are loco for locos. It's located 5km north of downtown Santa Elena; take the road toward Reserva Santa Elena and follow the signs.

Quakers in Monteverde

In 1949 four members of the Society of Friends, or Quakers, were jailed in Alabama for their refusal to be drafted into the Korean War. Since Quakers are obligated by their religion to be pacifists, the four men were eventually released from prison. However, in response to the incarceration, 44 Quakers from 11 Alabama families left the USA and headed for greener pastures, literally. The Quakers chose Monteverde (Green Mountain) for two reasons – a few years prior, the Costa Rican government had abolished its military, and the cool, mountain climate was ideal for grazing cattle. Ensconced in their isolated refuge they adopted a simple, trouble-free life of dairy farming and cheese production. In an effort to protect the watershed above its 15-sq-km plot in Monteverde, the Quaker community agreed to preserve the mountaintop cloud forests.

The Quaker community is still active in Monteverde – both in preservation of the land and in production of the cheese. Visit them at the **Monteverde Cheese Factory** (La Lechería; ☎2645-7090; www.monteverdecheesefactory.com; tours adult/child US$12/10; ☉tours 9am & 2pm Mon-Sat, store 7:30am-5pm Mon-Sat, to 4pm Sun).

HORSEBACK RIDING

Sabine's Smiling Horses
Horse Riding

(☎8385-2424, 2645-6894; www.smilinghorses. com; per person US$45-65) Conversant in four languages (in addition to equine), Sabine will make sure you are comfortable on your horse, whether you're a novice rider or an experienced cowboy. Her longstanding operation in Monteverde offers a variety of treks including a popular waterfall tour (three hours). And yes, the horses really really do smile.

Horse Trek Monteverde
Horse Riding

(☎8359-3485; www.horsetrekmonteverde. com; per person US$45-85) Owner and guide Marvin Anchia is a Santa Elena native, a professional horse trainer and an amateur naturalist who offers an excellent, intimate horse-riding experience. Tours range from scenic half-day rides in the cloud forest to all-day cowboy experiences to multiday treks. The horses are well cared for, well trained and a joy to ride.

Caballeriza El Rodeo
Horse Riding

(☎2645-5764, 2645-6306; elrodeo02@gmail. com; per person US$40-60) Based at a local *finca*, this outfit offers tours on private trails through field and forest. The specialty is a sunset tour to a spot overlooking the Golfo de Nicoya.

Sleeping

Casa Tranquilo
B&B $

(☎2645-6782; www.casatranquilohostel. com; dm/r per person incl breakfast US$10/15; P@☎) At Casa Tranquilo, the wonderful Tico hospitality starts first thing in the morning with homemade banana bread. In addition to the excellent breakfast, staff lead free guided hikes, sharing their in-depth local expertise. The rooms are simple and spotless, some featuring skylights and gulf views. Colorful murals adorn the outside, so you'll know you are in the right place.

Pensión Santa Elena
Hostel $

(☎2645-5051; www.pensionsantaelena. com; incl breakfast dm US$12, s/d/tr without bathroom from US$16/24/36, standard s/d/tr US$19/29/36, plus s/d US$25/37; P@☎) This full-service hostel right in central Santa Elena is a perennial favorite, offering budget travelers top-notch service and *pura vida* hospitality. Each room is different, with something to suit every budget. The 'plus' rooms in the annex feature perks like superior beds, stone showers and iPod docks.

Los Pinos Cabañas y Jardines Lodge $$
(☎2645-5252; www.lospinos.net; cabaña d/ste/q US$70/85/140, superior d US$115; P 📶) Fourteen freestanding *cabañas* are scattered around the peaceful, forested gardens of this 9-hectare property, which once formed part of the family *finca*. With plenty of space between them, each *cabaña* affords lots of privacy, plus a fully equipped kitchen and small terrace. It's a superb setting for those seeking a little solitude, with some great options for families.

Hotel Belmar Hotel $$$
(☎2645-5201; www.hotelbelmar.net; peninsula r US$150-160, deluxe chalets US$178-308; P @ 📶 🏊) Every room at the Belmar boasts a spectacular view of forest or gulf. (Indeed, you can see both from the 270 degrees of windows in some of the deluxe chalets.) The gorgeous light-filled rooms are decked out with hand-crafted furniture, high-thread-count linens and spectacular sunsets from the private balconies – and the higher you go, the more spectacular they are.

Eating

Taco Taco Mexican $
(mains US$5-8; ⏰noon-8pm; 📶) Quick and convenient, this *taquería* (taco stall) offers tasty Tex-Mex tacos, burritos and quesadillas filled with shredded chicken, slow-roasted short rib, pork *al pastor* (cooked on a spit), roasted veggies and battered mahi mahi. The only difficulty is deciding (but you really can't go wrong).

Orchid Cafe Bakery $
(☎2645-6850; mains US$2-12; ⏰7am-7pm; 📶) If you have a hankering for something sweet, go straight to this lovely little cafe. Take a seat on the front porch and take a bite of heaven. Aside from pastries and pies, crepes and cookies, there's a full menu of savories, such as ciabatta sandwiches, interesting and unusual salads and delicious quiche. Breakfast also gets an A+.

Sofia Fusion $$
(☎2645-7017; mains US$12-16; ⏰11:30am-9:30pm; 📶) Sofia has established itself as one of the best places in town with its Nuevo Latino cuisine – a modern fusion of traditional Latin American cooking styles. Think sweet-and-sour fig roasted pork loin, plantain-crusted sea bass, and shrimp with green-mango curry. The ambience is enhanced by groovy music, picture windows, romantic candle lighting and potent cocktails.

Monteverde Cloud Forest
MIKE LANZETTA/GETTY IMAGES ©

Café Caburé
Cafe **$$**

(2645-5020; www.cabure.net; mains US$10-12; 9am-8pm Mon-Sat; P) The Argentine cafe above the Bat Jungle specializes in creative and delicious everything, from sandwiches on homemade bread and fresh salads, to more elaborate fare like tortillas stuffed with chicken *mole*, chipotle-rubbed steak, curried potatoes, and lemon shrimp. Save room for dessert because the chocolate treats are high art.

Trio
Fusion **$$$**

(2645-7254; mains US$7-17; 11:30am-9:30pm;) In a funny location behind the SuperCompro, Trio has a classy, contemporary open-air dining room perched in the trees. The menu is all about blending unexpected elements into a delightful surprise for the taste buds, such as seabass *ceviche* in coconut milk, barbecue ribs with guava sauce, and a highly touted burger with figs. The dessert menu does amazing things with tropical fruits.

El Jardín
International **$$$**

(2257-0766; www.monteverde.com; mains US$16-23; 7am-10pm;) Arguably, the 'finest' dining in the area. The menu is wide ranging, always highlighting the local flavors. But these are not your typical *tipica:* beef tenderloin is served on a sugarcane kebab, pan-fried trout is topped with orange sauce. The setting – with windows to the trees – is lovely and service is superb. Romantics can opt for a private table in the garden. Located on the grounds of the Monteverde Lodge.

Drinking & Nightlife

Bar Amigos
Bar

(2645-5071; www.baramigos.com; noon-3am) With picture windows overlooking the mountainside, this Santa Elena mainstay evokes the atmosphere of a ski lodge. But no, there are DJs, karaoke, billiards, and sports on the screens. This is the one consistent place in the area to let loose, so there's usually a good mix of Ticos and tourists. Also, the food is surprisingly good.

La Taberna
Bar

(2645-5883; variable) Known by many names in recent years, this drinking establishment will always be remembered

Hiking, Monteverde Cloud Forest

MICHAEL BOYNY/GETTY IMAGES ©

as La Taberna. No matter what you call it, you'll find a friendly outdoor bar, drink specials, pub fare and live music.

Shopping

Luna Azul   Jewelry
(☎2645-6638; lunaazulmonteverde@gmail.com; ⏰9am-6pm) This super-cute gallery and gift shop is packed to the gills with jewelry, clothing, soaps, sculpture and macramé, among other things. The jewelry in particular is stylish and stunning, crafted from silver, shell, crystals and turquoise.

Monteverde Art House   Handicrafts
(Casa de Arte; ☎2645-5275; www.monteverdearthouse.com; ⏰9am-6:30pm) You'll find several rooms stuffed with colorful Costa Rican artistry. The goods run the gamut, including jewelry, ceramic work, Boruca textiles and traditional handicrafts. There's a big variety, including some paintings and more contemporary work, but it's mostly at the crafts end of the artsy-craftsy spectrum. Great for souvenirs.

Casem   Handicrafts
(Cooperativa de Artesanía Santa Elena Monteverde; ☎2645-5190; www.casemcoop.blogspot.com; ⏰8am-5pm Mon-Sat year-round, plus 10am-4pm Sun Dec-Apr) Begun in 1982 as a women's cooperative representing eight female artists, today Casem has expanded to reportedly include almost 150 local artisans (eight of whom are men). Honestly, it's an underwhelming selection, featuring embroidered clothing and painted handbags, polished wooden tableware, and some painted bookmarks and greeting cards. There are more interesting paintings and woodwork in the Sky Gallery upstairs.

ℹ Getting There & Away

After resident protesters took to the streets in 2013, the transportation ministry announced that it would invest the necessary US$16 million to pave the 18km road from Guacimal to Santa Elena, which is the main access route to Monteverde. There was no sign of asphalt at the time of research, but this plan is moving forward and may be completed by the time you read this. Enjoy the smooth ride. Travel times will obviously be greatly reduced, but that's not the only change that road will bring.

Bus

All buses stop at the bus terminal (☎2645-5159; ⏰5:45-11am & 1:30-5pm Mon-Fri, to 3pm Sat & Sun) in downtown Santa Elena, where most of the budget digs are, and do not continue into Monteverde. You'll have to walk or take a taxi if that's where you plan to stay. On the trip in, keep an eye on your luggage, particularly on the San José–Puntarenas leg, as well as on the Monteverde–Tilarán run. Keep all bags at your feet and not in the overhead bin. Stories of theft and loss are legion.

Reserva Monteverde US$1.20; 30 minutes; departs from in front of Banco Nacional at 6:15am, 7:30am, 9:30am, 1:30pm and 3pm; returns at 6:40am, 8:30am, 11am, 2pm and 4pm.

Reserva Santa Elena US$2; 30 minutes; departs from in front of Banco Nacional at 6:30am, 8:30am, 10:30am and 12:30pm; returns at 11am, 1pm and 4pm.

San José (Tilarán Transportes) US$5; five hours; departs the Santa Elena bus station at 6:30am and 2:30pm.

Tilarán, with connection to La Fortuna US$3; 2½ hours to Tilarán, seven hours in total; departs from the bus station at 4am and 12:30pm. This is a long ride, as you will need to hang around for two hours in Tilarán. If you have a few extra dollars, the jeep-boat-jeep option to La Fortuna is recommended.

Horseback

A number of outfitters offer transportation on horseback (per person US$65 to US$185, five to six hours) to La Fortuna, usually in combination with a boat ride. There are three main trails used: the Lake Trail (safe year-round), the Chiquito Trail (safe most of the year) and the gorgeous but infamous Castillo Trail (passable only in dry season by experienced riders).

Ask lots of questions and confirm the route before setting out.

Jeep-Boat-Jeep

The fastest route between Monteverde–Santa Elena and La Fortuna is a jeep-boat-jeep combo (US$22 to US$32, three hours), which can be arranged through almost any hotel or tour operator in either town. A 4WD minivan takes you to Río Chiquito, meeting a boat that crosses

Laguna de Arenal, where a van on the other side continues to La Fortuna. This is increasingly becoming the primary transportation between La Fortuna and Monteverde as it's incredibly scenic, reasonably priced and saves half a day of rough travel. In case you're wondering: no, absolutely no jeeps whatsoever are involved in the process.

BOSQUE NUBOSO MONTEVERDE

Here is a virginal **forest (Monteverde Cloud Forest Wildlife Biological Reserve;** ☎ 2645-5122; www.reservamonteverde.com; adult/concession US$18/9; ⏰ 7am-4pm) dripping with mist, dangling with mossy vines, sprouting with ferns and bromeliads, gushing with creeks, blooming with life and nurturing rivulets of evolution. It is so moving that when Quaker settlers first arrived in the area, they agreed to preserve about a third of their property in order to protect this watershed. By 1972, however, encroaching squatters threatened its sustainability. The community joined forces with environmental organizations to purchase 328 hectares adjacent to the already preserved area. It's one of Costa Rica's best natural attractions.

Visitors should note that the walking trails can be muddy, even during the dry season. You're essentially walking around in a cloud, so bring rain gear, suitable boots and a smile. Many of the trails have been stabilized with concrete blocks or wooden boards, but unpaved trails deeper in the reserve turn sloppy during the rainy season.

Because of the fragile environment, the reserve allows a maximum of 160 people at any time. During the dry season this limit is usually reached by 10am, so arrive early (before the gates open). Alternatively, head across town to the Santa Elena reserve, which gets about 10% of the number of visitors as Monteverde.

Activities

HIKING

There are 13km of marked and maintained trails – a free map is provided with your entrance fee. The most popular of the nine trails, suitable for day hikes, make a rough triangle (El Triángulo) to the east of the reserve entrance. The triangle's sides are made up of the popular **Sendero Bosque Nuboso** (1.9km), an interpretive walk through the cloud forest that begins at the ranger station, paralleled by the more open, 2km **El Camino**, a favorite of bird-watchers. The **Sendero Pantanoso** (1.6km) forms the far side of El Triángulo, traversing swamps, pine forests and the continental divide. Returning to the entrance, **Sendero Río** (2km) follows the Quebrada Cuecha past a few photogenic waterfalls.

Bisecting the triangle, the gorgeous **Chomogo Trail** (1.8km) lifts hikers to 1680m, the highest point in the triangle. Other little trails crisscross the region, including the worthwhile **Sendero Brillante** (300m), with bird's-eye views of a miniature forest. However, keep in mind that despite valiant efforts to contain crowd sizes, these shorter trails are among the most trafficked in the country.

The trail to the **Mirador La Ventana** (elevation 1550m) is moderately steep and leads further afield to a wooden deck overlooking the continental divide. To the west, on clear days you can see the Golfo de Nicoya and the Pacific. To the east you can see the Peñas Blancas valley and the San Carlos plain. Even on wet, cloudy days it's magical, especially when the winds are howling and fine swirling mist washes over you in waves. There's a 100m suspension bridge about 1km from the ranger station on **Sendero Wilford Guindon,** which rocks and sways with each step.

181

WILDLIFE-WATCHING

Monteverde is a bird-watching paradise, with the list of recorded species topping out at more than 400. The resplendent quetzal is most often spotted during the March and April nesting season, though you may get lucky any time of year. Keep your ears open for the three-wattled bellbird, a kind of cotinga that is famous for its distinctive call. If you're keen on birds, a specialized bird tour is highly recommended.

For those interested in spotting mammals, the cloud forest's limited visibility and abundance of higher primates (namely human beings) can make wildlife-watching quite difficult, though commonly sighted species (especially in the backcountry) include coatis, howler monkeys, capuchins, sloths, agoutis and squirrels (as in 'real' squirrel, not the squirrel monkey). Most animals avoid the main trails, so get off the beaten track.

❶ Information

The **visitors center** (☎2645-5122; www.cct.or.cr; park entry adult/student & child/child under 6yr US$17/9/free; ☺7am-4pm) is adjacent to the reserve gift shop, where you can get information and buy trail guides, bird and mammal lists and maps, as well as souvenirs and postcards. Leave your passport to rent a pair of binoculars (US$10).

The annual rainfall here is about 3000mm, though parts of the reserve reportedly get twice as much. It's usually cool, with high temperatures around 18°C (65°F), so wear appropriate clothing. It's important to remember that the cloud forest is often cloudy (!).

❶ Getting There & Away

Public buses (US$1.20, 30 minutes) depart the Banco Nacional in Santa Elena at 6:15am, 7:30am, 9:30am, 1:30pm and 3pm. Buses return from the reserve at 6:40am, 8:30am, 11am, 2pm and 4pm.

The 6km walk from Santa Elena is uphill but offers lovely views – look for paths that run parallel to the road. The birdwatching is magnificent, especially in the last 2km.

RESERVA SANTA ELENA

Though Monteverde gets all the attention, the misty Reserva Santa Elena has plenty to recommend. You can practically hear the epiphyte-draped canopy breathing in humid exhales as water drops onto the

Santa Elena cloud forest

leaf litter and mud underfoot. The odd call of the three-wattled bellbird and the low crescendo of a howler monkey punctuate the higher-pitched bird chatter. While Monteverde Crowd... er...Cloud Forest entertains almost 200,000 visitors annually, Santa Elena sees fewer than 20,000 tourists each year, which means its dewy trails through mysteriously veiled forest are usually far quieter.

This cloud forest is slightly higher in elevation than Monteverde's, and as some of the forest is secondary growth, there are sunnier places for spotting birds and other animals throughout. There's a stable population of monkey and sloth, many of which can be seen on the road to the reserve. Unless you're a trained ecologist, the old-growth forest in Santa Elena will seem fairly similar in appearance to Monteverde.

At 310 hectares, the community-run Santa Elena is much smaller than the other forest. More than 12km of trails are open for hiking, including four circular trails of varying difficulty and length. Guided hikes depart from the visitors center four times a day (reservations recommended).

The reserve is about 6km northeast of the village of Santa Elena, but the **reserve office** (☎2645-5693; ⊙8am-4pm Wed-Fri) is located at the high school. To reach the reserve itself, catch the bus (US$2, 30 minutes, four daily) from the Banco Nacional in town.

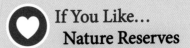

If You Like...
Nature Reserves

If you like the Reserva Santa Elena, we think you'll like these other protected areas in northern Costa Rica.

1 PARQUE NACIONAL GUANACASTE
(☎2666-5051; www.acguanacaste.ac.cr; adult/child US$10/1) One of the least-visited parks in Costa Rica; the land transitions from dry tropical forest to humid cloud forest.

2 REFUGIO NACIONAL DE VIDA SILVESTRE CAÑO NEGRO
(☎471-1309; US$6; ⊙8am-6pm; boat, car) The lagoons of Caño Negro attract a wide variety of birds year-round.

3 ECOCENTRO DANAUS
(☎2479-7019; www.ecocentrodanaus.com; admission with/without guide US$16/11, guided night tours US$35; ⊙8am-4pm Mon-Sat, 9am-3:30pm Sun, night tour 5:30pm) This small reserve has a well-developed trail system that's good for bird-watching, and spotting sloths, coatis and howler monkeys.

4 REFUGIO NACIONAL DE VIDA SILVESTRE BAHÍA JUNQUILLAL
(☎2666-5051; www.acguanacaste.ac.cr; adult/child 6-12yr/child 5yr & under US$13/5/free, camping per person US$2; ⊙8am-5pm) A small, peaceful protected site, this refuge has a beach backed by mangrove swamp and tropical dry forest.

LIBERIA

POP 63,000

The sunny rural capital of Guanacaste has long served as a transportation hub connecting Costa Rica with Nicaragua, as well as being the standard-bearer of Costa Rica's *sabanero* (cowboy) culture. Even today, a large part of the greater Liberia area is involved in ranching operations, but tourism is fast becoming a significant contributor to the economy. With an expanding international airport, Liberia is a safer and more chilled-out alternative Costa Rican gateway to San José, which means more travelers are spending a night or two in this small but sweet college town, knitted together by corrugated-tin fencing, mango trees and magnolias. And, though most of the historic buildings in the town center are a little rough around the edges, the 'white city' is a pleasant one. The streets in downtown Liberia are surprisingly well signed, a rarity in Costa Rica. Still, it's largely a launch pad for exploring Rincón de la Vieja National Park and the beaches of the Península de Nicoya.

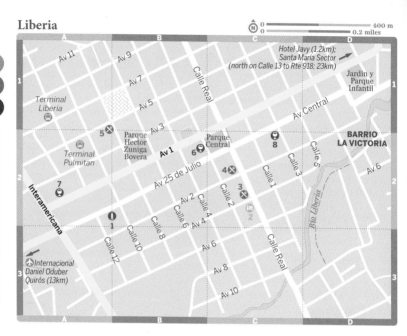

Liberia

◎ Sights

◎ Sights

Near the entrance of town, a **statue (Av 25 de Julio)** of a steely-eyed *sabanero*, complete with an evocative poem by Rodolfo Salazar Solórzano, stands watch over Av 25 de Julio, the main street into town. The blocks around the intersection of Av Central and Calle Real contain several of Liberia's oldest houses, many dating back about 150 years.

Africa Mía　　　　　Wildlife Reserve
(☎ 2666-1111; www.africamiacr.com; adult/child US$18/12, van tour US$30/24, safari tour US$65/55; ⏱ tours 9:30am, 11am, 1pm & 2pm) About 10km south of Liberia is a private wildlife reserve with free-roaming elephants, zebras, giraffes, ostriches and other animals. Splurge for the deluxe African Safari Wildlife Tour in an open-top Hummer, which allows you to get up close and personal with the giraffes.

🛌 Sleeping

Casa del Papel　　　　　B&B $$
(☎ 2666-0626; posadadelacallereal@gmail.com; cnr Calle Real & Av 4; r incl breakfast US$50-70; P ❄ 🛜 🏊) This historic house has been artfully converted into an exquisite guesthouse, easily recognizable by its newsprint facade. The rooms are simply and tastefully decorated with wooden floors, soaring ceilings and antique furniture. The common lounge is hung with original art and vintage furnishings, while gorgeous gardens, swimming pool with Jacuzzi and hammocks are at your disposal.

Hotel Javy
Hotel $$

(2666-9253; www.hoteljavy.com; cnr Av 19 & Calle 21; d incl breakfast US$50; P ❄ 🛜) Clara and Isabella are your hostesses with the *mostestes*. These charming ladies go out of their way to make sure their guests are happy, not least preparing an enormous, delicious breakfast to send you off feeling satisfied. The rooms are not going to win any style awards, but they are comfortable, with firm beds, incongruously formal furnishings and spotless new bathrooms.

✖ Eating

Donde Pipe
Cafe $

(2665-4343; www.dondepipe.com; cnr Calle 8 & Av 5; mains US$6-8; 7am-6pm Mon-Sat; 🛜 ⚡ 🚻) Perhaps the only proper cafe in Liberia, where you can sit for long hours inside or out, drinking strong coffee, munching homemade brownies and taking advantage of the free wi-fi. In addition to burgers, sandwiches and breakfast items, the menu features local specialties like *chifrijos* (rice, beans and fried pork topped with salsa and corn chips) and tamales, and of course refreshing fruit juices. This place is a local favorite.

Café Liberia
Organic $$

(2665-1660; Calle Real btwn Avs 2 & 4; mains US$8-15; 7am-10pm Mon-Sat; ❄ 🛜 ⚡) This beautifully restored colonial building has heavy wooden furniture and frescoed ceilings, creating a romantic ambience for rich coffee and gourmet fare. Simple food is taken to new levels: *ceviche* (seafood marinated in lemon or lime juice, garlic and seasonings) is served with irresistible, warm, fresh-baked tortilla chips. It's also an atmospheric setting for live music and other occasional performances.

Copa de Oro
Restaurant $$

(2666-0532; cnr Calle Central & Av 2; mains US$5-16; 11am-10pm Wed-Mon; 🛜 🚻) This congenial family restaurant is popular with locals and gringos alike. There's an extensive food and drink menu. Try the rice and seafood house specialty, *arroz copa de oro*. The *casados* (set meals) are excellent and there's a nice *ceviche* menu, too. With high quality and large portions, this place is great value.

Church, Liberia

185

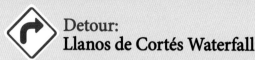

Detour:
Llanos de Cortés Waterfall

If you have time to visit only one waterfall in Costa Rica, make it **Llanos de Cortés** (by donation; ⊙8am-5pm). This beautiful hidden waterfall is located about 3km north of Bagaces; head north on the Interamericana, turn left on the dirt road after the Río Piedras bridge, then follow the bumpy road (4WD required) for about 1km, and turn right at the guarded gate, where you'll make a donation (US$2 will do the job) in exchange for your admission. Proceeds help fund the local primary school.

Continue down the dirt road about 300m to the parking area, then scramble down the short, steep trail to reach this spectacular 12m-high, 15m-wide waterfall, which you'll be able to hear from the parking lot. The falls drop into a tranquil pond with a white sandy beach that's perfect for swimming and sunbathing. Go 'backstage' and relax on the rocks behind the waterfall curtain, or shower beneath the lukewarm waters. On weekends this is a popular Tico picnic spot, but on weekdays you'll often have the waterfall to yourself.

There are no services here except for the occasional vendor selling fruit in the parking area. As always, don't leave valuables exposed in your car. If you don't have a car, any bus trawling this part of the Interamericana can drop you at the turnoff, but you'll have to hike from there to the falls.

🍷 Drinking & Nightlife

Palermo Lounge Cocktail Bar
(www.palermolounge.com; cnr Av Central & Calle 3) The city's most pleasant place for a drink is this tropical garden, lush with greenery and waterfalls. There are also sports and music videos on the big screen, but the volume is turned down so patrons can enjoy the tranquil atmosphere. The menu offers very tasty pub grub and Tico fare.

Ciro's Bar
(☏2665-3022; cirosbar.com; Calle 2 btwn Avs Central & 1; ⊙4pm-2am) The liveliest bar in Liberia belongs to this branch of the San José favorite. It's not much, just a handful of tables, a simple bar and doors that roll open onto the sidewalk. But the sound system rocks and the locals bring the party.

Morales House Bar
(☏2665-2490; cnr Av 1 & Calle 14; ⊙3pm-2am) A real Guanacaste *sabanero* hangout, this barnlike bar with cowboy motif has bulls' heads on the walls, blaring *ranchera* music and American sports on TV. Bonus: thick, juicy steaks for hungry buckaroos.

ⓘ Getting There & Away

Air
Since 1993 Aeropuerto Internacional Daniel Oduber Quirós (LIR), 12km west of Liberia, has served as the country's second international airport, providing easy access to all those beautiful beaches without the hassle of San José. In January 2012 it unveiled its sleek, mod new US$35-million terminal.

There are no car-rental desks at the airport; make reservations in advance, and your company will meet you at the airport with a car. There's a money-exchange, a cafe, gift shops and a fantastic, inexpensive duty-free shop (it's tucked away and hard to find – keep looking). Taxis to Liberia cost US$20.

Bus
Buses arrive and depart from Terminal Liberia (Av 7 btwn Calles 12 & 14) and Terminal Pulmitan (Av 5 btwn Calles 10 & 12). Routes, fares, journey times and departures are as follows:

Nicoya, via Filadelfia and Santa Cruz
US$2.25; 1½ hours; departs Terminal Liberia every 30 minutes from 3:30am to 9pm.

Playa Hermosa, **Playa Panamá** US$1.60; 1¼ hours; departs Terminal Liberia eight times from 4:50am to 5:30pm.

Playa Tamarindo US$2.75; 1½ to two hours; departs the Mercado Municipal hourly between 3:50am and 6pm. Some buses take a longer route via Playa Flamingo.

San José US$6; four hours; 12 departures from Pulmitan from 4am to 8pm.

Car

Liberia lies on the Interamericana, 234km north of San José and 77km south of the Nicaraguan border post of Peñas Blancas. Hwy 21, the main artery of the Península de Nicoya, begins in Liberia and heads southwest. A dirt road leads 25km from Barrio La Victoria to the Santa María entrance of Parque Nacional Rincón de la Vieja; the partially paved road to the Las Pailas entrance begins from the Interamericana, 5km north of Liberia (4WD is recommended).

There are more than a dozen rental-car agencies in Liberia (none of which have desks at the airport itself); rates can vary and you'll get steep discounts for rentals of a month or more. Most companies can arrange pickup in Liberia and drop-off in San José, though they'll charge you extra. Some companies will drop off your car in town upon request.

VOLCÁN MIRAVALLES AREA

Volcán Miravalles (2028m) is the highest volcano in the Cordillera de Guanacaste, and although the main crater is dormant, the geothermal activity beneath the ground has led to its rapid development as a hot-springs destination.

Miravalles isn't a national park or refuge, but the volcano itself is afforded a modicum of protection by being within the Zona Protectora Miravalles.

You can also take guided tours of the government-run Proyecto Geotérmico Miravalles, north of Fortuna de Bagaces, an ambitious project inaugurated in 1994 that uses geothermal energy to produce electricity. It produces about 18% of Costa Rica's electricity.

But the geothermal energy most people come here to soak up comes in liquid form. The hot springs are north of the tiny village of Fortuna de Bagaces (not to be confused with La Fortuna de Arenal or Bagaces). The sleeping options in the area aren't fabulous, so we suggest basing yourself in Parque Nacional Volcán Tenorio and visiting the springs on a day trip, as the two mountains are linked by a rather glorious back road.

🏃 Activities

Río Perdido   Hot Springs
(📞2673-3600; www.rioperdido.com; thermal canyon & river adult/child US$40/30) This fabulous new facility – set amid an otherworldly volcanic landscape – is a wonderful way to soak in the soothing waters of Miravalles. The 'thermal canyon experience' includes

Flower in grassland near Miravelles
KRYSSIA CAMPOS/GETTY IMAGES ©

a guided hike along the river, with plenty of opportunities to swim in the luscious coolness, before arriving at the thermal river, where temperatures range from 32°C to 46°C (89°F to 114°F). There's a swim-up bar, hanging bridges and glorious views all around.

Thermo Manía Hot Spring

(2673-0233; www.thermomania.net; adult/child US$12/10; 8am-10pm;) The biggest complex in the area has some Disney–Flintstone queso to it, but there are 11 thermal pools, which range from lukewarm to warm. The upper pool complex has a swim-up bar and waterslide. Much more tasteful are the five stone pools and sauna in the leafy lower sector. There's also a full spa (with private mud baths), playground, museum, soccer field and picnic tables. Families love it here.

El Guayacán Hot Spring

(2673-0349; www.termaleselguayacan.com; adult/child US$10/8; 8am-10pm;) Just behind Thermo Manía, this is a family finca that's hissing and smoking with vents

and mud pots. There are eight thermal pools and one cold pool with a water slide. You can also take a guided tour of the fumaroles (stay on the trail!). If you wish to spend the night, bed down in one of the clean, cold-water cabinas (singles/doubles from US$30/60) brushed in bright colors or in a spacious villa with kitchenette.

Termales Miravalles Hot Spring

(2673-0606, 8305-4072; adult/child US$5/3; 7:30am-10pm;) For some local flavor, Termales Miravalles has four pools and a super waterslide, all lying along a thermal stream. There's a small restaurant and space for camping. It's usually open on weekends year-round, and daily during high season. The access road is directly across from Yökö hot springs.

Las Hornillas Hiking

(2100-1233, 8839-9769; www.lashornillas.com; tours US$35-55; 9am-5pm) On the southern slopes of Miravalles, Las Hornillas has a unique lunar landscape, with bubbling pools and fumaroles on the property. Hike to explore a small volcanic crater and bathe in the mud pools. Or traverse a hanging bridge and discover a spectacular waterfall.

Getting There & Away

Volcán Miravalles is 27km northeast of Bagaces and can be approached by a paved road that leads north of Bagaces through the communities of Salitral and Torno, where the road splits. From the left-hand fork, you'll reach Guayabo, with a few sodas (lunch counters)and basic cabinas (cabins); to the right, you'll find Fortuna de Bagaces, with easier access to the hot springs. The road reconnects north of the two towns and continues toward Upala.

By bus, you can connect through Bagaces, which has hourly buses to and from Guayabo and Fortuna (US$1, 45 minutes).

Parque Nacional Rincón de la Vieja
BERNARD/GETTY IMAGES ©

Hottest Spots for Thermal Pools & Mud Pots

Costa Rica's volcano-powered thermal pools and mud pots provide plenty of good, clean fun for beauty queens and would-be mud wrestlers alike.

◦ On the slopes of Volcán Rincón de la Vieja, Hot Springs Rio Negro (p190) has several pools in a transporting jungle setting.

◦ While some hot spots around Arenal charge outrageous fees to soak in sparkly surrounds, **Eco Thermales Hot Springs** (☏2479-8787; www.ecotermalesfortunacr. com; adult/child US$34/29; ⏰10am-9pm; 👪) ✒ maintains its sense of elegance by limiting guest numbers.

◦ Thermal pools, hanging bridges and low-key luxury characterize the thermal canyon experience at Río Perdido (p187), near Volcán Miravalles.

◦ The pinnacle of indulgent dirt exists in the remote heights of Rincón de la Vieja at Borinquen Mountain Resort & Spa (p191), where, if mineral mud is not your thing, you can opt instead for a wine or chocolate skin treatment.

PARQUE NACIONAL RINCÓN DE LA VIEJA

Given its proximity to Liberia – really just a hop, a skip and a few bumps away – this 141-sq-km national park feels refreshingly uncrowded and remote. Named after the active Volcán Rincón de la Vieja (1895m), the steamy main attraction, the park also covers several other peaks in the same volcanic range, including the highest, Volcán Santa María (1916m). The park exhales geothermal energy. It bubbles with multihued fumaroles, tepid springs and steaming flatulent mud pots, as well as a young and feisty *volcancito* (small volcano). All of these can be visited on foot and horseback on well-maintained but sometimes steep trails.

The park was created in 1973 to protect a vital watershed that feeds 32 rivers and streams. Its relatively remote location means that wildlife, rare elsewhere, is out in force here, with the major volcanic crater a rather dramatic backdrop to the scene. Volcanic activity has occurred many times since the late 1960s, with the most recent eruption of steam and ash in 2012. At the moment, however, the volcano is gently active and does not present any danger – ask locally for the latest, as volcanoes do act up. (The crater itself is off-limits since the 2012 eruptions have made it unsafe.)

Elevations in the park range from less than 600m to 1916m, so visitors pass through a variety of habitats as they ascend the volcanoes, though the majority of the trees in the park are typical of those found in dry tropical forests throughout Guanacaste. The park is home to the country's highest density of Costa Rica's national flower, the increasingly rare purple orchid (*Guarianthe skinneri*), locally known as *guaria morada*.

Most visitors to the park are here for the hot springs, where you can soak to the sound of howler monkeys overhead. Many of the springs are reported to have therapeutic properties.

 Activities

HIKING

A circular trail east of Las Pailas ranger station – about 3km in total – takes you past boiling mud pools *(las pailas)*, sulfurous fumaroles and a *volcancito*.

About 350m west of the ranger station is the well-signed trail to Pozo Azul (Blue Lagoon), which offers a marvelous

Below: Hiking through the rainforest; **Right:** Fumarole, Área de Conservación Guanacaste (p193)

(BELOW) ADAM CLARK/GETTY IMAGES ©; (RIGHT) DAVID CAYLESS/GETTY IMAGES ©

river view and a stunning aquamarine swimming hole. Further away along the same trail are several waterfalls – the largest, Catarata La Cangreja, 5.1km west, is a classic, dropping 50m straight from a cliff into a small lagoon where you can swim. Dissolved copper salts give the falls a deep blue color. This trail winds through forest, past truly massive strangler figs, then on to open savanna spiked with yucca on the volcano's flanks, where you can enjoy views as far as the Palo Verde wetlands and the Pacific beyond.

The slightly smaller Cataratas Escondidas (Hidden Waterfalls) are 4.3km west on a different trail and a bit higher on the slope.

Since the 2012 eruptions, the trek to the summit of Rincón de la Vieja is no longer open to the public.

From the Santa María ranger station a trail leads 2.8km west through the 'enchanted forest' and past a waterfall to sulfurous hot springs with supposedly therapeutic properties. Don't soak in them for more than about half an hour (some people suggest much less) without taking a dip in the nearby cold springs, 2km away, to cool off. There's also a lovely 1.1km trail to the Catarata Bosque Encantado, Santa María's best waterfall. If you cobble all the Santa María trails together you'll have a gorgeous 12km day hike.

HOT SPRINGS & SPAS

Hot Springs Rio Negro   Hot Springs
(www.guachipelin.com; per person US$10; ⏱9am-5pm) Set in the dry forest along the Rio Negro, this magical place is managed by the Hacienda Guachipelín. Six natural, stone-crafted hot pools are accessible by a lovely wooded trail. Those closest to the hanging bridge, on either side of the river, are the hottest, topping out at 40°C (104°F). Admission comes with a short tour through the woods describing indigenous medicinal flora.

Canyon de la Vieja Adventure Lodge
Hot Springs

(✆ 2665-5912; www.thecanyonlodge.com; spa US$15, tours US$30-40) On the bank of the crystal-blue Río Colorado, this sprawling lodge operates a full-service spa, complete with warm pools, mud baths and a Tarzan swing dropping into the inviting river. The current is strong, but the swimming hole is glorious for cooling off on a hot, sunny day (unfortunately, there's not much shade here). In addition to the spa, the adventure lodge offers tours including horse tours, tubing, rafting and canopy tours.

Sleeping

Hacienda Guachipelín
Hotel $$

(✆ 2666-8075; www.guachipelin.com; s/d/ tr/q incl breakfast US$81/99/128/148; P ❄ @ 🛜 ☎) This appealing 19th-century working cattle ranch is set on 12 sq km of primary and secondary forest. The 54 rooms are simple and spacious with traditional wood furniture and wide, welcoming verandas. All rooms enjoy lovely views of the volcano and surrounding grounds. You'll appreciate the welcome drink that awaits you when you check in.

Borinquen Mountain Resort & Spa
Resort $$$

(✆ 2690-1900; www.borinquenresort.com; d incl breakfast US$218-373; 🕐 Anáhuac Spa 9am-6pm; ❄ 🛜) Splurge. The most luxurious resort in the area features nicely appointed bungalows with private decks and jaw-dropping mountain views. All the expected adventure tours are on offer. The hot springs, mud baths and natural saunas are gorgeous and surrounded by greenery; and a treatment at the elegant Anáhuac Spa – suspended over the steaming jungle – is the icing on this decadent mud pie.

ℹ Getting There & Away

The Las Pailas sector is accessible via a good 20km road that begins at a signed turnoff from the Interamericana, 5km north of Liberia; a private road is needed to reach the park and costs US$1.50 per person. There's no public transportation, but any of the lodges can arrange transport from Liberia to the park for around US$20 to US$30 per person each way (two or three people minimum). Alternatively, you can hire a 4WD taxi from Liberia for about US$35 to Las Pailas, or US$65 to Santa María, each way.

PARQUE NACIONAL VOLCÁN TENORIO

They say that when God finished painting the sky blue, he washed his paintbrushes in the Río Celeste. The heavenly blue river, waterfalls and lagoons of Parque Nacional Volcán Tenorio are among the most spectacular natural phenomena in Costa Rica, which is probably why the park is known to locals simply as Río Celeste.

Established in 1976 this magical 184-sq-km national park remains a blissfully pristine rainforest abundant with wildlife. Soaring 1916m above the cloud rainforest is the park's namesake, Volcán Tenorio, which actually consists of three peaked craters: Montezuma, Tenorio I (the tallest) and Tenorio II.

Your first stop will be the Puesto El Pilón ranger station, which houses a small exhibit of photographs and dead animals. Pick up a free English or Spanish hiking map.

 Activities

A well-signed trail begins at the ranger-station parking lot and winds 1.5km through the rainforest until you reach an intersection. Turn left and climb down a very steep but sturdy staircase to the Catarata de Río Celeste, a milky-blue waterfall that cascades 30m down the rocks into a fantastically aquamarine pool.

It's 400m further to the Mirador, where you'll have gorgeous views of Tenorio from the double-decker wooden platform. Further on is the Technicolor Pozo Azul (Blue Lagoon). The trail loops around the lagoon 400m until you arrive at the confluence of rivers known as Los Teñidores (The Stainers). Here, two small rivers – one whitish blue and one

brownish yellow – mix together to create the blueberry milk of Río Celeste.

Note that swimming is strictly prohibited everywhere along this trail. The nearby hot springs have also been closed, after some tourists were burned in 2011. Hiking to the volcano crater is also strictly prohibited.

Plans for a circuit trail are afoot, but for now the trail ends at Los Teñidores. Retrace your steps to return to the ranger station.

Allow three to four hours to complete the entire hike. It's about a 7km round trip, but parts of the trail are steep and rocky. And because this is a rainforest, the trail can be wet and muddy almost year-round. Good hiking shoes or boots are a must. After your hike, you'll find an area to wash your footwear near the trailhead.

Sleeping & Eating

Celeste Mountain Lodge
Lodge $$$
(2278-6628; www.celestemountainlodge.com; s/d/tr/q incl all meals US$150/190/225/260; P 🛜) Innovative and sustainable, this contemporary open-air hilltop lodge in the shadow of Volcán Tenorio is absolutely stunning. The 18 rooms are small but stylish, with wooden shutters that open onto immobilizing vistas. Winding through labyrinthine gardens, a trail is laid with geotextile (no more muddy shoes!), which makes for soundless hiking and prime bird-watching. The price includes meals at the excellent gourmet restaurant.

Tenorio Lodge
Lodge $$$
(2466-8282; www.tenoriolodge.com; s/d/tr/q incl breakfast US$130/140/170/190; P @ 🛜) Located on a lush hilltop with amazing views of Volcán Tenorio, this lodge has 12 romantic and roomy bungalows, featuring orthopedic beds, stone or wood floors and floor-to-ceiling windows with volcano views. On the 17-acre property you'll find a restaurant, two ponds, a heliconia garden and two hot tubs to enjoy after a long day of hiking. Located 1km south of Bijagua.

ℹ️ Getting There & Away

Buses between San José and Upala stop in Bijagua (US$8, four daily), the only sizable town in the Tenorio area. There are also six daily buses that run between Upala (US$1) and Cañas (US$1.25) via Bijagua.

ÁREA DE CONSERVACIÓN GUANACASTE

Among the oldest (established in 1971) and largest protected areas in Costa Rica, this sprawling 386-sq-km national refuge on the Península Santa Elena protects the largest remaining stand of tropical dry forest in Central America, some of the most important nesting sites of several species of sea turtle, and deep historical gravitas. Almost all of the worthy diversions can be found in a vast area known as the **Santa Rosa Sector** (☎ 2666-5051; www.acguanacaste.ac.cr; adult/child US$10/1, surfing surcharge US$15; ⊙ 8am-4pm).

However, the majority of travelers are here for one reason: the chance to surf the near-perfect beach break at **Playa Naranjo**, which is created by the legendary offshore monolith known as Witch's Rock (also known locally as Roca Bruja).

Santa Rosa is famous among Ticos as a symbol of historical pride. A foreign army has only invaded Costa Rica three times, and each time the attackers were defeated in Santa Rosa. The best known of these events was the Battle of Santa Rosa, which took place on March 20, 1856, when the soon-to-be-self-declared president of Nicaragua, an American named William Walker, invaded Costa Rica. Walker was the head of a group of foreign pirates and adventurers known as the 'Filibusters' that had already seized Baja and southwest Nicaragua, and were attempting to gain control over all of Central America. In a brilliant display of military prowess, Costa Rican president Juan Rafael Mora Porras guessed Walker's intentions and managed to assemble a ragtag group of fighters who proceeded to surround Walker's army in the main building of the old Hacienda Santa Rosa, known as La Casona. The battle was over in just 14 minutes, and Walker was forever driven from Costa Rican soil.

Catarata de Río Celeste

MICHAEL MIKE L. BAIRD/GETTY IMAGES ©

⊙ Sights & Activities

La Casona Historic Building

(📞2666-5051; www.acguanacaste.ac.cr; ⏱8-11:30am & 1-4pm) La Casona is the main edifice of the old Hacienda Santa Rosa. The battle of 1856 was fought around this building, and the military action is described with wonderful displays detailing (in English and Spanish) the old gold-rush route, William Walker's evil imperial plans, and the 20-day-battle breakdown. There are also exhibits on the region's natural history. Two hiking trails leave from behind the museum.

WILDLIFE-WATCHING

The wildlife is both varied and prolific, especially during the dry season, when animals congregate around the remaining water sources and the trees lose their leaves. More than 250 bird species have been recorded, including the raucous white-throated magpie jay, unmistakable with its long crest of manically curled feathers. The forests contain parrot and parakeet, trogon and tanager, and as you head down to the coast you'll be rewarded by sightings of a variety of coastal birds.

Bats are also very common (about 50 or 60 different species have been identified in Santa Rosa), as are reptile species that include lizards, iguanas, snakes, crocodiles and four species of sea turtle. The olive ridley sea turtle is the most numerous, and during the July to December nesting season tens of thousands of turtles make their nests on Santa Rosa's beaches. The most popular beach is **Playa Nancite**, where, during September and October especially, it's possible to see as many as 8000 of these 40kg turtles on the beach at the same time. The turtles are disturbed by light, so flash photography and flashlights are not permitted. Avoid the nights around a full moon – they're too bright and turtles are less likely to show up. Playa Nancite is strictly protected and entry is restricted, but permission may be obtained from park headquarters (p193) to observe; call ahead.

HIKING

Near Hacienda Santa Rosa is **El Sendero Indio Desnudo**, an 800m trail with signs

Área de Conservación Guanacaste

Detour:
Cinco Ceibas

On the grounds of the huge, 11 sqnca Pangola, there is a swathe of dense, green primary rainforest, home to some of the oldest and largest trees in all of Costa Rica. This is **Cinco Ceibas** (📞4000-0606; www.cincoceibas.com; half-day tour incl lunch US$40-60). And yes, there are five glorious ceiba trees that you can gawk at as you walk 1.2km along the raised wooden boardwalk through the jungle. The stroll is paired with horseback riding, kayaking, or an ox-cart ride, plus lunch, for a carefully choreographed adventure.

Transportation to Cinco Ceibas is offered for day-trippers from San José or La Fortuna. If you have your own wheels, it's a one-hour drive on mostly gravel roads from La Virgen. From the highway north of town, take the turn off to Pueblo Nuevo. There is supposed to be a new highway in the works, which will make this journey faster and easier, so ask around before you set out.

interpreting the ecological relationships among the animals, plants and weather patterns of Santa Rosa. The trail is named after the common tree, also called *gumbo limbo,* whose peeling orange-red bark can photosynthesize during the dry season, when the trees' leaves are lost (resembling a sunburned tourist...or 'naked Indian', as the literal translation of the trail name implies). Also seen along the trail is the national tree of Costa Rica, the *guanacaste*. The province is named after this huge tree species, which is found along the Pacific coastal lowlands. You may also see birds, monkeys, snakes and iguanas, as well as petroglyphs (most likely pre-Columbian) etched into rocks along the trail.

Behind La Casona a short 330m trail leads up to the **Monumento a Los Héroes** and a lookout platform. There are also longer trails through the dry forest, including a gentle 4km hike to the **Mirador**, with spectacular views of Playa Naranjo, which is accessible to hikers willing to go another 9km along the deeply rutted road to the sea. The main road is lined with short trails to small waterfalls and other photogenic natural wonders.

On the road to Playa Naranjo, and about 8km from shore, you'll pass a trailhead for the **Mirador Valle Naranjo**.

It's a short 600m hump to a viewpoint with magical Naranjo vistas.

From the southern end of Playa Naranjo there are two hiking trails: **Sendero Carbonal** is a 5km trail that swings inland along the mangroves and past Laguna El Limbo, where the crocs hang out; **Sendero Aceituno** parallels Playa Naranjo for 13km and terminates near the estuary across from Witch's Rock.

SURFING

The surfing at Playa Naranjo is truly world-class, especially near **Witch's Rock**, a beach break famous for its fast, hollow 3m rights (although there are also fun lefts when it isn't pumping). Beware of rocks near the river mouth, and be careful near the estuary as it's a rich feeding ground for crocodiles during the tide changes. Oh, and by the way, the beach is stunning, with a sweet, rounded boulder-strewn point to the north and shark-fin headlands to the south. Even further south, Nicoya and Papagayo peninsular silhouettes reach out in a dramatic attempt to out do each other.

The surfing is equally legendary at **Ollie's Point** off Playa Portero Grande, which has the best right in all of Costa Rica, with a nice, long ride, especially with a south swell. The bottom here is a mix of sand and rocks, and the year-round

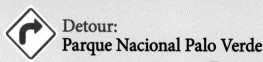

Detour:
Parque Nacional Palo Verde

The 184-sq-km **Parque Nacional Palo Verde** (☏ 2524-0628; www.ots.ac.cr; adult/ child US$10/1; ⏰ 8am-4pm) is a wetland sanctuary in Costa Rica's driest province. It lies on the northeastern bank of the mouth of the Río Tempisque and at the head of the Golfo de Nicoya. All the major rivers in the region drain into this ancient intersection of two basins, which creates a mosaic of habitats, including mangrove swamps, marshes, grassy savannas and evergreen forests. A number of low limestone hills provide lookouts over the park, and the park's shallow, permanent lagoons are focal points for wildlife. The park derives its name from its abundant *palo verde* (green tree), a small shrub that's green year-round.

Palo Verde has the greatest concentrations of waterfowl and shorebirds in Central America, and over 300 bird species have been recorded in the park. Bird-watchers come to see the large flocks of heron (including the rare black-crowned night heron), stork (including the endangered jabirú), spoonbill, egret, ibis, grebe and duck; and forest birds, including scarlet macaws, great curassows, keel-billed toucans and parrots, are also common. Frequently sighted mammals include deer, coati, armadillo, monkey and peccary, as well as the largest population of jaguarundi in Costa Rica. There are also numerous reptiles in the wetlands, including crocodiles that are reportedly up to 5m in length.

The dry season (December to March) is the best time to visit, as flocks of birds tend to congregate in the remaining lakes and marshes. Plus, the trees lose their leaves, allowing for clearer viewing. However, the entire basin swelters during the dry season, so bring adequate sun protection. During the wet months, large portions of the area are flooded, and access may be limited.

offshore is perfect for tight turns and slow closes. Shortboarding is preferred by surfers at both spots.

ⓘ Getting There & Away

The well-signed main park entrance can be reached by public transportation: take any bus between Liberia and the Nicaraguan border and ask the driver to let you off at the park entrance; rangers can help you catch a return bus. You can also arrange private transportation from the hotels in Liberia for about US$20 to US$30 per person round trip.

LA VIRGEN

Tucked into the densely jungled shores of the wild and scenic Río Sarapiquí, La Virgen was one of a number of small towns that prospered during the heyday of the banana trade. Although United Fruit has long since shipped out, the town remains dependent on its nearby pineapple fields, and it still leans on that river. For over a decade, La Virgen was the premier kayaking and rafting destination in Costa Rica. Dedicated groups of hard-core paddlers spent happy weeks running the Río Sarapiquí. But a tremendous 2009 earthquake and landslide altered its course and flattened La Virgen's tourist economy. Some businesses folded, others relocated to La Fortuna. But independent kayakers are starting to come back and there are now three river outfitters offering exhilarating trips on Class II-IV waters. There are cheap digs in town, or consider staying in one of the more interesting lodges on the outskirts or on the road to Puerto Viejo.

Sights

Snake Garden
Zoo

(☏ 2761-1059; snakegarden@hotmail.com; adult/student & child US$15/10, night tour US$24/18; ☺9am-5pm) This wildlife center is an entertaining rainy-day outing. Get face to face with 50 species of reptiles and amphibians, including poison-dart frogs, rattlesnakes, crocs and turtles. The star attraction is a gigantic 80kg Burmese python.

Activities

The Río Sarapiquí isn't as wild as the white water on the Río Pacuare near Turrialba, though it will get your heart racing. Even better, the dense jungle that hugs the riverbank is lush and primitive. You can run the Sarapiquí year-round, but December offers the biggest water. The rest of the year, the river fluctuates with rainfall. The bottom line is: if it's been raining, the river will be at its best. Where once there were nearly a dozen outfitters in La Virgen, now there are three. All offer roughly the same Class II-IV options at similar prices.

Sarapiquí Outdoor Center
Rafting

(☏ 8506-6889, 2761-1123; www.costaricaraft.com; 2/4hr rafting trip US$65/90, guided kayak trips US$90-120) Here is your local paddling authority. In addition to offering its own rafting excursions, it offers kayak rental, lessons and clinics. Indie paddlers should check in for up-to-date river information. If you need somewhere to sleep before you hit the water, you can pitch a tent here.

Aventuras del Sarapiquí
Rafting

(☏ 2766-6768; www.sara-piqui.com; river trips US$55-80) A highly recommend-ed outfitter, Adventuras del Sarapiquí offers mountain biking, and canopy, hiking and horseback tours, as well as a variety of river trips. It's set just out of town on the main highway in Chilamate.

Hacienda Pozo Azul Adventures
Adventure Tour

(☏ 2438-2616, in USA & Canada 877-810-6903; www.pozoazul.com; tours US$55-85;) Hacienda Pozo Azul Adventures specializes in adventure activities, including horseback-riding tours, a canopy tour over the lush jungle and river, rappelling, mountain biking, and assorted river trips. It is the most polished and best-funded tour concession in the area, catering largely to groups and day-trippers from San José.

Sleeping & Eating

Hacienda Pozo Azul Adventures
Bungalow $$

(☏ 2438-2616, 2761-1360; www.haciendapozoazul.com; s/d incl breakfast US$80/92; P @ 🛜) 🍃 Located near the southern end of La Virgen, Pozo Azul features luxurious 'tent

Black Ctenosaur, Parque Nacional Palo Verde

suites' scattered on the edge of the tree line, all on raised polished-wood platforms and dressed with luxurious bedding and mosquito nets. At night, the frogs and wildlife sing you to sleep as raindrops patter on the canvas roof.

Pozo Azul also has a restaurant-bar in town with a lovely riverside veranda.

Restaurante y Cabinas Tía Rosita
Soda $

(☎ 2761-1032; meals US$2-6; P 🛜) Tía Rosita is the best *soda* (lunch counter) in La Virgen, with excellent *casados* and Costa Rican–style *chiles rellenos* (stuffed fried peppers). The family also rents several *cabinas* with private hot-water bathrooms and plenty of breathing space, located about 100m down the road.

❶ Getting There & Away

La Virgen lies on Hwy 126, about 8km north of San Miguel and 17km southwest of Puerto Viejo de Sarapiquí. Buses originating in San José, San Miguel or Puerto Viejo de Sarapiquí make regular stops in La Virgen. If you're driving, the curvy road is paved between San José and Puerto Viejo de Sarapiquí, though irregular maintenance can make for a bumpy ride.

LA VIRGEN TO PUERTO VIEJO DE SARAPIQUÍ

This scenic stretch of Hwy 126 is home to a few excellent ecolodges. Good news for budget travelers: you don't have to stay at them to take advantage of their private trails and other interesting attractions. Any bus between La Virgen and Puerto Viejo de Sarapiquí can drop you off at the entrances, while a taxi from La Virgen will cost from US$8 to US$10.

◎ Sights & Activities

Tirimbina Rainforest Center & Lodge
Lodge $$

(☎ 2761-1579; www.tirimbina.org; d incl breakfast US$85-105; P ❄ @ 🛜) Located 2km from La Virgen, this is a working environmental research and education center. The spacious, comfortable accommodations are located at the lodge or at a more remote field station. Tirimbina reserve has more than 9km of trails (access US$15/9 per adult/child), and tours (US$22 to US$27) include birdwatching, frog and bat tours, night walks and a recommended chocolate tour.

Suspension bridge, Río Sarapiquí (p201)

Sleeping & Eating

Centro Neotrópico SarapiquíS
Lodge $$

(☎2761-1004; www.sarapiquis.org; d incl breakfast US$94; P🐕❄@🏊) 🍃 About 2km north of La Virgen, this ecolodge offers a place to stay and eat, as well as an education in environmental conservation and pre-Columbian culture. Modeled after a 15th-century pre-Columbian village, the *palenque*-style thatched-roof buildings each contain a clutch of luxuriously appointed rooms complete with huge solar-heated bathroom and private terrace. The restaurant incorporates ingredients used in indigenous cuisine, many grown on the premises.

What's really special about the lodge is the other attractions scattered about the grounds. The Alma Ata Archaeological Park is a Maleku archaeological site, estimated to be around 600 years old. Currently about 70 small stone sculptures marking a burial field are being excavated by Costa Rican archaeologists who have revealed a number of petroglyphs and pieces of pottery. Nearby is the **Sarapaquís Gardens & Museum** (www.sarapiquis.org; self-guided adult/child 4-16yr US$8/4, with guide US$15/8 ; ⊙9am-5pm), chronicling the history of the rainforest and of human interactions with it. It also displays hundreds of indigenous artifacts. The gardens boast one of the largest scientific collections of medicinal plants in Costa Rica.

La Quinta de Sarapiquí Lodge
Lodge $$

(☎2761-1052; www.laquintasarapiqui.com; d incl breakfast US$95; P❄🏊) 🍃 At this family-run lodge on the banks of the Río Sardinal, covered paths crisscross the landscaped garden, connecting thatched-roof, hammock-strung rooms. You can swim in the pretty saltwater pool or in the nearby river swimming hole; observe the creatures in the frog house, the caimen nursery and the butterfly garden; or hike the trails through secondary forest. Day passes are US$10.

Selva Verde Lodge
Lodge $$$

(☎2761-1800, in USA & Canada 800-451-7111; www.selvaverde.com; incl breakfast s/d US$116/134, bungalow s/d US$133/163; P🏊) In Chilamate, about 7km west of Puerto Viejo, this former *finca* is now an elegant lodge protecting 200 hectares of rainforest. Choose to stay at the river lodge, elevated above the forest floor, or in a private bungalow, tucked away in the nearby trees. Rooms have shiny wooden floors, solar-heated showers, and wide verandas with views to the forest.

There are three walking trails through the grounds and into the premontane tropical wet forest, as well as medicinal and butterfly gardens, various boat tours on the Río Sarapiquí, and an onsite Italian kitchen.

PUERTO VIEJO DE SARAPIQUÍ & AROUND

At the scenic confluence of Ríos Puerto Viejo and Sarapiquí, this was once the most important port in Costa Rica. Boats laden with fruit, coffee and other commercial exports plied the Sarapiquí as far as the Nicaraguan border, then turned east on the Río San Juan to the sea. Today, it is simply a gritty but pleasant palm-shaded market town. The town is adjusting to the new economy, as the local polytechnic high school offers students advanced tourism, ecology and agriculture degrees. The school even has its own reserve, laced with trails. Visitors, meanwhile, can choose from any number of activities in the surrounding area such as bird-watching, rafting, kayaking, boating and hiking. The *migración* (immigration office) is near the small wooden dock.

Activities

Taking the launch from Puerto Viejo to Trinidad, at the confluence of the Ríos Sarapiquí and San Juan, provides a rich opportunity to see crocodiles, sloths, birds, monkeys and iguanas sunning themselves on the muddy riverbanks or gathering in the trees. This river system is a historically important gateway from the Caribbean into the heart of Central America, and it's still off the beaten tourist track, revealing rainforest and ranches, wildlife and old war zones, deforested pasture land and protected areas.

Ruta Los Heroes
Boat Tour

(☎ 2766-5858; 2hr tour per person US$20; ⏱ 7am-3pm) The pink building near the dock is a boat-captain cooperative, offering river tours with ecological and historical emphasis. Make arrangements to leave as early as possible to beat the heat and see more wildlife. If the office is closed (as it sometimes is in the low season), you can negotiate directly with the captains you find at the dock. Or, try calling **Oscar** (☎ 8365-3683) or **Rafael** (☎ 8346-1220) directly.

Green Rivers
Rafting, Kayaking

(☎ 8884-0187, 2766-5274; tours US$50-70) Operating out of the Posada Andrea Cristina B&B, this is a new outfit run by the ever-amiable Kevín Martínez and his wife. They offer a wide variety of rafting and kayaking tours, from family-friendly floats to adrenaline-pumping, rapid-surfing rides. They also know their nature, so they do natural history and bird tours, too.

Sleeping

Posada Andrea Cristina B&B
B&B $$

(☎ 2766-6265; www.andreacristina.com; s/d incl breakfast from US$38/55; P 🛜) On the edge of town and at the edge of the forest, this charming B&B is a gem. The grounds are swarming with birds, sloths and monkeys, not to mention the frogs that populate the pond. Quaint cabins all have high, beamed ceilings, colorful paint jobs and private terraces. Or opt to stay in a funky tree house, built around a thriving Inga tree.

Your delightful host, Alex Martínez, is also a bird guide. He's active in environmental protection and runs **Tierra Hermosa** (www.tierrahermosacenter.org), a nearby wildlife reserve and rescue center. You'll see some of the 'clients' around the *posada* (guesthouse).

Hotel Gavilán
Hotel $$

(☎ 2234-9507; www.gavilanlodge.com; d US$65-75; P ❄ 🛜 🏊) Sitting on a 100-hectare reserve about 4km northeast of Puerto Viejo, this former cattle *hacienda* is a bird-watching haven, with 5km of private trails on the grounds. The cozy rooms have pastel paint jobs and wide porches, some with river views. Management is quite charming, offering private boat tours (US$50) and bird walks (US$18) upon request.

Hotel Ara Ambigua
Hotel $$

(☎ 2766-7101; www.hotelaraambigua.com; d/tr/q incl breakfast from US$86/106/128; P ❄ @ 🏊) About 1km west of Puerto Viejo, this countryside retreat offers

Poison-dart frog
JUDY BELLAH/GETTY IMAGES ©

oddly formal but well-equipped rooms, set on gorgeous grounds. There are birds buzzing in the luscious, blooming gardens, poison-dart frogs in the *ranario* (frog pond) and caimans in the small lake. Even if you're not staying here, the onsite pizzeria, **La Casona**, is an excellent place to grab lunch and spy on your feathered friends.

Getting There & Away

Puerto Viejo de Sarapiquí has been a transportation center longer than Costa Rica has been a country, and it's easily accessed by paved major roads from San José, the Caribbean coast and other population centers. There is a taxi stop across from the bus terminal, and drivers will take you to the nearby lodges for US$5 to US$10.

SOUTH OF PUERTO VIEJO DE SARAPIQUÍ

Adventure-oriented tour groups make up the majority of guests at **Sueño Azul** (☎ 2764-1000; www.suenoazulresort.com; **standard/superior d US$150/180**), a top-end adventure lodge upon a hill. It has an on-again off-again yoga retreat program and the secluded bamboo yoga platform is lovely, but that's one small, ephemeral slice of the business. Its perch on the stunning confluence of the Rios Sarapiquí and San Rafael, and vast property are the main draws. Here's a place with its own suspension bridge, canopy tour and waterfall. There is an enormous stable of gorgeous horses if you fancy a ride as well as hiking trails and hot tubs, a splashy pool, a bar and a huge tiled patio replete with leather rockers. Rooms are huge with terra cotta floors, log beds and river views, though some can smell musty.

Península de Nicoya

Península de Nicoya's simple allure: magical beaches and good surf. Archetypical tropical beaches edge this jungle-trimmed rich coast, whose shores have been imprinted on the memories of the millions of marine turtles who return to their birthplaces to nest. The travelers, too, descend on these beaches, seeking to witness such patterns of nature for themselves. And who can be blamed for wanting to play, beckoned by waves that never seem to close out, tropical forests teeming with wild things, the slow, sane pace of *la vida costarricense* (Costa Rican life) and what lies beyond that next turn down a potholed dirt road?

Humans, however, make more of an environmental impact than leatherbacks do. The Nicoya teeters on a balance between sane development and its intrinsic wildness.

Surfers, Playa Carmen (p235)
MAREMAGNUM/GETTY IMAGES ©

Península de Nicoya

Alajuela

San Rafael de Guatuso

Río Cote

Arenal

Unión

Laguna de Arenal

Volcán Tenorio (1916m)

Parque Nacional Volcán Tenorio

Río Chiquito

Santa Elena

Rancho Grande

Cordillera de Tilarán

Río Tenorio

Tilarán

Río Lagarto

Las Juntas de Abangares

1

Fortuna

Río Corobicí

Cañas

Reserva Biológica

Bebedero

Río Bebedero

Isla Chira

Bagaces

1

Refugio de Vida Silvestre Cipanci

Guanacaste

Pijije

Parque Nacional Palo Verde

Río Tempisque

Puente La Amistad

Hacienda Palo Verde

Puerto Humo

Quebrada Honda

18

LIBERIA

Valle de Tempisque

Parque Nacional Barra Honda

Mansión

Corillo

Santa Ana

Barra Honda

Reserva Indígena Matambú

Liberia International Airport

21

Río Liberia

Río Cañas

Laguna Mata Redonda

Guaitil

Parque Nacional Diriá

Nicoya

Río Quirimán

Río Tempisque

Belén

21

Santa Cruz

21

Golfo de Papagayo

Liberia

Filadelfia

155

Parque Nacional Diriá

Isla Santa Catalina

Comunidad

151

Sardinal

27 de Abril

Marbella

Playa Pan de Azúcar

Panamá

Playa Panamá

Playa Hermosa

Playa del Coco

Playa Ocotal

El Coco

Hotel Riu Guanacaste

Potrero

Huacas

Matapalo

160

Bahía de Culebra

Nacascolo

Bahía Potrero

Playa Flamingo

Playa Brasilito

Playa Conchal **4**

Parque Nacional Marino Las Baulas de Guanacaste

Refugio Nacional de Tamarindo

Villareal

Playa Grande

Playa Tamarindo

Tamarindo

San José de Pinilla

Hacienda Pinilla **5**

Paraíso

Playa Avellana

Playa Negra

Playa Junquillal

1 Surfing in Mal País
2 Montezuma
3 Playa Sámara
4 Playa Conchal
5 Playa Avellanas

Península de Nicoya Highlights

Surfing in Mal País

Península de Nicoya offers a great variety of surf spots for surfers of all skill levels. Though nearly every beach along the north Pacific coast is surfable, one of the most famous is Mal País (p235) near the southern tip of the peninsula. Waves are beautiful, board rentals inexpensive and après-surf amenities abundant.

1

2 Montezuma

One of Costa Rica's classic beach destinations, Montezuma (p230) is tucked away at Nicoya's southeastern end. A little effort is required to get here, but it's even harder to leave: abandoned stretches of winding coastline invite long bouts of beachcombing, while calm Pacific waters provide refreshing respite from the tropical heat.

Playa Sámara

3

This low-key beach destination (p227) seems to have it all. Families with little ones in tow positively rave about the spotless beach and tranquil town, while hipsters delight in the surprisingly sophisticated restaurants, cafes and bars. Though it's decidedly on the map, you can't help but feel you're in on a well-kept secret.

AARON MCCOY/GETTY IMAGES ©

4

Playa Conchal

Travelers from near and far flock to this lovely white-sand beach (p215), which boasts some of the Pacific's best snorkeling. Walking along the beach all day, you'll find increasingly wild and rugged shoreline. At night, a wash of colors lights up the sky in an epic sunset. One of the most idyllic beaches in the region.

5

Playa Avellanas

Appearing in the silver-screen surf classic *Endless Summer II,* this beach (p221) is thrashed on a daily basis by huge waves that are primarily the domain of intermediate and advanced surfers. Even if you don't surf at all, it's a great place to watch some of the best.

Península de Nicoya's Best...

Secret Spots

o **Playa Conchal** A secret beach of crushed seashells best accessed by foot – it's unlike the crowded beaches elsewhere. (p215)

o **Reserva Natural Absoluta Cabo Blanco** The country's first protected space helped give rise to the modern ecoboom. (p234)

o **Punta Islita** Gray-sand beaches and a colorful, cared-for little village. (p228)

o **Playa Cocolito** A two-hour hike from Montezuma to a secluded beach and waterfall. (p236)

Thrills

o **Zip Lines** Get ready for the superman pose, with many chances to whiz through the **jungle**. (p224)

o **Waterfall Jump** Take a leap into the swimming hole from 10m above at the Montezuma Waterfalls. (p232)

o **Surfing** Península de Nicoya is a surfing mecca. None surpass the righteous waves of Playa Grande. (p215)

o **Diving & Snorkeling** The shops near Playa del Coco know the clearest spots on this stretch of coast. (p212)

Splurges

o **Florblanca** Sets the standard for luxury in Mal País and Santa Teresa. (p236)

o **Moana Lodge** African art and jungle luxury on a Mal País hillside. (p238)

o **Sueño del Mar B&B** A secluded upmarket retreat that serves as a tranquil escape from nearby Tamarindo. (p219)

o **Villa Deevena** The most talked-about dinner spot in the Nosara area for good reason. (p223)

Eats

○ **Koji's** This is home to the best sushi in the country, bar none. (p237)

○ **Seasons by Shlomy** Thoughtfully created, perfectly prepared cuisine in Tamarindo. (p220)

○ **Playa de los Artistas** A romantic beachside eatery with local ingredients and artistic flourishes. (p233)

○ **Cocolores** A romantic place with Tico-Mediteranean dishes that consistently impress. (p233)

Need to Know

ADVANCE PLANNING

○ **Two months before** Book hotels for peak holiday seasons around Christmas and Semana Santa (Easter week).

○ **One month before** Getting around in the southern peninsula may require river crossings, so rent a 4WD – or high-clearance 4WD during rainy season.

Two weeks before If you're planning a surf trip, start following the surf reports to help plan your itinerary.

RESOURCES

○ **Nicoya Peninsula Guide** (www.nicoyapeninsula.com) Great overviews and general information about Península de Nicoya destinations, as well as local listings.

○ **CR Surf** (www.crsurf.com) With a surf map, surf reports, travel advice and business listings, this site is invaluable for planning a surf trip.

GETTING AROUND

○ **Boat** Jacó, located along the central Pacific coast, is a quick boat ride away from Montezuma.

○ **Bus** Intercity buses are frequent and cheap, which makes moving around a cinch.

○ **Car** Península de Nicoya is one region in particular where a 4WD vehicle can come in handy.

BE FOREWARNED

○ **Roads** If you're driving on unpaved roads during the rainy season, make sure you have a 4WD with high clearance, as well as a comprehensive insurance policy. Many roads will be impassable – always ask locally about conditions before setting out.

○ **Riptides** Get the local lowdown on ocean conditions before braving the waters.

Above left: Tuna and wine, Playa de los Artistas (p233); **Above right:** Zip lining, Montezuma (p231)

(ABOVE LEFT) YADID LEVY/GETTY IMAGES ©; (ABOVE RIGHT) MAREMAGNUM/GETTY IMAGES ©

Península de Nicoya Itineraries

A journey around Costa Rica's famous peninsula brings you to perfect beaches and iconic natural areas. You might not be alone, but these routes are well traveled for good reason: the landscape is stunning.

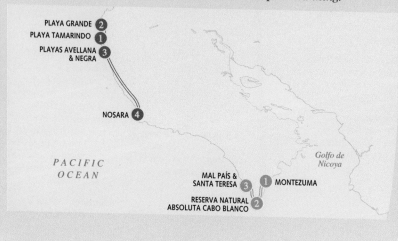

PLAYA TAMARINDO TO NOSARA

TAMARINDO & THE COAST

3 DAYS

A romp through this lovely peninsula starts in the famed beach getaway of ❶ **Playa Tamarindo** (p218). You'll have no problem keeping busy in this cosmopolitan tourist enclave, which is home to excellent restaurants, nightlife and a wealth of active pursuits: zip lining, hiking, sea kayaking, stand-up paddling and surfing. Tamarindo is an excellent place to take surfing lessons, with plenty of instructors and a forgiving beach break. Nature buffs can watch the ancient, entrancing ritual of sea turtles nesting on ❷ **Playa Grande** (p215). Surfers with some experience can cut loose at ❸ **Playas Avellanas & Negra** (p221); those

without can enjoy watching the action from the lovely beaches. These beaches are buffered by mangroves and lush, gentle hillsides allowing plenty of space for sunbathers to stretch out. If the area options dwindle, follow the coast south to ❹ **Nosara** (p223), a quieter, more laid-back alternative to the peninsula's most famous tourist destinations – Nosara's colorful denizens surf and perfect their yoga poses in this welcoming slice of paradise where ocean meets forest.

MONTEZUMA TO SANTA TERESA

THE FAR SOUTH CRAWL

5 DAYS

The southern tip of Península de Nicoya has a reputation for remoteness, but improved transport connections have made it possible to venture here and back in less than a week. Of course, once you set your eyes on the stunning wilderness, the beaches, and the overall lack of civilization, you might have second thoughts about heading anywhere else.

Head first for Jacó to catch a speedboat across the gulf to ❶ **Montezuma** (p230) and begin your adventure. The ride is lovely (sometimes involving impromptu dolphin-watching) and saves several long days of overland travel. With that time saved, don't

feel guilty about winding down to a slow crawl. If you can summon enough energy to leave the beach, you'll find some excellent hiking just around the corner in the ❷ **Reserva Natural Absoluta Cabo Blanco** (p234), where white-sand beaches are home to a number of migratory seabirds. And if that isn't exciting enough for you, grab a board and hit the monumental surf at ❸ **Mal País** & **Santa Teresa** (p235), where you can relax afterwards over a margarita, sushi or a yoga class.

Playa Tamarindo (p218)
JOHN COLETTI/GETTY IMAGES ©

Discover
Península de Nicoya

PLAYA DEL COCO

Sportfishing is the engine that built this place, and you'll mingle with the American anglers at happy hour (it starts early here). That said, there is an actual Tico community here, and plenty of Tico tourists. Stroll along the grassy beachfront plaza at sunset and gaze upon the wide bay, sheltered by long, rugged peninsular arms, the natural marina bobbing with motorboats and fishing *pangas*. All will be right in your world.

🏃 Activities

DIVING

Deep Blue Diving Adventures Diving, Snorkeling
(☏2670-1004; www.deepblue-diving.com; 2 tanks US$79-150, PADI Open Water Course US$415; ⏰7am-6pm) This outfitter runs two-tank dives in the local waters and further afield.

Rich Coast Diving Diving
(☏2670-0176, in USA & Canada 800-434-8464; www.richcoastdiving.com; 2 tanks from US$100, Open Water Course US$450; ⏰7:30am-6pm) On the main street, this Dutch-owned dive shop is the area's largest.

Summer Salt Diving
(☏2670-0308; www.summer-salt.com; 2 tanks US$80-110) This friendly Swiss-run dive shop has professional, bilingual staff. Trips to the Isla Murciélago are pricier.

SURFING

There's no surf in Playa del Coco, but the town is a jumping-off point for two legendary surf destinations: Witch's Rock and Ollie's Point, which are inside the Santa Rosa Sector of the Área de Conservación

Playa del Coco
TRAVEL INK/GETTY IMAGES ©

de Guanacaste. The best way to reach them is by boat, and several surf shops in Coco and Tamarindo are licensed to make the run.

OTHER ACTIVITIES

Sportfishing, sailing, horseback riding and sea kayaking are popular activities. Many places will rent sea kayaks, which are perfect for exploring the rocky headlands to the north and south of the beach.

Blue Marlin   Fishing
(2670-0707, 8828-8250; www.sportfish-ingbluemarlin.com; up to 6 people US$350-860; depart 6am) Offers high-quality sportfishing trips on either a 27ft *panga* or a larger 42ft boat. They cruise north of Coco and routinely hook mahi, mackerel, marlin, rooster fish and tuna.

Papagayo Golf & Country Club   Golf
(2697-0169; www.papagayo-golf.com; 9/18 holes US$55/95, putting green US$4-6; 6:30am-5pm Tue-Sun) An 18-hole course located 10km southeast of Playa del Coco.

 Sleeping

Pato Loco Inn   Guesthouse $$
(2670-0145; www.patolocoinn.com; d incl breakfast $58-78; P❄@🛜☀🐾) Richard and Mary Cox offer a warm welcome to Coco Beach, with a wide range of rooms, a friendly bar and the best American breakfast in town (think biscuits and gravy). Most of the rooms feature stenciling or thematic murals, hand-painted by Mary herself. Stop by for Monday or Friday happy hour to shoot the breeze with the expats.

Hotel Chantel   Boutique Hotel $$
(2670-0389; www.hotelchantel.com; r incl breakfast US$99, ste US$110, apt US$125; P❄🛜☀🐾) Perched on a cliff overlooking the coast, this intimate hotel is a step up from the local lodgings. Eleven rooms have tasteful wood and wicker furniture, contemporary artwork on the walls and private terraces with stunning vistas of Playa del Coco. The elegant infinity pool and the breezy rooftop restaurant share the same panoramic view.

Villa del Sol   Hotel $$
(2670-0085, in Canada 866-793-9523, in USA 866-815-8902; www.villadelsol.com; La Chorrera; r incl breakfast $65-75, apt US$100; P❄@🛜☀) About 1km north of the town center, this leafy, tranquil property attracts monkeys, iguanas and a good variety of bird life, in addition to the happy travelers lounging on hammocks. The main building has stylish rooms with sunset-view balconies. In the back building, studio apartments (sleeping four) offer excellent value. Walk to the beach in five minutes or less.

Hotel La Puerta del Sol   Hotel $$$
(2670-0195; www.lapuertadelsolcostarica. com; d incl breakfast US$113; P❄@🛜☀) A five-minute walk from town, this unpretentiously luxurious Mediterranean-inspired hotel has two large suites and eight huge pastel-colored rooms with polished brick and concrete floors, king-sized beds and private terraces. The well-manicured grounds house a glorious pool, a trellis-shaded gym and an Italian restaurant.

 Eating

Congo   Cafe $
(2670-2135; www.costaricacongo.com; mains US$6-10; 8am-8pm Mon-Sat, 8am-6pm Sun; P🛜🐾) Part cafe, part funky retail boutique, the interior is groovy with arched booths, rattan sofas and a deconstructed wood-and-granite coffee bar. They serve all the espresso drinks and an array of healthy sandwiches, salads and breakfasts.

Restaurante Donde Claudio y Gloria   Seafood $$
(2670-0256; www.dondeclaudioygloria.com; mains US$9-15; 8am-9pm) Founded by Playa del Coco pioneers Claudio and Gloria Rojas, this casual, beachfront seafood restaurant has been a local landmark since 1955. It's a must for seafood-lovers, with such interesting dishes as spicy mahi in an almond, raisin and white-wine sauce. Be warned: service can be painfully slow, but the solid jazz soundtrack will keep you buoyant.

La Dolce Vita
Italian $$

(☏2670-1384; www.ladolcevitacostarica.com; La Chorerra; mains US$10-18; ◷8am-10pm) Set in the Pueblito Sur development about 500m north of the main drag, this is the local expat choice for wood-fired pizza in Playa del Coco. The restaurant is lovingly set in a brick courtyard around a gurgling fountain, sprinkled with candlelit tables. They also do a range of pastas, unique preparations of seafood and traditional grills.

Citron
Fusion $$$

(☏2670-0942; www.citroncoco.com; mains US$15-20; ◷5:30-10pm Mon-Sat) The contemporary menu features fresh ingredients and innovative preparations, including a few enticing specials from the wok (think sea bass poached with scallions, soy sauce and sesame oil). Save room for a decadent Mediterranean dessert. Despite the shopping-mall setting, you can dine in the sophisticated, minimalist dining room or on an open-air deck, surrounded by pochote trees.

Getting There & Away

All buses arrive and depart from the main terminal next to Immigration.

Liberia US$1; one hour; departs hourly from 5am to 7pm.

San José (Pulmitan) US$8; five hours; departs 4am, 8am and 2pm.

PLAYA BRASILITO

Underrated Brasilito has an authentic *pueblo* feel, complete with town square, beachfront soccer pitch, pink-washed *iglesia* and friendly Tico community. All of which makes up for the beach, which has its (much) betters on either side. Still, it's just a short stroll along the sea to sugary Conchal.

🛏 Sleeping & Eating

Hotel Brasilito
Hotel $$

(☏2654-4237; www.brasilito.com; d/tr/q from US$50/60/70; P ❄ 🛜) On the beach side of the plaza, this recommended hotel offers simple, clean rooms with wood floors and ceiling fans, lined up along a wide balcony. Sea-view rooms are a little more,

Playa Brasilito

but worth the splurge. Otherwise, the patio's hammocks are ideal for soaking up the sunset.

Hotel y Restaurante Nany Hotel $$
(☎2654-4320; hotelnany.net; s/d US$50/60; P✿@🛜✈) Set well back from the road and shrouded in mango and palm trees, this impressive Tico-run property offers good value. The spacious rooms, painted in cheerful tropical colors, face an enticing saltwater pool. The restaurant is also recommended.

La Casita de Pescado Seafood $$
(☎2654-5171; mains US$4-20; ⊗9am-9pm) Set on either side of the sandy road to Conchal this beachfront, Tico-owned fish house has cheap yet delicious seafood. The affable owner also offers horse tours (per person US$35) through mountains to a secluded bay.

ℹ Getting There & Away

Buses to and from Playa Flamingo travel through Brasilito. There is a bus ticket office at the north end of Brasilito.

PLAYA CONCHAL

Just 1km south of Brasilito is Playa Conchal, one of the most beautiful beaches in Costa Rica. The name comes from the billions of *conchas* (shells) that wash up on the beach, and are gradually crushed into coarse sand. The shallows drift from an intense turquoise to sea-foam green deeper out, a rarity on the Pacific coast. If you have snorkeling gear, this is the place to use it.

On weekends, the beach is often packed with locals, tourists and countless vendors, but on weekdays during low season, Playa Conchal can be pure paradise. The further south you stroll, the wider, sweeter and more spectacular the beach becomes.

The easiest way to reach Conchal is to simply walk 15 minutes down the beach from Playa Brasilito. You can also drive along the sandy beach road, though you'll be charged US$2 to park.

PLAYA GRANDE

Playa Grande is a wide, gorgeous beach, famous among conservationists and surfers alike. By day, the offshore winds create steep and powerful waves, especially at high tide. By night, an ancient cycle continues, as leatherback sea turtles bearing clutches of eggs follow the ocean currents back to their birthplace. The beach stretches for about 5km from the Tamarindo estuary, around a dome rock – with tide pools and superb surf fishing – and onto equally grand Playa Ventanas. The water is exquisite, warm, clear and charged with dynamic energy. Even confident swimmers should obey those riptide signs, as people have drowned here.

Since 1991, Playa Grande has been part of the Parque Nacional Marino Las Baulas de Guanacaste, which protects one of the most important leatherback nesting areas in the world. During the day, the beach is free and open to all, which is a good thing as the breaks off Playa Grande are fast, steep and consistent. At night, however, it is only possible to visit the beach on a guided tour, to ensure that nesting cycles continue unhindered.

Surfing is most people's motivation for coming here, and it is indeed spectacular.

🛏 Sleeping & Eating

Hotels are signposted from the main road into Playa Grande. Bring a flashlight for walking around at night.

La Marejada Hotel Boutique Hotel $$
(☎2653-0594, in USA & Canada 800-559-3415; www.hotelswell.com; r incl breakfast US$79; ✿🛜✈) Hidden behind a bamboo fence, this stylish nest is a gem. The eight elegantly understated rooms have stone tile floors, rattan and wooden furnishings, and queen beds. Owners Gail and Carli are attentive to every need: if you treat yourself to an in-house massage, perhaps after a day of surfing, Carli will personally wring out all of your kinks.

Rip Jack Inn
Inn $$$

(☎ 2653-0480, in USA 800-808-4605; www.
ripjackinn.com; d from US$102; P ❄ @ ⚟ ☷)
Named for two canine amigos, this comfy,
convivial inn has a handful of rooms that
are clean, modern and artfully painted,
each featuring a small patio with a ham-
mock. In addition to a place to lay your
head, Rip Jack has a yoga shala with daily
classes, surf gear for rent and an amazing
'treetop' restaurant.

Mamasa
Brunch $

(☎ 5002-5468; www.mamasarestaurant.com;
mains US$4-15; ⊙ 10am-2pm Tue-Sun, 5:30-
9pm Wed & Sat) For brunch, feast on eggs
Benedict, breakfast burritos or to-die-for
lemon ricotta pancakes. Come back when
the sun sets, as that's when Jamie really
gets creative. Wednesday is for tapas,
while Saturday shows off a unique and
ever-changing menu of gastronomic
delights. If you're sick of *típica,* Mamasa
has the cure.

🛈 Getting There & Away

There are no buses to Playa Grande, but the road
was recently paved so it's an easy drive.

Alternatively, catch a boat across the estuary
from Tamarindo to the southern end of Grande
(around US$1 per person, from 7am to 4pm).

PARQUE NACIONAL MARINO LAS BAULAS DE GUANACASTE

Since 1991 Playa Grande has been part of
the Parque Nacional Marino Las Baulas De
Guanacaste (☎ 2653-0470; admission incl tour
US$25; ⊙ 8am-noon & 1-5pm, tours 6pm-2am),
which protects one of the world's most
important nesting areas for the *baula*
(leatherback turtle). The park encompass-
es the entire beach and adjacent land (700
hectares), along with 220 sq km of ocean.

The ecosystem is primarily composed
of mangrove swamp, ideal for caiman
and crocodile, as well as numerous bird

species, including the beautiful roseate spoonbill. But the main attraction is the nesting of the world's largest species of turtle, which can weigh in excess of 400kg. Nesting season is from October to March, and it's fairly common to see turtles lay their eggs here on any given night. Of course, it may not be a leatherback. Chances of seeing one of these giants hover around 10%, while you are 95% sure to see a green or black turtle nest.

During the day, the beach is free and open to all, which is a good thing as the breaks off Playa Grande are fast, steep and consistent. At night, however, it is only possible to visit the beach on a guided tour, to ensure that nesting cycles may continue unhindered.

🐾 Activities

The park office is by the northern entrance to Playa Grande. Reservations for turtle-watching can be made up to seven days in advance, and they're highly recommended as there is limited space. You can show up without one, as there are frequent no-shows, though this is less likely on weekends and during the holiday season.

Many hotels and tourist agencies in Tamarindo can book tours that include transportation to and from Playa Grande, admission to the park and the guided tour. The whole package costs about US$45. If you don't have your own transportation, this is the best way to go.

The show kicks off anytime from 9pm to as late as 2am. You might only have to wait for 10 minutes before a turtle shows up, or you could be there for five hours. Bring a book or a deck of cards for entertainment. It could be a very long night – but well worth it.

PLAYA TAMARINDO

Well, they don't call it Tamagringo for nothing. Tamarindo's perennial status as Costa Rica's top surf and party destination has made it the first and last stop for legions of tourists. It stands to reason, then, that this is the most developed beach on the peninsula with no shortage of hotels, bars and restaurants. Yet, despite its party-town reputation, Tamarindo is more than just drinking and surfing. It forms a part of the Parque Nacional Marino Las Baulas de Guanacaste, and the beach retains an allure for kids and adults alike. And Tamarindo's central location makes it a great base for exploring the northern peninsula.

Amazingly, there's no gas station here. For that, you'll have to drive 15 paved kilometers to Huacas, hang a right and go up the hill. The gas station is 4km ahead, on the right.

 Activities

SPORTFISHING

There are more than 30 fishing outfitters offering a variety of tour packages. Prices vary wildly depending on boat size, but expect to pay at least US$250 for a half-day tour.

SURFING

Like a gift from the surf gods, Tamarindo is often at its best when neighboring Playa Grande is flat. The most popular wave is a medium-sized right that breaks directly in front of the Tamarindo Diria hotel. The waters here are full of virgin surfers learning to pop up.

Kelly's Surf Shop   Surfing
(☎2653-1355; www.kellysurfshop.com; board rental per day/week US$20/120, group/private lesson US$50/90; ⊙9am-6pm) One of the very best surf shops in the area, it has a terrific selection of newish boards that it rents by the day or week. Premium boards cost a bit more.

Matos Surf Shop   Surfing
(☎2653-0734, 2653-0845; www.matossurfshop.com; Sunrise Commercial Center; ⊙8am-8pm, lessons 9-11am & 2-4pm) The granddaddy of local surf shops is owned by a Uruguayan DJ-photo-entrepreneur. It offer lessons, and rents and sells boards at the cheapest rates in town. There is another outlet in Playa Grande.

OTHER ACTIVITIES

Agua Rica Diving Center   Diving
(☎2653-2023, 2653-0094; www.aguarica.net; 2 tanks US$80-105) Italian-owned Agua Rica Diving Center, the area's scuba-diving expert, offers snorkeling and an assortment of dives in the Catalina Islands, including diving certification classes and trips to the Cocos Islands.

Blue Trailz   Surfing, Cycling
(☎2653-1705; www.bluetrailz.com; board rental per day US$15, group/private surf lesson US$45/80, bike rental per day US$20, bike tours US$55-75; ⊙7am-7pm Mon-Sat) Blue Trailz offers surf lessons, board rental and other more comprehensive surf packages. Lodging is at the same-named hostel, just across the street from the beach. This is also the local expert on mountain biking, distance cycling, bike tours and repairs.

Ser Om Shanti Yoga Studio   Yoga
(☎8346-8005; www.seryogastudio.com; US$15) There's a full schedule of daily yoga, tai chi and Pilates mat classes at this airy and bright studio on the top floor of Tamarindo plaza.

 Sleeping

Villa Amarilla   B&B $$
(☎2653-0038; www.hotelvillaamarilla.com; d incl breakfast from US$100; P❄🛜🐾) It's hard to resist this fun and funky yellow house backing up to the beach, its facade painted with happy animals and colorful fish. Newly renovated rooms feature flat-screen TVs, tile floors, comfy beds and whimsical paint jobs. An open-air massage area is on the grounds. The whole place is laid-back and lovely.

Playa Tamarindo

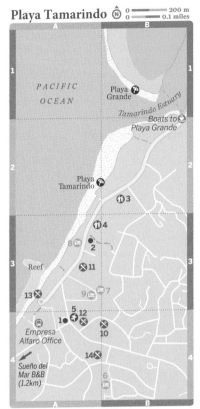

Playa Tamarindo Ⓝ 0 ▬▬▬ 200 m / 0 ▬▬▬ 0.1 miles

PACIFIC OCEAN

Playa Grande

Tamarindo Estuary

Boats to Playa Grande

Playa Tamarindo

Reef

Empresa Alfaro Office

Sueño del Mar B&B (1.2km)

in an otherwise frenzied town – it's also one of the best deals around. Beautiful modern villas with private hot showers, hammocks and patios surround a solar-heated pool and tropical garden, while larger apartments are equipped with full kitchens, making them ideal for families.

Hotel Luamey
Boutique Hotel $$$

(✆2653-1510; www.hotelluamey.com; d from US$135; 🅿❄🛜🏊) This brand new boutique hotel is simply exquisite. Spacious cabana suites are decorated in earth tones, with dark wood furnishings, stone showers and private patios. Service is super accommodating. Free use of surfboards. The on-site restaurant is highly recommended for breakfast or any other meal.

Sueño del Mar B&B
B&B $$$

(✆2653-0284; www.sueno-del-mar.com; d US$195, casitas US$220-295; 🅿❄@🛜🏊) This exquisite B&B on Playa Langosta is set in a stunning faux-dobe Spanish-style *posada*. The six rooms have four-poster beds, artfully placed crafts and open-air garden showers, while the romantic honeymoon suite has a wraparound window with sea views. There's private beach access beyond the pool and tropical garden, and a priceless, pervasive atmosphere of seclusion and beauty. No children allowed.

Casa Bambora
Apartment $$

(✆2653-0124; www.casabambora.com; studio US$70-110; 🅿❄🛜🏊) These five slick studio apartments include fully-equipped kitchens, private balconies and room to sleep three. They are perfectly practical and simply stylish, but enhanced by delicious ocean views. An outdoor kitchen and bar overlook the waterfall-soaked swimming pool. But the best scenery is from the 4th-floor sundeck, which offers 360 degrees of mountains, sea and sky.

Villas Macondo
Hotel $$

(✆2653-0812; www.villasmacondo.com; s/d/tr US$42/52/62, with air-con US$67/77/88, apt US$110-150; 🅿❄@🛜🏊) Although it's only 200m from the beach, this German-run establishment is an oasis of serenity

🍴 Eating

Green Papaya   Taquería $

(📞2652-0863; mains US$5-10; 🕐9am-10pm Tue-Sun; ❄🍴🚻) Swing on up to the bar for a breakfast burrito or pull up a tree-stump stool to sample the terrific tacos at this fantastic new addition. The mahi-mahi tacos are perfection in a tortilla, while non-meat-eaters will appreciate the multiple veggie options. You'll go loco for the Coco Loco dessert. Everything is funky, fresh and friendly – don't miss it.

El Casado del Carro   Costa Rican $

(casados US$4-6; 🕐noon-2pm) Doña Rosa has been delivering top-notch *casados* from her late-model Toyota hatchback for more than a decade. Her devoted Tico following lines up daily at noon, and she generally sells out by 2pm. You'll get your meal in a Styrofoam platter (nobody's *perfecto*), usually with yucca or plantains, rice, chicken or beef, and some tasty black beans.

Nogui's   Seafood $$

(📞2653-0029; mains US$9-22; 🕐11am-11pm) A fish shack with Mediterranean charm, this fabulously romantic, wooden and stained-glass, tin-roofed gem on the beach flaunts local seafood. Make a dinner reservation, or get sloshed at the bar with the occasionally rowdy (but not too rowdy) regulars.

Dragonfly Bar & Grill   Asian $$$

(📞2653-1506; www.dragonflybarandgrill.com; mains US$15-22; 🕐6-11pm Mon-Sat; P🛜🍴) Dragonfly is a local favorite, not just for its refined menu, but also for its lovely tiki-bar atmosphere. The chic open-air dining room has twinkling lights and lanterns, with a subtle dragonfly motif throughout. The menu has an Asian bent, featuring delights such as panko-crusted pork loin and Thai-style crispy fish cakes. The desserts are divine.

Seasons by Shlomy   Mediterranean $$$

(📞8368-6983; www.seasonstamarindo.com; Hotel Arco Iris; mains US$15-19; 🕐6-10pm Mon-Sat) Don't leave town without eating here. Israeli chef Shlomy offers a short list of carefully selected and perfectly prepared dishes. Depending on the availability of ingredients, you might start with sashimi, grilled octopus or spicy tuna tartare. Follow up with seared tuna in a honey chili marinade or filet mignon in red wine sauce.

ℹ Getting There & Away

Air

The airstrip is 3km north of town; a hotel bus is usually on hand to pick up arriving passengers, or you can take a taxi. During high season, Sansa has two daily flights to and from San José (one way US$114), while NatureAir

Riding on the beach, Playa Tamarindo
STEVE SMITH/GETTY IMAGES ©

(one way US$141) has three. Some flights transit through Liberia.

Bus

Buses for San José depart from the Empresas Alfaro office behind the Babylon bar. Other buses depart across the street from Zullymar Hostel.

Liberia US$3; 2½ hours; departs 12 times per day from 4:30am to 6pm.

San José US$11; 5½ hours; departs three times from 5:30am to 2:15pm. Alternatively, take a bus to Liberia and change for frequent buses to the capital.

Santa Cruz US$2; 1½ hours; departs 10 times per day from 5:45am to 10pm.

Car & Taxi

By car from Liberia, take Hwy 21 to Belén, then Hwy 155 via Huacas to Tamarindo. If you're coming from the southern peninsula, drive just past Santa Cruz, turn left on the paved road to 27 de Abril, then northwest on a decent dirt road to Tamarindo. These routes are well signed. A taxi costs about US$30 to or from Santa Cruz, and US$50 to or from Liberia.

PLAYAS AVELLANAS & NEGRA

About 15km south of Tamarindo, these popular surfing beaches were made famous in the surf classic *Endless Summer II,* and Playa Avellanas is an absolutely stunning pristine sweep of pale golden sand. Backed by mangroves in the center and two gentle hillsides on either end, there's plenty of room for surfers and sunbathers to have an intimate experience even when there are lots of heads in town. The wave here is decent for beginners and intermediate surfers.

Little Hawaii is the powerful and open-faced right featured in *Endless Summer II,* while **Beach Break** barrels at low tide. Playa Negra is also undeniably romantic, though the sand is a bit darker and the beach is broken up by rocky outcrops.

Surfing Península de Nicoya Don't Miss List

RECOMMENDATIONS FROM DEBBIE ZEC, PROFESSIONAL SURFER AND OPERATOR OF DOMINICAL SURF LESSONS

1 MAL PAÍS & SANTA TERESA

This long, sweeping stretch of coastline is one of the best places to surf along the peninsula. The waves are very consistent, and they have great shape during high and low tide. But there are some random rocks, so watch out! When you need a break from the crashing surf, the towns are full of hip restaurants and cafes.

2 PLAYA GRANDE

Famous for nesting sea turtles, this beach is also well known for the sheer number of waves that break along nearly 7km of coast. Tubes are easy to find here, so bring your board and get ready for some seriously hollow riding. In the evening, you can venture out onto the beach with the park rangers to witness newly hatched baby turtles scamper out to sea.

3 PLAYA TAMARINDO

The number-one party destination in the Nicoya is this tourist town, which has a well-developed infrastructure of resort hotels, sophisticated dining options and plenty of bars and dance clubs. The waves here are fairly tame, but they're great for beginners who need some time to practice standing up.

4 NOSARA AREA

Attracting both intermediate and advanced surfers, this collection of great wilderness beaches has simply amazing waves that are renowned for their beautiful shape and regular consistency. With so many different breaks to choose from, you could easily spend several days exploring the Nosara area without ever having to surf the same place twice.

🛏 Sleeping & Eating

PLAYA AVELLANAS

Casa Surf
Guesthouse $

(☎2652-9075; www.casa-surf.com; per person US$15; P) 🌿 Casa Surf is looking tropically teriffic after a recent makeover, featuring an all-new bamboo exterior and palm thatch roof. Inside, you'll find simple, clean rooms that share a bathroom and kitchen. The casa offers an excellent-value room, board and board option, which includes two meals daily and surfboard rental. Delicious filling meals (US$5 to US$7) are designed to sate hungry surfers. Also available: bike rental, book exchange, community guitar.

Las Avellanas Villas
Apartment $$

(☎2652-9212, 8821-3681; www.lasavellanasvillas.com; d/tr/q US$90/100/110; P❄❀🛜) Thoughtfully designed, these five stunning casitas are oases of tranquility and balance, with private terraces, polished concrete floors, indoor greenery, open-air showers, and large windows streaming with natural light. Full kitchens make this option perfect for families or groups. The grounds are about 800m from the beach.

Mauna Loa Surf Resort
Bungalow $$

(☎2652-9012; www.hotelmaunaloa.com; d/tr/q from US$90/113/136; P❄❀🛜🏊) This hip Italian-run spot offers a secure location that's a straight shot to the beach. Paths lead from the gorgeous pool area through a lush garden to attractive pod-like bungalows with pastel-brushed walls, and swaying hammocks on terraces.

Cabinas Las Olas
Bungalow $$

(☎2652-9315; www.cabinaslasolas.co.cr; s/d/tr US$90/100/110, air-con US$20; P❄❀🛜🏊) 🌿 Set on spacious grounds that are bursting with cocobolo, laurel and guanacaste trees, these 10 airy bungalows have shiny woodwork, stone detailing and private decks. There's an open-air restaurant and a surf shop where you can rent boards and kayaks. A purpose-built boardwalk leads 200m through the mangroves (good for wildlife) and down to the beach.

Lola's on the Beach
Cafe $

(☎2652-9097; meals US$8-13; ⊙10am-5pm Tue-Sun) If the water is looking glassy, this

Playa Avellanas

hauntingly stylish beach cafe is the place to hang out. Minimalist slanted wood chairs are planted in the sand beneath thatched umbrellas. A tree-stump bar overlooks an open kitchen, where the beachy cuisine is tops. In case you're wondering, Lola was an enormous and lovable pig, aka the queen of Avellanas. She has since passed, but her legacy lives on in 'little' Lolita!

PLAYA NEGRA

Café Playa Negra Guesthouse **$$**
(☎ 2652-9351; www.cafeplayanegra.com; s/d/tr/q US$45/65/80/90; P ❄ ☎ ☻) These stylish, minimalist digs upstairs from the cafe have polished concrete floors and elevated beds dressed with colorful bedspreads and other artistic touches. There's a groovy shared deck with plush lounges and an inviting swimming pool. The downstairs cafe (mains US$7 to US$13) serves delectable sandwiches, *ceviche* and super fresh seafood.

Hotel Playa Negra Bungalow **$$$**
(☎ 2652-9134; www.playanegra.com; s/d/tr/q from US$102/113/124/136; P ❄ ☎ ☻) This sweet compound of circular *rancho* bungalows is steps from a world-class reef break. The traditional thatch-roof *ranchos* have high ceilings and breezy porches. Higher-priced suites are further from the beach, but they have air-con, private decks with hammocks and outdoor showers. Restaurant and surf shop onsite.

Villa Deevena International
(☎ 2653-2328; www.villadeevena.com; ⊙7am-9pm) Like a beautiful sunset or a Da Vinci painting, the French chef at this boutique, family-run villa property off the main Negra drag is spoken about in hushed tones by local *extranjeros* up and down the coast. His creations include mahi baked with preserved lemon and rosemary, slow braised shortrib, duck confit and lobster ravioli. Patrick Jamon, the former executive chef at LA's famed Regency Club where he cooked for Fortune 500 CEOs and a handful of presidents, even makes his own goat cheese from his herd in the hills.

Getting There & Away

There is no public transportation to/from Playa Tamarindo to Playas Avellanas or Negra, though surf camps often organize trips. The only bus connections are heading inland, via Santa Cruz (US$1.50, 1½ hours, two daily). The schedule seems to change frequently, so inquire locally.

NOSARA AREA

Nosara is a cocktail of international surf culture, stunning back-road topography, jungled microclimates, moneyed expat mayhem and yoga bliss. Three stunning beaches are stitched together by a network of swerving, rutted earth roads that meander over coastal hills and kiss the coast just west of the small Tico village of Nosara. From the south, the first beach you'll come to is **Playa Garza**, still a sleepy Tico fishing village with an arc of pale brown sand and headlands on either side of the rippling bay.

But there's a reason the majority of visitors descend on **Playa Guiones**. It's an easygoing place for surfers, surf dogs and surf babies – you might just see unattended strollers lodged in the wet sand at low tide.

Playa Pelada, just north, is rough and rugged, dry and less endowed with surfers and luxury, which could be viewed as a luxury in itself. Things feel at once a touch spookier and more profound in Pelada. This beach lacks surf, so it's wonderful for children.

Activities

SURFING

Coconut Harry's Surfing
(☎ 2682-0574; www.coconutharrys.com; board rental per day US$15-20, lessons US$45; ⊙7am-5pm) At the main intersection in Guiones, this surf shop offers private lessons, board rental, and stand-up paddle rental, and they even rent snorkels and fins. Conveniently, there's a second location near the main break at Playa Guiones.

Detour:
Refugio Nacional de Fauna Silvestre Ostional

This 248-hectare coastal refuge extends from Punta India in the north to Playa Guiones in the south, and includes the beaches of Playa Nosara and Playa Ostional. It was created in 1992 to protect the *arribadas,* or mass nestings of the olive ridley sea turtles, which occur from July to November with a peak from August to October. Along with Playa Nancite in Parque Nacional Santa Rosa, Ostional is one of two main nesting grounds for this turtle in Costa Rica.

The olive ridley is one of the smallest species of sea turtle, typically weighing around 45kg. Although they are endangered, there are a few beaches in the world where ridleys nest in large groups that can number in the thousands. Scientists believe that this behavior is an attempt to overwhelm predators.

Rocky Punta India at the northwestern end of the refuge has tide pools that abound with marine life, such as sea anemone, urchin and starfish. Along the beach, thousands of almost transparent ghost crabs go about their business, as do the bright-red Sally Lightfoot crabs. The sparse vegetation behind the beach consists mainly of deciduous trees and is home to iguanas, crabs, howler monkeys, coatis and many birds. Near the southeastern edge of the refuge is a small mangrove swamp where there is good bird-watching.

Juan Surfo's Surf Shop Surfing
(2682-1081; www.surfocostarica.com; board rental per day US$15-20, lessons per hour US$45; 8am-6pm) Juan Surfo is a highly recommended surf teacher. His shop offers lessons and rents boards, as well as organizing transportation and tours. Located on the northern loop road, 200m from the beach. Juan also rents rooms at the nearby Surf Lodge.

YOGA

Nosara Yoga Institute Yoga
(2682-0071; www.nosarayoga.com; per class US$15) This well-known yoga institute hosts a wide variety of drop-in classes (six daily during high season) ranging from Vinyasa to restorative to core strengthening. If you want more, they also hold workshops, retreats and instructor training courses for beginner and advanced students in a beautiful jungle setting. In the hills near Playa Guiones.

Pilates Nosara Yoga
(8663-7354; www.pilatesnosara.com; per person US$10) Set in the Heart of Guiones Wellness Center, this studio offers Pilates mat and reformer classes (six daily during the high season). Teacher training and retreats are also held here.

TURTLE-WATCHING

Most hotels in the area can arrange guided tours to Refugio Nacional de Fauna Silvestre Ostional, where you can watch the *arribadas* (mass arrivals) of olive ridley turtles.

OTHER ACTIVITIES

Miss Sky Outdoor
(2682-0969; www.missskycanopytour.com; adult/child 5-12 US$65/45; office 7am-5pm) Miss Sky has brought a canopy tour to Nosara, with a total length of 11,000m above a pristine, private reserve. The zip lines don't go from platform to platform but from mountainside to mountainside, and have double cables for added safety. Your top speed will be about 45km/h.

Tours leave twice daily, at 8am and 2pm. The morning tour is slightly longer.

Reserva Biológica Nosara   Hiking

(2682-0035; www.lagarta.com; US$6, guided nature walks US$15) The private 35-hectare reserve behind the Lagarta Lodge has trails leading through a mangrove wetland down to the river (five minutes) and beach (10 minutes). This is a great spot for bird-watching, and there's a good chance you'll see some reptiles as well (look up in the trees as there are occasionally boa constrictors here). Non-guests can visit the reserve for self-guided hikes or guided nature walks.

Tica Massage   Spa

(2682-0096; www.ticamassage.com; US$35-65; 9am-6pm) After a hard day of surfing, treat yourself to a (totally legit) spa treatment at Tica Massage, in the Heart of Guiones Wellness Center. Services cater especially to surfers; or opt for a foot massage, a face massage or an invigorating 'Sea Glow' massage.

Sleeping & Eating

PLAYA GUIONES

Kaya Sol   Hostel $$

(2682-1459; www.kayasol.com; dm US$18, d US$50-120;) The heart of this sprawling surfer-and-seeker retreat is the dorm-style accommodations. The shared bathrooms are spotless and the pool, with waterfall shower, is perfect for cooling off. There are also a few rooms and private cabins, some of which have kitchenettes. The on-site restaurant/bar is fun and tasty, though it can be noisy at night.

Gilded Iguana   Hotel $$

(hotel 2682-0450, restaurant 2682-0259; www.thegildediguana.com; r with/without air-con from US$85/57, ste US$85-113;) Down the second access road to Guiones, this long-standing hotel for anglers and surfers has well-furnished rooms with tile floors, big windows and shared terraces. The cheaper rooms are close to the bar and tend to be noisy. The tasty restaurant (mains US$9 to US$14) serves generous platters of fish tacos, fajitas and seafood specials, and the attached bar is a popular

Local dish of black beans and fish, Nosara

gringo hangout, with live music on Tuesday and Friday nights.

Living Hotel & Spa
Boutique Hotel **$$$**

(☎2682-5201; www.livinghotelnosara.com; room incl breakfast with/without bathroom US$108/86; P ✳ @ 🛜 🏊) Relax amid the simplicity and serenity of this tropical paradise. Pristine white rooms have tile floors, shined wood ceilings and pretty stencilled walls. Tropical gardens surround the sparkling swimming pool, with plenty of communal space in the thatchroof *rancho*. Located on the north beach access road.

Beach Dog Café
Cafe **$**

(☎2682-1293; mains US$6-10, dinner mains US$12-15; ⏰7am-3pm daily, also to 10pm Wed & Sat; P 🛜 🐕) Just steps from the beach, this groovy cafe is decadent and delicious. Try banana bread French toast for breakfast, or uber-popular fish tacos for lunch. Dinner is only a couple of nights a week, but they occasionally host live music and show movies on the beach.

Robin's Cafe & Ice Cream
Cafe **$**

(☎2682-0617; www.robinsicecream.com; mains US$5-8; ⏰8am-5pm Mon-Sat, 10am-4pm Sun; 🛜 🐕) Perfectly suited to the health-conscious yogis and surfers who live in and visit Nosara. You'll see Robin working the kitchen, preparing a welcome menu of sweet and savory crepes, tempting wraps, and sandwiches on homemade, whole-wheat focaccias. If you must indulge your sweet tooth, the ice cream is homemade and sublime.

Taco! Taco!
Taquería **$**

(☎2682-0574; tacos US$4-8; ⏰11am-4pm; 🐕 🛒) Every beach town needs an open-air *taquería* where surfers and beach bums can get a quick fix. In Nosara, it's Taco! Taco!, right on the main road into town. They do tacos and only tacos, stuffed with slow-cooked meat, fresh fish or grilled veggies, and topped with savory salsas and delectable guacamole. This place has earned its exclamation points.

Marlin Bill's
Seafood, Burgers **$$**

(☎2682-0458; meals US$11-25; ⏰11am-10pm Mon-Sat) Across the main road from the Guiones swirl, this is one of the few restaurants with views of the ocean. The casual, open-air dining room is a perfect place to feast on grilled tuna, *ceviche* and other fresh seafood. Bill is famous for his burgers, so if you are hankering for the taste of home, he's your man.

PLAYA PELADA

Refugio del Sol
Guesthouse **$$**

(☎8825-9365, 2682-0287; www.refugiodelsol.net; s/d US$35/55, d with kitchen US$65; P 🛜) A short stroll from the sand, this rustic lodge is decked out with ceramic tiled floors, beamed ceilings, wood furnishings, candles and lanterns, and other soulful touches that

Sunset, Playa Pelada
ROB FRANCIS/GETTY IMAGES ©

make it feel like home. Rooms open onto a wide L-shaped patio with hammocks. The gorgeous young owners make tasty Italian food for guests every night, and are generous of heart.

Lagarta Lodge
Lodge $$

(☎ 2682-0035; www.lagarta.com; r s/d/tr/q US$85/90/96/102, ste s/d/tr/q US$120/125/130/136, air-con US$10; P ✱ @ ☎ ✖) At the northern end of Pelada, a road dead-ends at this 12-room lodge, a recommended choice set high on a steep hill above a 50-hectare reserve (bird-watching and wildlife-spotting are good here). Large rooms have high ceilings, stucco walls and private patios, while suites take advantage of floor-to-ceiling windows and extra living space. The panoramas are priceless.

La Luna
International $$

(☎ 2682-0122; dishes US$9-24; ⊙11am-11pm Mon-Fri, 8am-11pm Sat & Sun) Located on the beach, this trendy restaurant-bar has cushy couches right on the sand, perfect for sunset drinks. The interior is equally appealing, with soaring ceilings, a gorgeous hardwood bar and walls adorned with work by local artists. Asian and Mediterranean flourishes round out the eclectic menu, and the views (and cocktails) are intoxicating. Call ahead for reservations.

Getting There & Away

Air
NatureAir has two daily flights to and from San José for about US$103 one way.

Bus
Local buses depart from the *pulpería* (corner grocery store) by the soccer field. Traroc buses depart for Nicoya (US$2, two hours, five daily). Empresas Alfaro buses going to San José (US$9, six hours) depart from the pharmacy by the soccer field at 2:45pm.

Car
From Nicoya, a paved road leads toward Playa Sámara. About 5km before Sámara (signed), a windy, bumpy (and, in the dry season, dusty) dirt road leads to Nosara village (4WD recommended). Ask around before trying this in the rainy season, when Río Nosara becomes impassable.

PLAYA SÁMARA

Is Sámara the black hole of happiness? That's what more than one expat has said after stopping here on vacation and never leaving. And perhaps it is more than the sum of its parts? Because on the surface it's just an easy-to-navigate beach town with barefoot, three-star appeal, and a crescent-shaped strip of pale-gray sand spanning two rocky headlands, where the sea is calm and beautiful. Not spectacular, just safe, mellow, reasonably developed, easily navigable on foot and accessible by public transportation. Not surprisingly, you'll find it's popular with vacationing Tico and foreign families and backpackers, who enjoy Sámara's palpable ease and tranquility. But be careful, the longer you stay the less you'll want to leave.

If you've got some extra time and a 4WD, explore the hidden beaches north of Sámara, such as Playa Barrigona, equally famous for its pristine beach as for its celebrity resident, Mel Gibson.

Activities

Pato Surf School
Surfing

(☎ 8761-4738; www.patossurfingsamara.com; board rental per day US$15, lessons US$25-35) Set right on the beach, Pato offers inexpensive and quality board rental, and beginner surf instruction. Pay for a lesson and get free board rental for five days! Also on offer: stand-up paddle rental and lessons; kayak rental and tours; and snorkel gear. Plus, massage on the beach and occasional beach yoga. What else do you want?

Wing Nuts
Outdoors

(☎ 2656-0153; www.wingnutscanopy.com; adult/child US$60/40; ⊙tours 8am, 9am, noon & 1pm) One entrepreneurial family found a way to preserve their beautiful, wild patch of dry tropical forest: by setting up a small-scale canopy tour. Family-owned and professionally run, this 10-platform operation is unique for its personal approach, as groups max out at 10 people. The price includes transportation from your hotel in Sámara.

Detour:
Islita Area

The coast southeast of Playa Carrillo remains one of the peninsula's most isolated and wonderful stretches of coastline, mainly because much of it is inaccessible and lacking in accommodations.

There are a few small breaks in front of the Hotel Punta Islita, where you'll find a gorgeous cove punctuated with that evocative wave-thrashed boulder that is Punta Islita. At high tide the beach narrows, but at low tide it is wide and as romantic as those vistas from above. Another good beach and point break lies north of Punta Islita at **Playa Camaronal** – officially known as **Refugio Nacional de Vida Silvestre Camaronal** (⏱8am-6pm) – a charcoal gray stretch of sand strewn with driftwood and sheltered by two headlands. Nearby hotels and tour operators can make arrangements for nighttime turtle tours here.

Also worth a visit is the pretty little town of Islita, home to the **Museo Islita** (⏱8am-4pm Mon-Sat), an imaginative contemporary art house crusted with mosaic murals, and featuring carvings and paintings that adorn everything from houses to tree trunks. The Hotel Punta Islita channels funding into the local community, resulting in this museum as well as a partnership with the **Ara Project** (www.thearaproject.org), a local NGO dedicated to the conservation of Costa Rica's two species of macaw: the Great Green Macaw and the Scarlet Macaw. Thanks to the hotel's donation, the Ara Project has opened a new breeding center in Islita, as well as an education and viewing center, Lapa Lookout, where guests can learn more.

Flying Crocodile   Scenic Flights
(☎2656-8048; www.flying-crocodile.com; flights 20/30/60min US$110/150/230, lessons per hour US$230) About 6km north of Sámara in Playa Buenavista, the Flying Crocodile offers ultralight flights and lessons.

Sleeping

Tico Adventure Lodge   Lodge $$
(☎2656-0628; www.ticoadventurelodge.com; tw/d/q US$57/68/84; P✳🛜🏊) The US owners are proud of the fact that they built this lodge without cutting down a single tree, and they have every reason to be – it's stunning. Nine double rooms and several larger apartments are surrounded by lush vegetation and old-growth trees. There's an outdoor kitchen and cookout area for communal use, as well as an on-site massage studio.

Sámara Palm Lodge   Guesthouse $$
(☎2656-1169; www.samarapalmlodge.com; d US$60-80; P✳🛜🏊) An inviting little lodge on the edge of town. Eight spotless rooms feature a tropical decor, with natural wood furniture, tile floors and bold colorful artwork. They face a lush garden and enticing swimming pool. Your hosts, Brigitte and Lothar, are delightful.

El Pequeño Gecko Verde   Bungalow $$$
(☎2656-1176; www.gecko-verde.com; r US$95-105, bungalow US$100-175; P✳🛜🏊) A hidden slice of heaven. Contemporary and beautifully decorated bungalows have beds dressed in plush linens, artisanal carvings on the walls, private terraces with hammocks and outdoor dining areas, plus our favorite feature – outdoor stone showers. Onsite amenities include a saltwater swimming pool with waterfall, lush gardens and a fabulous open-air restaurant and bar.

Sámara Tree House Inn
Bungalow $$$

(📞2656-0733; www.samaratreehouse.com; bungalows incl breakfast US$150; 🅿️❄️@🛜🏊) These five stilted tree houses for grownups are so appealing that you might not want to leave. Fully equipped kitchens have pots and pans hanging from driftwood racks, huge windows welcome light and breezes, and hammocks are hung underneath the raised bungalows. Four of the units face the beach. You can't get much closer than this.

 ## Eating

Ahora Sí
Vegetarian $

(📞2656-0741; ahorasi.isamara.co; mains US$5-11; 🕐noon-9pm; 🅿️🛜🍴) A Venetian-owned vegetarian restaurant and all-natural cocktail bar. They do smoothies with coconut milk; gnocchi with nutmeg, sage and smoked cheese; soy burgers and yucca fries; wok stir-fries; and thin-crust pizzas. All served on a lovingly decorated tiled patio. Required eating.

Lo Que Hay
Mexican $

(📞2656-0811; tacos US$2, meals from US$6; 🕐7am-late) This rocking beachside *taquería* and pub offers six delectable taco fillings (fish, chorizo, chicken, beef, pork, veggie). Try the grilled avocados stuffed with *pico de gallo* (tomato salsa). And even *sin* (without) tacos, it's a good time, as the bar crowd sips into the wee smalls.

Cafe Carola
Cafe $

(📞8994-9171; items US$4; 🕐7am-6:30pm daily, 7-10pm Wed & Fri; 🛜) Stop by this shady German bakery for breakfast, for sandwiches on homemade bread or for something to sate your sweet tooth. The book exchange, board games and strong espresso drinks complete the picture. This friendly place is also open for live music on Wednesday nights and Chinese food on Friday nights.

Gusto Beach
International $$

(📞2656-0252; mains US$9-17; 🕐9am-11pm; 🅿️🛜) Good food, great location. Enjoy pastas, salads and seafood, as well as phenomenal smoothies and creative cocktails, all while watching the action on the beach. If you care to linger, there are lounge chairs on the sand, lockers and beach volleyball.

Poolside, Hotel Punta Islita

ALBERTO COTO/GETTY IMAGES ©

Getting There & Away

The beach lies about 35km southwest of Nicoya on a paved road. No flights were operating out of the Sámara airport (PLD) at research time.

Bus

Empresas Alfaro has a bus to San José (US$8, five hours) that departs at 4am and 8am. All buses depart from the main intersection just south of Entre Dos Aguas guesthouse. Buy your San José bus tickets at the Alfaro office behind Bazar d'Liss on the main intersection in town.

MONTEZUMA

Montezuma is an immediately endearing beach town that demands you abandon the car to stroll, swim and, if you are willing to stroll even further, surf. The warm and wild ocean and that remnant, ever-audible jungle has helped this rocky nook cultivate an inviting, boho vibe. Typical tourist offerings such as canopy tours do a brisk trade here, but you'll also bump up against Montezuma's internationally inflected, artsy-rootsy beach culture in yoga classes, volunteer corps, veggie-friendly dining rooms and neo-Rastas hawking uplifting herbs. No wonder locals lovingly call this town 'Montefuma.' It's not perfect. The lodging is particularly poor value, and the eateries can be that way too (though there are some absolute gems). But in this barefoot *pueblo,* which unfurls along several kilometers of rugged coastline, you're never far from the rhythm and sound of the sea, and that is a beautiful thing.

Sights & Activities

Picture-perfect white-sand beaches are strung along the coast, separated by small rocky headlands, offering great beachcombing and ideal tidepool contemplation. Unfortunately, there are strong rip tides, so inquire locally before going for a swim.

The beaches in front of the town are nice enough, but the best beach is just north of Cocolores restaurant, where the sand is powdery and sheltered from big swells. This is your glorious sun-soaked

crash pad, and the further northeast you walk the more solitude you'll find. The water's shade of teal is immediately nourishing, the temperature is perfect and fish are abundant.

During low tide, the best snorkeling is at **Playa Las Manchas**, 1km west of downtown.

Montezuma Gardens   Gardens
(✆8888-4200, 2642-1317; www.montezum-agardens.com; adult/student/child US$8/6/4; ⊙8am-4pm) About 1km south of town, alongside the waterfall trail, you can take a tour through this lush *mariposario* (butterfly garden) and nursery where the mysterious metamorphoses occur. You'll learn about the life cycles and benefits of a dozen local species, of which you'll see many colorful varieties. There's also a B&B here (rooms US$57 to US$80).

Playa Grande   Beach
About 7km north of town, Playa Grande is the best surf beach in the area. It's a 3km-plus stretch of waves and sand, which doesn't get too crowded as it requires a 30-minute hike to get here. But what a hike it is, wandering along between the turquoise waters of the Pacific and the lush greenery of the Montezuma Biological Reserve.

Young Vision Surf School   Surfing
(✆8669-6835; www.youngvisiontest.net76.net; lessons from US$40) Manny and Alvaro get rave reviews for their knowledge, enthusiasm and patience with new surfers of all ages. Daily lessons include two hours of instruction, the use of a surfboard and rash guard, and fresh fruits.

Montezuma Yoga   Yoga
(✆8704-1632; www.montezumayoga.com; per person US$14; ⊙classes 8:30am Mon-Fri, 6pm Fri-Sun) Anusara-inspired instruction, which pairs Iyengar alignment principles with a Vinyasa flow, is available in a gorgeous studio kissed by ocean breezes, lit by paper lanterns and sheltered by a peaked tin roof. On the grounds of Hotel Los Mangos.

Montezuma

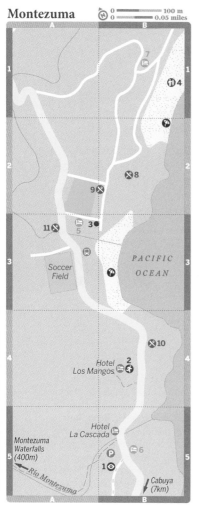

sweet stone lodge built into a lush inlet of remnant jungle, just a few steps from the beach. The upstairs 'suites' have high palm-beamed ceilings, wood furnishings, and new tile throughout. The cheaper downstairs rooms are not all that, but they all have access to a lovely pool area (with kiddie pool), an open-air *rancho* and shady grounds with abundant wildlife.

El Sano Banano   Boutique Hotel **$$**
(📞2642-0638; d US$86; 🅿❄@📶❄) A well-run boutique hotel in the center of town. Although its many businesses take up an entire city block, it has just 12 prim and comfortable rooms. The attached restaurant has appetizing baked goods and an inviting terrace on the main drag. It's also worth showing up in the evening when the restaurant shows nightly films in the garden out back.

Hotel Amor de Mar   B&B **$$$**
(📞2642-0262; www.amordemar.com; d with/without ocean view US$135/102, villas from US$278; 🅿📶) A lovable, German-owned B&B with 11 unique rooms, replete with exquisite touches like timber-framed mirrors, organic lanterns, and rocking chairs on a terrace laced with fishing netting and dotted with hundreds of potted plants. Then there's the palm-dappled lawn that rolls out to the tide pools and the Pacific beyond. They also have two exquisite private beach villas.

Sun Trails   Outdoors
(📞2642-0808; www.montezumatraveladventures.com; US$40; ⊙9am-3pm) After you've flown down nine zip lines, this 2.5-hour canopy tour winds up with a hike down – rather than up – to the waterfalls; bring your swimsuit. Book at its office in town.

 Sleeping

Luz de Mono   Lodge **$$**
(📞2642-0090; www.luzdemono.com; standard/ste incl breakfast US$75/90; 🅿📶❄) A

TRAVELSTOCK44 TRAVELSTOCK44/GETTY IMAGES ©

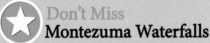

Don't Miss
Montezuma Waterfalls

A 40-minute river hike south of Montezuma takes you to a set of three scenic waterfalls. The main attraction is to climb the second set of falls and jump in.

The first waterfall has a good swimming hole, but it's shallow and rocky and unsafe for diving. From here, continue on the well-marked trail that leads around and up to the second set of falls. These falls offer a good clean 10m leap into deep water. To reach the jumping point, follow the trail up the side of the hill until you reach the diving area. Do not attempt to scale the falls; this is exactly how several people have died here. From this point, the trail continues up the hill to the third and last set of falls. These are not safe for jumping; however, there's a rope swing that will drop you right over the deeper part of the swimming hole (just be sure to let go on the outswing!). A lot of travelers enjoy the thrill, but indulge at your own risk.

As you head south past Hotel La Cascada, there's a parking area, then take the trail to the right just after the bridge.

NEED TO KNOW
Parking US$2

Ylang-Ylang Beach Resort
Resort $$$

(✆2642-0636, in USA 888-795-8494; www.ylangylangresort.com; standard/ste/bungalow incl breakfast & dinner US$237/288/322; ❋🛜🏊) Walk 15 minutes north along the beach to this lush four-star property,

complete with beautifully appointed rooms and bungalows, a palm-fringed swimming pool, yoga center, gourmet organic restaurant and spa. The decor is lovely and tropical, with tile floors, stenciled walls and colorful tapestries. All accommodations have outdoor terraces facing the glorious sea. You can't actually drive here, though staff will pick you up in their custom beach cruisers from El Sano Banano.

Eating

Orgánico   Organic $
(mains US$7-11; 8am-9pm;) When they say 'pure food made with love,' they mean it – this healthy cafe turns out vegetarian and vegan dishes such as spicy Thai burgers, a *sopa azteca* with tofu, burritos, falafel, smoothies and other meat-free treats you can feel good about. But they do meat dishes, like spaghetti Bolognese, too. Whaddaya want? They're Italian. There's live music almost nightly, including an open mic on Monday nights.

Playa de los
Artistas   International $$
(2642-0920; www.playamontezuma.net/ playadelosartistas.htm; mains US$9-13; 5-9pm Mon-Fri, noon-9pm Sat) Most romantic dinner ever. If you're lucky, you'll snag one of the tree-trunk tables under the palms. The interior tables – covered by a bamboo roof but open to sea breezes – are also inviting. The international menu with heavy Mediterranean influences changes daily depending on locally available ingredients, though you can always count on fresh seafood roasted in the wood oven. The service is flawless, the cooking is innovative and delicious, and the setting is downright dreamy. Cash only (back to reality).

Puggo's   Middle Eastern $$
(2642-0308; mains US$9-20; noon-11pm) A locally beloved restaurant decorated like a bedouin tent that specializes in Middle Eastern cuisine, including falafel, hummus, kebabs and aromatic fish, which they dress in imported spices and herbs and roast whole. Cap it off with a strong cup of Turkish coffee.

Cocolores   International $$
(2642-0348; mains US$9-22; 5-10pm Tue-Sun) Set on a beachside terrace lit with lanterns, Cocolores is one of Montezuma's top spots for an upscale dinner. The wide-ranging menu includes curries, pasta, fajitas and steaks, all prepared and served with careful attention to delicious details. Prices aren't cheap but portions are ample.

Getting There & Away

Boat
A fast passenger ferry connects Montezuma to Jacó in an hour. At US$40 or so, it's not cheap, but it'll save you a day's worth of travel. Boats depart at 9:30am daily and the price includes van transfer from the beach to the Jacó bus terminal. Book in advance from any tour operator. Dress appropriately; you will get wet.

Bus
Buses depart Montezuma from the sandy lot on the beach, across from the soccer field. Buy tickets directly from the driver. To get to Mal País and Santa Teresa, go to Cóbano and change buses.

Cabo Blanco via Cabuya US$1.50; 45 minutes; departs 8:15am, 10:15am, 12:15pm and 4:15pm.

Paquera, via Cóbano US$3; two hours; departs 5:30am, 8am, 10am, noon, 2pm and 4pm.

San José US$14; five hours; departs 6:20am and 2:20pm.

Car & Taxi
During the rainy season the stretch of road between Cóbano and Montezuma is likely to require a 4WD. In the village itself, parking can be a problem, though it's easy enough to walk everywhere.

A 4WD taxi can take you to Mal País (US$70) or Cóbano (US$12).

Montezuma Expeditions (www.montezuma expeditions.com) Operates private shuttles to San José (US$50), La Fortuna (US$55), Monteverde (US$55), Jacó, (US$55), Manuel Antonio (US$60), Dominical (US$70), Tamarindo (US$45), Sámara (US$45) and Liberia (US$55).

RESERVA NATURAL ABSOLUTA CABO BLANCO

Just 11km south of Montezuma is Costa Rica's oldest protected wilderness area. Cabo Blanco comprises 12 sq km of land and 17 sq km of surrounding ocean, and includes the entire southern tip of the Península de Nicoya. The moist microclimate on the tip of the peninsula fosters the growth of evergreen forests, which are unique when compared with the dry tropical forests typical of Nicoya. The park also encompasses a number of pristine white-sand beaches and offshore islands that are favored nesting areas for various bird species.

The park was originally established by a Danish–Swedish couple, the late Karen Mogensen and Olof Nicolas Wessberg, who settled in Montezuma in the 1950s and were among the first conservationists in Costa Rica. In 1960 the couple was distraught when they discovered that sections of Cabo Blanco had been clear-cut. At the time, the Costa Rican government was primarily focused on the agricultural development of the country, and had not yet formulated its modern-day conservation policy. Karen and Nicolas, as he was known, were instrumental in convincing the government to establish a national park system, which eventually led to the creation of the Cabo Blanco reserve in 1963. The couple continued to fight for increased conservation of ecologically rich areas, but, tragically, Olof was murdered in 1975 during a campaign in the Península de Osa. Karen continued their work until her death in 1994, and today they are buried in the Reserva Absoluta Nicolás Wessberg, the site of their original homestead.

Cabo Blanco is called an 'absolute' nature reserve because prior to the late 1980s visitors were not permitted. Even though the name hasn't changed, a limited number of trails have been opened to visitors, but the reserve remains closed on Monday and Tuesday to minimize environmental impact.

Nesting booby seabird, Reserva Natural Absoluta Cabo Blanco

ℹ️ Getting There & Away

Buses (US$1.50, 45 minutes) depart from the park entrance for Montezuma at 7am, 9am, 11am and 3pm. A taxi from Montezuma to the park costs about US$16.

During dry season, you can drive (4WD required) for 7km from Cabuya to Mal País via the stunningly scenic Star Mountain Rd.

MAL PAÍS & SANTA TERESA

Get ready for tasty waves, creative kitchens and babes in board shorts and bikinis, because the southwestern corner of Península de Nicoya has all that and more. Which is why it's become one of Costa Rica's most life-affirming destinations. Here, the sea is alive with wildlife and is almost perfect when it comes to shape, color and temperature. The hills are dotted with stylish boutique sleeps and sneaky good kitchens run by the occasional runaway, top-shelf chef. Sure, there is a growing ribbon of mostly expat development on the coastline, but the hills are lush and that road is still rutted earth (even if it is intermittently sealed with aromatic vats of molasses). The entire area unfurls along one coastal road that rambles from Santa Teresa in the north through Playa Carmen, the area's commercial heartbeat, then terminating in the fishing hamlet of Mal País. The whole region is collectively known as Mal País.

🐾 Activities

Surfing is the be-all and end-all for most visitors to Mal País, but the beautiful beach stretches north and south for kilometers on end, and many accommodations can arrange horseback-riding tours and fishing trips. Or you could find the fishing harbor in Mal País and arrange your own fishing tour. It does help to speak some Spanish, however.

SURFING

The following beaches are listed from north to south.

❤️ If You Like…
Parks & Reserves

If you like Reserva Absoluta Cabo Blanco, we think you'll like these other parks and reserves on the Península de Nicoya:

1 **PARQUE NACIONAL BARRA HONDA CAVERNS**
(☎ 2659-1091, 2659-1551; park admission adult/child US$10/1; guided tour per person US$26; ⏱ trails 8am-4pm, caverns 8am-1pm) Best in the dry season, you can go spelunking in the limestone caves of this underground wonderland.

2 **REFUGIO NACIONAL DE VIDA SILVESTRE CURÚ**
(☎ 2641-0100; www.curuwildliferefuge.com; day fee adult/child 3-11/child 2 & under US$10/5/free; ⏱ 7am-3pm) Hike, kayak, snorkel, ride horseback or simply sunbathe in this tiny park that encompasses beaches, dry tropical forest and mangrove swamp.

3 **RESERVA BIOLÓGICA NOSARA**
(☎ 2682-0035; www.lagarta.com; US$6, guided nature walks US$15) The private 35-hectare reserve behind the Lagarta Lodge has trails leading through a mangrove wetland down to the river and beach – a great spot for bird-watching.

About 8km north of the Playa Carmen intersection, **Playa Manzanillo** is a combination of sand and rock that's best surfed when the tide is rising and there's an offshore wind.

The most famous break in the area is at **Playa Santa Teresa**, and it's fast and powerful. This beach can be surfed at virtually any time of day, though be cautious as there are scattered rocks. To get here take the lane just north of La Lora Amarilla from the main road.

Playa Carmen, downhill from the main intersection, is a good beach break that can also be surfed anytime. The beach is wide and sandy and curls into successive coves, so it makes good beachcombing and swimming terrain too.

Detour:
Playa Cocolito & El Chorro Waterfall

Here's your chance to see a waterfall crashing down a cliff, straight onto the rocks and into the ocean. And yes, it is as spectacular as it sounds. El Chorro Waterfall is the pièce de résistance of Playa Cocolito, which is itself pretty irresistible. The waters here are a dreamy, irridescent azure, with pink rocky cliffs creating two inviting swimming areas. It's far enough away from the action that you are likely to have the place to yourself.

It's a two-hour, 12km hike from Montezuma: leave at sunrise to spot plenty of wildlife along the way. Alternatively, this is a popular destination for horseback riding.

The entire area is saturated with surf shops, and competition has kept prices low. This is a good place to pick up an inexpensive board, and you can probably get most of your money back if you sell it elsewhere.

Al Chile Surf Shop
Surfing

(☎2640-0959; www.alchilesurfshop.com; board rental per day US$10, lessons per person US$40-45) 'Al Chile' is a slang phrase that means something like 'For real!' As in 'In one lesson you'll be riding the white water – *al chile!*' The charming husband–wife team here guarantees it. If you don't want a lesson, they will still rent you a top-notch board. And if you're bringing your own board, check out the custom surfboard art by local surfer-artist William Borges.

Freedom Ride SUP
Surfing

(☎2640-0521; www.sup-costarica.com; rental half-/full day US$25/35, lessons per person

US$50; ⊙9am-6pm) A stand-up paddle (SUP) place with sharp, English-speaking management, set in Mal País proper. It offers half- and full-day rentals, as well as SUP lessons and tours. Lessons should be arranged in advance.

YOGA
Casa Zen
Yoga

(☎2640-0523; www.zencostarica.com; per person US$9) Offers two or three classes daily, in a lovely 2nd-story, open-air studio, surrounded by trees. Most of the classes are a Hatha-inspired Vinyasa flow, but there's also a more relaxing flow class, cardio fit and other styles. Multi-class packs available.

Sleeping & Eating

SANTA TERESA
Horizon Yoga Hotel
Hotel $$$

(☎2640-0524; www.horizon-yogahotel.com; d US$120-140, q US$210; ⓟ❄️📶🏊) Replete with fountains and profound beauty, this stunning terraced property on the Santa Teresa hillside offers barefoot elegance at its best. There is a range of rooms, including family-friendly villas with private pools. A better choice is the stilted bamboo bungalows, which have decks with hammocks and massive 180-degree ocean views.

Canaima Chill House
Apartment $$$

(☎2640-0410; www.hotel-canaima-chill-house. com; d US$100-130; ⓟ📶🏊) A 'chill house' is an apt desciptor for this eight-room boutique eco chic hotel. Super stylish suites have breezy indoor-outdoor living areas, awesome hanging bamboo beds and loads of natural materials (such as stone grotto showers). Guests share the Jacuzzi and plunge pool off the sunken pillow lounge. It's set in the hills, 500m from the main road, so you'll want wheels.

Florblanca
Villas $$$

(☎2640-0232; www.florblanca.com; villas incl breakfast US$350-800; ⓟ❄️@🏊) Truly in a class of its own, these 11 romantic villas are scattered around 3 hectares of land next to a pristine white-sand beach. Indoor–outdoor spaces are flooded with natural light and replete with design details, such as an open-air bathroom and sunken indoor–outdoor living area. Complimentary yoga and Pilates classes are offered, as are free use of bikes, surfboards and snorkeling equipment. The tour desk is innovative and will create personalized and adventurous itineraries (think: spear fishing and lobster diving) you won't find elsewhere. The sensational restaurant, Nectar (mains US$11 to US$24), is open to the public and is highly recommended for its innovative, seasonal, farm-fresh Latin American cuisine. If they have it, order the seared sesame-crusted tuna drizzled in jalapeño-ponzu sauce. Treatments at their Spa Bambu are addictive and open to the public, as well. Children under 13 are not allowed.

Brisas Del Mar   Seafood $$
(☎ 2640-0941; www.buenosairesmalpais.com; mains US$14-18; ⏰ 8-11am & 4-10pm Tue-Sun; P ⛵) It's worth the steep climb for sensational views and delectable seafood at the poolside patio restaurant at the Hotel Buenos Aires. Begin with a specialty cocktail as you peruse the day's menu written on the blackboard. Look for fresh *fruits de mer* prepared with international influences, such as chipotle lime-marinated tuna with roasted-tomato salsa and jalapeño cilantro cream. Brisas del Mar is open for breakfast too.

Koji's   Japanese $$$
(☎ 2640-0815; www.santa-teresa.com/kojis; sushi US$5-10; ⏰ 5:30-9:30pm Wed-Sun) Koji Hyodo's sushi shack in nearby Playa Hermosa is a twinkling beacon of fresh raw excellence. The atmosphere and service are superior, of course, but his food is a higher truth. The grilled octopus is barely fried and sprinkled with sea salt; and there's a sweet crunch to his lobster sashimi, sliced trace-paper thin and sprinkled with fresh ginger.

PLAYA CARMEN

Frank's Place   Hotel $$
(☎ 2640-0096; www.franksplacecr.com; standard s/d US$55/75, superior s/d US$95/115; P ❄ @ 🛜 🏊) Coming into town from Cóbano the first place you'll see is this historic surfer outpost. But Frank has

Surfing, Playa Carmen

grown up, and this is no longer the backpackers' paradise it once was. The rooms are plain but clean and comfortable (all include breakfast). The location has its advantages: not the least, the road is paved here so it's not nearly as dusty as elsewhere in town.

Casa Azul   Guesthouse $$

(☎2640-0379; www.hotelcasaazul.com; r with/without ocean view US$125/60, casita US$150, ste US$400; [P][🛜][♨]) You can't get much closer to the waves than this fabulous electric-blue house, looming over the garden, pool and beach. Sharing a communal kitchenette and an outdoor barbecue, the three downstairs rooms are attractive with ceramic-tile floors, wrought-iron beds and plenty of light. The secluded garden *casita* has a private patio with sea views.

Pizzeria Playa Carmen   Pizza $

(☎2640-0110; mains US$8-23; ⏱11am-9pm) Playa Carmen's most conspicuous pizza joint is this splashy restaurant right on the *playa*, which makes it ideal for sundowners. The tasty pizza is cooked in the wood-fired oven and beer is cheap.

MAL PAÍS

The Place   Boutique Hotel $$

(☎2640-0001; www.theplacemalpais.com; d/bungalow incl breakfast US$69/135; [P][❄][🛜][♨]) A waterfall-fed pool is surrounded by cushy blood-red lounge chairs and day beds at this Euro-chic boutique hotel. Attractive tile rooms are draped in linens, but it's absolutely worth it to splurge on the more expensive bungalows. Set amid tropical gardens, each one is creatively and uniquely decorated according to a different theme.

Moana Lodge   Boutique Hotel $$$

(☎2640-0230, toll-free in USA 888-865-8032; www.moanalodge.com; r standard/deluxe US$99/135, ste US$235-260) A simply stunning boutique property etched into the wooded hillside above Mal País. Standard rooms are all-wood garden cottages, decked out with African art, and close to the pool and reception. Make the climb to the junior suites for 180-degree views of the coast, as well as wood floors throughout, rain showers inside and outside, a wet bar and sliding glass door entry. The top-shelf **Papaya Lounge** (☎2640-0230; tapas US$6-9; ⏱7:30-10am & 5-10pm) shares that stunning perch.

Scarlet macaw
PAUL SOUDERS/GETTY IMAGES ©

Mary's Restaurant

International, Organic **$**

(8348-1285; www.maryscostarica.com; mains US$7-17; 5:30-10pm Thu-Tue) At the far end of Mal País village, this unassuming, open-air restaurant has polished concrete floor, wood oven, pool table and chalkboard menu. It offers delicious wood-fired pizzas, homemade bacon and sausage, grilled seafood, sashimi tasting plates and fresh produce straight from the farm. It's all fabulous. Its secret? Using only fresh, organic ingredients from local farms and fishermen.

Getting There & Around

All buses begin and end at Ginger Café, 100m south of Cuesta Arriba hostel; you can flag the bus down anywhere along the road up to Frank's Place, at which point buses turn left and head inland toward Cóbano.

A direct bus from Mal País to San José via the Paquera ferry departs at 6am and 2pm (US$13, six hours). Local buses to Cóbano (US$2, 45 minutes) depart at 7am and noon.

A taxi to or from Cóbano costs approximately US$32. Taxis between Mal País, Playa el Carmen and Santa Teresa range from US$4 to US$8. A taxi to the ferry in Paquera is US$55.

Montezuma Expeditions (2642-0919; www.montezumaexpeditions.com; Centro Comercial Playa El Carmen) organizes shuttle-van transfers to San José, Tamarindo and Sámara (US$50); Jacó, La Fortuna, Liberia and Monteverde (US$50); Manuel Antonio (US$60); and Dominical (US$70).

Central Pacific Coast

Beaches, wildlife and rainforests: this is Costa Rica in miniature.

Stretching from the rough-and-ready port city of Puntarenas to the tiny town of Uvita on the shores of Bahía Drake, the central Pacific coast is brimming with killer surfing, a suite of excellent national parks, and miles of coastline where visitors spot migrating whales and pods of dolphins. With so much biodiversity packed into a small geographic area, it offers a taste of the whole country.

Given its proximity to San José and its well-developed system of paved roads, the region has traditionally served as a weekend getaway for city folk fleeing for the beaches – and boasts plentiful animals and activities to keep kids entertained for weeks on end.

Jacó (p250)

Central Pacific Coast

Esparza

Barranca

PUNTARENAS

Chacarita

Ferry

Isla
San
Lucas

Playa
Doña Ana

Boca Barranca

Mata de
Limón

Puerto
Caldera

Playa Tivives
& Valor

Paquera

Curú

Isla Tortuga

Golfo de Nicoya

Punta
Leona

Playa
Herradura

2 Jacó

Playa
Hermosa

Refugio Nacional de
Playa Hermosa

Playa
Esterillos

Playa
Palo Seco

Isla
Damas

ALAJUEL

Alajuela

Atenas

San
Mateo

Orotina

Zona Protectora
Cerro Atenas

Turu Ba Ri
Tropical Park

San Pablo de
Turrubares

Ciudad
Colón

Reserva
Indígen
Quitirris

Santiago de
Puriscal

Río Candela

Parque
Nacional
Carara

Tárcoles

Bijagual

Río Tárcoles

San José

Río P

Puntarena

Valle de Parrita

Parrita

PACIFIC

OCEAN

1 Manuel Antonio Area

2 Jacó

3 Dominical

4 Parque Nacional Marino
Ballena

5 Kayaking Around Uvita

N

0   40 km
0   20 miles

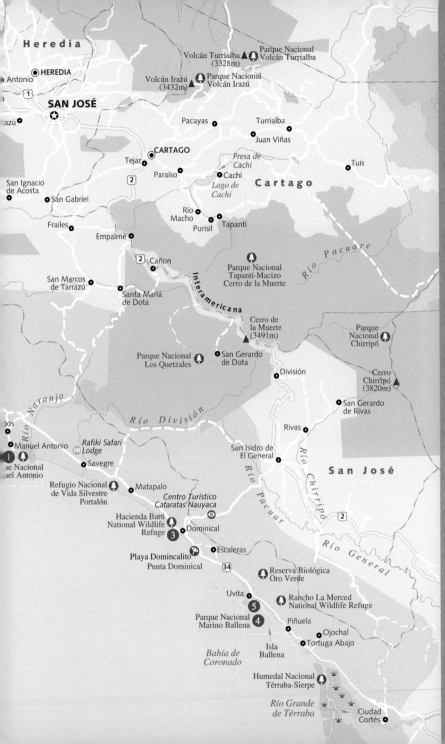

Central Pacific Coast Highlights

Manuel Antonio Area

Pristine beaches, luscious rainforests and an incredible variety of flora and fauna make it the complete nature experience. Where the jungle meets the ocean, you can follow well-designed trails in search of wildlife, lie on golden sands and swim in crystal-clear waters. (p261)

1

2 Jacó

The big city of the central Pacific coast, Jacó (p250) is loud and proud and unapologetic about it. Home to resident expats from around the world, Jacó has a cosmopolitan mix of restaurants, boutique hotels and a couple of large resorts. The beach is shaped by decent novice-friendly surf, and there's a laundry list of activities for anyone who can't sit still.

JODI JACOBSON/GETTY IMAGES ©

Dominical

3

A legendary surf town, Dominical (p265) has been drawing in legions of surfers for decades. Even if you happen to be a self-professed newbie, Dominical still warrants a visit as the incredibly laid-back ambiance of the beach is positively infectious. Don't be surprised if you get stuck here for much longer than you intended.

4

Parque Nacional Marino Ballena

This sleepy marine park (p270) lies at the extreme southern end of the central Pacific coast and has miles of empty, coconut-strewn beaches. Shaped like a giant whale's tale stretching out into the Pacific, Marino Ballena is a stunning slice of shore that harbors astonishing marine life including pods of dolphins and migrating whales.

5

Kayaking Around Uvita

The coastal area around Uvita (p269) has a great diversity of kayaking trips in a relatively small area. Visitors navigate challenging ocean waves and lazy mangrove channels... sometimes both in the same afternoon. The wildlife-spotting is good, but the rare treat is a visit to local ocean caves, where you can break for a picnic of fresh local fruit.

Central Pacific Coast's Best...

Wildlife

○ **Scarlet macaws** Catch a glimpse of red birds amid green trees in Parque Nacional Carara. (p250)

○ **Squirrel monkeys** Adorable little fur balls in **Parque Nacional Manuel Antonio**. (p261)

○ **Humpback whales** Migrating pods swim through **Parque Nacional Marino Ballena**. (p270)

○ **Tapir** Get off the tourist trail and onto the 'Path of the Tapir' at the **Hacienda Barú National Wildlife Refuge**. (p263)

Activities

○ **Surfing** A string of surf towns, including Playa Hermosa, make this region ideal for surfing. (p253)

○ **Canopy Tours** Zip-line your way through the lofty treetops along 'the Flight of the Toucan' at **Hacienda Barú National Wildlife Refuge**. (p263)

○ **Hiking** Navigate the easy trails of **Parque Nacional Manuel Antonio** to spot monkeys, macaws and lush tropical forests. (p261)

○ **Yoga** Get perfectly aligned with yoga and movement classes at Dominical's **Bamboo Yoga Play**. (p265)

Splurges

○ **Hotel Sí Como No** A family-friendly hotel with the government's highest rating for ecofriendliness. (p259)

○ **Arenas del Mar** This luxury ecoresort offers unmatched intimacy and excellent coast views. (p259)

○ **Docelunas** A teak-accented mountain retreat surrounded by virgin rainforest. (p252)

○ **Makanda by the Sea** With minimalist design and unmatched views, this tiny set of villas is a stunner. (p258)

Need to Know

Eats & Drinks

○ **Citrus** Mouthwatering Pan-Asian cuisine highlights the bounty of the Pacific Ocean. (p273)

○ **La Luna** Take in views of the Pacific and jungle over tapas or a romantic dinner. (p260)

○ **El Avión** Savor an ice-cold beer in the shadow of a 1954 Fairchild C-123. (p268)

○ **Exotica** French execution and cozy ambience make this Ojochal eatery a surprising delight. (p273)

ADVANCE PLANNING

○ **Two months before** Flights are packed in the high season, so book and pay for your ticket well ahead of time and reconfirm often.

○ **One month before** Because getting around the peninsula usually means a few rough roads, and the southern peninsula may require some river crossings, be sure to rent a 4WD vehicle as early as possible as they go quickly.

○ **One week before** Check the surf report so you can plan your destinations accordingly.

RESOURCES

○ **Quepolandia** (www.quepolandia.com) Quepos and Manuel Antonio news, resources and local tidbits.

GETTING AROUND

○ **Boat** The beach town of Montezuma on the tip of the Península de Nicoya is a quick boat ride away from Jacó.

○ **Bus** Intercity buses are frequent and cheap, which makes moving around a cinch.

○ **Car** The smoothly paved and well-signed coastal highway is conducive to self-driving.

BE FOREWARNED

○ **Prostitution** Jacó has a seedy underbelly at night, so be mindful of your surroundings and choose your nightlife venues with discretion.

○ **Petty theft** Opportunistic theft is too common on the well-trodden Central Pacific coast, but it's easily preventable. As anywhere in Costa Rica, never leave anything in your vehicle or unattended on the beach, and use common street sense elsewhere.

○ **Riptides** Currents here can be very strong, even in shallow waters. Ask locals for advice about when and where it's safe to swim.

ove left: Scarlet macaws; **Above right:** Beach Parque Nacional Manuel Antonio (p261)

(ABOVE LEFT) PAUL SOUDERS/GETTY IMAGES ©;
(ABOVE RIGHT) HOLGER METTE/GETTY IMAGES ©

Central Pacific Coast Itineraries

A newly paved coastal road invites an ideal road trip into less-developed areas that evoke the 'Old Costa Rica'. From a quick escape to a rambling escapade, the region holds all of Costa Rica's colorful charms.

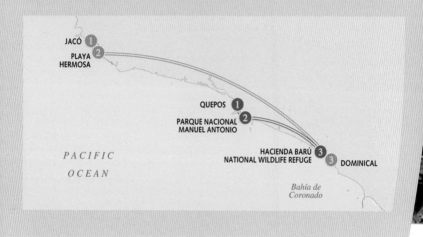

3 DAYS

QUEPOS TO HACIENDA BARÚ NATIONAL WILDLIFE REFUGE
MANUEL ANTONIO & BEYOND

It takes time to traverse the full length of the coast, though fortunately this itinerary will give you a quick but fulfilling taste of Pacific wonder. You can cruise this route with your own wheels or on public transportation, on the smoothly paved Costanera Sur between tropical ocean and jungle-clad coastal mountains.

Your first destination is the friendly, authentic Tico town of ❶ **Quepos** (p254), which has great restaurants, tons of services for travelers and a healthy nightlife. While it's worth a stop, the primary reason to visit is as the gateway for ❷ **Parque Nacional Manuel Antonio** (p261). One of

the country's top national parks, Manuel Antonio can be summed up with three words: beaches, rainforests and monkeys. The park has good hiking for families and some of the best swimming beaches in the Pacific. For more wildlife, take a guided hike through ❸ **Hacienda Barú National Wildlife Refuge** (p263), a small reserve that encompasses a range of tropical habitats and is part of a major biological corridor protecting a wide range of species.

SURFER'S PARADISE

5 DAYS

If you're looking to burn off some adrenaline, the central Pacific is home to a string of spectacular beach towns with fairly consistent year-round surf. Don't fret if you're not an expert and don't have your own board: there are plenty of shops where you can get geared up, and the surf schools are abundant. Even if the surf isn't up, there's still plenty of sun, sea and sand to enjoy.

With modest waves and a gentle beach break, ❶ **Jacó** (p250) is a great place to take surfing lessons; most instructors guarantee that they'll get you standing up. Whether you do or not, you'll still enjoy your evenings in the unofficial party capital of the Pacific coast. More-experienced surfers can test their skills a bit further south at ❷ **Playa Hermosa** (p253), where sharper curls and faster swells present a mighty challenge. Finally, sink into the laid-back charms of ❸ **Dominical** (p265), a true surfer's paradise, with its unpaved roads, budget-friendly lodgings, surf shops and open-air eateries.

Suspension bridge in Parque Nacional Manuel Antonio (p261)

LUCAS GILMAN/GETTY IMAGES ©

Discover
Central Pacific Coast

At a Glance

○ **Jacó** The regions's biggest town has a notorious party scene and great surf.

○ **Quepos** (p254) Gateway to the country's most popular national park, Manuel Antonio.

○ **Dominical** (p265) Learn to surf, surf, party, lather, rinse, repeat.

Relaxing in Quepos (p254)
KEVIN HATT/GETTY IMAGES ©

PARQUE NACIONAL CARARA

Straddling the transition between the dry forests of Costa Rica's northwest and the sodden rainforests of the southern Pacific lowlands, this national park is a biological melting pot of the two. Acacias intermingle with strangler figs, and cacti with deciduous kapok trees, creating hetergeneous habitats with a blend of wildlife to match. It's not the biggest, not the wildest and not the most beautiful, but the significance of this park cannot be understated. Surrounded by a sea of cultivation and livestock, it is one of the few areas in the transition zone where wildlife finds sanctuary. The park can be easily explored in half a day's expedition.

Carara is also the famed home to one of Costa Rica's most charismatic bird species, the scarlet macaw. While catching a glimpse of this tropical wonder is a rare proposition in most of the country, macaw sightings are common at Carara. And there are more than 400 other avian species flitting around the canopy, as well as Costa Rica's largest crocodiles in the waterways – best viewed from afar!

Any bus traveling between Puntarenas and Jacó can leave you at the park entrance. If you're driving, the entrance to Carara is right on the Costanera and clearly marked.

JACÓ

Few places in Costa Rica generate such divergent opinions and paradoxical realities as Jacó. Partying surfers, North American retirees and international developers laud it for its devil-may-care atmosphere, bustling streets and booming real-estate opportunities. Observant ecotourists, marginalized Ticos and loyalists of the 'old Costa Rica' absolutely despise the place for the *exact* same reasons.

While Jacó's lackadaisical charm is not for everyone, the surfing is excellent, the restaurants and bars are generally great and the nightlife can be a blast. It's impossible to deny Jaco's good side, which put it on the map in the first place: the sweeping beauty of the beach, the consistently fine surf and the lush tropical backdrop.

🏃 Activities

SURFING

Although the rainy season is considered best for Pacific coast surfing, Jacó is blessed with consistent year-round breaks. If you're looking to rent a board for the day, shop around as the better places will rent you a board for US$15 to US$20 for 24 hours.

OTHER ACTIVITIES

Discovery Horseback Tours Horse Riding
(☎ 8838-7550; www.horseridecostarica. com; rides from US$75) Nearby beach and rainforest rides are available through this highly recommended outfit, run by an English couple who offer an extremely high level of service and professionalism.

Kayak Jacó Kayaking
(☎ 2643-1233, 8869-7074; www.kayakjaco.com; tours from US$70) This reliable company facilitates kayaking and sea-canoeing trips that include snorkeling excursions to tropical islands, in a wide variety of customized day and multiday trips. Though it does have a presence at Playa

Agujas, 250m east of the beach, it's best to phone or email in advance.

🛏 Sleeping

AparHotel Vista Pacífico Hotel $$
(☎ 2643-3261; www.vistapacifico.com; d incl breakfast from US$68-121; P 🅿 @ 🛜 ☎) Located on the crest of a hill just north of Jacó (off Bulevar), this gem of a hotel is run by a warm young Canadian couple. Homey, comfortable rooms and suites with kitchen facilities come in a variety of configurations. Its favorable elevation offers not only panoramic views of the coastline and valley but also blessedly cool breezes.

Sonidos del Mar Guesthouse $$$
(☎ 2643-3912, 2643-3924; www.sonidos-delmar.com; Calle Hidalgo; houses US$250; P 🅿 @ 🛜 ☎) Set within a mature tropical garden, these guesthouses may be two of the most beautiful in Costa Rica. The design is impeccable, from the vaulted Nicaraguan hardwood ceilings to the hand-laid volcanic-rock and pebble showers. Owner Lauri is a skilled artist

Kayakers
DREAMPICTURES/GETTY IMAGES ©

Jacó

and a collector who has lovingly filled each room with original paintings, sculptures and indigenous crafts.

Docelunas
Hotel $$$

(☎2643-2211; www.docelunas.com; Costanera Sur; d/junior ste incl breakfast US$169/197; P ⊖ ✳ @ 🛜 ☲) Situated in the foothills across the highway, 'Twelve Moons' is a heavenly mountain retreat consisting of only 20 rooms sheltered in a pristine landscape of tropical rainforest. Each teak-accented room is uniquely decorated with original artwork, and the luxurious bathrooms feature double sinks and bathtubs. Yoga classes, offered regularly, are free with room rates.

Hotel Poseidon
Hotel $$$

(☎2643-1642; www.hotel-poseidon.com; Calle Bohío; d incl breakfast from US$107; P ✳ @ 🛜 ☲) It's hard to miss the huge Grecian wooden carvings that adorn the exterior of this small American-run hotel. On the inside, sparkling rooms are perfectly accented with stylish furniture and mosaic tiles, and include amenities like fridges and hair dryers. There's a pool with swim-up bar, a small Jacuzzi and an open-air restaurant serving some of the best food in Jacó.

Eating

Graffiti
International $$

(☎2643-1708; www.graffiticr.com; mains US$8-22; ⏱5-10pm Mon-Sat; 🖍) The decor is what you might expect from the name, and live music on weekends ups its game, but the spotlight here is fixed on the plate. Those in the know come for the famous cacao-and-coffee-encrusted filet mignon, macadamia-and-passionfruit catch of the day, decadent cheesecake and creative cocktails. Reservations are highly recommended.

Caliche's Wishbone
International $$

(☎2643-3406; Av Pastor Díaz; meals $9-18; ⏱noon-10pm Thu-Tue) Overseen by the charming Caliche, this has been a Jacó favorite for years and years. The eclectic menu includes pizzas, pitas, stuffed potatoes, pan-seared sea bass and tuna-sashimi salads, though its justifiable fame comes from the fact that everything is quite simply fresh, delicious and good value. It's south of Calle Bohío.

Lemon Zest
Fusion $$$

(☎ 2643-2591; www.lemonzestjaco.com; Av Pastor Díaz; mains US$10-30; ⏱ 5-10pm; ❄ 🛜 🖋) Chef Richard Lemon (a former instructor at Le Cordon Bleu Miami) wins many accolades for Jacó's most swish menu. The roster of upscale standards – Caribbean-style jerk pork chop; seared duck in blackberry sauce – might lack a creative concept, but they're carried out with due sophistication, accompanied by a well-matched wine list.

Drinking & Nightlife

Le Loft
Club

(☎ 2643-5846; Av Pastor Díaz; cover US$10; ⏱ 9pm-2am) The Loft is Jacó's sleekest nightlife venue, offering some much-needed urban sophistication. Live DJs spin essential mixes while the pretty people preen to be seen. There's a calendar of special events and a balcony perch for checking out the street life.

Getting There & Away

Air

NatureAir (www.natureair.com) and **Alfa Romeo Aero Taxi** (www.alfaromeoair.com) offer charter flights. Prices are dependent on the number of passengers, so it's best to try to organize a larger group if you're considering this option.

Boat

The jet-boat transfer service that connects Jacó to Montezuma is, far and away, the most efficient to connect the central Pacific coast to the Península de Nicoya. The journey across the Golfo de Nicoya only takes about an hour (compared to about seven hours overland), though at US$40 it's not cheap. Reservations are required and can be made at most tour operators in town.

Bus

Buses for San José stop at the Plaza Jacó mall, north of the center. The bus stop for other destinations is opposite the Más x Menos supermarket. (Stand in front of the supermarket if you're headed north; stand across the street if you're headed south.) The departure times listed here are approximate since buses originate in Puntarenas or Quepos.

Quepos US$2, 1½ hours, departs hourly from 6:30am to 2:30pm and 6pm and 7pm.

San José US$5, three hours, departs 5am, 7am, 9am, 11am, 1pm, 3pm and 5pm.

PLAYA HERMOSA

While newbies struggle to stand up on their boards in Jacó, a few kilometers south in Playa Hermosa seasoned veterans are thrashing their way across the faces of some monster waves. Regarded as one of the most consistent and powerful breaks in the whole country, Hermosa (Spanish for 'beautiful') serves up serious surf that commands the utmost respect. Still, even if you're not a pro, the vibe here is excellent, the surfers are chilled out and the beach lives up to its name.

Crocodile Bridge

If you're driving from Puntarenas or San José, pull over immediately after crossing the Río Tárcoles bridge, also known as Crocodile Bridge. Parking touts may also wave you down just short of the bridge. Either way, you can walk along the narrow pedestrian curbs to check out the sandbanks below. Chances are, you'll see as many as 30 truly ginormous basking crocodiles. Although they're visible year-round, the best time for viewing is low tide during the dry season. Binoculars will help a great deal.

Crocodiles this large are generally rare in Costa Rica as they've been hunted vigorously for their leather. However, the crocs are tolerated here as they feature prominently in a number of wildlife tours that depart from Tárcoles. And, of course, the crocs don't mind, as they're hand-fed virtually every day.

🛏 Sleeping & Eating

Tortuga del Mar
Lodge $$

(☎ 2643-7132; www.tortugadelmar.net; r US$89, studios from US$99; P ❄ @ 🛜 🐾) Top-end accommodations with a recession-proof midrange price tag, this newish lodge is sheltered amid shady grounds, and has just a handful of rooms housed in a two-story building. Tropical modern is the style, making excellent use of local hardwoods to construct lofty ceilings that catch every gust of the Pacific breezes.

Hermosa Beach Bungalows
Bungalow $$$

(☎ 2643-7190, 2643-1513; www.hermosabeach-bungalows.com; bungalows US$200-250) These attractive, two-bedroom bungalows on stilts are individually owned, but a third are managed by onsite concierge Twinka. Most are pet-friendly, and all have modern bathrooms, washers, dryers and balconies. Trimmed in bright, tropical colors, the bungalows surround a pool and community *rancho,* and the property faces a long stretch of beach 1km south of town.

Backyard Bar
Breakfast $

(☎ 2643-7011; meals US$5-10; ⏱ noon-late; 🛜) Backyard Bar's expansive menu reaches beyond the usual surfer fare, though the burritos are a good bet if you're in the mood for the usual. As the town's de facto nightspot, the Backyard Bar occasionally hosts live music, heavy pours at its nightly happy hour and a local surf contest every Saturday from 4pm until sunset. The property's adjacent hotel offers enticingly cushy rooms, if you don't mind the noise next door.

ℹ Getting There & Away

Located only 5km south of Jacó, Playa Hermosa can be accessed by any bus heading south from Jacó.

QUEPOS

Located just 7km from the entrance to Manuel Antonio, the small, busy town of Quepos serves as the gateway to the national park, as well as a convenient port of call for travelers in need of goods and services. Although the Manuel Antonio area was rapidly and irreversibly transformed following the ecotourism boom, Quepos has largely retained an authentic Tico feel, particularly when you get out of the middle of town. Exuding an ineffable charm absent from so much of the central Pacific, Quepos still has glimmers of traditional Latin America, even while being a heavily traveled stop on the tourist-packed gringo trail.

Activities

Titi Canopy Tours
Adventure Tour

(☎ 2777-3130; www.titi-canopytour.com; Costanera Sur; daytime/nighttime tours US$65/80; ⏱ tours 7:30am, 11am & 2:30pm) Offering zip-lining adventures during the day and

Beach, Quepos
MACDUFF EVERTON/GETTY IMAGES ©

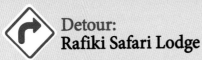

Detour:
Rafiki Safari Lodge

Nestled into the rainforest, with a prime spot right next to the Río Savegre, the **Rafiki Safari Lodge** (☎ 2777-5327, 2777-2250; www.rafikisafari.com; s/d/ste incl all meals US$189/327/420, child under 5yr free; Ⓟ @ 🛜 ♨) ✎ combines all the comforts of a hotel with the splendor of a jungle safari – and getting here is half the fun. The owners, South African expats who have lived in the area for years, have constructed 10 luxury tents on stilts equipped with modern bathroom, private porch and hydroelectric power. All units are screened in, allowing you to see and hear the rainforest without actually having creepy-crawlies in your bed. There's a spring-fed pool with a serious waterslide and ample opportunity for horseback riding, bird-watching (more than 350 species have been identified), hiking, white-water rafting and unplugging. And of course, South Africans are masters on the *braai* (barbecue), so you know that you'll eat well alongside other guests in the *rancho*-style restaurant. This place makes for a great three-day stay; it's too remote to warrant the transport for only one night, but guests exhaust all the activities on offer after three days.

The entrance to the lodge is located about 15km south of Quepos in the small town of Savegre. From here, a 4WD dirt road parallels the Río Savegre and leads 7km inland, past the towns of Silencio and Santo Domingo, to the lodge. However, if you don't have private transportation, the lodge can arrange all of your transfers with advance reservations. Word to the wise: bring your own flashlight to supplement the standard-issue loaner that comes with your room keys.

at night, this outfit has friendly, professional guides and a convenient location just outside of central Quepos (150m south of the hospital). Tour rates include drinks, snacks and local transportation; group discounts are available.

Oceans Unlimited
Diving

(Map p257; ☎ 2777-3171; www.scubadivingcostarica.com; 2-tank dive US$98) ✎ This shop takes its diving very seriously, and runs most of its excursions out to Isla Larga and Isla del Caño, which is south in Bahía Drake (connected via a two-hour bus trip). It also has a range of specialized PADI certifications, and regular environmental-awareness projects that make it stand out from the pack.

Quepos Sailfishing Charters
Fishing

(Map p257; ☎ 2777-2025, toll free in USA 800-603-0015; www.queposfishing.com) This Quepos-based outfitter gets good reviews from travelers and offers charters on a fleet of variously sized boats. Rates vary significantly depending on season, number of people and size of boat. It also offers packages that include accommodations and transfers.

H2O Adventures
Adventure Tour

(Rios Tropicales; Map p257; ☎ 2777-4092; www.h2ocr.com) The venerable Costa Rican rafting company Ríos Tropicales has a franchise in Quepos called H2O Adventures. Rates for Class II to IV rapids start at US$67 in low season. In summer they are US$82.

🛏 Sleeping

Hotel Sirena
Hotel $$

(Map p257; ☎ 2777-0572; www.lasirenahotel.com; s/d/tr incl breakfast from US$82/94/105; Ⓟ ❄ @ 🛜 ♨) This intimate boutique hotel is a welcome and warm addition to the Quepos scene, and is easily the best midrange option in town. The Sirena's whitewashed walls, blue trim and aromatherapy offer a slice of breezy Mediterranean serenity. In their rooms, guests enjoy crisp white linens, air-conditioning, cable and a minifridge. Rooms upstairs get much better light.

Hotel Villa Romántica — Hotel $$$

(Map p257; 2777-0037; www.villaroman-tica.com; s/d incl breakfast from US$77/111; P✱@🛜🏊) A short walk southeast from the town center brings you to this peaceful garden oasis, which is overflowing with verdant greens and tropical flowers; rooms are bright and open. If you're looking for a compromise between the convenience of staying in Quepos and the intimate proximity to nature found in Manuel Antonio, this is an excellent choice.

🍴 Eating

Tropical Sushi — Japanese $$

(Map p257; 2777-1710; meals US$10-27, all-you-can-eat sushi US$26; ⏱4-10:30pm) This is without doubt the best sushi on the central Pacific coast. Chef Fuji (originally from Japan, and a resident of Costa Rica for 15 years) serves up delicious sushi and other authentic Japanese cuisine in this cozy little spot. As he's the only one manning the kitchen, expect to have a leisurely dining experience.

Gran Inca — Peruvian $$

(Map p257; 2777-4347; mains US$7-15; ⏱5-10pm Tue-Sun) The no-frills look of this Peruvian-run spot belies the excellent food you'll find here. The menu encompasses a variety of traditional dishes, ranging from Peruvian-style *ceviche* to steak sautéed with peppers and onions. While the dishes might sound similar to Tico fare found everywhere, the flavors are lively and distinctive, and a welcome change of pace.

Escalofrío — Italian $$

(Map p257; 2777-1902; gelato $2, mains US$9-20; ⏱2:30-10:30pm Tue-Sun; 🛜) Gelato lovers should make a point of stopping here, to choose from more than 20 flavors of the heavenly stuff. This spacious alfresco restaurant may also be the only game in town on Sunday night during slow

season, a godsend especially if you enjoy wood-fired pizza, pasta and gnocchi.

Getting There & Away

Air

Both **NatureAir** (www.natureair.com) and **Sansa** (www.sansa.com) service Quepos. Prices vary according to season and availability, though you can expect around US$75 for a flight from San José or Liberia.

Bus

Jacó US$2.80, 1½ hours, 10 departures daily from 4:30am to 5:30pm.

San Isidro de El General, via Dominical US$4, three hours, departs 5:30am, 11:30am and 3:30pm.

San José (Tracopa) US$9, three hours, departs 4am, 6am, 7:30am, 9:30am, noon, 1pm, 2:30pm and 5pm.

Uvita, via Dominical US$8, two hours, departs 6:30am, 9:30am and 5:30pm.

QUEPOS TO MANUEL ANTONIO

From the Quepos waterfront, the road swings inland for 7km before reaching the beaches of Manuel Antonio Village and the entrance to the national park. This route, home to some of the region's best hotels and restaurants, passes over a number of hills awash with picturesque views of forested slopes leading down to the palm-fringed coastline.

If driving this winding road, be particularly aware of pedestrians, especially at night.

◎ Sights & Activities

Manuel Antonio Nature Park & Wildlife Refuge — Wildlife Reserve

(Map p257; 2777-0850; www.wildliferefugecr.com; adult/child US$15/8; ⏱8am-4pm; 🚻) Formerly known as Fincas Naturales, this private rainforest preserve and butterfly garden breeds about three dozen species of butterfly – a delicate population compared to the menagerie of lizards, reptiles and frogs that inspire gleefully grossed-out

Manuel Antonio Area

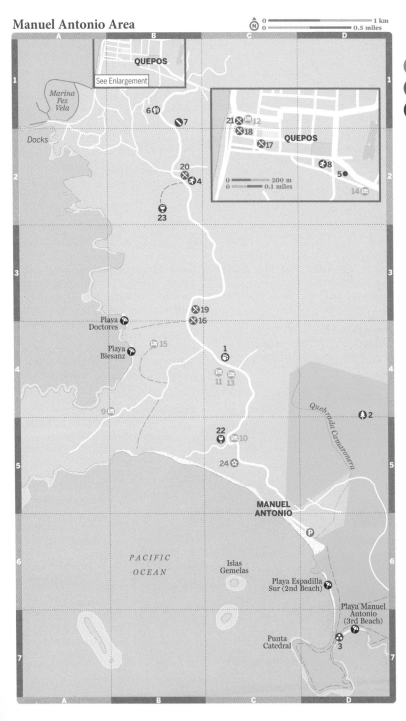

QUEPOS

See Enlargement

Marina
Pez
Vela

Docks

QUEPOS

Playa
Doctores

Playa
Biesanz

Quebrada Camaronera

**MANUEL
ANTONIO**

PACIFIC
OCEAN

Islas
Gemelas

Playa Espadilla
Sur (2nd Beach)

Playa Manuel
Antonio
(3rd Beach)

Punta
Catedral

Manuel Antonio Area

squeals from the little ones. A jungle night tour (US$39 for adults, US$29 for children) showcases the colorful local frogs and their songs.

Amigos del Río Adventure Tour
(Map p257; ☎ 2777-0082; www.adradventurepark.com; tours US$130; ⊙ tours depart 6:45am, 8:30am & 10:30am) Pack all of your canopy-tour jungle fantasies into one day on Amigos del Ríos's '10-in-One Adventure', featuring zip-lining, a Tarzan swing, rappelling down a waterfall and more. The seven-hour adventure tour includes a free transfer from the Quepos and Manuel Antonio area as well as breakfast and lunch. Amigos del Río is also a reliable outfit for white-water rafting trips.

Manuel Antonio Surf School Surfing
(MASS; Map p257; ☎ 2777-1955, 2777-4842; www.manuelantoniosurfschool.com; group lesson US$65) MASS offers friendly, safe and fun small-group lessons daily, lasting for three hours and with a three-to-one student-instructor ratio. Find its stand about 500m up the Manuel Antonio road south of Quepos.

Sleeping

Makanda by the Sea Villa $$$
(Map p257; ☎ 2777-0442; www.makanda.com; studios/villas incl breakfast from US$299/452; P ❄ @ 🛜 🌊)

Parque Nacional Manuel Antonio (p261)
SLOW IMAGES/GETTY IMAGES ©

Comprising just six villas and five studios, Makanda has an unmatched air of intimacy and complete privacy. Villa 1 (the largest) will take your breath away – one entire wall is open to the rainforest and the ocean. The other villas and studios are air-conditioned and enclosed, though they draw upon the same minimalistic, Eastern-infused design schemes.

Hotel Costa Verde   Hotel $$$

(Map p257; ☎2777-0584; www.costaverde.com; efficiency units/studios from US$130/168, Boeing 727 fuselage home US$565; P ✲ @ 🛜 🏊) The collection of comfortable rooms and studios at Costa Verde occupy a verdant setting frequented by troops of monkeys. Efficiency units incorporating teak trim and furnishings are attractively tiled and face the encroaching forest, while more expensive studios have full ocean views. But the most coveted accommodation is the airplane–tree house hybrid made out of a decommissioned Boeing 727 fuselage.

Arenas del Mar   Boutique Hotel $$$

(Map p257; ☎2777-2777; www.arenasdelmar.com; r incl breakfast US$350-825; P ✲ @ 🛜 🏊) ✿ This visually arresting hotel and resort complex is consistently shortlisted among Costa Rica's finest upscale hotels. Despite the extent and breadth of the grounds, there are only 40 rooms, which ensures an unmatched degree of personal service and privacy. It has won numerous ecotourism awards since its establishment and was designed to incorporate the beauty of the natural landscape.

Hotel Sí Como No   Hotel $$$

(Map p257; ☎2777-0777; www.sicomono.com; r US$260-328, child under 6yr free; P ✲ @ 🛜 🏊) ✿ The flawless design of this hotel is an example of how to build a resort while maintaining environmental sensibility. Ecofriendliness aside, the hotel is also gorgeous and packed full of family-friendly amenities. The rooms

Gay Guide to Manuel Antonio

For jet-setting gay and lesbian travelers the world over, Manuel Antonio has long been regarded as a dream destination. Homosexuality has been decriminalized in Costa Rica since the 1970s – a rarity in all-too-often machismo-fueled, conservative Central America – and a well-established gay scene blossomed in Manuel Antonio soon after. Gay and lesbian travelers will find that it's unlike any other destination in the country.

During the daylight hours, the epicenter of gay Manuel Antonio is the famous **La Playita**, a beach with a long history of nude sunbathing for gay men. Alas, the days when you could sun in the buff are gone, but La Playita still is widely regarded as a playful pick-up scene for gay men on the prowl.

A significant number of hotels in the Manuel Antonio area advertise themselves as being gay-friendly and even the ones that don't are unlikely to discriminate. But if you want to enjoy the freedom and peace of mind that comes with staying at exclusively gay accommodations, book a room at the gay-owned and operated **Hotel Villa Roca** (Map p257; 2777-1349; www.villaroca.com; d/apt incl breakfast from $113/192; P @), a collection of brightly whitewashed rooms and apartments situated around a central pool and sundeck.

While there are no exclusively gay restaurants and bars, there are a few with particularly good gay-oriented events. Check out the friendly **Bar Mogambo** (Map p257; 2777-6310; 4pm-midnight Tue-Sun) for happy hour, and the nightclub **Liquid** (Map p257; 2777-5158; 9pm-3am Tue-Sun) later in the evening.

themselves are accented by rich woods and bold splashes of tropical colors, and they feature enormous picture windows and sweeping balconies.

Eating & Drinking

Café Milagro Cafe $$
(Map p257; 2777-0794; www.cafemilagro.com; mains US$6-19; 7am-9:30pm; P) With a menu full of vibrant, refreshing delectables – like gazpacho, or salads tossed with mango and chayote squash in passionfruit dressing, or fish tacos with chunky guacamole, or banana-macadamia pancakes – this appealing cafe is worth a stop morning, noon or night. Like its sister cafe in Quepos, it also serves a mean cuppa joe.

Claro Que Sí Seafood $$
(Map p257; 2777-0777; Hotel Sí Como No; meals US$8-20) A casual, family-friendly restaurant that passes on pretension without sacrificing quality, Claro Que Sí proudly serves organic and locally sourced food items that are in line with the philosophy of its parent hotel, Sí Como No. Guilt-free meats and fish are expertly complemented with fresh produce, resulting in flavorful dishes typical of both the Pacific and Caribbean coasts.

Kapi Kapi Restaurant Fusion $$$
(Map p257; 2777-5049; www.restaurantekapikapi.com; meals US$15-40; 4-10pm) While there is some stiff competition for the title of best restaurant in the area, this Californian creation certainly raises the bar on both quality and class. The menu at Kapi Kapi (*kapi kapi* is a traditional greeting of the indigenous Maleku people) spans the globe from America to Asia. Pan-Asian–style seafood features prominently, brought to life with rich Continental-inspired sauces.

La Luna International $$$
(Map p257; 2777-9797; mains US$8-55; 7am-11pm;) Unpretentious, friendly

and first rate, La Luna makes a lovely spot for a special-occasion dinner, with a spectacular backdrop of jungle and ocean. An international menu offers everything from pizza to lobster tails, with a Tico-style twist – such as grouper baked en papillote, with plantain puree and coconut milk. Or enjoy the inexpensive tapas menu from 4pm to 6pm.

ⓘ Getting There & Away

A good number of visitors who stay in this area arrive by private or rented car. The public bus from Quepos will let you off anywhere along the road.

PARQUE NACIONAL MANUEL ANTONIO

A place of swaying palms and playful monkeys, spakling blue water and riotous tropical birds, **Parque Nacional Manuel Antonio** (Map p257; ☏ 2777-0644; park entrance US$10, parking US$3; ⌚ 7am-4pm Tue-Sun) embodies Costa Rica's postcard charms. It was declared a national park in 1972, preserving it (with just minutes to spare) from being bulldozed and razed to make room for a coastal development project. Although Manuel Antonio was enlarged to its present-day size of 19.83 sq km in 2000, it is still the country's smallest national park. Space remains at a premium, and as this is one of Central America's top tourist destinations, you're going to have to break free from the camera-clicking tour groups and actively seek out your own idyllic spot of sand.

That said, Manuel Antonio is absolutely stunning, and on a good day, at the right time, it's easy to convince yourself that

you've died and gone to a coconut-filled paradise. The park's clearly marked trail system winds through rainforest-backed tropical beaches and rocky headlands, and the views across the bay to the pristine outer islands are unforgettable. As if this wasn't enough, add an ubiquitous population of iguanas, howlers, capuchins, sloths and squirrel monkeys.

◉ Sights & Activities

HIKING & SWIMMING

After the park entrance, it's about a 30-minute hike to **Playa Espadilla Sur** and **Playa Manuel Antonio**, the park's idyllic beaches, which is where most people spend a good part of their time in the park. There will be numerous guides leading clusters of groups along the flat hike, so a bit of eavesdropping will provide solo shoestring travelers an informal lesson on the many birds, sloths and monkeys along the way. Eventually, the obvious, well-trodden trail veers right and through forest to an isthmus separating Playas

Parque Nacional Manuel Antonio
KATHRIN ZIEGLER/GETTY IMAGES ©

Monkey Business

There are a number of stands on the beach that cater to hungry tourists, though everything is exuberantly overpriced and of dubious quality. Plus, all the food scraps have negatively impacted the monkey population. Before you offer a monkey your scraps, consider the following risks to their health:

○ Monkeys are susceptible to bacteria transmitted from human hands.

○ Irregular feeding will lead to aggressive behavior as well as create a dangerous dependency (picnickers in Manuel Antonio suffer downright intimidating mobs of them sometimes).

○ Bananas are not their preferred food, and can cause serious digestive problems.

○ Increased exposure to humans facilitates illegal poaching as well as attacks from dogs.

It should go without saying: don't feed the monkeys. And, if you do happen to come across someone doing so, take the initiative and ask them politely to stop.

Espadilla Sur and Manuel Antonio. This is also where there's a park ranger station and information center (its hours are random, but we've yet to see it open, so be pleasantly surprised if it is staffed).

Geography fun fact: this isthmus is called a *tombolo* and was formed by the accumulation of sand between the mainland and the peninsula beyond, which was once an island. Along this bridge are the park's two amazing beaches, Playa Manuel Antonio, on the ocean side, and the slightly less visited (though occasionally rough) Playa Espadilla Sur, which faces Manuel Antonio Village. With their turquoise waters, shaded hideouts and continual aerial show of brown pelicans, these beaches are dreamy.

At its end, the isthmus widens into a rocky peninsula, with thick forest in the middle. Several informal trails lead down the peninsula to near the center of it, the **Punta Catedral**. If you bushwhack your way through, there are good views of the Pacific Ocean and various rocky islets that are bird reserves and form part of the national park. Brown boobies and pelicans nest on these islands.

At the western end of Playa Manuel Antonio you can see a semicircle of rocks

at low tide. Archaeologists believe that these were arranged by pre-Columbian indigenous people to function as a **turtle trap** (Map p257). (Turtles would swim in during high tide, but when they tried to swim out after the tide started receding, they'd be trapped by the wall.) The beach itself is an attractive one of white sand and is popular for swimming. It's protected and safer than the Espadilla beaches.

Beyond Playa Manuel Antonio, if visitors return towards the trail from the entrance of the park, the trail divides and leads deeper into the park. The lower trail is steep and slippery during the wet months and leads to the quiet **Playa Puerto Escondido**. This beach can be more or less completely covered by high tides, so be careful not to get cut off. The upper trail climbs to a **lookout** on a bluff overlooking Puerto Escondido and Punta Serrucho beyond – a stunning vista. Rangers reportedly limit the number of hikers on this trail to 45.

WILDLIFE-WATCHING

Increased tourist traffic has taken its toll on the park's wildlife, as animals are frequently driven away or – worse still – taught to scavenge for tourist handouts.

To its credit, the park service has reacted by closing the park on Monday and limiting the number of visitors to 600 per day during the week and 800 per day on weekends and holidays.

Even though visitors are funneled along the main access road, you should have no problem seeing animals here, even as you line up at the gate. White-faced **capuchins** are very used to people, and normally troops feed and interact within a short distance of visitors; they can be encountered anywhere along the main access road and around Playa Manuel Antonio.

 Tours

Hiring a guide costs US$25 per person for a two-hour tour. The only guides allowed in the park are members of Aguila (a local association governed by the park service), who have official ID badges, and recognized guides from tour agencies or hotels. This is to prevent visitors from getting ripped off and to ensure a good-quality guide. Aguila guides are well trained and multilingual (French-, German- or English-speaking guides can be requested).

Visitors report that hiring a guide virtually guarantees wildlife sightings.

 **Getting There & Away**

The entrance and exit to Parque Nacional Manuel Antonio lies in Manuel Antonio Village.

HACIENDA BARÚ NATIONAL WILDLIFE REFUGE

Located on the Pacific coast 3km northeast of Dominical on the road to Quepos, this **wildlife refuge** (2787-0003; www.haciendabaru.com; admission US$7, each extra day US$2, guided tours US$20-60) forms a key link in a major biological corridor called the 'Path of the Tapir'. It comprises more than 330 hectares of private and state-owned land that has been protected from hunting since 1976. The range of tropical habitats that may be observed here include pristine beaches, riverbanks, mangrove estuaries, wetlands, selectively logged forests, secondary forests, primary forests, tree plantations and pastures.

Capuchin monkey

CYRIELLE BEAUBOIS/GETTY IMAGES ©

Detour:
Matapalo

For years, Matapalo has been off most travelers' radar screens, though without good reason, as this palm-fringed, gray-sand beach has some truly awesome surf. With two river-mouth breaks generating some wicked waves, Matapalo is recommended for intermediate to advanced surfers who are comfortable dealing with rapidly changing conditions. As you might imagine, Matapalo is not the best beach for swimming as the transient rips here are about as notorious as they come.

Near the end of the road you'll find the friendly and laid-back **Rafiki Beach Camp** (☏2787-5014; www.rafikibeach.com; d/tents incl breakfast US$60/125; ☃), with luxury safari-style beachfront tents and cabinas. All of the tents are fully furnished and have electricity, tiled bathroom with hot shower, hand-painted sink and ocean views. The cabinas across the road are also beautifully decorated and come ornamented with fresh flowers. There's a pool overlooking the ocean, adjacent to a *rancho* (open-air structure) with communal kitchen.

Buses between Quepos and Dominical can drop you off at the turnoff to the village; from there it's a couple of kilometers to this off-the-beaten-track beach.

This diversity of habitat plus its key position in the Path of the Tapir account for the multitude of species that have been identified in Hacienda Barú. These include 351 birds, 69 mammals, 94 reptiles and amphibians, 87 butterflies and 158 species of tree, some of which are more than 8.5m in circumference. Ecological tourism provides this wildlife refuge with its only source of funds with which to maintain its protected status, so guests are assured that money spent here will be used to further the conservation of tropical rainforest.

There is an impressive number of guided tours on offer. You can experience the rainforest canopy in three ways – a platform 36m above the forest floor, tree climbing and a zip line called 'Flight of the Toucan'. In addition to the canopy activities, Hacienda Barú offers bird-watching tours, hiking tours, and two overnight camping tours in both tropical rainforest and lowland beach habitats. Hacienda Barú's naturalist guides come from local communities and have lived near the rainforest all of their lives. Even if you don't stop here for the sights, the onsite store carries an excellent selection of specialist titles for bird-watchers.

For people who prefer to explore the refuge by themselves, there are 7km of well-kept and marked self-guided trails, a bird-watching tower, 3km of pristine beach, an orchid garden and a butterfly garden.

The **Hacienda Barú Lodge** (d incl breakfast $96) consists of six clean, two-bedroom cabins located 350m from Barú beach. Guests staying here receive free admission to the refuge. The red-tile–roofed, open-air restaurant serves a variety of tasty Costa Rican dishes (restaurant meals US$6 to US$10).

The Quepos–Dominical–San Isidro de El General bus stops outside the hacienda entrance. The San Isidro de El General–Dominical–Uvita bus will drop you off at the Río Barú bridge, 2km from the hacienda office. A taxi from Dominical costs about US$5.

If you're driving, the El Ceibo gas station, 50m north of the Hacienda Barú Lodge, is the only one for a good distance in any direction. Groceries, fishing gear, tide tables and other useful sundries are available, and there are clean toilets.

DOMINICAL

Dominical hits a real sweet spot with the travelers who wander up and down its rough dirt road with a surfboard under an arm, balancing the day's activities between surfing and hammock hang time. And although some may decry the large population of expats and gringos who have hunkered down here, proud residents are quick to point out that Dominical recalls the mythical 'old Costa Rica' – the days before the roads were all paved, and when the coast was dotted with lazy little towns that drew a motley crew of surfers, backpackers and affable do-nothings alike. Dominical has no significant cultural sights, no paved roads and no chain restaurants, and if you're not here to learn to surf or to swing in a hammock it might not be the place for you. It remains the sort of place that reminds you to slow down, unwind and take things as they come.

 **Sights & Activities**

Centro Turístico
Cataratas Nauyaca   Waterfall
(📞 2787-0542, 2787-0541; www.cataratasnauyaca.com; horseback tour US$60, hike admission US$5; ⏲ tours depart 8am Mon-Sat; 🏇) This Costa Rican family–owned and operated center is home to a series of wonderful waterfalls that cascade through a protected reserve of both primary and secondary forest. The family runs horseback-riding tours to the falls, where visitors can swim in the inviting natural pools. Led by experienced guides, the six-hour tours include breakfast, lunch and transfers from Dominical – reservations required. Alternatively, you can pay US$5 and hike to the falls independently if you're in decent shape.

Bamboo Yoga Play   Yoga
(📞 2787-0229, in USA 323-522-5454; www.bamboyogaplay.com; class US$14) Complementary as yoga is to surfing, it's no wonder the practice is sweeping across Costa Rica. This lovely Dominical studio

Learning to Surf in Dominical

Although Dominical attracts some serious surfers and the waves can be gnarly, the quality of surf instruction here is among the best and most affordable in the country. For beginners who need lots of time and attention, the two most important questions to ask are about the ratio of students to instructors and if rates include board rental. There are scores of shops and instructors who offer services with a wide range of quality; the following come highly recommended.

Costa Rica Surf Camp (📞 2787-0393, 8812-3625; www.crsurfschool.com; Hotel DiuWak; all-inclusive packages per week from US$1105) This fantastic, locally owned surf school prides itself on a two-to-one student-teacher ratio, with teachers who have CPR and water-safety training and years of experience. The amiable owner, Cesar Valverde, runs a friendly, warm-hearted program.

Sunset Surf (📞 8827-3610, 8917-3143; www.sunsetsurfdominical.com; Domilocos; all-inclusive packages per week from US$1315; ⏲ 8am-4:30pm) Operated by Dylan Park, who grew up surfing the waves of Hawaii and Costa Rica, Sunset offers a variety of packages (including one for women only). It has a three-to-one student-instructor ratio and Park is an excellent teacher.

offers a variety of classes for all levels, including unique dance–yoga flow hybrid styles and even burlesque dance. The studio also serves as a center for yoga and arts retreats and offers several tidy accommodations for people interested in yoga-intensive stays.

Dominical Surf Adventures
Rafting, Surfing

(☎ 8897-9540, 2787-0431; www.dominicalsur-fadventures.com; ⏱ 8am-5pm Mon-Sat, 9am-3pm Sun) A bit of an adventurer's one-stop shop, visitors can book white-water trips, kayaking, snorkel and dive trips and surf lessons from this humble little desk on the main drag. Rafting trips start at US$80 (for runs on the Class II and III Guabo) and include a more challenging run on the Rio Coto Brus' Class IV rapids. Thankfully, there's no hustling sales pitch.

Pineapple Kayak Tours
Kayaking

(☎ 8362-7655, 8873-3283; www.pineapple-kayaktours.com; tours US$) Run by a friendly young Tico-American couple, Pineapple Kayak Tours runs kayaking and stand-up paddle trips to local caves, rivers and mangrove forests. Find their office next to the police station in Dominical.

Sleeping

IN TOWN

Posada del Sol
Hotel $

(☎ 2787-0085, 2787-0082; d from US$30; P ⏰) There are only five rooms at this charming, secure, tidy little place, but if you score one, consider yourself lucky (no advance reservations are taken). Posada del Sol hits the perfect price point and has basic comforts – hammocks outside each room, a sink to rinse out your salty suit and a clothesline to dry it. It's no place to party (it's a short stroll to the beach or to the bars in town), but

the warm-hearted, watchful proprietor, Leticia, makes the place so inviting. Single travelers should check out the tiny single in the back – a great deal. Located 30m south of the school.

Hotel DiuWak Hotel $$$

(☎2787-0087; www.diuwak.com; r US$105-145, ste US$200; P ❄ @ 🛜 ⛲) While the location in the center of town is super-convenient, this hotel could use a bit of an upgrade for these prices. Rooms range greatly in size and are quite comfort-able, with hot water and all the modern conveniences you would expect, amid a lovely tropical garden. Onsite amenities include a bar, restaurant, convenience store, fitness center and spa.

AROUND DOMINICAL

Albergue Alma de Hatillo B&B $$

(☎8850-9034; www.cabinasalma.com; r US$70-140; P ❄ @ ⛲) One of the most loved B&Bs on the entire Pacific coast, this hid-den gem is run by Sabina, a charming Pol-ish woman who has legions of dedicated

fans the world over. If you're looking for a quiet base from which to explore the Dominical area, this tranquil spot is home to immaculate cabins spread among several hectares of fruit trees.

Hotel Villas Río Mar Hotel $$

(☎2787-0052; www.villasriomar.com; bungalows US$89, ste US$140; P ❄ @ 🛜 ⛲) 🍃 From the turnoff into town, a right turn will bring you to this property about 800m from the village. Here you'll find a few dozen polished-wood bungalows, each with a private hammock-strung terrace, as well as a handful of luxury suites that accommodate small groups. Río Mar also offers a pool, Jacuzzi, tennis court, playground, equipment rental, restaurant and bar.

Costa Paraíso Boutique Hotel $$$

(☎2787-0025; www.costa-paraiso.com; d US$140-150; P ❄ 🛜 ⛲) In a prime spot overlooking a rocky cove in Playa Domini-calito, this snug hideaway lives up to its name. Each of the five rooms is beautifully

If You Like...
Watering Holes

If you like drinking an ice-cold Imperial during sunset, we think you'll like these watering holes with amazing Pacific views:

1 RONNY'S PLACE
(Map p257; ☎2777-5120; www.ronnysplace.com; mains US$6-14; ⊙noon-10pm) The insane views at Ronny's Place, of two pristine bays and jungle on all sides, make it worth a detour off the road to Manuel Antonio. Look for the well-marked dirt road off the main drag.

2 HOTEL VILLA CALETAS
(☎2630-3000; www.hotelvillacaletas.com; r US$224-641; P❋🛜🏊) The romantic, terraced cocktail lounge here is simply gorgeous, as are the expertly mixed drinks. Killer views from this blufftop aerie are unmatched.

3 EL AVIÓN
(Map p257; ☎2777-3378; mains US$6-14; 🛜🎶) This unforgettable bar-restaurant was constructed from a 1954 Fairchild C-123, which was carted piece by piece to Manuel Antonio. It's a great spot for a sundowner; during the dry season there are regular live-music performances.

appointed in a modern tropical style, with cool tile floors, wood beams and furniture and windows oriented to catch ocean breezes and views. Bonus: the in-house restaurant is a destination in itself.

Eating & Drinking

The restaurant scene in Dominical is of a high standard, catering mostly to foreign guests. The town also loves to party, though the scene changes from night to night. Maracutú hosts lots of live music and DJs; the late-night scene unfolds at San Clemente on Friday and Hotel y Restaurante Roca Verde on Saturday.

IN TOWN

Soda Nanyoa   Costa Rican $
(☎2787-0195; mains US$3-7; ⊙6am-10pm) In a town that caters to gringo appetites with inflated price tags, Nanyoa is a gratifying find: an authentic, moderately priced, better-than-most Costa Rican *soda*. The big pinto breakfasts and fresh-squeezed juice are ideal after a morning session on the waves, and at night it lets patrons bring their own beer from the grocery across the street.

Maracutú   Vegetarian, Asian $$
(☎2787-0091; www.maracatucostarica.com; meals US$6-12; ⊙11am-1am; 🌱) This 'natural restaurant and world music' spot hits a lovely high note in Dominical, serving mostly vegetarian and vegan dishes of international provenance, but skewing towards Asian. From vegan pad thai to shiitake soba salad, the food is made from organic and locally sourced produce as much as possible. For your aural pleasure, the musical rotation changes genres nightly.

Tortilla Flats   Bar
(☎2787-0033) The beachfront Tortilla Flats is the de facto place for surfers to enjoy session beers and tacos after a morning in the water. Its open-air atmosphere is pleasant, the surf videos on continuous loop and the good times abundant, but the staff is unfortunately surly.

AROUND DOMINICAL

¿Por Qué No?   Fusion $$
(☎2787-0025; www.cpporqueno.com; mains US$5-14; ⊙7am-2pm & 5:30-9:30pm, closed Mon night; 🌱) ¿Blackberry-and-cream-cheese-stuffed French toast, anyone? (Served with *real* maple syrup – this Canadian-run establishment doesn't mess around.) If breakfast doesn't turn you on, it's worth making a reservation for any other time of day, as the creative, well-executed Tico fusion cuisine at this restaurant at the Costa Paraíso hotel represents some of the best eats around here.

Getting There & Away

Buses pick up and drop off passengers along the main road in Dominical.

Quepos US$8, two hours, departs 5:30am, 8:30am, 1pm, 1:20pm and 3pm.

Uvita US$1.20, 20 minutes, departs 4:45am, 8:30am, 10:30am, 12:40pm, 1pm, 3pm, 5pm and 9:40pm.

UVITA

Just 17km south of Dominical, this sweet little hamlet is really nothing more than a loose straggle of farms, houses and tiny shops, though it should give you a good idea of what the central Pacific coast looked like before the tourist boom. Uvita serves as the base for visits to Parque Nacional Marino Ballena, a pristine marine reserve famous for its migrating pods of humpback whales and its virtually abandoned wilderness beaches.

Sights & Activities

Uvita is a perfect base for exploring Costanera Sur, which is home to some truly spectacular beaches that don't see

Movies in the Jungle

The decade-long (give or take) tradition of Friday and Saturday night movies, high on the hillside in Escaleras, had taken an indefinite hiatus on our last visit. The creators of this magical event may revive **Cinema Escaleras** (2787-8065; www. moviesinthejungle.com) at some point in the future; check the website for signs of life.

anywhere near the number of tourists that they should attract. All the better for you, if crowds aren't your thing.

Tours

Bahía Aventuras   Adventure Tour
(8846-6576, 2743-8362; www.bahiaaventuras. com) A well-regarded tour operator in Uvita, Bahía Aventuras has tours running the gamut, from surfing to diving to hiking,

Uvita

MARCAUX/GETTY IMAGES ©

and spanning the Costa Ballena to Corcovado. Tour rates are variable.

Uvita Adventure Tour
Kayaking, Mountain Biking

(📞8918-5681, 2743-8008; www.uvitadventure-tours.com; mountain-biking/kayaking tours from US$35/65) Run by the young owner Victor, this small tour company offers tours kayaking through the mangroves, snorkeling at the marine park and mountain biking, among others.

🛏 Sleeping & Eating

Flutterby House
Hostel $

(📞2743-8221, 8341-1730; www.flutterbyhouse.com; campsites US$6, dm US$12, d US$30-80; P@🛜) 🏄 Is it possible to fall in love at first sight with a hostel? If so, the ramshackle collection of colorful *Swiss Family Robinson*–style tree houses and dorms at Flutterby has us head over heels. Run by a pair of beaming Californian sisters, the hostel is friendly, fun and well situated within a short stroll of Marino Ballena's beaches.

Bungalows Ballena
Bungalow $$$

(📞8309-9631, 2743-8543; www.bungalows-ballena.com; apt/bungalows US$125/250; P🛜🏊) These fully outfitted apartments and stand-alone bungalows are an excellent mid-market option for families and large groups. All have kitchens, wi-fi and satellite television. The place is outfitted for kids – there's a playground and a big, welcoming pool in the shape of a whale's tail. Find it 300m north of the park's main entrance.

Sabor Español
Spanish $$

(📞8768-9160, 2743-8312; Playa Colonia; mains US$7-22; ⏰noon-3pm & 6-9:30pm Tue-Sun) Having had a successful run in Monteverde, charming Spanish couple Heri and Montse realized that they wanted to live by the ocean – to Uvita's good fortune. Thus, their sublime gazpacho, paella, tortilla *española* and other Spanish specialties can now be savored with sangria at the end of a dirt road in Playa Uvita, in a lovely *rancho* setting.

ℹ Getting There & Away

Most buses depart from the two sheltered bus stops on the Costanera in the main village.

San Isidro de El General US$1.25, two hours, departs 6am and 2pm.

San José US$5, 3½ hours, departs 5:15am and 1:15pm.

PARQUE NACIONAL MARINO BALLENA

This stunner of a **marine park** (📞2743-8236; admission US$7) protects coral and rock reefs surrounding several offshore islands. Its name comes not only from the humpback whales that breed here but also

Waterfalls, Centro Turistico Cataratas Nauyaca (p265)
OGPHOTO/GETTY IMAGES ©

because of the Punta Uvita 'Whale Tail', a distinctive sandbar extending into a rocky reef that, at low tide, forms the shape of a whale's tail when viewed from above. Despite its small size, the importance of this area cannot be overstated, especially since it protects migrating humpback whales, pods of dolphins and nesting sea turtles, not to mention colonies of sea-birds and several terrestrial reptiles.

Although Ballena is relatively off the radar of many coastal travelers, this can be an extremely rewarding destination for beach-lovers and wildlife-watchers. The lack of tourist crowds means that you can enjoy a quiet day at the beach in near solitude – a rarity in Costa Rica. And, with a little luck and a bit of patience, you just might catch a glimpse of a humpback breaching or a few dolphins gliding through the surf.

◉ Sights & Activities

The beaches at Parque Nacional Marino Ballena are a stunning combination of golden sand and polished rock. All of them are virtually deserted and perfect for peaceful swimming and sunbathing. And the lack of visitors means you'll have a number of quiet opportunities for good bird-watching.

Although the park gets few human visitors, the beaches are frequently visited by a number of animal species, including nesting seabirds, bottle-nose dolphins and a variety of lizards. And from May to November, with a peak in September and October, olive ridley and hawksbill turtles bury their eggs in the sand nightly. However, the star attraction are the pods of humpback whales that pass through the national park from August to October and December to April.

Scientists are unsure as to why humpback whales migrate here, though it's possible that Costa Rican waters may be one of only a few places in the world where the whales mate. There are actually two different groups of humpbacks that pass through the park – whales seen in the fall migrate from Californian waters,

while those seen in the spring originate from Antarctica.

From the ranger station you can walk out onto Punta Uvita and snorkel (best at low tide). Boats from Playa Bahía Uvita to Isla Ballena can be hired for up to US$45 per person for a two-hour snorkeling trip, though you are not allowed to stay overnight on the island.

To delve into the underwater beauty of the park, take a dive with the Argentinean-run **Mad About Diving** (☎ 2743-8019; www.madaboutdivingcr.com).

There is also some decent surfing near the river mouth at the southern end of Playa Colonia.

❶ Getting There & Away

Parque Nacional Marino Ballena is best accessed from Uvita or Ojochal, by either private vehicle or a quick taxi ride; inquire at your accommodations for the latter.

OJOCHAL AREA

Beyond Uvita, the Costanera Sur follows the coast as far as Palmar, approximately 40km away. This route provides a coastal alternative to the Interamericana, as well as convenient access to points in the Península de Osa. En route, about 15km south of Uvita, you'll pass the tiny town of Ojochal, on the inland side of the highway.

Ojochal also serves as a convenient base for exploring nearby Parque Nacional Marino Ballena, and there are plenty of accommodations here to choose from, despite its small size. Though Ojochal has attracted quite a multicultural expat population, its friendly, well-integrated vibe has a distinctly different cultural feel from that of surfer-dominated Dominical.

Just north of Ojochal, about 14km south of Uvita, is the wilderness beach of Playa Tortuga, which is largely undiscovered and virtually undeveloped, but it's home to some occasional bouts of decent surf.

Reviving Roots

Ojochal's namesake, once on the verge of extinction in the area, is making a slow comeback. Though the tall, leafy *ojoche* tree (*Brosimum alicastrum*) takes about 30 years to mature, making this a long-term project, the local community has begun putting the *ojoche* back into Ojochal.

As Ojochal's population grew through the 1950s, most stands of *ojoche* were felled for cattle grazing and lumber. But in the same decade the tree's starchy fruit provided nourishment to many local families during severe drought. The pulp of the fruit can be eaten raw, boiled or made into flour. The fruit (also known as the 'Maya nut', though not a true nut) has a low glycemic index and high protein content, and it's rich in fiber, fat, folate, iron and antioxidants.

Around 2009, the grassroots community group Comité de Ojochal began to replant *ojoche* trees in the area in an effort to re-establish Ojochal's connection with its roots (so to speak), and to save the tree from local extinction while reforesting the area with a nutritious and culturally valuable food source.

Hotel Villas Gaia (below) offers walking tours of the 'Ojoche Route', and you can buy *ojoche* flour from the local women's entrepreneurial association, which helps to fund the *ojoche*-revival project.

Sleeping

Lookout at Playa Tortuga
Boutique Hotel **$$**

(☏2786-5074; www.hotelcostarica.com; d US$79-110; [P][❄][@][🛜][🏊]) This beautiful hilltop sanctuary is home to a dozen brightly painted bungalows awash in calming pastels. The grounds are traversed by a series of paths overlooking the beaches below, but the highlight is the large deck in a tower above the pool. Here you can pursue some early-morning bird-watching, or perhaps better yet, some late-afternoon slothful lounging.

Hotel Villas Gaia
Cabina **$$**

(☏8382-8240; www.villasgaia.com; r incl breakfast from US$85, casa US$153; [P][@][🛜][🏊])
🖉 Along the beach side of the road is this beautifully kept collection of shiny wooden cabins with shaded porches, set in tranquil forested grounds. An excellent restaurant serves a variety of international standards, and the hilltop pool boasts a panoramic view of Playa Tortuga. The

beach is a pleasant 20-minute hike along a dirt path that winds down the hillside.

Diquis del Sur
B&B **$$**

(☏2786-5012; diquiscostarica.com; r per day/ week from US$55/330; [P][❄][@][🛜][🏊]) In Ojochal proper, this bed and breakfast is run by a delightful French-Canadian couple who make it feel like a home away from home. Accommodations are in a variety of fairly modest rooms, though all have kitchenettes conducive to self-catering. There's also a good restaurant onsite, and the well-maintained property is landscaped with flowers and fruit trees.

Finca Bavaria
Boutique Hotel **$$**

(☏8355-4465; www.finca-bavaria.de; s/d from US$64/74; [P][🛜][🏊]) This quaint German-run inn comprises a handful of pleasing rooms with wooden accents, bamboo furniture, romantic mosquito net–draped beds and...high-tech German toilets. The lush grounds are lined with walkways and hemmed by forest, though you can take in sweeping views of the ocean from the hilltop pool. Look for the signed dirt road at Km 167.

La Cusinga
Ecolodge $$$

(📞2770-2549; www.lacusingalodge.com; Finca Tres Hermanas; s/d US$136/172; P) 🌿 Awarded the CST's five leaves of sustainability, this lovely ecolodge is a model of sustainable practices. It's also a relaxing place to unplug – in place of televisions there are yoga classes. Located on a private reserve that borders on Parque Nacional Marino Ballena, it has access to hiking, bird-watching, snorkeling and swimming in the national park.

Eating

Ballena Bistro
Cafe $$

(📞2786-5407; Costanera Sur, Km 169; ⏱11am-4pm Tue-Sun, to 8pm Thu; P 📶) The main attraction of multiuse Goathouse 169, this bistro offers substantial and fresh dishes, such as lentil, beet and feta salad, Brazilian coconut fish soup and Belgian beef stew. Salads, burgers, wraps, fresh juices and cold beers round out the menu. This is a smashing spot to break up a long drive or pick up some damn good picnic fixings.

Citrus
International $$$

(📞2786-5175; meals US$10-30; ⏱11am-9pm Mon-Sat;) With its fresh, bright, Moroccan-inspired flavors Citrus is a standout, even among the excellent choices within strolling distance. Offering New World dishes that are heavily influenced by Southeast Asian and north African culinary traditions, and benefiting from its candlelit riverside location, Citrus welcomes patrons with flair and bravado.

Exotica
International $$$

(📞2786-5050; dishes US$10-30; ⏱11am-9pm Mon-Sat) This phenomenal gourmet restaurant certainly sets a high benchmark for Ojochal. The nouveau French dishes each emphasize a breadth of ingredients brought together in masterful combinations. Some of the highlights include oil-drizzled fish carpaccio, wild-duck breast topped with tropical-fruit tapenades and homemade desserts.

ⓘ Getting There & Away

Daily buses between Dominical and Palmar can drop you off near any of the places described here. However, given the infrequency of transportation links along this stretch of highway, it's recommended that you explore the area by private car.

Southern Costa Rica & Península de Osa

Costa Rica's wild side still thrives in the south. From the chilly heights of Cerro Chirripó to the dense coastal jungles of the Península de Osa, this sector of Costa Rica encompasses some of the country's least-explored and least-developed lands. Vast tracts of wilderness remain untouched in Parque Internacional La Amistad, and the country's most visible indigenous groups maintain traditional ways of living in their remote territories. Wildlife-watchers visiting Parque Nacional Corcovado are often rewarded with sightings of slumbering tapir, while the flash of scarlet macaws overhead is quite common all along these coasts. Abandoned wilderness beaches, world-class surf and opportunities for rugged exploration draw intrepid travelers yearning for something truly wild.

Parque Nacional Corcovado (p294)

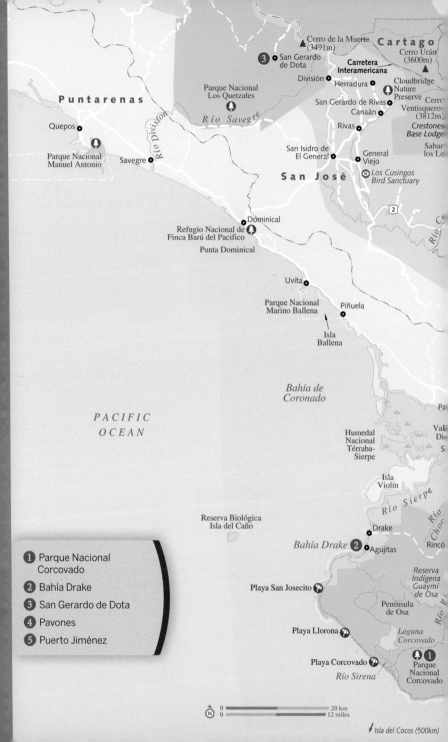

Cartago

Cerro de la Muerte (3491m) ▲

Cerro Urán (3600m) ▲

San Gerardo de Dota ③

Carretera Interamericana

División

Herradura

Cloudbridge Nature Preserve

Cerro Ventisqueros (3812m)

Puntarenas

Parque Nacional Los Quetzales

San Gerardo de Rivas

Canaán

Río Savegre

Rivas

Crestones Base Lodge

Quepos

Sabar los Le

Parque Nacional Manuel Antonio

Río División

San Isidro de El General

General Viejo

Savegre

San José

Los Cusingos Bird Sanctuary

Dominical

Refugio Nacional de Finca Barú del Pacifico

Punta Dominical

Río C

②

Uvita

Parque Nacional Marino Ballena

Piñuela

Isla Ballena

Bahía de Coronado

PACIFIC OCEAN

Pa

Val Di S

Humedal Nacional Térraba-Sierpe

Isla Violín

Río Sierpe

Río Choc

Reserva Biológica Isla del Caño

Drake

Bahía Drake ②

Agujitas

Rincó

Playa San Josecito

Reserva Indígena Guaymí de Osa

Península de Osa

Río

Laguna Corcovado

Playa Llorona

Playa Corcovado

Río Sirena

Parque Nacional Corcovado ①

① Parque Nacional Corcovado

② Bahía Drake

③ San Gerardo de Dota

④ Pavones

⑤ Puerto Jiménez

Ⓝ

0 ————— 20 km

0 ————— 12 miles

↙ *Isla del Cocos (500km)*

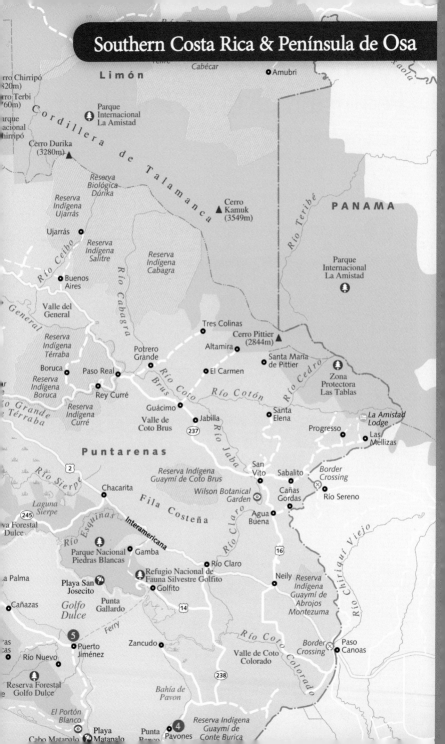

Southern Costa Rica & Península de Osa's Highlights

Parque Nacional Corcovado

Although Costa Rica is dotted with patches of rainforest, none are as exciting as Parque Nacional Corcovado (p294), huge and wild, inviting rugged adventure. Trekking muddy trails through the wet, wild, fascinating park offers a view of the jungle filled with mind-blowing flora, exotic animals and empty beaches.

Bahía Drake

Put your boots on and head south from Bahía Drake (p284) along the muddy coastal trail towards Corcovado. You will find the country's wildest beaches and lodges tucked amid thickly forested rocky points. Or take a daylong boat trip to snorkel at Isla del Caño, then picnic and catnap on a jungle-fringed peninsula beach.

CHRIS CHEADLE/GETTY IMAGES ©

San Gerardo de Dota

JUDY BELLAH/GETTY IMAGES ©

3

Quetzal-spotting, the refreshing crispness of cool air and cold mountain streams full of trout – the bucolic highland village of San Gerardo de Dota (p306) is the antidote for the sunburned and beach-weary. Birds abound in this out-of-the-way mountain refuge. Green violetear hummingbird

4

Pavones

Devoted surfers won't mind sacrificing a chunk of time to get out here, for it's worth the effort to access this far-flung beach if you wish to surf what is arguably the world's longest left-hand surf break (p299). Even if you're not a hard-core surfer, this comparatively undeveloped corner of the country makes a quiet getaway.

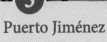

5

Puerto Jiménez

The closest town of any real size to Parque Nacional Corcovado, Puerto Jiménez (p289) is a great place to stock up on supplies and organize a guide for park expeditions. The town itself is loaded with character, with frequent wildlife encounters in addition to diverse accommodations and eating options.

Southern Costa Rica & Península de Osa's Best...

Wildlife

○ **Dolphins & Whales** The waters of Bahía Drake are incredibly rich in marine life. (p284)

○ **Tapirs** The largest land mammal in Costa Rica is found throughout Parque Nacional Corcovado. (p294)

○ **Sloths & Crocs** The mangrove swamps near Zancudo harbor all manner of creatures. (p299)

○ **Scarlet macaws** Scarlet macaws are common throughout the Osa, even around town in Puerto Jiménez. (p289)

Splurges

○ **Luna Lodge** Eco-retreat literally next-door to Corcovado. (p294)

○ **Lapa Ríos** Expansive views of Cabo Matapalo, and all-inclusive luxury. (p294)

○ **Monte Azul** This luxury getaway is a masterful marriage of artistic and natural wonders. (p303)

○ **Copa de Arbol** Beachside *cabinas* (cabins) on Bahía Drake. (p289)

○ **Dantica Cloud Forest Lodge** Elegant stone cabins high in the mountains. (p306)

Secret Spots

○ **Reserva Indígena Boruca** The indigenous reserve for the Boruca population welcomes visitors for homestays. (p309)

○ **Parque Nacional Isla del Coco** This island chain in the Pacific is a true Lost World. (p300)

○ **Wilson Botanical Garden** This out-of-the-way mountain reserve is excellent for spotting a huge variety of birds. (p310)

○ **Cloudbridge Nature Reserve** Scenic and quiet, most people skip the extensive network of trails here while rushing up Cerro Chirripó. (p307)

Epic Hikes

o **Parque Nacional Corcovado** Through-hike or day hike – this wilderness is a Costa Rica classic. (p296)

o **Cerro Chirripó** Watch the sun rise from the country's highest peak. (p304)

o **Parque Internacional La Amistad** Rugged and mostly inaccessible, trekking here takes you into true wilderness. (p312)

o **Bahía Drake** Hike along the muddy coastal trail with detours to remote beaches. (p284)

Need to Know

ADVANCE PLANNING

o **One month before** Make accommodations arrangements in remote locations such as Bahía Drake; hire guides for treks in Parque Nacional Corcovado or Parque Internacional La Amistad; make reservations for dive trips to Isla del Coco.

o **Two weeks before** Break in those hiking boots!

RESOURCES

o **Corcovado Guide** (www.corcovadoguide. com) Useful background information for Corcovado visitors.

o **San Gerardo de Rivas** (www.sangerardocostarica. com) Great resource for those planning to climb Cerro Chirripó.

GETTING AROUND

o **Air** Small planes and charters to Puerto Jiménez can save you lots of time-consuming overland travel.

o **Car** Brave souls who want to take on an exploration of Osa with their own four wheels will absolutely need a 4WD vehicle. The roads here are extremely rough, even in the dry season.

o **Boat** Lodges in Bahía Drake are accessed by boat from Sierpe.

o **Bus** Large cities in southern Costa Rica are surprisingly well served by public buses.

BE FOREWARNED

o **Climate** Bring adequate clothing if you're planning to climb Cerro Chirripó – it's cold and wet at high altitudes.

o **Accommodation** The lodges around Bahía Drake are largely all-inclusive, due to the difficulty of getting supplies into the area by boat. For a more DIY experience, approach Corcovado from the Puerto Jiménez side.

bove left: Three-toed sloth; **Above right:** Fishing, Parque Nacional Corcovado (p294)

Southern Costa Rica & Península de Osa Itineraries

Much of southern Costa Rica is rough and rugged, and travel in the region is a slow-going but thrilling adventure through mountains and jungles.

3 DAYS

SIERPE TO CORCOVADO
BAHÍA DRAKE & AROUND

Southern Costa Rica is off the main tourist circuit, but it's possible to dip in and out within a few days if you plan carefully. If this sounds like your cup of shade-grown coffee, the resorts lining Bahiá Drake are fairly expensive, but bedding down in eco-paradise is worth the splurge.

First get to ❶ **Sierpe** (p289; those on a tight schedule should fly directly to Bahía Drake from San José). A boat will take you on a scenic ride through the sparkling-clear waters of ❷ **Bahía Drake** (p284). On the ride, you may even be chased by schools of dolphins. Upon arriving at your destination, expect to spend your entire stay swimming,

hiking, boating and searching for wildlife. Take a day trip to hike around ❸ **Parque Nacional Corcovado** (p294); most lodges around Bahía Drake run boat trips to the park, which include hiking with a guide and lunch, along with a round-trip boat ride. Spend another day snorkeling the pristine waters of ❹ **Isla del Caño** (p284), swimming among rays, sharks, and colorful reef fish, before heading back into so-called civilization.

PUERTO JIMÉNEZ TO CORCOVADO
HIKING CORCOVADO

5 DAYS

One of the quintessential Costa Rican experiences is a multiday expedition through Parque Nacional Corcovado. It's not easy to get here, and all visitors now must be accompanied by a licensed guide, but trekking through this gem of a national park remains profoundly rewarding. Though some trails have closed due to overgrowth, there are several routes to take, and the following is only one option.

In ❶ **Puerto Jiménez** (p289), make arrangements with your guide, gather last-minute provisions, enjoy a good meal and rest well. You'll catch the *colectivo* (collective truck taxi) or private vehicle to ❷**Carate** (p293), from where you'll hike 3.5km along the beach

to the park. After hiking through the jungle looking for scarlet macaws, monkeys and coatis, you'll overnight at ❸**Sirena ranger station** (p295), where you may see sleeping tapirs. If you can, spend a second night at Sirena to spend the day exploring the trails and beaches. Wake up early the next day for the 18km hike from Sirena to ❹ **Los Patos ranger station**. After bidding farewell to the park, spend a restful night at ❺ **Danta Corcovado Lodge** (p294), the perfect waypoint between Corcovado wilderness and the world at large.

Diving, Isla del Caño (p287)
JOHNNY HAGLUND/GETTY IMAGES ©

Discover Southern Costa Rica & Península de Osa

BAHÍA DRAKE

As one of Costa Rica's most isolated destinations, Bahía Drake (*'drah-kay'*) is a veritable Lost World filled with tropical landscapes and abundant wildlife. In the rainforest canopy, howler monkeys greet the rising sun with their haunting bellows, while pairs of macaws soar between the treetops, filling the air with their cacophonous squawking. Offshore in the bay itself, pods of migrating dolphins flit through turquoise waters.

🏃 Activities

HIKING

All of the lodges offer tours to Parque Nacional Corcovado, usually a full-day trip to San Pedrillo or Sirena ranger stations (from US$85 to US$150 per person), including boat transportation, lunch and guided hikes. Indeed, if you came all the way to the Península de Osa, it's hard to pass up a visit to the national park that made it famous.

If you'd prefer to hike independently, take the long coastal trail that heads south out of Agujitas and continues about 10km to the border of the national park. Note that visitors intending to enter or spend the night in the park must have secured reservations in advance and must be accompanied by a guide. Hikers along this narrow, muddy trail should remember that sunset descends swiftly around 5:30pm.

SWIMMING & SNORKELING

About 20km west of Agujitas, **Isla del Caño** is considered the best place for snorkeling in this area.

Boat tour, Bahía Drake
JOHN BORTHWICK/GETTY IMAGES ©

Bahía Drake & Around

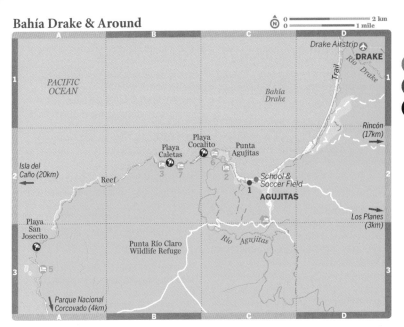

There are other opportunities for snorkeling on the coast between Agujitas and Corcovado.

KAYAKING & CANOEING

A fantastic way to explore the region's biodiversity is to paddle through it. The idyllic Río Agujitas attracts a huge variety of birdlife and lots of scaly reptiles. The river conveniently empties out into the bay, which is surrounded by hidden coves and sandy beaches ideal for exploring in a sea kayak. Paddling at high tide is recommended because it allows you to explore more territory. Most accommodations in the area have kayaks and canoes for rent for a small fee.

SPORTFISHING

Bahía Drake claims more than 40 fishing records, including sailfish, marlin, yellowfin tuna, wahoo, cubera snapper, mackerel and roosterfish. Fishing is excellent year-round, although the catch may vary according to the season. The peak season for tuna and marlin is from August to December. Sailfish are caught year-round, but experience a slowdown

in May and June. Dorado and wahoo peak between May and August. Other species are abundant year-round, so you are virtually assured to reel in something. Many lodges can arrange fishing excursions, but you need to be prepared to pay for the experience – half-/full-day excursions cost around US$600/1000.

DOLPHIN- & WHALE-WATCHING

Bahía Drake is rife with marine life, including more than 25 species of dolphin and whale that pass through on their migrations throughout the year. This area is uniquely suited for whale-watching: humpback whales come from both the northern and the southern hemispheres to calve, resulting in the longest humpback whale season in the world. Humpbacks can be spotted in Bahía Drake year-round (except May), but the best months to see whales are late July through early November.

Sleeping

This area is off the grid, so many places do not have 24/7 electricity. Reservations are recommended in the dry season (mid-December to mid-April).

Finca Maresia Bungalow $$
(☏8888-1625, 2775-0279; www.fincamaresia. com; Camino a Los Planes; budget s/d US$30/40, standard s/d US$50/60, superior s/d US$75/90, all incl breakfast) After traveling the world for more than 20 years, the owners of this absolute gem of a hotel decided to settle down in their own veritable slice of paradise. Here amid a large *finca* (farm) that stretches across a series of hills, Finca Maresia beckons to budget travelers by offering a combination of low prices, high value and good design sense. All seven rooms overlook lush environs, and play a near-continuous audio track of jungle sounds. Beyond the show-stopping natural setting, the good taste of the owners is evident as you walk from room to room and view the transition from modernist glass walls to Japanese-style sliding rice-paper doors.

Aguila de Osa Inn Lodge $$$
(☏2296-2190, toll-free in USA 866-924-8452; www.aguiladeosa.com; s/d 2-night package US$673/1130) On the east side of the Río Agujitas, this swanky lodge consists of roomy quarters with shining wood floors, cathedral ceilings and private decks with expansive ocean views. Diving and sportfishing charters are available to guests, as are significant discounts if you stay beyond two nights. Rates include all meals, plus an Isla del Caño tour and a Corcovado tour.

La Paloma Lodge Lodge $$$
(☏2293-7502, 2775-1684; www.lapalomalodge. com; 3-/4-/5-day package per person from US$1119/1379/1667; ❄🛜♨) Perched on a lush hillside, this exquisite lodge provides guests with an incredible panorama of ocean and forest, all from the comfort of the sumptuous, stylish quarters. Rooms have shiny hardwood floors and queen-sized orthopedic beds, draped in mosquito netting, while shoulder-high walls in all the bathrooms offer rainforest views while you bathe. Each room has a large balcony (with hammock, of course) that catches the cool breeze off the ocean. Rates for stays of three days or more include a tour to both Isla del Caño and Corcovado.

Getting There & Away

Air

Departing from San José, **Nature Air** (www. natureair.com) and **Sansa** (www.flysansa.com) have daily flights to the **Drake airstrip**, which is 2km north of Agujitas. Prices vary according to season and availability, though you can expect to pay around US$140 to/from San José.

Alfa Romeo Aero Taxi (☏8632-8150; www.alfaromeoair.com) offers charter flights connecting Bahía Drake to Puerto Jiménez, Golfito, Carate and Sirena. Flights are best booked at the airport in person; one-way fares are typically less than US$100.

Most lodges provide transportation to/from the airport or Sierpe, which involves a jeep or a boat or both.

Boat

Unless you charter a flight, you'll arrive here by an exhilarating boat ride through mangrove channels and the ocean. It's one of the true thrills of visiting the area. All of the hotels offer boat transfers between Sierpe and Bahía Drake with prior arrangements. Most hotels in Drake have beach landings, so wear appropriate footwear.

BAHÍA DRAKE TO CORCOVADO

This craggy stretch of coastline is home to sandy inlets that disappear at high tide, leaving only the rocky outcroppings and luxuriant rainforest. Virtually uninhabited and undeveloped beyond a few tourist lodges, the setting here is magnificent

BORUT FURLA/GETTY IMAGES ©

Don't Miss
Reserva Biológica Isla del Caño

Reserva Biológica Isla del Caño is a 326-hectare island that is among Bahía Drake's most popular destinations, not only for fish and marine mammals, but also for snorkelers, divers and biologists. It's the tip of numerous underwater rock formations, which is evident from the rocky cliffs along the coastline, some towering 70m over the ocean. This is not your stereotypical tropical island: the few white-sand beaches are small to start with, and they disappear to nothing when the tide comes in.

The submarine rock formations are among the island's main attractions, drawing divers to explore the underwater architecture. Snorkelers can investigate the coral and rock formations along the beach, right in front of the ranger station. The water is much clearer here than along the mainland coast, though rough seas can cloud visibility. Fifteen different species of coral have been recorded, as well as threatened animal species such as the Panulirus lobster and the giant conch. Dolphins and whales are frequently spotted swimming in the outer waters, and hammerhead sharks, manta rays and sea turtles also inhabit the area.

Local lodges can arrange day trips to Isla del Caño (from US$80 per person), including the park fee, snorkeling equipment and lunch on Playa San Josecito. The clarity of the ocean and the variety of the fish fluctuate according to water and weather conditions: it's worth inquiring before booking.

and wild. If you're looking to spend a bit more time along the shores of Bahía Drake before penetrating the depths of Parque Nacional Corcovado, consider a night or two in some of the country's most remote accommodations.

Detour:
Danta Corcovado Lodge

Conveniently located midway between the Los Patos ranger station and the town of La Palma on the Península de Osa, the unpretentious Danta Corcovado Lodge (☎ 2735-1111; www.dantalodge.com; r/bungalow incl breakfast US$108/137) is an ideal stopover for those starting or ending a Corcovado through-hike at Los Patos. Each of its delightful room and bungalow designs are dreamed up by the staff, ranging from comfortable wood cabins to a funky concrete dome – with open-air bathrooms and hot water. Winding through this family-run property are 4km of trails, and the lodge offers tours and activities, including day trips to Corcovado. Reserve as far in advance as possible, as this lovely spot fills up fast.

Sights & Activities

A public trail follows the coastline for the entire spectacular stretch, and it's excellent for wildlife-spotting. Among the multitude of animal species you're likely to see and hear are scarlet macaws, chestnut-mandibled toucan, white-faced capuchin and howler monkeys.

Scenic little inlets punctuate this entire route, each with a wild, windswept beach. Just west of Punta Agujitas, a short detour off the main trail leads to the picturesque **Playa Cocalito**, a secluded cove perfect for sunning, swimming and body surfing. With no lodges in the immediate vicinity, it's often deserted. **Playa Caletas**, in front of the Corcovado

Adventures Tent Camp, is excellent for snorkeling.

Further south, the Río Claro (there are two; the other is near Sirena ranger station) empties out into the ocean. Water can be waist-deep or higher, and the current swift, so take care when wading across.

South of this Río Claro, **Playa San Josecito** is the longest stretch of white-sand beach on this side of the Península de Osa. It is popular with swimmers, snorkelers and sunbathers, though you'll rarely find it crowded.

The border of Parque Nacional Corcovado is about 5km south of Playa San Josecito (it's about 16km and four hours in total from Agujitas to Corcovado).

Sleeping

Las Caletas Lodge   Lodge **$$**
(☎ 8863-9631, 8826-1460, 2560-6602; www.caletas.cr; Playa Caletas; tents/r per person from US$70/80; @ 🛜) 🍃 This adorable lodge consists of cozy wooden cabins and safari tents perched above the picturesque beach of the same name. The Swiss and Tico owners are warm hosts who established this convivial spot before there was phone access or electricity (now mostly solar- and hydro-powered). The food is delicious and bountiful, the staff friendly and the environment beautifully chill.

Guaria de Osa   Lodge **$$$**
(☎ 2235-4313, in USA 510-235-4313; www.guariadeosa.com; per person US$150; 🛜) Cultivating a new-age ambience, this Asian-style retreat center offers yoga, tai chi and 'Sentient Experiential' events, along with the more typical rainforest activities. The lovely grounds include an ethnobotanical garden, which features exotic local species. The architecture of this place is unique: the centerpiece is the Lapa Lapa Lounge, a spacious multistory pagoda built entirely from reclaimed hardwood.

Copa de Arbol
Lodge $$$

(📞 8935-1212, in USA 831-246-4265; www.
copadearbol.com; Playa Caletas; s/d from
US$382/610; 🛜 🏊) Though they look a
bit rustic from the outside with their
thatch roofs and stilts, these *cabinas* are
gorgeously outfitted inside – built with
sustainably grown wood and recycled
materials, each has a private terrace and
air-con. The lodge, steps from the beach,
is all laid-back luxury, run smoothly by
super-friendly staff. Paddleboards and
kayaks are available to rent.

ⓘ Getting There & Away

Boat
All of the hotels offer boat transfers between
Sierpe and Bahía Drake with prior arrangements.
If you have not made advance arrangements
with your lodge for a pick-up, two *colectivo* boats
depart daily from Sierpe at 11:30am and 4:30pm,
and from Bahía Drake back to Sierpe at 7:15am
(US$15) and 2:30pm (US$20).

SIERPE

This sleepy village on the Río Sierpe is
the gateway to Bahía Drake, and if you've
made a reservation with any of the jungle
lodges further down the coast, you will be
picked up here by boat.

ⓘ Getting There & Away

Air
Scheduled flights and charters fly into Palmar Sur,
14km north of Sierpe.

Boat
If you are heading to Bahía Drake, your lodge
will arrange the boat transfer. Should things go
awry or if you're traveling independently, there's
no shortage of water taxis milling about – be
prepared to negotiate a fair price.

PUERTO JIMÉNEZ

Sliced in half by the swampy, overgrown
Quebrada Cacao, and flanked on one side
by the emerald waters of the Golfo Dulce,
the vaguely Wild West outpost of Puerto
Jiménez is shared equally by local residents
and wildlife. It's not too hard to understand
why scarlet macaws hang out above the
soccer field or monkeys swing through the
town treetops, since Puerto Jiménez lies on
the edge of Parque Nacional Corcovado.

Humpback whale, Parque Nacional Corcovado (p294)

LUISMIX/GETTY IMAGES ©

Puerto Jiménez

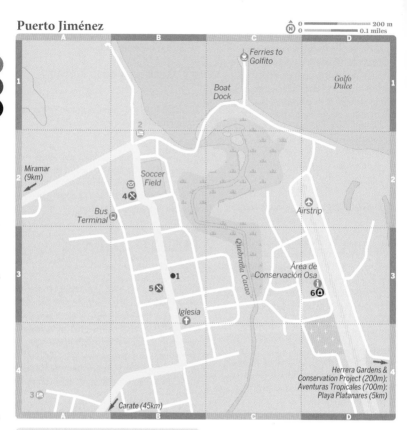

Puerto Jiménez

As the preferred jumping-off point for travelers heading to the famed Sirena ranger station, the town is a great place to organize an expedition, stock up on supplies, eat a hot meal and get a good night's rest before hitting the trails.

👉 Tours

Puerto Jiménez has a host of tour operators, taxi drivers and touts hungry for the tourist dollar. Ask lots of questions, consult with fellow travelers and choose carefully.

Osa Wild   Tour
(📞 8765-3330, 8376-1152, 2735-5848; www.
osawildtravel.com; Rte 245, downtown Puerto Jiménez; tours from US$25, one-day Corcovado tour US$75; ⏰ 8:30am-noon & 2:30-7pm) 🎫
Osa Wild is just what the area so desperately needed: a resource for travelers to connect with community-oriented initiatives that go to the heart of the real Osa through homestays, farm tours and sustainable local cultural exchanges. Of course it also offers the more typical

stuff like kayaking tours and guided trips through Corcovado, but its focus on sustainability, environmental protection and community development puts it in a league of its own.

Surcos Tours
Nature Tour

(www.surcostours.com) A trio of excellent guides make Surcos the best company tours into Osa that focus on wildlife and bird-watching. Arrangements for tours are made through the website.

Aventuras Tropicales
Adventure Tour

(☑2735-5195; www.aventurastropicales.com) Aventuras Tropicales is a professional, Tico-run operation that offers all sorts of active adventures. Some of its most popular excursions include kayaking tours of the mangroves, which start at $45 per person. Located 2km east on the road to Platanares.

Sleeping

Cabinas Jiménez
Cabina $

(☑2735-5090; www.cabinasjimenez.com; s/d from US$35/50; P ❄ @ 🛜 ⛵) Cabinas Jiménez is hands-down the nicest place to stay in town. All of the rooms have jungle scenes painted on the walls, with underwater murals in the hot-water bathrooms. Refrigerators and safes are practical, while details such as carved wooden furniture, woven textiles and batik curtains add an elegant flair. Pricier rooms have kitchenettes and fantastic views of the lagoon. Bikes and kayaks are free for guests' use, and the bilingual staff is friendly and helpful.

Cacao Monkeys
Cabina $$

(☑2735-5248; www.cacaomonkeys.com; s/d incl breakfast from US$40/60; P 🛜) On the fringes of downtown on a cacao farm, this jungle joint has a set of five brightly painted wooden *cabinas,* and an excellent riverside cafe (meals US$8). One *cabina* has a small kitchen, two are set up with a double and two single beds for families, and all have shiny hardwood floors and porches. It's a good option for families as it's a bit removed from the noise of town

and there is loads of wildlife right out the door.

Iguana Lodge
Hotel $$$

(☑8848-0752, in USA & Canada 800-259-9123; www.iguanalodge.com; d incl breakfast US$150, casitas per person incl 2 meals from US$186, villa US$599; P ❄) This luxurious lodge fronting Playa Platanares has the most architecturally alluring cabins in the area: four two-story bungalows have huge breezy decks, bamboo furniture, ortho-pedic beds draped in mosquito netting and lovely stone bathrooms with garden showers. The on-site restaurant serves three delectable meals a day: the creative cuisine is a highlight.

Eating

Soda Valeria
Soda $

(Rte 245; mains US$3-8) Clean, cute and smack-dab in the middle of town, this *soda* (lunch counter) is a dream – the kind of place you know is good because the local government workers all pile in at lunch. The heaping, fresh *casados* (set meals) change daily and are delivered with homemade tortillas and sided with fresh fruit. Add considerate, quick service and Valeria is short-listed among our favorite *sodas* in all of Costa Rica.

Pizzamail.it
Pizza $$

(pizzas US$9-18; ⊗4-10:30pm; 🛜) A pizzeria may not instill lots of confidence when its name sounds more like a website. Still, all doubts will be cast aside when a server at Pizzamail.it brings out the pie: a thin-crust, wood-fired piece of Italy in the middle of the jungle. From its small patio, diners can watch squawking macaws in the trees over the soccer field. *Bellissimo!*

 Shopping

Jagua Arts & Crafts
Arts & Crafts

(Map p290; ☑2735-5267; ⊗6:30am-3:30pm) A superb collection of art and jewelry by local and expat craftspeople, including some amazing Boruca masks.

ℹ️ Getting There & Away

Air

Nature Air (📞2735-5428; www.natureair.com; ⏰6am-2pm) and **Sansa** (📞2735-5890; www.flysansa.com) have daily flights to/from San José; one-way flights are approximately US$130.

Alfa Romeo Aero Taxi (📞8632-8150; www.alfaromeoair.com) has light aircraft (for three and five passengers) for charter flights to Golfito, Carate, Bahía Drake, Sirena, Palmar Sur, Quepos and Puerto Limón. Prices are dependent on the number of passengers, so it's best to try to organize a larger group if you're considering this option. Sometimes, if there's already a trip planned into the park, the cost can be as low as US$60 per person.

Boat

Several fast ferries travel to Golfito (US$6, 30 minutes), departing at 6am, noon and 2pm daily. Double-check current schedules, as they change often and without notice.

Bus

Most buses arrive at the peach-colored terminal on the west side of town.

San Isidro de El General US$9.50; 5½ hours; departs 5am, 9am and 1pm.

San José US$15; eight hours; departs 5am and 9am.

Car & Taxi

The *colectivo* (shared truck taxi) runs daily to Cabo Matapalo (US$6, 1½ hours) and Carate (US$10, 2½ hours) on the southern tip of the national park. Departures are from Soda Deya at 6am and 1:30pm, returning at 8:30am and 4pm.

4WD taxis usually charge up to US$90 for the ride to Carate, about US$55 for the ride to Matapalo, and more than US$100 for the overland trek to Bahía Drake.

Left: Lush forests, Península de Osa; **Below:** Howler monkey

CABO MATAPALO & CARATE

Cabo Matapalo occupies the southern tip of the Osa peninsula, along the rough road from Puerto Jiménez and Carate. And if you make it to Carate on the *colectivo*, congratulations. A bone-rattling 45km south of Puerto Jiménez, this is where the dirt road rounds the peninsula and comes to an abrupt dead end.

Carate is nothing to see by itself, but it's a beautifully remote getaway and the southern gateway for anyone hiking to Sirena ranger station in Parque Nacional Corcovado.

This area is an excellent place in which to unplug, or to rest before or after a foray into Corcovado.

Sleeping

Because of the area's end-of-the-line remoteness, all accommodations listed include all meals in their rates, with some including tours and transfers to Puerto Jiménez.

Lookout Inn   Hut $$$
(☏ 2735-5431; www.lookout-inn.com; r per person from US$115; P @ ☎) Perched up the side of a steep hillside overlooking the ocean, Lookout Inn has comfortable, open-air quarters with mural-painted walls, hardwood floors, beautifully carved doors and unbeatable views. Accommodations are accessible only by a wooden walkway winding through the trees. Interesting gimmick: if you don't spot a scarlet macaw during your stay, your lodging is free!

La Leona Eco-Lodge   Ecolodge $$$
(☏ 2735-5704; www.laleonaecolodge.com; s/d from US$160/280; ☎) ⁄ On the edge of Parque Nacional Corcovado, this friendly lodge offers all the thrills of camping, without the hassles. Sixteen comfy forest-

293

green tents are nestled between the palm trees, with decks facing the beach. All are fully screened and comfortably furnished. Solar power provides electricity in the restaurant. All guests must hike the 2.5km in from the Carate airstrip.

Lapa Ríos Lodge $$$

(☎2735-5130; www.laparios.com; rd to Carate, Km 17; s/d US$576/904; P ☀) ✎ This top-notch wilderness resort combines the right amount of luxury with a rustic, tropical ambience. On the site are 16 spacious, thatched bungalows, all decked out with queen-sized beds, bamboo furniture, garden showers and private decks with panoramic views. An extensive trail system allows exploration of the 400-hectare reserve, while swimming, snorkeling and surfing are within easy reach. Rates include round-trip transfer from Puerto Jiménez plus tours, classes and workshops. Make reservations as far in advance as possible.

Luna Lodge Lodge $$$

(☎2206-5859, in USA & Canada 888-760-0760; www.lunalodge.com; s/d from US$140/250; P ☎ ☀) ✎ A steep road crisscrosses the Río Carate and up the valley to this enchanting mountain retreat on the border of Parque Nacional Corcovado. Accommodations in this dreamy wilderness retreat range from tent cabins to thatched bungalows with open-air garden showers and private terraces, but all have stunning views of the gardens and the pristine jungle rolling down to the ocean. This isolated luxury spot is the result of owner Lana's passion for conservation, and her energy is infectious.

ℹ Getting There & Away

If you are driving, a 4WD is highly recommended even in the dry season as roads frequently get washed out. There are several shallow rivers to cross on the way here. Otherwise, the *colectivo* (US$6) from Puerto Jiménez will drop you here.

PARQUE NACIONAL CORCOVADO

Famously labeled by *National Geographic* as 'the most biologically intense place on earth,' this national park is the last great original tract of tropical rainforest in Pacific Central America. The bastion of biological diversity is home to Costa Rica's

Scarlet macaw

MARCO SIMONI/GETTY IMAGES ©

largest population of scarlet macaws, as well as countless other endangered species, including Baird's tapir, the giant anteater and the world's largest bird of prey, the harpy eagle. Corcovado's amazing biodiversity has long attracted a devoted stream of visitors who descend from Bahía Drake and Puerto Jiménez to explore the remote location and spot a wide array of wildlife.

Activities

WILDLIFE-WATCHING

The best wildlife-watching in Corcovado is at Sirena, but the coastal trails have two advantages: they are more open, and the constant crashing of waves covers the sound of noisy walkers. White-faced capuchin, red-tailed squirrel, collared peccary, white-nosed coati and northern tamandua are regularly seen on both of the following trails.

The coastal trail from Carate to Sirena produces an endless pageant of birds. Sightings of scarlet macaws are guaranteed, as the tropical almond trees lining the coast are a favorite food. The sections along the beach shelter mangrove black hawk by the dozens and numerous waterbird species.

The Los Patos–Sirena trail attracts lowland rainforest birds such as great curassow, chestnut-mandibled toucan, fiery-billed aracari and rufous piha. Encounters with mixed flocks are common. Mammals are similar to those near coastal trails, but Los Patos is better for primates and white-lipped peccary.

For wildlife-watchers frustrated at the difficulty of seeing rainforest mammals, a stay at Sirena ranger station is a must. Baird's tapirs are practically assured – a statement that can be made at few other places in the world. This endangered and distant relative of the rhinoceros is frequently spotted grazing along the airstrip after dusk.

Around Parque Nacional Corcovado Don't Miss List

RECOMMENDATIONS FROM DIONISIO 'NITO' PANIAGUA, PARQUE NACIONAL CORCOVADO GUIDE

1 THREE-DAY TREK CORCOVADO
You have to spend one night at the Sirena ranger station. This is the best way to spot wildlife such as tapirs, wild pigs, bull sharks and crocodiles, among others, and it also provides a good chance for catching a glimpse of pumas or ocelots. The ranger station is not a lodge but not as basic as travelers sometimes expect.

2 MATAPALO
The perfect place for a combination of beach, rainforest and waterfall. Here you can spot all four types of monkeys, sloths, coatis, agoutis, scarlet macaws and blue morpho butterflies. Matapalo is also good for seeing the poisonous dart frogs and giant trees of the rainforest. It is perfect for families and travelers who are short on time.

3 ISLA DE CAÑO
There is access from Bahía Drake and the possibility of snorkeling and scuba diving. The visibility under water is great and lots of colorful fish can be spotted. It's a perfect day tour with the option to hike in the rainforest and spend some time on the beach.

4 KAYAKING IN THE GOLFO DULCE
On a marvelous three-hour kayaking trip in the mangroves around Puerto Jiménez you'll spot boas, white-faced capuchin monkeys, water birds and giant crabs. The return to Jiménez is along the Golfo Dulce and with some luck dolphins will accompany the kayaks.

Corcovado is the only national park in Costa Rica with all four of the country's primate species. Spider monkey, mantled howler and white-faced capuchin can be encountered anywhere, while the Los Patos–Sirena trail is best for the fourth and most endangered species, the Central American squirrel monkey. Sirena also has fair chances for the extremely hard-to-find silky anteater, a nocturnal animal that frequents the beachside forests between the Río Claro and the station.

HIKING

Paths are primitive and the hiking is hot, humid and insect-ridden, but the challenge of the trek and the interaction with wildlife at Corcovado are thrilling. Carry plenty of food, water and insect repellent.

The most popular route traverses the park from Los Patos to Sirena, then exits the park at La Leona (or vice versa). This allows hikers to begin and end their journey in or near Puerto Jiménez, offering easy access to La Leona and Los Patos.

Hiking is best in the dry season (from December to April), when there is still regular rain but all of the trails are open. It's still muddy, but you won't sink quite as deep.

Sleeping & Eating

Simple dormitory lodging (US$8 per person) is available at Sirena ranger station only. Here, you'll find simple vinyl mattresses and simple bunk beds. The station serves decent meals (breakfast is US$20, lunch or dinner is US$25) by advance reservation only; if packing in your own food, no cooking is allowed, so be sure it's edible as is or with cold preparation.

All visitors are required to pack out all of their trash.

Information

Changes to park regulations in early 2014 mean that all visitors to Corcovado must be accompanied by an ICT-certified guide. Besides their intimate knowledge of the trails, local guides are amazingly informed about flora and fauna, including the best places to spot various species. Most guides also carry telescopes, allowing for up-close views of wildlife.

Guides are most often hired through the Área de Conservación Osa **park office** **(ACOSA; Osa Conservation Area Headquarters;** ☎ 2735-5036; **Corcovado park fee per person per day US$10;** ⊗ **8am-noon & 1-4pm Mon-Fri)** in Puerto Jiménez, or through hotels and tour operators. Two recommended local offices are the super-reliable, locally run Osa Wild in Puerto Jiménez and **Corcovado Info Center** (☎ 8846-4734, 2775-0916; **www.corcovadoinfocenter. com**) in Bahía Drake. Prices vary considerably depending on the season, availability, size of your party and type of

Masked tree frog, Parque Nacional Piedras Blancas
JOHN SULLIVAN/ALAMY ©

expedition you want to arrange. In any case, you will need to negotiate a price that includes park fees, meals and transportation.

Getting There & Away

From Bahía Drake

From Bahía Drake, you can walk the coastal trail that leads to San Pedrillo station (about four hours from Agujitas). Many lodges run day tours here, with a boat ride to San Pedrillo (30 minutes to an hour, depending on the departure point) or Sirena (one to 1½ hours).

From Carate

In the southeast, the closest point of access is Carate, from where La Leona station is a one-hour, 3.5km hike west along the beach.

Carate is accessible from Puerto Jiménez via a poorly maintained, 45km dirt road. This journey is an adventure in itself, and often allows for some good wildlife-spotting along the way. A 4WD *colectivo* travels this route twice daily for US$10.

If you have your own car, the *pulpería* (corner store) in Carate is a safe place to park for a few days; tip the manager before setting out.

GOLFITO

With a long and sordid history, Golfito is a rough-around-the-edges port that stretches out along the Golfo Dulce. The town was built on bananas – the United Fruit Company moved its regional head-quarters here in the '30s. In the 1980s, declining markets, rising taxes, worker unrest and banana diseases forced the company's departure.

In an attempt to boost the region's economy, the federal government built a duty-free facility, the so-called Zona Americana, in Golfito. This surreal shopping center attracts Ticos from around the country, who descend on the otherwise dying town for 24-hour shopping sprees. And as charmless as it is by day, by night the place is home to surly ex-military men, boozy yachters, prostitutes and shady characters.

Still, as the largest town in Golfo Dulce, Golfito is a transportation hub for hikers heading to Corcovado, surfers heading to Pavones and sportfishers.

Detour: Parque Nacional Piedras Blancas

Formerly known as Parque Nacional Esquinas, this national park was established in 1992 as an extension of Corcovado. Piedras Blancas has 120 sq km of undisturbed tropical primary rainforest, as well as 20 sq km of secondary forests, pasture land and coastal cliffs and beaches.

As one of the last remaining stretches of lowland rainforest on the Pacific, Piedras Blancas is also home to a vast array of flora and fauna. According to a study conducted at the biological station at Gamba, the biodiversity of trees in Piedras Blancas is the densest in all of Costa Rica, even surpassing Corcovado.

To really get to know the place, stay a few nights nestled at the **Esquinas Rainforest Lodge** (☏2741-8001; www.esquinaslodge.com; s/d incl meals US$161/256; P 🛜 🏊) 🐾, which is integrally affiliated with community and rainforest.

Sights

Fundacíon Santuario Silvestre de Osa   Wildlife Reserve
(Osa Wildlife Sanctuary; ☏8888-3803, 8861-1309; www.osawildlife.org; Caña Blanca; minimum donation US$25; ◷8am–noon) Run by Earl and Carol Crews, who began with a lodge that became a bird sanctuary, which then turned into a sanctuary for injured and orphaned animals of all kinds, this nonprofit reserve now rehabilitates and releases all manner of local wildlife. Those that can't be rein-troduced into the wild – like the resident spider and howler monkeys – remain at the sanctuary, where visitors can meet them up close and personal.

Sleeping & Eating

Samoa del Sur
Hotel $$

(☎2775-0233; www.samoadelsur.com; s/d incl breakfast US$79/96; P❄️🛜🏊) This French-run facility offers comfortable rooms outfitted with tiled floors, wood furniture and thick towels. The bar, with its huge dome ceiling, is a popular spot in the evenings, and the restaurant serves typical Tico fare as well as beautiful French specialties like mussels Provençal. *Colectivo* (shared) boats to Zancudo leave from the Samoa dock, but it's also near the Muellecito (main dock).

Casa Roland Marina Resort
Resort $$$

(☎2775-0180; www.casarolandgolfito.com; d from US$170; P❄️@🛜🏊) Casa Roland is Golfito's most swish hotel, and primarily caters to duty-free shoppers looking for an amenity-laden base. You can expect to find all the usual top-end standards including a swimming pool, restaurants and bars, tennis courts and a health spa, as well as a few extras such as a movie theatre and casino.

Restaurante Buenos Días
Breakfast $

(☎2775-1124; meals US$5-10; ⊙6am-10pm; P) Rare is the visitor who passes through Golfito without stopping at this cheerful spot opposite the Muellecito. Brightly colored booths, bilingual menus and a super-convenient location ensure a constant stream of guests – whether for an early breakfast, a typical Tico *casado* or a good old-fashioned burger.

ℹ️ Getting There & Away

Air

The airport is 4km north of the town center near the duty-free zone. Nature Air (www.natureair.com) and Sansa (www.flysansa.com) have daily flights to/from San José. One-way tickets are approximately US$100.

Boat

Fast ferries travel to Puerto Jiménez from the Muellecito (main dock) (US$6, 30 minutes), departing at 6am, 11:30am and 2pm daily. Because this schedule changes frequently, it's best to check for current times at the dock; in any event, show up early to ensure a spot.

The boat taxi for Zancudo (US$6, 30 minutes) departs from the dock at Samoa del Sur at noon, Monday through Saturday. The return trip is at 7am the next day (except Sunday).

Bus

Most buses stop at the depot opposite the small park in the southern part of town.

Pavones US$4; two hours; departs 10am and 3pm. This service may be affected by road and weather conditions, especially in the rainy season.

San José, via San Isidro de El General (Tracopa) US$14.70; seven hours; departs from the terminal near Muelle Bananero at 5am and 1:30pm.

Zancudo US$4; three hours; departs 1:30pm.

Pier, Golfito (p297)
HOLGER LEUE/GETTY IMAGES ©

ZANCUDO & PAVONES

Occupying a slender finger of land that juts into the Golfo Dulce, the tiny village of Zancudo is about as laid-back a beach destination as you'll find in Costa Rica. On the west side of town, gentle, warm Pacific waters lap onto black sands, and seeing more than a handful of people on the beach means it's crowded. On the east side, a tangle of mangrove swamps attracts birds, crocodiles and plenty of fish, which in turn attract fishers hoping to reel them in. Unlike nearby Pavones, an emerging surf destination, Zancudo is content to remain a far-flung village in a far-flung corner of Costa Rica.

Pavones, on the other hand, has been well known among surfers for a couple of generations since it boasts one of the longest left-hand breaks in the world. The town itself is a hodgepodge of lodges, *cabinas* and *sodas*. Connect a few dots along rough, mostly unmarked roads and you've got a zig-zag route between these two sister-villages.

Activities

The main activities at Zancudo and Pavones are undoubtedly swinging on hammocks, strolling on the beach and swimming in the aqua-blue waters of the Golfo Dulce. In Zancudo the surf is gentle, and at night the water sometimes sparkles with bioluminescence – tiny phosphorescent marine plants and plankton that light up if you sweep a hand through the water. The effect is like underwater fireflies.

The mangrove swamps around Zancudo offer plenty of opportunities for exploration: birdlife is prolific, while other animals such as crocodile, caiman, monkey and sloth are also frequently spotted. The boat ride from Golfito gives a glimpse of these waters, but you can also paddle them yourself: rent kayaks from any of the accommodations listings following.

If You Like...
Parks & Reserves

If you like Parque Nacional Corcovado, we think you'll like these other parks and nature reserves in Southern Costa Rica:

1 HUMEDAL NACIONAL TÉRRABA-SIERPE
Approximately 330 sq km of protected mangrove wetlands that harbor numerous species of aquatic birds; you can set up tours in Sierpe.

2 REFUGIO NACIONAL DE VIDA SILVESTRE GOLFITO
(☑ SINAC Office in Golfito 2775-2620; park fee US$10; ⏰ 8am-4pm) This tiny 28-sq-km reserve surrounding the town of Golfito is home to rare cycads (living plant 'fossils').

3 TISKITA JUNGLE LODGE
(☑ 2776-2194, 2776-2193; www.tiskita. com; guided hike US$25) In the Pavones area, this private reserve consists of 100 hectares of virgin rainforest, through which trails lead to waterfalls and freshwater pools suitable for swimming. Hikes led by knowledgeable local guides are available with advance reservations.

In Pavones surfing is the draw – when the surf's up, this beach town attracts hordes of international elite, usually between April and October. However, because Pavones is inside Golfo Dulce, it can go for weeks without seeing any waves. When Pavones is flat, head south to **Punta Banco**, a reef break with decent rights and lefts.

🛏 Sleeping & Eating

ZANCUDO

Sol y Mar   Cabina **$**
(☑ 2776-0014; www.zancudo.com; cabins from US$45; **P** **@** 🛜) This popular hangout offers various lodging options, from smallish dwellings further from the water to private deluxe units with fancy tile showers and unobstructed ocean views. Even if you're not staying here, the

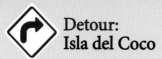

Detour: Isla del Coco

Even though it's a tiny speck of green amid the endless Pacific, Isla del Coco looms large in the imagination of the adventurer: jagged mountains and tales of treasure, a pristine and isolated ecosystem filled with wildlife and some of the world's best diving. Remember the opening shot of *Jurassic Park,* where the helicopter sweeps over a tropical island? That was here.

Isla del Coco (aka Cocos Island) is around 500km southwest of the mainland in the middle of the eastern Pacific. As it's the most far-flung part of Costa Rica, you'll have to pay through the nose to get here, though few other destinations in the country are as wildly exotic and visually arresting.

As beautiful as the island may be, its terrestrial environs pale in comparison to what lies beneath. Named by PADI as one of the world's top 10 dive spots, the surrounding waters of Isla del Coco harbor abundant pelagics including one of the largest known schools of hammerhead sharks in the world.

Since the island remains largely uninhabited and is closed to overnight visitors, visits require either a private yacht or a liveaboard dive vessel. While non-divers are certainly welcome to make the trip, it pays to have some significant underwater experience in your logbook – sites around Isla del Coco are as challenging as they are breathtaking.

open-air restaurant and thatched bar is a Zancudo favorite – and it's the only game in town during low season.

Au Coeur du Soleil
Cabina $$
(☎2776-0112; www.aucoeurdusoleil.com; d US$50-60; P☎) These brightly painted, lovingly maintained cabins have fans, fridges, big windows and a central barbecue – some have kitchenettes and all have a homey charm. The French hosts are warm and gregarious and offer guests the use of bikes for cruising around Zancudo.

El Coquito
Costa Rican $
(☎2776-0000; meals US$7-8; ⊙7am-8pm Sun-Wed, later Thu-Sat) Bright, cheerful and right in the middle of Zancudo's main drag, this *soda* is a charmer. It offers a filling *casado* for US$7 of fresh fish, rice and fruit, and the *licuado* (smoothies) are magically refreshing after the long, dusty ride into town. On weekends the adjoining space transforms into a nightclub, with booming music and dancing.

PAVONES

Cabinas La Ponderosa
Cabina $$
(☎2776-2076; www.cabinaslaponderosa.com; r US$60-140, houses US$235-275; P☀☎) Housed on six lovely landscaped hectares, these cozy cabins are tenderly cared for by Marshall and Angela McCarthy, who have spent years living in their adopted home of Pavones. The common lounge offers all kinds of entertainment, including a table-tennis table and a massive video library, but the real appeal of staying here is the warm hospitality of the McCarthy's.

Tiskita Jungle Lodge
Lodge $$$
(☎in San José 2296-8125; www.tiskita-lodge. co.cr; r from US$570 for 3 nights; P@☎☒) Set amid extensive gardens and orchards, this lodge is arguably the most beautiful and intimate in all of Golfo Dulce. Accommodations are in various stunning wooden cabins accented by stone garden showers that allow you to freshen up while bird-watching. Rates include all meals and guided walks (there's a three-night minimum). Reservations must be made in advance.

Café de la Suerte   Cafe $

(☎ 2776-2388; meals US$4-9; ⏰ 8am-5pm Mon-Sat; 📶 🍴) Simple breakfasts, omelets and veggie dishes dominate the menu here, all light fare to be washed down with a tropical-fruit smoothie. They also have a handful of simple, colorful rooms for rent (from US$35 to US$70).

❶ Getting There & Away

Boat

The boat dock is near the north end of the beach on the inland, estuary side. A water taxi to Golfito (US$6, 30 minutes) departs from this dock at 7am, returning at noon, Monday through Saturday. Inquire locally, however, as times are subject to change.

Bus

The bus for Golfito (US$4) leaves at 5am for the three-hour trip, with a ferry transfer at the Río Coto Colorado. Service is erratic in the wet season, so inquire before setting out.

From Pavones, two daily buses go to Golfito (US$4, two hours). The first leaves at 5:15am, departing from the end of the road in Punta Banco and stopping opposite the Riviera. The second leaves at 12:30pm from the school. Most connections go through Zancudo.

Car

It's possible to drive to Zancudo by taking the road south of Río Claro for about 10km. Turn left at the Rodeo Bar and follow the signs across the bridge. From there, 30km of poorly maintained dirt road gets you to Zancudo.

If going on to Pavones, the roads are signed sporadically; best to ask directions as you go.

SAN ISIDRO DE EL GENERAL

With a population of only 45,000, San Isidro de El General is little more than a sprawling, utilitarian town at the crossroads between some of Costa Rica's prime destinations. Still, the strolling lovers and teenage troublemakers give the town square some charm, as does its unexpectedly lively bar scene.

'El General' (often referred to as Pérez Zeledón, the name of the municipality)

San Isidro de El General

is the region's largest population center and major transportation hub. If you're traveling to the southern Pacific beaches or Chirripó, a brief stop is inevitable.

🛏 Sleeping & Eating

Options in San Isidro proper serve as one-night crash pads of varying levels of style and sophistication, while options outside the town generally have more character and warrant a longer stay.

Thunderbird Hotel & Casino   Hotel $$

(☎ 2770-6230; www.tbrcr.com/hotelcostarica; cnr Av 3 & Calle 4; r standard/luxury from US$49/62; 🅿 ❄ @ 📶) 'Executive Elegance' is the boast of this upscale business hotel. After a series of upgrades it's surprisingly swish. The quarters are brightly painted and fitted with shiny black-lacquer furniture. There's a small casino downstairs where you can drink for free while feeding the slots.

Talari Mountain Lodge   Lodge $$

(☎ 2771-0341; www.talari.co.cr; Rivas; s/d incl breakfast US$62/90; 🅿 📶 ♨) This secluded mountain lodge is a bird-watcher's haven, with over 200 species of bird spotted on the riverside property. Accommodations are in simple wooden cabins hemmed in by the forest. To get here from San Isidro, follow the road to San Gerardo de Rivas for 7km; the driveway will be on the right (find directions on the website).

La Casa del Marisco
Seafood $

(☎ 8366-1880, 2772-2862; mains US$4-10; ⏰ 10am-10pm Mon-Sat) Since this unpretentious seafood spot is usually slammed at lunchtime, it's best to come during off hours for its several daily varieties of *ceviche,* fresh fish or shrimp prepared as you like it, and pastas, burgers, salads and soups. The crowd of local clientele not-so-subtly hints at the choice sustenance served here.

Kafe de la Casa
Cafe $

(☎ 2770-4816; Av 3 btwn Calles 2 & 4; meals US$6-13; ⏰ 6am-8pm Mon-Fri, 7am-3pm Sun; 📶) Set in an old Tico house, this bohemian cafe features eclectic artwork, an open kitchen and breezy garden seating.

The menu has excellent breakfasts, light lunches, gourmet dinners and plenty of coffee drinks.

ℹ Getting There & Away

Bus

Buses to San José depart from Terminal Tracopa; buses to central Pacific coast towns depart from Terminal Quepos.

San José US$7; three hours; departs 7:30am, 8:30am, 9am, 10:30am, 1pm, 4pm, 5:30pm and 8:30pm.

Dominical US$3; 1½ hours; departs 7am, 9am, 11:30am, 3:30pm and 4pm.

Puerto Jiménez (via Palmar Norte) US$9.50; five hours; departs 6:30am, 11am and 3pm.

Quepos US$5; three hours; departs 7am, 11:30am and 3:30pm.

Uvita US$3.50; two hours; departs 9am and 4pm.

Taxi

A 4WD taxi to San Gerardo de Rivas will cost between US$25 and US$30. To arrange one, it's best to inquire through your accommodations.

SAN GERARDO DE RIVAS

If you have plans to climb Cerro Chirripó, you're in the right place – the tiny, tranquil town of San Gerardo de Rivas is at the doorstep of the national park. This is a place to get supplies, a good night's rest and a hot shower before embarking on the trek.

Although hikers are keen to press on to the park as quickly as possible, the logistics of getting up the mountain and the infrequent bus schedule will almost certainly require a night in San Gerardo before the

Dolphin and fish, Isla del Coco (p300)
DMITRY MIROSHNIKOV/GETTY IMAGES ©

hike, the night after or both. Luckily, the boulder-strewn Río Chirripó and bird-filled alpine scenery make it a beautiful place to linger.

 Sights & Activities

Cocolisos Truchero
Fishing

(☎2742-5023; ⏰8am-6pm Sat & Sun, & by appointment; 👫) Down the hill 500m from the middle of town is this lovely little trout farm, operated by the Marin family. If you're hanging out the day before or after a trip into Parque Nacional Chirripó, a perfect afternoon can be made out of sitting by the trout pools and taking in the celebrated orchid collection. Naturally, the fish is the best part; matronly Garita puts together a feast of trout and home-cooked sides for US$7.

Thermal Hot Springs
Health & Fitness

(Aguas Termales; ☎2742-5210; Herradura; admission US$6; ⏰7am-5:30pm) About 2km north of San Gerardo above the ranger station the road forks; take the left fork and walk for about 1km on a paved road for these hot springs. Turn right and take the rickety suspension bridge over the river. A switchback trail will lead you another 1km to a house with a *soda* (lunch counter), which is the entrance to the springs.

Sleeping & Eating

Most options are situated along the narrow road parallel to the river. The majority rent out equipment (sleeping bags, air mattresses, cooking stoves etc), though supplies are limited and quality varies. Note that many accommodations close when Parque Nacional Chirripó closes, during the last half of May and all of October.

Casa Mariposa
Hostel $

(☎2742-5037; www.hotelcasamariposa.net; dm US$15, d US$36-60; P @) 🚲 Just a short walk from the entrance of the park, this adorable lodge is built into the side of the mountain and has a warm, glowing atmos-

Meeting Your Maker

Although the treacherous drive across the Cerro de la Muerte might offer ample opportunities to meet your maker, look to the heavens about 6km north of San Isidro. There you'll see a towering statue of Christ, perched precariously on the edge of a cliff above.

phere. Traveler-oriented details – warm clothes to borrow for the hike, laundry service, assistance with booking the Chirripó lodge – make it ideal.

Talamanca Reserve
Hotel $$

(☎2742-5080; www.talamancareserve.com; r/ste $70/80; P @ 🛜) 🚲 With over 4000 acres of primary and secondary cloud forest, this private reserve has trails leading to its 10 waterfalls and cabins nestled into a garden and forest setting. The lovely garden and river cabins on the property have hot water, terraces and beautifully embellished wood and tile interiors. There's also a good onsite restaurant and a cozy lounge area.

Monte Azul
Boutique Hotel $$$

(☎2742-5222, in USA 415-967-4300; www.monteazulcr.com; Rivas; s/d incl 2 meals from US$359/416; P 🍽 🛜) 🚲 The luxurious, elegant and carbon-neutral Monte Azul single-handedly boosts the quality of accommodations within a stone's throw of Chirripó. Set on a private 125-hectare reserve, the luxury riverfront suites have tasteful contemporary art, small kitchens, luxury mattresses and linens, and custom-designed furniture. The gourmet restaurant offers international fusions using organic produce from its garden. Note that this place is in the village of Rivas, which is down the mountain from San Gerardo de Rivas.

Day Hiking Chirripó

Although it might be possible to leave San Gerardo de Rivas, summit Chirripó and return to town in a single day, don't do it. It would be an utterly exhausting slog for even the most fit hikers, and nearly guarantee returning in the dark over the muddiest parts of the trail. If you don't have the time, consider a long day hike in the Cloudbridge Nature Reserve (p307).

 Information

The Chirripó ranger station (SINAC; 2742-5083; 6:30am-noon & 1-4:30pm) is about 1km below the soccer field on the road from San Isidro. Stop by early to check for availability at Crestones Base Lodge (p305), and to confirm and pay fees before setting out. The Base Lodge holds 10 first-come-first-served beds, which can only be reserved the day prior to arrival.

Getting There & Away

Arriving via public transportation requires a connection through San Isidro. Buses to San Isidro depart from the soccer field at 5:15am, 11:30am and 4pm (US$1.80, 1½ to two hours). Any of the hotels can call a taxi for you (about US$30).

Driving from San Isidro, head south on the Interamericana and cross Río San Isidro south of town. About 500m further on, cross the unsigned Río Jilguero and take the first, steep turn up to the left, about 300m beyond the Jilguero. Note that this turnoff is not marked (if you miss the turn, it *is* signed from the northbound side).

PARQUE NACIONAL CHIRRIPÓ

Costa Rica's highest peak, **Cerro Chirripó**, at 3820m above sea level, is the focus of popular **Parque Nacional Chirripó** (2742-5083; park fee for two days US$15, plus US$15 for each additional day; closed 2nd half of May & all of Oct). Of course, while Chirripó is the highest and most famous summit

in Costa Rica, it is not unique: two other peaks inside the park top 3800m, and most of the park's 502 sq km lies above 2000m.

Like a tiny chunk of the South American Andes, Parque Nacional Chirripó's rocky high-altitude features are an entirely unexpected respite from the heat and humidity of the rainforest (it's downright cold at night). Above 3400m, the landscape is *páramo*, which is mostly scrubby trees and grasslands, and supports a unique spectrum of highland wildlife. Rocky outposts punctuate the otherwise barren hills, and feed a series of glacial lakes that earned the park its iconic name: Chirripó means 'eternal waters.'

The only way up Chirripó is by foot. Although the trekking routes are long and challenging, watching the sunrise from such lofty heights, literally above the clouds, is an undeniable highlight of Costa Rica. You will have to be prepared for the cold – and at times wet – slog to the top, though your efforts will be rewarded with some of the most sweeping vistas that Costa Rica can offer. The vast majority of travelers visit Chirripó over three days: one to get to San Gerardo de Rivas to secure permits, one to hike to the Crestones Base Lodge and one to summit the peak and return to San Gerardo.

The dry season (from late December to April) is the most popular time to visit Chirripó. February and March are the driest months, though it may still rain. The park is closed in May and October.

The maps available at the ranger station are serviceable for the major trails.

Activities

CLIMBING CHIRRIPÓ

The park entrance is at San Gerardo de Rivas, which lies 1350m above sea level; from here the summit is 2.5km straight up! A well-marked 16km trail leads all the way to the top and no technical climbing is required. It would be nearly impossible to get lost.

The amount of time it takes to get up varies greatly – it can take as little as five and as many as 14 hours to cover the 10km from the trailhead to the hostel, depending on how fit you are: the recommended departure time is 5am or 6am. The trailhead lies 50m beyond Albergue Urán in San Gerardo de Rivas (about 4km from the ranger station). The main gate is open from 4am to 10am to allow climbers to enter; no one is allowed to begin the ascent after 10am (although it is unlikely that a fast-moving latecomer would be turned away). Inside the park the trail is clearly signed at every kilometer.

Reaching the hostel is the hardest part. From there the hike to the summit is about 5km on relatively flatter terrain (although the last 100m is very steep): allow at least two hours if you are fit, but carry a warm jacket, rain gear, water, snacks and a flashlight just in case. From the summit on a clear day, the vista stretches to both the Caribbean Sea and the Pacific Ocean.

WILDLIFE-WATCHING

The varying altitude means an amazing diversity of fauna in Parque Nacional Chirripó. Particularly famous for its extensive birdlife, the national park is home to several endangered species, including the harpy eagle (the largest, most powerful raptor in the Americas) and the resplendent quetzal (especially visible between March and May).

In addition to the prolific birdlife, the park is home to some unusual high-altitude reptiles, such as the green spiny lizard and the highland alligator lizard. Mammals include puma, Baird's tapir, spider monkey, capuchin and – at higher

elevations – Dice's rabbit and the coyotes that feed on them.

 ## Sleeping & Eating

The only accommodations in Parque Nacional Chirripó are at **Crestones Base Lodge** (Centro Ambientalista el Parámo; dm US$10), which houses up to 60 people in dorm-style bunks that have serviceable vinyl-coated mattresses. The basic stone building has a solar panel that provides electric light for limited hours and sporadic heat for showers. Amazingly, it also has wi-fi. All crude comforts – sleeping bags, cooking stoves, blankets and the like – should be rented in San Gerardo de Rivas, where they're ubiquitous.

The lodge reserves 10 spaces per night for travelers who show up in San Gerardo and are ready to hike on the following day. This is far and away the more practical option for most travelers. Even though there is no certainty that there will be space available on the days you wish to hike, showing up immediately when the ranger station opens at 6:30am usually works.

Cerro Chirripó
CHRISTIAN KOBER/GETTY IMAGES ©

ℹ Information

It is essential that you stop at the Chirripó ranger station (p304) at least one day before you intend to climb Chirripó so that you can get a space at the mountaintop hostel and pay your park entry fee (US$15 for two days, plus US$15 for each additional day).

ℹ Getting There & Around

From opposite the ranger station, in front of Cabinas El Bosque, there is free transportation to the trailhead at 5am. Also, several hotels offer early-morning trailhead transportation for their guests.

SAN GERARDO DE DOTA

San Gerardo de Dota is unlike any other place in Costa Rica – a bucolic mountain town run through by a clear, rushing river and surrounded by forested hills that more resemble the alps than the tropics. It's set deep within a mountain valley; the air is crisp and fresh, and chilly at night, and orchard-lined Savegre basin hosts high-altitude species that draw bird-watchers from around the world.

The elusive quetzal is such a celebrity in these parts that in 2005 the national government demarcated a national park in its honor.

Visiting the national park is largely a self-organized DIY affair since it has no permanent infrastructure, but the town of San Gerardo provides easy access to the trailheads and offers a wide assortment of tourist lodges. In stunning contrast to Costa Rica's famous tropical regions, San Gerardo de Dota is a charmer, well worth seeking out for a quiet couple of days of fresh mountain air.

🌿 Activities

SPORTFISHING

The trout-fishing in the Río Savegre is excellent: May and June is the time for fly-fishing and December to March for lure-fishing. A number of trout farms surround the village as well.

BIRD-WATCHING & HIKING

The best place to go bird-watching and hiking in the area is Parque Nacional Los Quetzales. While there are no information facilities for tourists in the park, you can hire terrific local guides through the hotels. Travelers who wish to do extensive hiking in the area are advised to collect maps before they arrive.

🛏 Sleeping & Eating

Note that many of the lodges offer dinner with their accommodation.

Dantica Cloud Forest Lodge   Lodge **$$$**
(📞 2740-1067; www.dantica.com; r/ste incl breakfast from US$189/217; 🅿 ❄ @ 🛜) Definitely the most elegant place in San Gerardo, if not the

WHIT RICHARDSON/ALAMY ©

 Don't Miss
Cloudbridge Nature Reserve

About 2km past the trailhead to Cerro Chirripó you will find the entrance to the mystical, magical Cloudbridge Nature Reserve. Covering 182 hectares on the side of Cerro Chirripó, this private reserve is an ongoing reforestation and preservation project spearheaded by New Yorkers Ian and Genevieve Giddy. A network of trails traverses the property, which is easy to explore independently. Even if you don't get far past the entrance, you'll find two waterfalls, including the magnificent Catarata Pacifica.

NEED TO KNOW

📞USA 917-494-5408; www.cloudbridge.org; admission by donation; ☉sunrise-sunset

whole southern zone, this upscale lodge consists of lovely stucco bungalows with colorful Colombian architectural accents. The modern comforts – leather sofas, plasma TVs, Jacuzzis and track lighting – are nice, but the stunning vistas over the cloud forest steal the scene.

Savegre Hotel de Montaña
Lodge **$$$**

(📞2740-1028, in USA & Canada 866-549-1178; www.savegre.com; s/d/ste incl 3 meals US$136/190/254; 🅿@🛜) Owned and operated by the Chacón family since 1957, this lodge is a local institution,

especially among bird-watchers keen to catch a glimpse of the quetzal. The rooms and suites are gorgeous: wrought-iron chandeliers hang from the high wooden ceilings, while rich wooden furniture surrounds a stone fireplace.

Café Kahawa
Cafe **$**

(📞2740-1081; mains US$5-10; ☉7am-8pm; 🅿) With alfresco tables sitting above the river, funky skull art and sparkling fish tanks filled with fingerling trout, this atmospheric spot prepares trout in numerous excellent ways. There isn't much on the menu that doesn't feature this

local fish, but variations on the theme – such as trout in coconut sauce and trout *ceviche* (seafood marinated in lemon or lime juice, garlic and seasonings) – can't be found just anywhere.

ⓘ Getting There & Away

The turnoff to San Gerardo de Dota is near Km 80 on the Interamericana. From here, the steep road alternates between paved and dirt. Take it slowly, as two-way traffic necessitates a bit of negotiation. Buses between San José and San Isidro de El General can drop you at the turnoff.

PARQUE NACIONAL LOS QUETZALES

Formerly known as Reserva Los Santos, **Parque Nacional Los Quetzales** (☎2206-5020; admission US$5; ☺7:30am-3:30pm) officially became a national park in 2005. Spread along both banks of the

Río Savegre, at an altitude of 2000m to 3000m, Los Quetzales covers 50 sq km of rainforest and cloud forest lying along the slopes of the Cordillera de Talamanca.

The lifeblood of the park is the Río Savegre, which starts high up on the Cerro de la Muerte and feeds several mountain streams and glacial lakes before pouring into the Pacific near the town of Savegre. Although relatively small, this region is remarkably diverse – the Savegre watershed contains approximately 20% of the registered bird species in Costa Rica.

True to the park's new name, the beautiful quetzal is here, along with the trogon, hummingbird and sooty robin. Avians aside, the park is home to endangered species including jaguars, Baird's tapirs and squirrel monkeys. The park is also home to premontane forests, the second-most endangered life zone in Costa Rica.

The park has no facilities for tourists aside from the small **ranger station** (☎2206-5020; admission US$5; ⏰ 7:30am-3:30pm), which collects fees. From here, a modest network of bird-watching trails radiates into the forest. All the lodges around San Gerardo de Dota organize hiking and bird-watching tours.

The park is bordered by the Interamericana; the entrance is just past Km 76. Any bus along this route can drop you off at the ranger station, though most people arrive in a private vehicle.

RESERVA INDÍGENA BORUCA

The picturesque valley of the Río Grande de Térraba cradles several mostly indigenous villages that comprise the reserve of Brunka (Boruca) peoples. At first glance it is difficult to differentiate these towns from typical Tico villages, aside from a few artisans selling their handiwork. In fact, these towns hardly cater to the tourist trade, which is one of the main reasons why traditional Brunka life has been able to continue without much distraction.

Be sensitive when visiting these communities – dress modestly, avoid taking photographs of people without asking permission, and respect the fact that these living communities are struggling to maintain traditional culture amid a changing world.

Tours to Boruca, which include homestays, hikes to waterfalls, handicraft demonstrations and storytelling, can be arranged through Galería Namu (p69) in San José. Note that transportation is not included.

GENEVIEVE VALLEE/ALAMY ©

★ Don't Miss
Wilson Botanical Garden

Covering 12 hectares and surrounded by 254 hectares of natural forest, Wilson Botanical Garden lies about 6km south of San Vito. This world-class garden was established by Robert and Catherine Wilson in 1963 and thereafter became internationally known for its collection.

The gardens are well laid out, many of the plants are labeled and a trail map is available for self-guided walks featuring exotic species such as orchids, bromeliads and medicinal plants. The many ornamental varieties are beautiful, but the tours explain how they are useful, too (the delicate cycad, for one, is used by the Cabécar and Bribrí people as a treatment for snakebites). The gardens are very popular among bird-watchers, who may see several rare species.

If you want to stay overnight at the botanical gardens, make reservations well in advance: facilities often fill with researchers. Accommodations are in comfortable cabins in the midst of the gorgeous grounds. Rooms are simple but each has a balcony with an amazing view.

Buses between San Vito and Neily pass the entrance to the gardens. Take the bus that goes through Agua Buena, as buses that go through Cañas Gordas do not stop here.

NEED TO KNOW

☎ 2773-4004; www.ots.ac.cr/lascruces; Las Cruces Biological Station; admission US$8, half-/full-day guided tours US$28/54; ⊙ 7am-5pm Mon-Fri, 8am-5pm Sat & Sun

Shopping

The Brunka are celebrated craftspeople and their traditional art plays a leading role in the survival of their culture. While most make their living from agriculture, some indigenous people have begun producing fine handicrafts for tourists. The tribe is most famous for its ornate masks, carved from balsa or cedar, and sometimes colored with natural dyes and acrylics. Brunka women also use pre-Columbian backstrap looms to weave colorful, natural cotton bags, placemats and other textiles. These crafts are not widely available elsewhere in the country.

Getting There & Away

Drivers will find a good road that leaves the Interamericana about 3km south of Rey Curré – look for the sign. This route follows a ridgeline and affords spectacular views of the valleys below. In total, it's about 8km to Boruca from Rey Curré, though the going is slow, and a 4WD is recommended.

SAN VITO

Although the Italian immigrants who founded little San Vito in the 1850s are long gone, this hillside village proudly bears traces of their legacy in linguistic, cultural and culinary echoes. As such, the town serves as a base for travelers in need of a steaming plate of pasta and a good night's sleep before descending into the deep wilderness.

The proximity of the town to the Reserva Indígena Guaymí de Coto Brus means that indigenous peoples pass through this region (groups of Ngöbe – also known as Guaymí – move back and forth across the border with Panama). You might spot women in traditional clothing – long, solid-colored *nagua* dresses trimmed in contrasting hues – riding the bus or strolling the streets.

Tucked in between the Cordillera de Talamanca and the Fila Costeña, the Valle de Coto Brus offers some glorious geography, featuring the green, rolling hills of coffee plantations backed by striking mountain facades. The principal road leaves the Interamericana at Paso Real (near Rey Curré) and follows the Río Jaba to San Vito, then continues south to rejoin the Interamericana at Neily. This winding mountain road offers spectacular scenery and a thrilling ride.

Sights

Finca Cántaros   Park
(2773-3760; www.fincacantaros.com; admission US$5; 7am-5pm;) About 3km south of town, Finca Cántaros is a recreation center and reforestation project. Over 18 acres of grounds – formerly coffee plantations and pasture land – are now a lovely nature reserve with trails, picnic areas and a dramatic lookout over the city. Especially interesting are the pre-Columbian cemetery and a large petroglyph that was discovered on the property in 2009. Though its meaning and age are unclear, the petroglyph is estimated to be about 1600 years old.

Sleeping & Eating

Casa Botania   B&B $$
(2773-4217; www.casabotania.com; s/d incl breakfast US$62/73;) This, the freshest B&B in the region, is exquisitely run by a sweet young Belgian-Tico couple. It hits every note with pitch-perfect elegance, from the modern, beautifully adorned rooms, to the library of bird-watching guides, to the gourmet meals, which are served on a polished deck overlooking the steaming foliage of the valley below. If you don't stay, book a dinner reservation; the three-course, locally sourced, ever-changing menu of smart European-touched Costa Rican fare wins raves. It's located 5km south of town on the road between the Wilson Botanical Garden and San Vito.

Cascata del Bosco   Bungalow $$
(2773-3208; www.cascatadelbosco.com; camping US$20, d US$75;) The four round cabins at Cascata del Bosco overlook the forested valley below and enclose guests in treehouse-like comfort. Each cabin has a large terrace, kitchenette and lovely interior of bamboo and tile. A short

trail winds through the property (there are also plans for a canopy walkway) to the roadside restaurant, a convivial gathering spot for locals and expats. Located 200m north of Wilson Botanical Garden.

ⓘ Information

If you're planning on heading to Parque Internacional La Amistad, San Vito is home to the Minae parks office (Ministry of Environment & Energy; ☎2773-3955; Calle 2 btwn Avs 4 & 6; ⏱9am-4pm), which can help you get your bearings before heading to the national park.

ⓘ Getting There & Away

Bus

The main Tracopa bus terminal (☎2773-3410) is about 150m down the road to Sabalito from downtown.

San Isidro US$7.85; three hours; departs 6:45am, 1:30pm.

San José US$13.45; seven hours; departs 5am, 7:30am, 10am, 3pm.

Car

The drive north from Neily is a scenic one, with superb views of the lowlands dropping away as the road winds up the hillside. The paved road is steep,

Tree frog, Parque Internacional La Amistad

narrow and full of hairpin turns. You can also get to San Vito from San Isidro via the Valle de Coto Brus – an incredibly scenic and less-used route with fantastic views of the Cordillera de Talamanca to the north and the lower Fila Costeña to the south.

PARQUE INTERNACIONAL LA AMISTAD

The 4070-sq-km Parque Internacional La Amistad is an enormous patch of green sprawling across the borders of Panama and Costa Rica (hence its Spanish name La Amistad – 'Friendship'). This is by far the largest protected area in Costa Rica. Standing as a testament to the possibilities of international cooperation and environmental conservation, the park was established in 1982 and declared a UNESCO World Heritage Site just eight years later. It then became part of the greater Mesoamerican Biological Corridor, which protects a great variety of endangered habitats. Its cultural importance is also significant as it includes several scattered indigenous reserves.

Although most of the park's area is high up in the Talamanca and remains virtually inaccessible, there is no shortage

of hiking and camping opportunities available for intrepid travelers at lower altitudes.

Sleeping & Eating

Asoprola (2743-1184, in Canada 877-206-4642, in USA 866-393-5889; www.actuarcos-tarica.com; Altamira; ⏰7am-8pm) runs a simple lodge and restaurant in the village of Altamira and can make arrangements for lodging in local homes in Altamira and Santa Elena de Pittier for a reasonable fee (usually US$10 to US$15 per person). For an intimate look at the lives of people living on the fringes of the rainforest, there is no better way than to arrange a homestay.

Getting There & Away

If you have a tight schedule, a 4WD drive is required to get around this area – the buses are unreliable, the roads are bumpy and things run on a very loose schedule.

SOUTHERN COSTA RICA & PENÍNSULA DE OSA PARQUE INTERNACIONAL LA AMISTAD

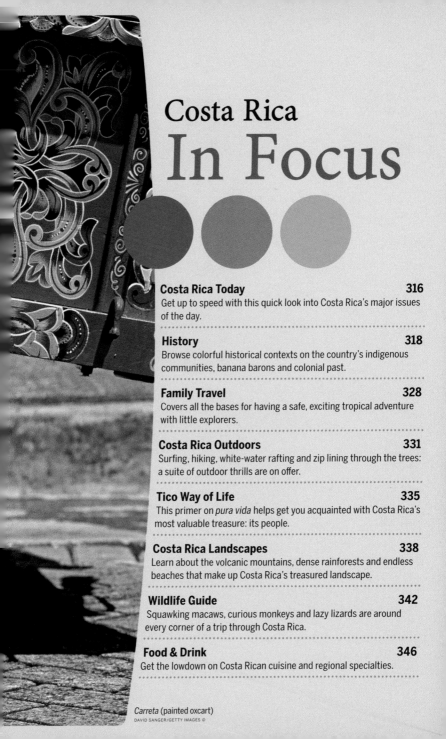

Costa Rica
In Focus

Carreta (painted oxcart)
DAVID SANGER/GETTY IMAGES ©

Costa Rica Today

Harvesting coffee plants

> *The progress made in the next few years will reveal whether Costa Rica's vision of carbon neutrality can coalesce into reality by 2021.*

belief systems
(% of population)

75 Roman Catholic
13 Evangelical
Other
4 None
2 Jehovah's Witnesses
other Protestant

if Costa Rica were 100 people

94 would be white & *mestizo*
3 would be black
1 would be Chinese
1 would be indigenous
1 would be other

population per sq km

≈ 6 people

COSTA RICA   USA   MEXICO

Changing of the Guard

After Costa Rica's first female president, Laura Chinchilla, termed out in 2014, Luis Guillermo Solís won the runoff election – the second in the country's history – for president.

Though Costa Rica's political landscape is unlikely to change dramatically, Solís' win may signal a sea change for the National Liberation Party (PLN), which has dominated Costa Rican politics for more than half a century but has been dogged by corruption scandals.

Solís, affiliated with the center-left Citizens' Action Party (PAC), ran on promises to fight corruption and to address the country's social and economic inequality. As a scholar of Latin American studies and former professor at the University of Costa Rica, he is still considered somewhat of a political outsider. From the results of the election, it seems that many Costa Ricans view Solís as an agent of much-needed but not-too-radical change.

DREAMPICTURES/GETTY IMAGES ©

Río San Juan Saga

Forming the eastern stretch of the border between Nicaragua and Costa Rica is the Río San Juan, a silty river studded with small marshy islands and floating rafts of water lettuce.

The border area is complicated, not only because the river is an evolving geographical entity. The 1858 Cañas-Jerez Treaty asserts that Nicaragua owns the Río San Juan but that Costa Rica retains navigation rights on its side of the river. Border spats between the two countries have arisen over the years, flaring up again recently.

The latest tensions started with Nicaragua dredging a river delta in late 2010. With Nicaraguan soldiers present during the process, the Costa Rican government called it an invasion, and the situation deteriorated from there. In March 2011, when the International Court of Justice considered the case and reiterated the validity of the Cañas-Jerez Treaty, both sides interpreted the language as a win.

Subsequently, Costa Rica's then-president Laura Chinchilla called for emergency funds to begin construction of a riverside road on the Costa Rican side, without proper environmental or engineering reviews. This caused consternation not only in Nicaragua but also on Costa Rican soil about the road's environmental and political impact.

The latest development comes from Nicaragua's president Daniel Ortega, who has hinted that he wishes to extend an olive branch across the river to the incoming president. Stay tuned.

Carbon Neutrality

Costa Rica has long had a reputation for being green, but, to paraphrase Kermit: it ain't easy. Back in 2009, then-president Óscar Arias set an ambitious goal – that Costa Rica achieve carbon neutrality by the year 2021. Meeting this goal would make Costa Rica the first carbon-neutral country in the world and would coincide auspiciously with the country's bicentennial.

Although some measures have not yet been implemented as scheduled, the numbers suggest that it's still possible to hit the 2021 target. The first phase – as yet incomplete – addresses energy and agriculture, both major contributors to carbon-dioxide emissions.

The progress made in the next few years will reveal whether Costa Rica's vision of carbon neutrality can coalesce into reality by 2021. In the meantime, one of the proposals announced by new president Luis Guillermo Solís during his electoral campaign is an extension of the carbon-neutrality goal to 2025.

Alajuela (p86)

JOSE FUSTE RAGA/CORB

Although humans have inhabited Central America for at least 10,000 years and some 400,000 people were in today's Costa Rica before Europeans arrived, our knowledge of these pre-Columbian cultures has been lost to natural disasters and the brutalities of the Spanish colonization.

Heirs of Columbus

On his fourth and final voyage to the New World in 1502, Christopher Columbus was forced to drop anchor near present-day Puerto Limón after a hurricane damaged his ship. While waiting for repairs, Columbus ventured into the verdant terrain and exchanged gifts with hospitable and welcoming chieftains. He returned from this encounter, claiming to have seen 'more gold in two days than in four years in Española.' Columbus dubbed the stretch

11,000 BC

The first humans occupy Costa Rica and populations flourish due to the rich land and marine resources along both coastlines.

of shoreline from Honduras to Panama 'Veraguas', but it was excited descriptions of *la costa rica* (the rich coast) by subsequent explorers that gave the country its lasting name.

To the disappointment of Columbus' conquistador heirs, the region was not abundant with gold and the locals were considerably less than affable. Spain's first colony in present-day Panama was abruptly abandoned when tropical disease and warring tribes decimated its ranks. Successive expeditions launched from the Caribbean coast also failed, as pestilent swamps, oppressive jungles and volcanoes made Columbus' paradise seem more like a tropical hell.

New World Order

It was not until the 1560s that a Spanish colony was firmly established in Costa Rica. Hoping to cultivate the rich volcanic soil of the Central Valley, the Spanish founded the village of Cartago on the banks of the Río Reventazón. Although the fledgling colony was extremely isolated, it survived under the leadership of its first governor, Juan Vásquez de Coronado. Preferring diplomacy over firearms to counter indigenous resistance, Coronado used Cartago as a base to survey the lands south to Panama and west to the Pacific, and secured deed and title to make the loose network of indigenous tribes and their surrounding lands into a unified colony.

Though Coronado was later lost at sea in a shipwreck, his legacy endured: Costa Rica was an officially recognized province of El Virreinato de Nueva España (Viceroyalty of New Spain), which was the name given to the viceroy-ruled territories of the Spanish empire in North America, Central America, the Caribbean and Asia. Coronado's long-lasting legacy as the father of Costa Rica's political elite was also something that lasted generations. In the 1970s his family tree included some 29 heads of state and more than 200 members of parliament.

For roughly three centuries the Captaincy General of Guatemala (also known as the Kingdom of Guatemala), which extended from modern-day Texas to Panama, with the exception of Belize, was a loosely administered colony in the vast Spanish empire. Since the political-military headquarters of the kingdom was in Guatemala, Costa Rica became a minor provincial outpost that had little, if any, strategic significance or exploitable riches. Additionally, Costa Rica's relatively small indigenous population

The Best...
Places To
Feel History

1 Guayabo (p102)

2 San José (p60)

3 Cartago (p95)

4 Alajuela (p86)

5 Heredia (p92)

1000 BC

The Huetar power base in the Central Valley is solidified around Guayabo, continuously inhabited until its mysterious abandonment in 1400.

AD 800

Indigenous production of granite spheres begins in the Diquis region, but archaeologists remain divided as to their function and significance.

1522

Spanish settlement develops in Costa Rica, though it will be several decades before the colonists get a sturdy foothold on the land.

Pre-Columbian Costa Rica

The early inhabitants of Costa Rica were part of an extensive trading zone that extended as far south as Peru and as far north as Mexico. The region hosted roughly 20 small tribes, organized into chiefdoms, indicating a permanent leader, or *cacique,* who sat atop a hierarchical society that included shamans, warriors, toilers and slaves.

Adept at seafaring, the Carib dominated the Atlantic coastal lowlands, and served as a conduit of trade with the South American mainland. In the northwest, several tribes were connected to the great Mesoamerican cultures. Aztec religious practices and Maya jade and craftsmanship are in evidence in the Península de Nicoya, while Costa Rican quetzal feathers and golden trinkets have turned up in Mexico. In the southwest three chiefdoms showed the influence of Andean indigenous cultures, including the cultivation of coca leaves for medicine and yucca and sweet potatoes in their diets – all of which were staples of the Andean societies.

There is also evidence that the language of the Central Valley, Huetar, was known by Costa Rica's indigenous groups, which may be an indication of their power and influence. The Central Valley is home to the only major archaeological site uncovered in Costa Rica, namely Guayabo. Thought to be an ancient ceremonial center, Guayabo once featured paved streets, an aqueduct and decorative gold. Here, archaeologists uncovered exquisite gold ornaments and unusual life-size stone statues of human figures, as well as distinctive types of pottery and *metates,* stone platforms that were used for grinding corn. For travelers interested in Costa Rica's pre-Columbian history, it is far and away the most significant site in the country. Today, the site consists of little more than ancient hewed rock and stone, though Guayabo continues to stand as a testament to a once-great civilization of the New World.

played a role in limiting the development of the country during this period. With fewer indigenous workers to be used in forced labor, Spanish and European settlers had to work much of the difficult terrain on their own, and weren't able to establish the kind of large haciendas that existed elsewhere in Central America and Mexico.

1540
The Kingdom of Guatemala is established by the Spanish, and covers much of Central America, including present-day Costa Rica.

1562
Spanish conquistador Juan Vásquez de Coronado arrives in Costa Rica as governor, determined to move settlers to Central Valley.

1563
The first permanent Spanish colonial settlement in Costa Rica is established by Juan Vásquez de Coronado in Cartago.

The Fall of an Empire

On October 27, 1807, the Treaty of Fontainebleau, which defined the occupation of Portugal, was signed between Spain and France. Under the guise of reinforcing the Franco-Spanish army occupying Portugal, Napoleon moved tens of thousands of troops into Spain. In an act of military genius, Napoleon ordered his troops to abandon the ruse and seize key Spanish fortifications. Without firing a single shot, Napoleon's troops captured Barcelona after convincing the city to open its gates for a convoy of wounded soldiers. Although Napoleon's invasion by stealth was successful, the resulting Peninsular War was a horrific campaign of guerrilla combat that crippled both countries. As a result of the conflict, as well as the subsequent power vacuum and internal turmoil, Spain lost nearly all of its colonial possessions in the first third of the 19th century.

In 1821 the Americas wriggled free of Spain's imperial grip following Mexico's declaration of independence for itself and the whole of Central America. Of course, the Central American provinces weren't too keen on having another foreign power reign over them and subsequently declared independence from Mexico. However, all these events hardly disturbed Costa Rica; it learned of its liberation a month after the fact.

The newly liberated colonies pondered their fates: to stay together in a United States of Central America or to go their separate national ways. At first, they came up with something in between, namely the Central American Federation (CAF), though it could neither field an army nor collect taxes. Accustomed to being at the center of things due to its size, wealth and long-standing strategic advantages as a hub of trade and military power, Guatemala also attempted to dominate the CAF, alienating smaller colonies and hastening its demise.

Meanwhile, an independent Costa Rica was taking shape under Juan Mora Fernández, first head of state (1824–33). He tended toward nation-building and organized new towns, built roads, published a newspaper and coined a currency. His wife even partook in the effort by designing the country's flag.

Life returned to normal, unlike in the rest of the region where post-independence civil wars raged on. In 1824 the Nicoya-Guanacaste Province seceded from Nicaragua and joined its more easygoing southern neighbor, defining the territorial borders. In 1852 Costa Rica received its first diplomatic emissaries from the USA and Great Britain.

Coffee Rica

In the 19th century, the riches Costa Rica had long promised were uncovered when it was realized that the soil and climate of the Central Valley highlands were ideal for coffee cultivation. Costa Rica led Central America in introducing the caffeinated bean, which transformed the impoverished country into the wealthiest in the region.

1737

The future capital of San José is established, sparking a rivalry with neighboring Cartago that will eventually culminate in a civil war.

1821

Following a unanimous declaration by Mexico on behalf of all of Central America, Costa Rica gains its independence from Spain.

April 1823

The Costa Rican capital officially moves to San José after intense skirmishes with the conservative residents of Cartago.

Fast Fact

In the 1940s children in Costa Rica learned to read with a text that stated 'Coffee is good for me. I drink coffee every morning.'

When an export market was discovered, the government actively promoted coffee to farmers by providing free saplings. At first, Costa Rican producers exported their crops to nearby South Americans, who processed the beans and re-exported the product to Europe. By the 1840s, however, local merchants had already built up domestic capacity and learned to scope out their own overseas markets. Their big break came when they persuaded the captain of the HMS *Monarch* to transport several hundred sacks of Costa Rican coffee to London, percolating the beginning of a beautiful friendship.

The Costa Rican coffee boom was on. The drink's quick fix made it popular among working-class consumers in the industrializing Northern Hemisphere. The aroma of riches lured a wave of enterprising German immigrants to Costa Rica, enhancing technical and financial skills in the business sector. By century's end, more than one-third of the Central Valley was dedicated to coffee cultivation, and coffee accounted for more than 90% of all exports and 80% of foreign-currency earnings.

Coffee wealth became a power resource in politics. Costa Rica's traditional aristocratic families were at the forefront of the enterprise. At midcentury three-quarters of the coffee barons were descended from just two colonial families. The country's leading coffee exporter at this time was Juan Rafael Mora Porras (president from 1849 to 1859), whose lineage went back to the colony's founder Juan Vásquez de Coronado.

Banana Empire

The coffee trade unintentionally gave rise to Costa Rica's next export boom – bananas. Getting coffee out to world markets necessitated a rail link from the Central Highlands to the coast, a costly and difficult proposition, but well worth it considering the potential for exporting the lucrative beans to North America. Puerto Limón's deep harbor made an ideal port but inland was dense jungle and insect-infested swamps, which prompted the government to contract the task to Minor Cooper Keith, nephew of a North American railroad tycoon.

The project was a disaster. Malaria and accidents churned through workers as Tico (people from Costa Rica) recruits gave way to US convicts and Chinese indentured servants, who were in turn replaced by freed Jamaican slaves. Some 4000 men, including three of Keith's brothers, died in the process of laying the first 25 miles of track. To entice Keith to continue, the government turned over 3200 sq km of land along the route and provided a 99-year lease to run the railroad. In 1890 – nearly 20

December 1823
The Monroe Doctrine declares the intentions of the USA to be the dominant imperial power in the western hemisphere.

1824
The Nicoya-Guanacaste region votes to secede from Nicaragua and become a part of Costa Rica.

1856
William Walker's army is defeated at the Battle of Santa Rosa.

years after the plan had been approved – the line was finally completed and running at a loss.

Keith had begun to grow banana plants along the tracks as a cheap food source for the workers. Desperate to recoup his investment, he shipped some bananas to New Orleans in the hope of starting a side venture. He struck gold, or rather yellow. Consumers went crazy for the elongated finger fruit. By the early 20th century, bananas surpassed coffee as Costa Rica's most lucrative export and the country became the world's leading banana exporter. Unlike in the coffee industry, however, the profits were exported to the USA.

Costa Rica was transformed by the rise of Keith's banana empire. His first venture, the Tropical Trading and Transport Company, made him among the richest and most powerful men in the country. When he joined forces with another North American importer to found the infamous United Fruit Company, Keith's side business in bananas had become the largest employer in Central America. To the locals, it was known as *el pulpo* (the octopus) – its tentacles stretching across the region, becoming entangled with the local economy and politics. United Fruit owned huge swaths of lush lowlands, much of the transportation and communication infrastructure and bunches

Bunch of bananas
EISENHUT & MAYER/GETTY IMAGES ©

1889
Costa Rica's first democratic elections are held, though blacks and women are prohibited by law to vote.

1890
The railroad between San José and Puerto Limón is completed despite years of hardship and countless deaths.

1900
The population reaches 50,000 as the country prospers due to lucrative international coffee and banana trades.

of bureaucrats. The company sparked a wave of migrant laborers from Jamaica, changing the country's ethnic complexion and provoking racial tensions.

If travelers look close enough today, the rusting remains of the United Fruit Company are still all over the country, including rusting railroad tracks near Puntarenas and along the Pacific coast, and the historic buildings that housed the company headquarters in Golfito.

Birth of a Nation

The inequality of the early 20th century led to the rise of José Figueres Ferrer, a self-described farmer-philosopher and the father of Costa Rica's unarmed democracy. The son of Catalan immigrant coffee planters, Figueres excelled in school and went to MIT, in Boston, to study engineering. Upon returning to Costa Rica to set up his own coffee plantation, he organized the hundreds of laborers on his farm into a utopian socialist community and appropriately named the property La Lucha Sin Fin (The Struggle Without End).

Parque Central, San José

1919

Federico Tinoco Granados is ousted as the dictator of Costa Rica in an episode of brief violence in an otherwise peaceful political history.

1940

Rafael Ángel Calderón Guardia is elected president and enacts minimum-wage laws as well as an eight-hour day.

1940s

José Figueres Ferrer becomes involved in national politics and opposes the ruling conservatives and President Calderón.

In the 1940s Figueres became involved in national politics as an outspoken critic of President Rafael Ángel Calderón Guardia. In the midst of a radio interview in which he badmouthed the president, police broke into the studio and arrested Figueres. He was accused of having fascist sympathies and banished to Mexico. While in exile he formed the Caribbean League, a collection of students and democratic agitators from all over Central America, who pledged to bring down the region's military dictators. When he returned to Costa Rica, the now 700-man-strong Caribbean League went with him and helped protest against the powers that be.

When government troops descended on the farm with the intention of arresting Figueres and disarming the Caribbean League, it touched off a civil war. Figueres emerged victorious from the brief conflict and seized the opportunity to put into place his vision of Costa Rican social democracy. After dissolving the country's military, Figueres quoted HG Wells: 'The future of mankind cannot include the armed forces.'

As head of a temporary junta government, Figueres enacted nearly 1000 decrees. He taxed the wealthy, nationalized the banks and built a modern welfare state. His 1949 constitution granted full citizenship and voting rights to women, blacks, indigenous groups and Chinese minorities. Today, Figueres' revolutionary regime is regarded as the foundation for Costa Rica's unarmed democracy.

The American Empire

Throughout the 1970s and '80s, the USA played the role of watchful big brother in Latin America, challenging the sovereignty of smaller nations. Big sticks, gunboats and dollar diplomacy were instruments of a US policy to curtail socialist politics, especially the military oligarchies of Guatemala, El Salvador and Nicaragua.

In 1979 the rebellious Sandinistas toppled the American-backed Somoza dictatorship in Nicaragua. Alarmed by the Sandinistas' Soviet and Cuban ties, anticommunist President Ronald Reagan decided to intervene in the 1980s. The Cold War arrived in the hot tropics.

The organizational details of the counterrevolution were delegated to Oliver North, a lieutenant colonel working out of the White House basement. North's can-do creativity helped to prop up the famed Contra rebels to resist the Sandinistas in Nicaragua.

1948
Conservative and liberal forces clash, resulting in a six-week civil war that leaves 2000 Costa Ricans dead.

1949
The temporary government enacts a new constitution that abolishes the army and grants women and blacks the right to vote.

1963
Reserva Natural Absoluta Cabo Blanco becomes Costa Rica's first federally protected conservation area.

While both sides invoked the rhetoric of freedom and democracy, the war was really a turf battle between left-wing and right-wing forces.

Under intense US pressure, Costa Rica was reluctantly dragged in. The Contras set up camp in northern Costa Rica, from where they staged guerrilla raids. Not-so-clandestine CIA operatives and US military advisers were dispatched to assist the effort and there were multiple allegations in Costa Rican and American media that Costa Rican authorities were bribed to keep quiet. A secret jungle airstrip was built near the border to fly in weapons and supplies. To raise cash for the rebels, North allegedly used his covert supply network to traffic illegal narcotics through the region. Although North vehemently denied the US government had ever helped the Nicaraguan resistance with 'running drugs', a congressional investigation found that North and other senior officials helped create a network that attracted drug traffickers and then turned a blind eye to reports of narcotic trafficking.

The war polarized Costa Rica. Conservatives wanted to re-establish the military and join the anticommunist crusade, but more than 20,000 demonstrators marched through San José in a demonstration for peace. The debate climaxed in the 1986

Teatro Nacional (p61)

1987

President Oscar Arias Sánchez wins the Nobel Peace Prize for his work on the Central American peace accords.

2000

The population of Costa Rica tops four million, though the number may be far greater due to illegal settlements on the fringes of the capital.

2007

A referendum narrowly passes Cafta; opinion is divided on whether opening up trade with the USA will be beneficial in the long run.

presidential election, which went to Oscar Arias Sánchez who was an intellectual reformer in the mold of Figueres.

Once in office, Arias affirmed his commitment to a negotiated resolution and reasserted Costa Rican national independence. He vowed to uphold his country's pledge of neutrality and to vanquish the Contras from the territory, which prompted the US ambassador to suddenly quit his post. In a public ceremony, Costa Rican school children planted trees on top of the CIA's secret airfield. Arias became the driving force in uniting Central America around a peace plan, which ended the Nicaraguan war and earned him the Nobel Peace Prize in 1987.

In 2006 Arias once again returned to the presidential office, winning the popular election by a 1.2% margin, and subsequently ratifying the controversial Central American Free Trade Agreement (Cafta).

The Best...
Historic
Buildings

1 Basílica de Nuestra Señora de los Ángeles (p96)

2 Teatro Nacional (p61)

3 La Casona (p194)

4 Iglesia de la Inmaculada Concepción (p92)

5 Iglesia San Bartolomé (p94)

2010
Costa Rica elects its first woman president, National Liberation Party candidate Laura Chinchilla.

2011
Regional drug wars encroach on Costa Rica's borders; the country is named among the USA's list of major drug trafficking centers.

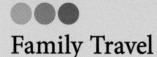

Family Travel

Zip lining

Costa Rica is a kid-friendly country, especially since Ticos (people of Costa Rica) themselves tend to be extremely family-oriented and will go out of their way to lavish attention on children. In fact, Costa Rica is arguably the most accessible family destination in Latin America, so check your worries and concerns along with the baggage and get ready for what may be the best family vacation you've ever taken.

Where to Go

Although you will have to take certain precautions to ensure the health and safety of little ones, Costa Rica's standards of safety are more similar to North America and Europe than they are to other countries in Central America.

Families could go just about anywhere in Costa Rica and be perfectly happy. Even San José has a few sights for children, but it's best to get out of the cities and towns and into the countryside or along the coastlines.

Snorkeling on the Caribbean coast, taking a surfing roadtrip along the central Pacific coast, and spotting monkeys and tropical birds in Manuel Antonio National Park are highlights they'll never forget. Families who want to maximize their time should look into the Nicoya Peninsula and central Pacific coast, as these regions are packed with activities, natural highlights and excellent infrastructure.

What to Eat

Costa Rican cuisine is simple and hearty, if somewhat bland (beans, rice and grilled chicken, steak or fish are omnipresent). The ubiquity of these dishes might be a bit dull for adults with adventurous appetites, but it makes it easier to cater to finicky young eaters. Special kids' meals are not normally offered in restaurants, though some fancy lodges prepare them. However, most local eateries will accommodate two children splitting a meal or can produce child-size portions on request.

If you're traveling with an infant, stock up on milk formula and baby food before heading to remote areas, and always carry snacks for long drives in remote areas – sometimes there are no places to stop for a bite.

Tired of juice and water? Here are some local drinks that your kids are sure to love: *batidos* (fresh fruit shakes), either *al agua* (made with water) or *con leche* (with milk); coconut water (sipped through a straw straight from the cracked-open coconut); and *horchata* (cinnamon-spiked rice milk).

And don't worry too much – generally speaking, tap water and ice cubes in Costa Rica are safe for foreigners to consume.

The Best... Places for Kids

1 Monteverde & Santa Elena (p168)

2 Parque Nacional Manuel Antonio (p261)

3 Parque Nacional Tortuguero (p123)

4 Playa Sámara (p227)

5 Volcán Arenal (p158)

IN FOCUS FAMILY TRAVEL

Where to Stay

When it comes to accommodation in Costa Rica, families have a lot to choose from. From plush jungle ecolodges to beachside tents, you can find the type of accommodation your family needs at most tourist destinations. There are many rooms to accommodate families on a tight budget, and most midrange and top-end hotels have reduced rates for children under 12, provided the child shares a room with parents.

Need to Know

Breastfeeding OK in public

Changing facilities In upmarket hotels and resorts

Cribs In upmarket hotels and resorts (best to book in advance)

Diapers (nappies) Widely available except in rural areas

Health Food-borne and infectious diseases are of very minor concern

Highchairs In most tourist-friendly restaurants

Strollers Bring your own if lightweight and collapsible, or better yet, bring a baby hiking harness

Transport Consider private shuttles or rental car

Can You Drink the Water?

Yes. Yes. Yes. The tap water is perfectly safe to drink in Costa Rica. You can drink from the tap in all but the most remote regions of the country's wilderness areas.

Top-end hotels will provide cribs and usually have activities for children, swimming pools and play areas.

Additional Tips

○ Children under the age of 12 get a 25% discount on internal air travel, while children under two fly free (provided they sit on an adult's lap).

○ If you're traveling with an infant, bring disposable diapers, baby creams or toiletries, baby aspirin and a thermometer from home, or stock up in San José. Supplies may be difficult to find in rural areas, though cloth diapers are more widespread.

○ Strollers may help you get around high-end resorts, but are challenging anywhere else in the country. Few national parks are set up to accommodate them, so consider investing in a quality hiking baby harness if you plan to spend much time in the parks.

○ Young kids won't have a problem with the paths in most of Costa Rica's national parks, which are easy, short and well marked. Notable exceptions are Parque Nacional Corcovado, Parque Nacional Chirripó and Parque Nacional La Amistad, which are more challenging to navigate.

○ Although many surf schools allow for very young students, kids under 10 will likely have to take the class with a parent or guardian.

Costa Rica Outdoors

Canopy trams

MICHAEL MARQUAND/GETTY IMAGES ©

What truly distinguishes Costa Rica is the diversity and accessibility of the outdoors. While hard-core enthusiasts can seek out complete solitude in absolute wilderness, families and novices are equally well catered for. From jungle treks and beachcombing to rafting snaking rivers and surfing crashing waves – whatever you're looking for, Costa Rica has most definitely got it.

Canopy Tours

Costa Rica's lofty tally of national parks and reserves provides an incredible stage for lovers of the outdoors. Natural spaces are so entwined with Costa Rica's ecofriendly image that it's difficult to envisage the country without them. For the vast majority of travelers, Costa Rica equals rainforest, and you're certain to encounter charismatic wildlife, including primates, birds and butterflies galore. As you'll quickly discover, no two rainforests are created equal, providing a constantly shifting palette of nature.

Life in the rainforest takes place at canopy level. But with trees extending 30m to 60m in height, the average human has a hard time getting a look at what's going on up there. Indeed, it was only a matter of time before someone in Costa Rica invented the canopy tour.

The Best...
Hikes

Some companies have built elevated walkways through the trees that allow visitors to stroll through. SkyTrek, in Monteverde, and Rainmaker Aerial Walkway, near Quepos, are two of the most established operations in the country.

For adrenaline-seekers, consider zipping from tree to tree while harnessed into a sophisticated cable-suspension system. With a total length of 11,000m connecting no fewer than 21 platforms, Miss Sky is the longest canopy tour in the world, stretching from mountainside to mountainside and finishing on the top floor of a disco-bar.

Major tourist centers, such as Monteverde, Santa Elena and La Fortuna, offer the largest number of canopy-tour operators.

Hiking

Whether you're interested in taking a walk in the park or embarking on a rugged mountaineering circuit, the hiking opportunities around Costa Rica are seemingly endless. Nearly every visitor to the country will have a hike or trek on their agenda – whether they know it before they arrive or not. With its extensive mountains, canyons, dense jungles, cloud forests and two coast-lines, Costa Rica is one of Central America's best and most varied hiking destinations.

These hikes come in an enormous spectrum of difficulty. At tourist-packed destinations such as Monteverde and Santa Elena, trails are clearly marked and even lined with cement blocks in parts. This is very appealing if you're traveling with little ones, or if you're lacking navigational prowess. For long-distance hiking, there are lots more options in the remote corners of the country.

Opportunities for moderate hiking are also available in most parks and reserves, particularly once you leave the well-beaten tourist path. As this is Costa Rica you can, for the most part, still rely on signs and maps for orientation, though it helps to have a bit of route-finding experience. Tourist information centers at park entrances are great resources for planning out your intended route.

If you're properly equipped with camping essentials, the country's longer and more arduous multiday treks are at your disposal. Costa Rica's top challenges are scaling Cerro Chirripó, traversing Corcovado and penetrating deep into the heart of La Amistad. Cerro Chirripó can be undertaken either solo or with trusted companions; however, local guides are required for Corcovado and most of La Amistad. The advantage to trekking with a guide, aside from their expertise on the terrain, is that they are usually experts on the local ecology and can point out flora and fauna you might otherwise miss.

Surfing

Point and beach breaks, lefts and rights, reefs and river mouths, warm water and year-round waves make Costa Rica a favorite surfing destination. For the most part, the Pacific coast has bigger swells and better waves during the latter part of the rainy season, but the Caribbean cooks from November to May. Basically, there is a wave somewhere waiting to be surfed at any time of the year.

For the uninitiated, lessons are available at almost all of the major surfing destinations – especially popular towns include Jacó, Dominical and Tamarindo on the Pacific coast.

Throughout Costa Rica, waves can get big (though not Hawaii-big), and many offer hollow and fast rides that are perfect for intermediates. Experienced, skilled surfers can tackle some of the sport's most famous waves.

White-Water Rafting & Kayaking

Since the birth of the ecotourism-based economy in the mid-1980s, white-water rafting has emerged as one of Costa Rica's top-billed outdoor pursuits. Ranging from family-friendly Class II swells to borderline unnavigable Class V rapids, Costa Rica's rivers offer highly varied white-water experiences.

First-time runners are catered for year-round, while seasoned enthusiasts arrive en masse during the wildest months from June to October. There is also much regional variation, with gentler rivers located near Manuel Antonio along the central Pacific coast, and truly world-class runs along the Pacuare and Reventazón rivers in the Central Valley. Since all white-water rafting in Costa Rica requires the presence of a certified guide, you will need to book trips through a reputable tour agency.

River kayaking is not as popular as rafting, though it has its share of loyal fans. The tiny village of La Virgen in the northern lowlands is the unofficial kayaking capital of Costa Rica, and the best spot to hook up with other like-minded lovers of the sport. The Río Sarapiquí has an impressive variety of runs that cater to all ages and skill levels.

With 1228km of coastline, two gulfs and plentiful mangrove estuaries, Costa Rica is ideal for sea kayaking. This is a great way for paddlers to access remote areas and catch rare glimpses of birds and wildlife. Difficulty of access varies considerably and is largely dependent on tides and currents.

The Best...
Rafting & Kayaking

1 Turrialba (p99)

2 La Virgen (p196)

3 Quepos and Manuel Antonio (p254)

4 Parque Nacional Tortuguero (p123)

5 Bahía Drake (p284)

IN FOCUS COSTA RICA OUTDOORS

Diving & Snorkeling

The good news is that Costa Rica offers body-temperature water with few humans and abundant marine life. The bad news is that the visibility is low because of silt and plankton, and soft corals and sponges are dominant. If you are looking for turquoise waters and plenty of hard coral, head for Belize and Honduras.

However, those who do venture underwater will find massive schools of fish and larger marine animals such as turtles, sharks, dolphins and whales. It's also worth pointing out that there are few places in the world where you can dive in the Caribbean and the Pacific on the same day, albeit with a good amount of effort and some advanced planning.

The Caribbean Sea is better for novice divers and snorkelers, with the beach towns of Manzanillo and Cahuita particularly well suited to beginners. Puerto Viejo lays claim to a few decent sites that can be explored on a discovery dive. Along the Pacific, Playa del Coco and Isla del Caño up the ante slightly, offering a variety of beginner- and intermediate-level sites.

Isla del Coco is the exception to the rule – this remote island in the deep Pacific is regarded by veteran divers as one of the best dive spots in the world. In order to catch

333

The Best...
Wildlife-Watching

a glimpse of the underwater world of Cocos, you'll need to visit on a liveaboard, and have some serious experience in your logbook.

Wildlife- & Bird-Watching

Costa Rica's biodiversity is legendary, so it should come as no surprise that the country offers unparalleled opportunities for watching birds and wildlife. As a bonus, people of all ages are already familiar with Costa Rica's most famous, commonly spotted, animals. You'll instantly recognize monkeys bounding through the treetops, sloths clinging to branches and toucans gliding beneath the canopy. Young children, even if they've been to the zoo dozens of times, typically enjoy the thrill of spotting creatures in the wild.

For the slightly older, keeping checklists is a fun way to add an educational element to your travels. Want to move beyond the novice level? Check out your local bookstore prior to landing in Costa Rica to pick up wildlife and bird guides – look for ones with color plates that make positive identification a cinch.

A quality pair of binoculars is highly recommended and can make the difference between far-off movement and a face-to-face encounter. A spotting scope is essential for expert bird-watchers, and multipark itineraries will allow you to quickly add dozens of new species to your all-time list. Finally, it's worth pointing out that Costa Rica is brimming with wildlife at every turn, so always keep your eyes peeled and your ears pricked – you never know what's waiting for you just ahead!

Tico Way of Life

HOLGER LEUE/GETTY IMAGES ©

'Pura vida' – pure life – is more than just a slogan that rolls off the Tico tongue and emblazons souvenirs: uttered in a laid-back tone, the phrase is a mantra for the Costa Rican way of life. Perhaps the essence of the pure life is something better lived than explained, but hearing it again and again across this beautiful country as a greeting, farewell or acknowledgement of thanks makes it evident that the concept lives deep within the DNA of this country.

Lifestyle

The living seems particularly pure when Costa Rica is compared with its Central American neighbors such as Nicaragua and Honduras: there's little poverty, illiteracy or political tumult here.

With the lack of war, a high standard of living and a relatively sturdy economy, Costa Ricans (Ticos) live fairly rich and comfortable lives for the most part, even by North American standards. As in many places in Latin America, the family unit remains the nucleus of life in Costa Rica.

Life expectancy in Costa Rica is almost the same as in the USA, partly due to a comprehensive socialized health-care system, proper sanitation and generally low-stress lifestyles.

The Best...
Cultural Hot Spots

Economy

Despite the economic tumult that has rocked the world since 2008, Costa Rica's economy has remained remarkably stable thanks to consistently growing returns on tourism, a sector that outpaces agriculture and industry for the biggest slice of the economy. If you're concerned about the availability of an English menu, take note: North Americans account for nearly half of the 2.2 million annual tourists.

Poverty levels have been in check for more than 20 years thanks to strong welfare programs. Although approximately 24% of the populace lives below the poverty line, beggars are few and far between, and you won't see the street kids you would in other Latin American capitals.

Population

In the 1940s Costa Rica was overwhelmingly an agricultural society. These days the service sector employs more than half of the labor force, while industry (especially agro-industry) employs another one-fifth.

Most inhabitants are *mestizos,* having a mix of Spanish and indigenous and/or African roots, though the vast majority of Ticos consider themselves to be white. Although it's difficult to offer a precise explanation for this cultural phenomenon, it is partly due to the fact that Costa Rica's indigenous populations were virtually wiped out by the Spanish *conquistadors* (conquerors). As a result, most Costa Ricans trace their ancestry back to the European continent and take considerable pride in the purity of their Spanish heritage.

Indigenous Costa Ricans, Chinese immigrants and black Costa Ricans together make up only 5% of the population. In recent years North American and European immigration has greatly increased, and it is estimated that roughly 50,000 expats from these two regions presently live in the country.

Literature

Costa Rica has a relatively young literary history and few works of Costa Rican writers or novelists are available in translation. Carlos Luis Fallas (1909–66) is widely known for *Mamita Yunai* (1940), an influential novel that took the banana companies to task for their labor practices, and he remains very popular among the Latin American left.

Carmen Naranjo (1928–2012) is one of the few contemporary Costa Rican writers to receive international acclaim. Her collection of short stories, *There Never Was a Once Upon a Time,* is widely available in English. Another important figure is José León Sánchez (1930–), an internationally renowned memoirist of Huetar descent. After being convicted for stealing from the famous Basílica de Nuestra Señora de Los Ángeles in Cartago, he authored one of the continent's most poignant books: *La isla de los hombres solos* (God Was Looking the Other Way).

Visual Arts

The visual arts in Costa Rica first took on a national character in the 1920s, when Teodorico Quirós, Fausto Pacheco and their contemporaries began painting landscapes that differed from European styles and depicted distinctly Costa Rican scenes.

The contemporary scene is varied, making it difficult to define a unique Tico style. Look out for the magical realism of Isidro Con Wong, and surreal paintings and primitive engravings from Francisco Amighetti. The Museo de Arte y Diseño Contemporáneo in San José is the top place to see modern work.

Best Book for the Beach

If you're looking for a bit of beach reading, pick up *Costa Rica: A Traveler's Literary Companion*, edited by Barbara Ras. This fine collection of 26 short stories by modern Costa Rican writers offers a valuable glimpse of society from Ticos themselves.

Music

San José features a regular lineup of domestic and international rock, folk and hip-hop artists, but you'll find that regional sounds also survive, each with its own special rhythm, instruments and style. Popular dance music includes salsa, merengue, bolero and cumbia.

The Península de Nicoya has a rich musical history, most of it made with guitars, maracas and marimbas (wooden percussion instruments similar to a xylophone), and the traditional sound on the Caribbean coast is calypso, which has roots in Afro-Caribbean culture.

Costa Rica Landscapes

Golfo de Papagayo

PANORAMIC IMAGES/GETTY IMAGES

Despite its diminutive size of 51,000 sq km, Costa Rica is an explosion of Technicolor contrasts and violent contradictions. Between the breezy skies and big waves of the Pacific coast and the muggy, languid shores of the Caribbean (only 119km away) lie active volcanoes, alpine peaks, and crisp high-elevation forest. Few places on earth can compare with this little country's spectacular interaction of natural, geological and climatic forces.

The Pacific Coast

Start by twisting and turning around the endless gulfs, sandy peninsulas and deserted bays of Costa Rica's 1016km-long Pacific coast. Rugged, rocky headlands give way to classic white- and black-sand beaches bedecked with palms. Strong tidal action creates an excellent habitat for waterbirds, a dramatic crash of waves and some exquisite surfing.

Two major peninsulas hook out into the Pacific along this coast: Nicoya in the north and Osa in the south. The two could hardly be more different. Nicoya is one of the driest places in the country and holds some of Costa Rica's most developed tourist infrastructure; Osa is wet and rugged, run through by wild, seasonal rivers and rough dirt roads that are always under threat from the creeping jungle.

Just inland from the coast, the Pacific lowlands are a narrow strip of land backed by mountains. This area is equally dynamic, ranging from dry deciduous forests to misty, mysterious tropical rainforests.

Central Costa Rica

Just inland from the Pacific coast ascends the jagged spine of the country: the majestic Cordillera Central in the north and the rugged, largely unexplored Cordillera de Talamanca in the south. Continually being revised by earthquakes and volcanic activity, these mountains are part of the majestic Sierra Madre chain that runs north through Mexico.

A land of active volcanoes, clear trout-filled streams and ethereal cloud forest, these ranges generally follow a northwest to southeast line, with the highest and most dramatic peaks in the south near the Panamanian border. The highest in the country is the rugged, windswept 3820m peak of Cerro Chirripó.

In the midst of this powerful landscape, surrounded on all sides by mountains, are the highlands of Meseta Central – the Central Valley. This fertile central plain, some 1000m above sea level, is the agricultural heart of the nation and enjoys abundant rainfall and mild temperatures. It includes San José and is home to more than half the country's population.

The Best...
Iconic Geography

1 Volcán Arenal (p158)

2 Monteverde Cloud Forest (p180)

3 Cerro Chirripó (p304)

4 Parque Nacional Tortuguero (p123)

5 Parque Nacional Marino Ballena (p270)

6 Parque Nacional Manuel Antonio (p261)

The Caribbean Coast

Cross the mountains and drop down the eastern slope and you'll reach the elegant line of the Caribbean coastline – a long, straight 212km along low plains, brackish lagoons and waterlogged forests.

A lack of strong tides allows plants to grow right over the water's edge along coastal sloughs, creating walls of green vegetation. Broad, humid plains that scarcely rise above sea level and murky waters characterize much of this region. As if taking cues from the slow-paced Caribbean-influenced culture, the rivers that rush out of the central mountain take on a languid pace here as they curve towards the sea.

Compared with the smoothly paved roads and popular beaches of the Pacific coast, much of the land here is still inaccessible except by boat or plane. The best access points for travelers is the Parque Nacional Tortuguero, which allows intimate visits to this little-discovered border between land and sea.

National Parks & Protected Areas

The vibrancy of its natural resources has made Costa Rica something of a comeback kid: the deforestation here in the early 1990s was among the worst in Latin America. Today, the country is a global leader in tropical conservation. Now in charge of an exemplar system of well-managed and accessible parks, Costa Rica is among the best places in the world to experience rainforest habitats.

Six Ways To Save the Rainforest

Here are a few simple measures you can take to actually help save the rainforests.

Plant a tree At **Selva Bananito Lodge** (☎ 8375-4419, 2253 8118; www.selvabananito. com; 3-day package US$432) 🖋 on the Caribbean coast, visitors can help to reforest a former banana plantation.

Drink the water Tap water in Costa Rica is perfectly safe to drink. Bringing a refillable water bottle is a simple way to reduce plastic waste.

Drink organic, shade-grown coffee Organic coffee-growing avoids the use of chemical pesticides and fertilizers, minimizing their environmental impact.

Say no to beef The number-one reason for forest clearing in Central America is to feed cows, mostly for export.

Green impact Choose local tour operators who give back to their communities and employ local guides, such as Osa Wild (p290).

Bring it home Sustainability practices that protect Costa Rica are just as urgent at home. Take the inspiration to protect the rainforest home with you.

The national-park system began in the 1960s and has since been expanded into a National Conservation Areas System with an astounding 186 protected areas, including 32 national parks, eight biological reserves, 13 forest reserves and 51 wildlife refuges. At least 10% of the land is strictly protected and another 17% is included in various multiple-use preserves. The most amazing number might be the smallest of all: Costa Rica's parks are a safe haven to approximately 5% of the world's wildlife species.

Most national parks can be entered without permits, though a few limit the number they admit on a daily basis and others require advance reservations for accommodation within the park's boundaries (Chirripó, Corcovado and La Amistad). The average entrance fee to most parks is US$10 per day for foreigners, plus additional fees for overnight camping where permitted.

Most parks in the country have a ranger station of some kind and, though these are largely administrative offices with few formal services for travelers, it is worth dropping in if you plan to deeply explore the park. The *guardeparques* (park rangers) know the parks inside and out and can offer tips on trail conditions, good camping spots and places to see wildlife. Naturally, these conversations will be most helpful if you speak Spanish.

With Costa Rican parks contributing significantly to national and local economies through the huge influx of tourist money, there is little question that the country's healthy natural environment is important to its citizens. In general, support for land preservation remains high because it provides income and jobs to so many people, plus important opportunities for scientific investigation.

Geology

If the proximity to all this wildly diverse beauty makes Costa Rica feel like the crossroads between worlds, that's because it is. As part of the thin strip of land that separates two continents with vastly different wildlife and topographical characteristics and sitting in between the world's two largest oceans, it's little wonder that Costa Rica boasts such a colorful collision of climates, landscapes and wildlife.

Costa Rica's geological history began when the Cocos Plate, a tectonic plate that lies below the Pacific, crashed headlong into the Caribbean Plate, which is off the isthmus' east coast. At a rate of about 10cm every year, it might seem slow by human standards but the collision was a violent wreck by geological standards, creating the area's 'subduction zone' that is rife with geological drama. The plates continue to collide, with the Cocos Plate pushing the Caribbean Plate toward the heavens and making the area prone to earthquakes and ongoing volcanic activity.

But despite all the violence underfoot, these forces have blessed this country with some of the world's most beautiful and diverse tropical landscapes.

Plants

Simply put, Costa Rica's floral biodiversity is mind-blowing – close to 12,000 species of vascular plants have been described in Costa Rica, and the list gets more and more crowded each year. Orchids alone account for about 1400 species.

The diversity of habitats created when this many species mix is a wonder to behold; one day you're canoeing in a muggy mangrove swamp, and the next you're squinting through bone-chilling fog to see orchids in a montane cloud forest. Jump on a bus and after a short ride you'll be fighting your way through the vines of a tropical rainforest. Sure, everyone loves Costa Rica's celebrated beaches, but travelers would be remiss to visit the country without seeing some of its most distinctive plant communities, including rainforests, mangrove swamps, cloud forests and dry forests.

Experiencing a tropical forest for the first time can be a bit of a surprise for visitors from North America or Europe, who are used to temperate forests with little variety. Such regions are either dominated by conifers, or have endless tracts of oaks, beech and birch. Tropical forests, on the other hand, have a staggering number of species – in Costa Rica, for example, almost 2000 tree species have been recorded. If you stand in one spot and look around, you'll see scores of different plants, and if you walk several hundred meters you're likely to find even more.

Wildlife Guide

Keel-billed toucan

STUART WESTMORLAND/GETTY IMAGES

Nowhere else are so many types of habitat squeezed into such a tiny area. In Costa Rica species from different continents have been mingling for millennia. Costa Rica tops the list of countries for number of species per 10,000 sq km, at 615 species. To compare, wildlife-rich Rwanda has 596 and the comparatively impoverished USA has 104 species per 10,000 sq km. This fact alone (not to mention the ease of travel and friendly residents) makes Costa Rica the world's premier destination for nature-lovers.

Birds

Costa Rica's amazing biodiversity includes approximately 850 species of birds, including six endemics. The country holds a greater variety of birds than Europe, North America or Australia.

Of the 16 parrot species in Costa Rica, none are as spectacular as the scarlet macaw. Unmistakable due to its large size, bright-red body, blue-and-yellow wings, long red tail and white face, it's common in Parque Nacional Carara and the Península de Osa. Macaws have long, monogamous relationships and can live 50 years.

The quetzal, Central America's most dazzling bird, has great cultural importance and was of high ceremonial significance to the Aztecs and the Maya. Look for its bright-blue mohawk, red breast and long green tail at high elevations and near Parque Nacional Los Quetzales.

With their dark bodies, yellow chests and brilliant beaks, toucans are classic rainforest birds; six species are found in Costa Rica. Huge bills and vibrant plumage make the chestnut-mandibled toucan and the keel-billed toucan hard to miss, and they are common across the country. Listen for the keel-billed's song: a repetitious 'carrrick!' at dusk.

The descriptively named roseate spoonbill has a white head and a distinctive spoon-shaped bill, and feeds by touch, swinging its open bill back and forth underwater. It's the only pink bird in Costa Rica and is common around the Península de Nicoya and along Pacific lowlands.

There are 42 species of tanager in the country – many are brightly colored and all have bodies that are about the size of an adult's fist. Look for these songbirds everywhere except at high elevation. Their common name in Costa Rica is *viuda*, meaning widow.

More than 50 species of hummingbird have been recorded – and most live at high elevations. The largest is the violet sabrewing, with a striking violet head and body with dark-green wings.

The Best...
Bird-Watching Spots

1 Parque Nacional Tortuguero (p123)

2 Parque Nacional Carara (p250)

3 Wilson Botanical Garden (p310)

4 Parque Nacional Corcovado (p295)

5 Parque Nacional Los Quetzales (p308)

IN FOCUS **WILDLIFE GUIDE**

Land Mammals

A wild selection of land mammals inhabit Costa Rica's multitudinous biomes, but the rainforest has the stars: fierce predators, crafty prey and more than a few playful primates.

Costa Rica is home to the brown-throated three-toed sloth and Hoffman's two-toed sloth. Both are 50cm to 75cm in length, have stumpy tails, and tend to hang motionless from branches or slowly progress upside down along a branch toward leaves, their primary food. Look for them in Parque Nacional Manuel Antonio.

The spider monkey is named for its long, thin legs, arms and tail, which enable it to pursue an arboreal existence in forests near Monteverde. It swings from arm to arm through the canopy and can hang supported just by its prehensile tail.

The king of Costa Rica's big cats, the jaguar, is extremely rare, shy and well camouflaged, so the chance of seeing one is virtually nonexistent – though your best chance is in Parque Nacional Corcovado. They have large territories, however, so you may see their prints or droppings, or even hear their roars – a sound more like a series of deep coughs.

The loud vocalizations of a male mantled howler monkey can carry for more than 1km even in dense rainforest and will echo through many of the nation's national parks including Corcovado, Tortuguero and Monteverde. This crescendo of noise is one of the most characteristic and memorable of all rainforest sounds.

The small and inquisitive white-faced capuchin monkey has a prehensile tail that is typically carried with the tip coiled. Capuchins occasionally descend to the ground for food and count corn and even oysters as part of their diet.

The diminutive squirrel monkey travels in small to medium-sized groups during the day, squealing or chirping noisily and leaping and crashing through vegetation in search of insects and fruit. It lives only along the Pacific and is common in Parque Nacional Manuel Antonio and the Península de Nicoya.

The white-nosed coati is a frequently seen member of the raccoon family, but is brownish, longer and slimmer than a common raccoon. Its most distinctive feature is a long, mobile, upturned whitish snout with which it snuffles around in search of food.

Other mammals you might encounter in the remote forests include the bristly, stinky little white-lipped peccary and collared peccary and Baird's tapir, a large pudgy, pig-like browsing animal.

Marine Mammals

Costa Rica has one of the most biologically diverse marine ecosystems in the world and an astounding variety of marine animals. Deepwater upwellings are constant year-round, making these waters extremely productive and creating ideal viewing conditions at any season.

The smallest of Costa Rica's sea turtles, the little olive ridley, is easy to love – it has a heart-shaped shell. It nests during the rainy season, and between September and October arrives in huge numbers at Ostional beach in the Guanacaste province. This species is legendary for its synchronized nesting – 200,000 emerge from the sea during a short period of a few days.

The massive 360kg leatherback sea turtle is much, much bigger than the olive ridley, and is distinguished by its soft, leathery carapace with seven ridges. It nests on the Pacific beaches of the Osa and Nicoya Peninsulas.

Divers are relatively likely to encounter the whale shark, the world's biggest fish, in the waters off Reserva Biológica Isla del Caño, the Golfo Dulce or Isla del Coco. These majestic, harmless creatures can reach 20ft long and can weigh over 2 tons, and adult males have been known to live 70 years.

With wings that can reach 7m, the elegant manta ray is common in the warm Pacific waters and can be seen when diving off the coast of Guanacaste and around the Bat and Catalina islands. Sometimes you don't have to don a wetsuit to see them, either – fortunate visitors might glimpse one jumping from the waves in what is thought to be a sign of play.

Bottle-nosed dolphins are year-round residents in Costa Rica and also quite common. These charismatic cetaceans are among the most intelligent animals on the planet, and have been observed exhibiting complex sociocultural behaviors. Keep a lookout for them on the boat ride to Bahía Drake; they sometimes chase water taxis across the bay.

Migrating whales, which arrive from both the northern and southern hemispheres, include orca, blue and sperm whales, and several species of relatively unknown beaked whale. Humpback whales are commonly spotted along the Pacific coast by tour boats. The best place to see them is in Bahía Drake.

Reptiles & Amphibians

More than half of the 220 species of reptiles in Costa Rica are snakes, though only a couple could be deadly – and then only without treatment. Of the 160 species of amphibians, frogs and toads garner the most attention as early-warning indicators of climate change.

The stocky green iguana is regularly encountered draping its 2m-long body across a branch over water. Despite their enormous bulk, iguanas are vegetarians, and prefer to eat young shoots and leaves. You'll see them just about everywhere in Costa Rica.

The bright-green basilisk lizard is notable for the huge crest running the length of its head, body and tail. Common along watercourses in lowland areas (particularly around Golfo Dulce), it has the appearance of a small dinosaur.

Costa Rica's Most Venomous Critters

Note that bites from any of these are exceptionally rare and non-lethal.

Bark scorpion A jab from this common brown variety is painful but not lethal.

Vampire bat After anticoagulant saliva inhibits blood clotting, these bats lick up their dinner.

Roadguarders A bite from this large brown snake of the northwest can cause vomiting, headache and bleeding, but won't kill.

Yellow-bellied sea snake Though no deaths have been recorded, a bite from this bi-colored sea snake attacks the nervous system.

Tarantula hawk This wasp packs a wallop that kills tarantulas, though it only stings humans when provoked.

The poison-dart frog has skin glands exuding toxins that can cause paralysis and death in animals. Indigenous populations traditionally used them as a poison for the tips of hunting arrows.

With a shimmering blue throat and sharp, feather-like black-spotted green scales, the green spiny lizard is a common reptile in the driest parts of the country. It's often seen lazing on fenceposts or exposed tree branches on the Península de Nicoya.

The unofficial symbol of Costa Rica, the red-eyed tree frog has a green body, yellow and blue side stripes, and orange feet. Despite this vibrant coloration, it's well camouflaged in the rainforest and rather difficult to spot. This species is widespread, apart from on the Península de Nicoya, which is too dry.

The crocodile is an ancient species that has changed little over millions of years. The best place to spot one is at the Crocodile Bridge, on the central Pacific coast.

Food & Drink

Pargo rojo (whole red snapper)

OGPHOTO/GETTY IMAGES

Traditional Costa Rican fare, for the most part, is basic, mild comfort food. The diet consists largely of rice and beans or beans and rice – thatched country kitchens all over Costa Rica serve up hearty home-cooked specials known as comida típica (literally 'typical food'). In well-traveled towns all over the country, you'll usually find decent international restaurants ranging from Italian wood-fired pizza joints to sushi bars.

What to Eat & Drink

Breakfast for Ticos (Costa Ricans) is usually *gallo pinto* (literally 'spotted rooster'), a stir-fry of last night's rice and beans. When combined, the rice gets colored by the beans, and the mix obtains a speckled appearance. Served with eggs, cheese or *natilla* (sour cream), *gallo pinto* is generally cheap, filling and sometimes downright tasty. If you plan to spend the whole day surfing or hiking, you'll find that *gallo pinto* is great energy food.

Most restaurants offer a set meal at lunch and dinner called a *casado* (literally 'married'), a cheap, well-balanced plate of rice, beans, meat, salad and sometimes *plátanos maduros* (fried sweet green plantains) or *patacones* (twice-fried plantains), which taste something like french fries.

Food is not heavily spiced, unless you're having traditional Caribbean-style cuisine.

Most local restaurants will lay out a bottle of Tabasco-style sauce, homemade salsa and/or Salsa Lizano, the Tico version of Worcestershire sauce and the 'secret' ingredient of *gallo pinto*.

Specialties

Considering the extent of the coastline, it is no surprise that seafood is plentiful, and fish dishes are usually fresh and delicious. While not traditional Tico fare, *ceviche* (seafood marinated in lemon or lime juice, garlic and seasonings) is on most menus, usually made from *pargo* (red snapper), *dorado* (mahi-mahi), octopus or tilapia. Raw fish is marinated in lime juice with some combination of chilis, onions, tomatoes and herbs. Served chilled, it is a delectable way to enjoy fresh seafood. Emphasis is on 'fresh' here – it's raw fish, so if you have reason to believe it is not fresh, don't risk eating it.

Caribbean cuisine is the most distinctive in Costa Rica, having been steeped in indigenous, *criollo* (Creole) and Afro-Caribbean flavors. It's a welcome cultural change of pace after seemingly endless *casados*. Regional specialties include *rondón* (whose moniker comes from 'rundown', meaning whatever the chef can run down), a spicy seafood gumbo; Caribbean-style rice and beans, made with red beans, coconut milk and curry spices; and *patí,* the Caribbean version of an *empanada* (savory turnover), the best street food, bus-ride snack and picnic treat.

The Best...
Spots for Sampling Regional Specialties

1 Caribbean Kalisi Coffee Shop (p115)

2 La Casona del Maíz (p89)

3 Restaurant Betico Mata (p101)

4 Selvin's Restaurant (p138)

IN FOCUS FOOD & DRINK

Drinks

Coffee is probably the most popular beverage in the country and, wherever you go, someone is likely to offer you a *cafecito*. Traditionally, it is served strong and mixed with hot milk to taste, also known as *café con leche*. Purists can get *café negro* (black coffee); if you want a little milk, ask for *leche al lado* (milk on the side). Many trendier places serve espresso drinks.

For a refresher, nothing beats *batidos* – fresh fruit shakes made either *al agua* (with water) or *con leche* (with milk). The array of available tropical fruit can be intoxicating and includes mango, papaya, *piña* (pineapple), *sandía* (watermelon), *melón* (cantaloupe), *mora* (blackberry), *carambola* (starfruit), *cas* (a type of tart guava), *guanabana* (soursop or cherimoya) or *tamarindo* (fruit of the tamarind tree). If you are wary about the condition of the drinking water, ask that your *batido* be made with *agua enbotellada* (bottled water) and *sin hielo* (without ice), though water is generally safe to drink throughout the country.

Pipas are green coconuts that have had their tops hacked off with a machete and spiked with a straw for drinking the coconut water inside – super refreshing when you're wilting in the tropical heat. If you're lucky enough to find it, *agua dulce* is sugarcane water, a slightly grassy, sweet juice that's been pressed through a heavy-duty, hand-cranked mill. On the Caribbean coast, look for *agua de sapo* (literally 'toad water'), a beautiful lemonade laced with fresh ginger juice and *tapa de dulce* (brown sugar; also known as *tapa dulce*). *Resbaladera,* found mostly in the Guanacaste countryside, is a sweet milk – much like *horchata* (Mexican rice drink) – made from rice, barley, milk and cinnamon. Other local drinks you may encounter include *linaza,* a flaxseed drink said to aid digestion, and *chan,* a drink made from chia seed and lemon – an acquired taste due to its slimy (yum!) texture.

The most popular alcoholic drink is *cerveza* (beer; sometimes called *birra* locally), and there are several national brands. Imperial is the most popular – either for its smooth flavor or for the ubiquitous merchandise emblazoned with the eagle-crest logo. Pilsen, which has a higher alcohol content, is known for its saucy calendars featuring *las chicas Pilsen* (the Pilsen girls). Both are tasty pilsners. Bavaria produces a lager and Bavaria Negro, a delicious, full-bodied dark beer; this brand is harder to find. A most welcome burgeoning craft-beer scene is broadening the variety of Costa Rican beers and deepening the tastes of local palates.

After beer, the poison of choice is *guaro,* which is a colorless alcohol distilled from sugarcane and usually consumed by the shot, though you can order it as a sour. It goes down mighty easily but leaves one hell of a hangover.

How to Eat & Drink

Places to Eat

The most popular eating establishment in Costa Rica is the *soda*. These are small, informal lunch counters dishing up a few daily *casados*. Other popular cheapies include the omnipresent fried- and rotisserie-chicken stands.

A regular *restaurante* is usually higher on the price scale and has slightly more atmosphere. Many *restaurantes* serve *casados,* while the fancier places refer to the set lunch as the *almuerzo ejecutivo* (literally 'executive lunch').

For something smaller, *pastelerías* and *panaderías* are shops that sell pastries and bread, while many bars serve *bocas,* which are snack-sized portions of main meals.

Vegetarians & Vegans

If you don't mind rice and beans, Costa Rica is a relatively comfortable place for vegetarians to travel.

Most restaurants will make veggie *casados* on request and many are now including them on the menu. They usually include rice and beans, cabbage salad and one or two selections of variously prepared vegetables or legumes.

With the high influx of tourism, there are also many specialty vegetarian restaurants or restaurants with a veggie menu in places like San José and tourist towns. Lodges in remote areas that offer all-inclusive meal plans can accommodate vegetarian diets with advance notice.

Vegans, macrobiotic and raw food–only travelers will have a tougher time, as there are fewer outlets accommodating those diets. If you intend to keep to your diet, it's best to choose a lodging where you can prepare food yourself. Many towns have health-food stores (*macrobióticas*), but selection varies. Fresh vegetables can be hard to come by in isolated areas and will often be quite expensive, although farmers markets are cropping up throughout the country.

Habits & Customs

When you sit down to eat in a restaurant, it is polite to say *buenos días* (good morning), *buenas tardes* (good afternoon) or *buenas noches* (good evening) to the waitstaff and any people you might be sharing a table with – and it's generally good form to acknowledge everyone in the room this way. It is also polite to say *buen provecho,* which is the equivalent of *bon appetit,* at the start of the meal.

Survival Guide

Crocodiles

S.B. NACE/GETTY IMAGES ©

Directory

Accommodations

o Rates in listings are for the high (dry) season, generally between December to April. Many lodges lower their prices during the low (rainy) season, from May to November. Prices change quickly, so view prices as approximations. Expect to pay a premium during Christmas, New Year and Easter week (Semana Santa).

o Prices are inclusive of tax and given in US dollars, which is the preferred currency for listing rates in Costa Rica. However, colones are accepted everywhere and are usually exchanged at current rates without an additional fee.

o A sales tax of 13% is added to all room and meal fees. Paying with a credit card often incurs additional fees. Listings include taxes in the prices throughout.

o Many hotels charge per person rather than per room – read rates carefully.

o The term *cabina* (cabin) is a catch-all that can define a wide range of prices and amenities – from rustic rooms to very expensive stand-alone dwellings.

o It is always advisable to ask to see a room – and a bathroom – before committing to a stay, especially in budget lodgings. Rooms within a single hotel can vary greatly.

Rates

Budget

o Budget accommodation in the most popular regions of the country are competitive and need to be booked well in advance during the high season.

o At the top end of the budget scale, rooms will frequently include a fan and a bathroom with hot water.

o Hot water in showers is often supplied by electric showerheads, which will dispense hot water if the pressure is kept low.

o Wireless internet is increasingly available at budget accommodations, particularly in popular tourist destinations.

Midrange

o Midrange rooms will be more comfortable than budget options, and will generally include a bathroom with gas-heated hot water, a choice between fans and air-con, and cable or satellite TV.

o Most midrange hotels have wireless internet, though often it is limited to the area near reception or the office.

o Many midrange places offer tour services, and will have an onsite restaurant or bar and a swimming pool or Jacuzzi.

o Many hotels in this price range offer kitchenettes or even full kitchens.

Top End

o This price bracket includes many ecolodges, all-inclusive resorts, and business and chain hotels, in addition to a strong network of intimate boutique hotels, remote jungle camps and upmarket B&Bs.

Price Ranges

The following price ranges refer to a standard double room with bathroom in high season. Unless otherwise stated a combined tourism and sales tax of 13% is included in the price.

$ less than $50

$$ $50–100

$$$ more than $100

- Top-end places in Costa Rica adhere to the same standards of quality and service as similarly priced accommodation in North America and Europe.

- Staff will likely speak English.

- Many lodgings in this category include amenities such as hot-water bath tubs, private decks, satellite TV and air-con as well as concierge, tour and spa services.

Apartments & Villas

The network of long-term rentals has grown dramatically in recent years. These can be an excellent option for families, as they typically include a kitchen and several bedrooms. The following networks of rental apartments are peer reviewed and cover a spectrum of prices, sophistication and amenities.

Airbnb Costa Rica (www. airbnb.com)

Escape Villas (www. villascostarica.com) Has high-end villas across Costa Rica, most near Manuel Antonio. Suitable for families and honeymooners looking for luxury.

Vacation Rentals by Owner (VRBO) (www.vrbo. com) Worldwide network of vacation rentals by owner; has hundreds of properties listed in Costa Rica.

B&Bs

Generally speaking, B&Bs in Costa Rica tend to be mid-range to top-end affairs, often run by resident European and North American expats. You can find B&Bs listed in the *Tico Times* and on the following websites:

BedandBreakfast.com (www.bedandbreakfast.com/costa-rica.html)

Costa Rica Innkeepers Association (www. costaricainnkeepers.com)

Practicalities

- **Emergency** The local tourism board, Instituto Costarricense de Turismo (ICT), is located in San José and distributes a helpful brochure with up-to-date emergency numbers for every region. Dialing 911 will contact emergency services and an English-speaking operator, though response time is slow.

- **DVDs** DVDs in Costa Rica are region 4.

- **Weights & Measures** Costa Ricans use the metric system for weights, distances and measures.

- **Electricity** While Costa Rica uses a 120V/60Hz power system that is compatible with North American devices, power surges and fluctuation are frequent.

Climate

Costa Rica's diverse landscapes and its geographical position create a number of varied climates in close proximity to each other. The highlands are cold, the cloud forest is misty and cool, and San José and the Central Valley live in 'eternal spring'. Both the Pacific and Caribbean coasts are pretty

Reserving by Credit Card

- Some pricier hotels will require confirmation of a reservation with a credit card. Before doing so, note that some top-end hotels require a 50% to 100% payment upfront when you reserve. This rule is not always clearly communicated. In addition, many hotels charge a hefty service fee for credit-card use.

- In most cases advance reservations can be canceled and refunded with enough notice. Ask the hotel about its cancellation policy before booking. (In Costa Rica it's a lot easier to make the reservation than to unmake it.)

- Have the hotel fax or email you a confirmation. Hotels often get overbooked, and if you don't have confirmation, you could be out of a room.

Climate

San José

°C/°F **Temp**

Rainfall inches/mm

J F M A M J J A S O N D

Puerto Limón

°C/°F **Temp**

Rainfall inches/mm

J F M A M J J A S O N D

Puntarenas

°C/°F **Temp**

Rainfall inches/mm

J F M A M J J A S O N D

Electricity

120V/60Hz

120V/60Hz

much sweltering year-round, though are rainier from May to November.

Customs Regulations

○ All travelers over the age of 18 are allowed to enter the country with 5L of wine or spirits and 500g of processed tobacco (400 cigarettes or 50 cigars).

○ Camera gear, binoculars, and camping, snorkeling and other sporting equipment are readily allowed into the country.

○ Dogs and cats are permitted entry providing they have obtained both general health and rabies vaccination certificates.

○ Pornography and illicit drugs are prohibited.

Discount Cards

Costa Rica Card (www. costaricacard.org; individual/ couple/family US$30/40/60) Hotel and restaurant discounts through affiliated network; must be picked up in-country and used with photo ID.

Food

For information about food in Costa Rica, see Food & Drink (p346).

Gay & Lesbian Travelers

In Costa Rica the situation facing gay and lesbian travelers is better than in most Central American countries and some areas of the country – particularly Quepos and Parque Nacional Manuel Antonio – have been gay vacation destinations for two decades. Homosexual acts are legal. Still, most Costa Ricans are tolerant of homosexuality only at a 'don't ask, don't tell' level. Same-sex couples are unlikely to be the subject of harassment, though public displays of affection might attract unwanted attention.

Since 1998 there have been laws on the books to protect 'sexual option', and discrimination is generally prohibited in most facets of society, including employment. And though the country is becoming increasingly more gay friendly along with the rest of the world, this traditional culture has not always been quick to adopt equal protection.

Legal recognition of same-sex partnerships has been a hot topic since 2006 and was a major point of contention in the 2010 presidential race. In January 2012 Costa Rica's primary newspaper La Nación conducted a poll in which 55% of the respondents believed that same-sex couples should have the same rights as heterosexual couples. Then in July 2013 the Costa Rican legislature 'accidentally' passed a law legalizing gay marriage, due to a small change in the bill's wording.

At the time of writing, it had not been vetoed; however, the country's courts have not granted marriage rights to couples who have applied thus far.

The undisputed gay and lesbian capital of Costa Rica is Manuel Antonio; while there, look for the gay magazine *Playita*. The monthly newspaper *Gayness* and the magazine *Gente 10* (in Spanish) are both available at gay bars in San José.

Health

Before You Go

o Get necessary vaccinations four to eight weeks before departure.

o Bring medications in their original containers, clearly labeled.

o If carrying syringes or needles, be sure you have a physician's letter documenting their medical necessity.

o Understand your health care coverage abroad and arrange for travel insurance if you do not have it.

Price Ranges

The following price ranges refer to a standard meal. Prices at small *sodas* (lunch counters) will be the most economical, and will always be posted in colones. Unless otherwise stated, tax is included in the price.

$ less than $10

$$ $10–15

$$$ more than $15

Insurance

o A list of medical evacuation and travel insurance companies can be found on the website of the US State Department under the 'Before You Go' tab.

o Worldwide travel insurance is available at www.lonelyplanet.com/travel_services. You can buy, extend and claim online any time – even if you're already on the road.

Availability & Cost of Health Care

o Good medical care is available in most major cities but may be limited in rural areas.

o For an extensive list of physicians, dentists and hospitals visit http://costarica.usembassy.gov/medical.html.

o Most pharmacies are well supplied and a handful are open 24 hours. Pharmacists are licensed to prescribe medication. If you're taking any medication on a regular basis, make sure you know its generic (scientific) name, since many pharmaceuticals go under different names in Costa Rica.

Infectious Diseases

Dengue Fever (Breakbone Fever)

Dengue is transmitted by Aedes aegypti mosquitoes, which often bite during the daytime and are usually found close to human habitations, often indoors. Dengue is especially common in densely populated urban environments. It usually causes flu-like symptoms including fever, muscle aches, joint pains, headaches, nausea and vomiting, often followed by a rash. Most cases resolve uneventfully in a few days. There is no treatment for dengue fever except taking analgesics such as acetaminophen/paracetamol (Tylenol) and drinking plenty of fluids. Severe cases may require hospitalization for intravenous fluids and supportive care. There is no vaccine. The key to prevention is taking insect-protection measures.

Hepatitis A

The second most common travel-related infection (after traveler's diarrhea). It's a viral infection of the liver that is usually acquired by ingestion of contaminated water, food or ice, though it may also be acquired by direct contact with infected persons. Symptoms may include fever, malaise, jaundice, nausea, vomiting and abdominal pain. Most cases resolve without complications, though hepatitis A occasionally causes severe liver damage. There is no treatment. The vaccine for hepatitis A is extremely safe and highly effective.

Leishmaniasis

This is transmitted by sand flies. Most cases occur in newly cleared forest or areas of secondary growth; the highest incidence is in Talamanca. It causes slow-growing ulcers over exposed parts of the body. There is no vaccine. To protect yourself from sand flies, follow the same precautions as for mosquitoes.

Malaria

Malaria is very rare in Costa Rica, occurring only occasionally in rural parts of the Limón province. It's transmitted by mosquito bites, usually between dusk and dawn. Taking malaria pills is not necessary unless you are making a long stay in the province of Limón (not Puerto Limón). Protection against mosquito bites is most effective.

Traveler's diarrhea

Tap water is safe and of high quality in Costa Rica, but when you're far off the beaten path it's best to avoid tap water unless it has been boiled, filtered or chemically disinfected (with iodine tablets). To prevent diarrhea, be wary of dairy products that might contain unpasteurized milk and be highly selective when eating food from street vendors. If you develop diarrhea, be sure to drink plenty of fluids, preferably with an oral rehydration solution containing lots of salt and sugar. If diarrhea is bloody or persists for more than 72 hours, or is accompanied by fever, shaking chills or severe abdominal pain, seek medical attention.

Typhoid

Caused by ingestion of food or water contaminated by a species of salmonella known as Salmonella typhi. Fever occurs in virtually all cases. Other symptoms may include headache, malaise, muscle aches, dizziness, loss of appetite, nausea and abdominal pain. Possible complications include intestinal perforation, intestinal bleeding, confusion, delirium or (rarely) coma. A pre-trip vaccination is recommended.

Environmental Hazards

Animal Bites

Do not attempt to pet, handle or feed any animal. Any bite or scratch by a mammal, including bats, should be promptly and thoroughly cleansed with large amounts of soap and water, and an antiseptic such as iodine or alcohol should be applied. Contact a local health authority in the event of such an injury.

Insect Bites

No matter how much you safeguard yourself, getting bitten by mosquitoes is part of every traveler's experience here. The best prevention is to stay covered up – wear long pants, long sleeves, a hat, and shoes, not sandals.

Bring a good insect repellent, preferably one containing DEET. Apply to exposed skin and clothing (but not to eyes, mouth, cuts, wounds or irritated skin). Compounds containing DEET should not be used on children under the age of two and should be used sparingly on children under 12.

Invest in a bug net to hang over beds (along with a few thumbtacks or nails with which to hang it). Many hotels in Costa Rica don't have windows (or screens), and a cheap little net will save you plenty of nighttime aggravation. The mesh size should be less than 1.5mm. Dusk is the worst time for mosquitoes, so take extra precautions.

Sun Exposure

Stay out of the midday sun, wear sunglasses and a wide-brimmed hat, and apply sunblock with SPF 15 or higher, with both UVA and UVB protection. Drink plenty of fluids and avoid strenuous exercise when the temperature is high.

Internet Access

○ Costa Rica has plenty of internet cafes and many businesses have wi-fi.

○ Expect to pay US$1 to US$2 per hour in San José and tourist towns.

○ Wi-fi is common in all midrange and top-end hotels; most hotels of all budget ranges have a computer for guest use and/or wi-fi.

Legal Matters

○ If you are arrested your embassy can offer limited assistance. Embassy officials will not bail you out and you are subject to Costa Rican laws, not the laws of your own country.

○ Keep in mind that travelers may be subject to the laws of their own country in regard to sexual relations.

Drivers & Driving Accidents

○ Drivers should carry their passport and driver's license at all times.

○ If you have an accident, call the police immediately to make a report (required for insurance purposes). Leave the vehicles in place until the report has been made and do not make any statements except to members of law-enforcement agencies.

Money

ATMs

○ ATMs, or *cajeros automáticos*, are ubiquitous in all but Costa Rica's smallest towns.

○ Most ATMs dispense US dollars or Costa Rican colones.

Cash & Currency

○ The Costa Rican currency is the colón (plural colones), named after Cristóbal Colón (Christopher Columbus).

○ Bills come in 1000, 2000, 5000, 10,000, 20,000 and 50,000 notes, while coins come in denominations of five, 10, 20, 25, 50, 100 and 500.

○ Paying for things in US dollars is common, and at times is encouraged, since the currency is viewed as being more stable than colones.

○ Newer US dollars (ie big heads) are preferred throughout Costa Rica.

○ When paying in US dollars at a local restaurant, bar or shop the exchange rate can be unfavorable.

Credit Cards

○ Expect a transaction fee on all international credit-card purchases.

○ Cards are widely accepted at midrange and top-end hotels, as well as at top-end restaurants and some travel agencies.

Dollars Versus Colones

While colones are the official currency of Costa Rica, US dollars are virtually legal tender. Case in point: most ATMs in large towns and cities will dispense both currencies. However, it pays to know where and when you should be paying with each currency.

In Costa Rica you can use US dollars to pay for hotel rooms, midrange to top-end meals, admission fees for sights, tours, domestic flights, international buses, car hire, private shuttle buses and large-ticket purchase items. Local meals and drinks, domestic bus fares, taxis and small-ticket purchase items should be paid for in colones.

All of our listings have prices in US dollars.

○ All car-rental agencies require drivers to have a credit card for the deposit (debit cards may not be accepted).

Exchanging Money

All banks will exchange US dollars, and some will exchange euros and British pounds; other currencies are more difficult. Most banks have excruciatingly long lines, especially at the state-run institutions (Banco Nacional, Banco de Costa Rica, Banco Popular), though they don't charge commission on cash exchanges. Private banks (Banex, Banco Interfin, Scotiabank) tend to be faster. Make sure the bills you want to exchange are in good condition or they may be refused.

Tipping

On guided tours, tip the guide a few dollars per person per day. Top-end restaurants may add a 10% service charge to the bill. If not, you might leave a small tip to show your appreciation, but it is not required.

Opening Hours

○ **Restaurants** Usually open from 7am and serve dinner until 9pm, though upscale places may open only for dinner. In remote areas, even the small *sodas* (inexpensive eateries or lunch counters) might open only at specific meal times.

○ **Government offices** Typically open between 8am and 5pm Monday to Friday, but often closed between 11:30am and 1:30pm.

Bargaining

○ A high standard of living along with a steady stream of international tourist traffic means that the Latin American tradition of haggling is uncommon in Costa Rica.

○ Do not try to bargain for hotel room rates as it is very uncommon.

○ Negotiating prices at outdoor markets is acceptable, and bargaining is accepted when hiring long-distance taxis.

○ **Banks** Hours are variable, but most are open at least from 9am to 4pm Monday to Friday.

○ **Shops** Most are open from 8am to 6pm Monday to Saturday.

○ Unless otherwise stated, count on sights, activities and restaurants to be open daily.

Public Holidays

Días feriados (national holidays) are taken seriously in Costa Rica. Banks, public offices and many stores close. During these times, public transport is tight and hotels are heavily booked. Many festivals coincide with public holidays.

○ **New Year's Day** January 1

○ **Semana Santa** (Holy Week; March or April) The Thursday and Friday before Easter Sunday is the official holiday, though most businesses shut down for the whole week. From Thursday to Sunday bars are closed and alcohol sales are prohibited; on Thursday and Friday buses stop running.

○ **Día de Juan Santamaría** (April 11) Honors the national

hero who died fighting William Walker in 1856; major events are held in Alajuela, his hometown.

○ **Labor Day** May 1

○ **Día de la Madre** (Mother's Day; August 15) Coincides with the annual Catholic Feast of the Assumption.

○ **Independence Day** September 15

○ **Día de la Raza** (Columbus Day) October 12

○ **Christmas Day** (December 25) Christmas Eve is also an unofficial holiday.

○ **Last week in December** The week between Christmas and New Year is an unofficial holiday; businesses close and beach hotels are crowded.

Safe Travel

For the latest official reports on travel to Costa Rica, see the websites of the **US State Department** (www.travel.state.gov) or the **UK Foreign & Commonwealth Office** (www.fco.gov.uk).

Earthquakes & Volcanic Eruptions

Costa Rica lies on the edge of active tectonic plates, so it is decidedly earthquake-prone. Recent major quakes occurred in 1990 (7.1 on the Richter scale) and 1991 (7.4). Smaller quakes and tremors happen quite often – particularly on the Península de Nicoya – cracking roads and knocking down telephone lines. The volcanoes in Costa Rica are not really dangerous, though, as long as you stay on designated trails and don't try to peer into the crater of an active volcano. As a precaution, always check with park rangers before setting out in the vicinity of active volcanoes.

Hiking Hazards

Hikers setting out into the wilderness should be adequately prepared for their trips.

◦ Know your limits and don't set out to do a hike you can't reasonably complete.

◦ Carry plenty of water, even on very short trips.

◦ Carry maps, extra food and a compass.

◦ Let someone know where you are going, so they can narrow the search area in the event of an emergency.

◦ Be aware that Costa Rica's wildlife can pose a threat to hikers, particularly in Parque Nacional Corcovado.

Ocean Hazards

Each year Costa Rican waters see approximately 200 drownings, 90% of which are caused by riptides (strong currents that pull the swimmer out to sea). Many deaths in riptides are caused by panicked swimmers struggling to the point of exhaustion. If you are caught in a riptide, do not struggle. Simply float and let the tide carry you out beyond the breakers, after which the riptide will dissipate. Then swim parallel to the beach and allow the surf to carry you back in.

Thefts & Muggings

The biggest danger that most travelers face is petty theft, primarily from pickpockets and car break-ins. Be aware of your surroundings at all times and never leave anything in your car.

Telephone

◦ Cellular service now covers most of the country and nearly all of the country that is accessible to tourists.

◦ To call Costa Rica from abroad, use the country code (506) before the eight-digit number.

◦ Due to the increasing popularity of voice-over IP services such as Skype, and more reliable ethernet connections, traveling with a smartphone can be the cheapest way to call internationally.

Time

Costa Rica is six hours behind GMT, so Costa Rican time is equivalent to Central Time in North America. There is no daylight-saving time.

Important Numbers

Emergency ☏911

Fire ☏118

Police ☏117

Red Cross ☏128, 2542-5000

Traffic Police ☏2222-9330

Tourist Information

The government-run tourism board, the **ICT** (☏ in USA 800-343-6332; www.visitcostarica.com), has two offices in the capital. The ICT can provide you with free maps, a master bus schedule and information on road conditions in the hinterlands. English is spoken. Consult the ICT's English-language website for information. From the USA call the ICT's toll-free number for brochures and information.

Travelers with Disabilities

Although Costa Rica has an equal-opportunity law for disabled people, the law applies only to new or newly remodeled businesses and is loosely enforced. Therefore, very few hotels and restaurants except for the most top end have features specifically suited to wheelchair use. Many don't have ramps, while room or bathroom doors are

Passport

○ Citizens of all nations are required to have a passport that is valid for at least six months beyond the dates of your trip.

○ Though seldom enforced, the law requires that you carry your passport at all times.

rarely wide enough to accommodate a wheelchair.

Visas

Passport-carrying nationals of the following countries are allowed 90 days' stay with no visa: Argentina, Australia, Canada, Chile, Iceland, Ireland, Israel, Japan, Mexico, New Zealand, Panama, South Africa, the USA and most Western European countries. Most others require a visa from a Costa Rican embassy or consulate.

For the latest info on visas, check the websites of the ICT (p357) or the **Costa Rican Embassy** (www.costarica-embassy.org) in Washington, DC.

Extensions

Extending your stay beyond the authorized 30 or 90 days is time consuming; it's easier to leave the country for 72 hours and then re-enter.

Women Travelers

Most female travelers experience little more than a *'mi amor'* ('my love') or an appreciative hiss from the local men. But, in general, Costa Rican men consider foreign women to have looser morals and to be easier conquests than Ticas (female Costa Ricans). Men will often make flirtatious comments to single women, particularly blondes, and women traveling together are not exempt. The best response is to do what Ticas do: ignore it completely. Women who firmly resist unwanted verbal advances from men are normally treated with respect.

Transport

●●●

Getting There & Away

Entering the Country

○ Entering Costa Rica is mostly free of hassle, with the exception of some long queues at the airport.

○ Overland border crossings are straightforward and travelers can move freely between Panama to the south and Nicaragua to the north.

○ Some foreign nationals will require a visa. Be aware that you cannot get a visa at the border.

✈ Air

○ Costa Rica is well connected by air to other Central and South American countries, as well as the USA.

○ International flights arrive at Aeropuerto Internacional Juan Santamaría, 17km northwest of San José, in the town of Alajuela.

○ Aeropuerto Internacional Daniel Oduber Quirós in Liberia also receives international flights from the USA, the Americas and Canada. It serves a number of American and Canadian airlines and some charters from London in the UK.

○ The national airline, Avianca (part of the Central American airline consortium Grupo TACA), flies to the USA and Latin America, including Cuba.

○ The US Federal Aviation Administration has assessed Costa Rica's aviation authorities to be in compliance with international safety standards.

Sea

Cruise ships stop in Costa Rican ports and enable passengers to make a quick foray into the country. Typically, ships dock at either the Pacific ports of Caldera, Quepos and Bahía Drake, or the Caribbean port of Puerto Limón.

●●●

Getting Around

✈ Air

Scheduled Flights

○ Costa Rica's domestic airlines are **Nature Air** (☏ 2220-3054; www.natureair.com) and **Sansa** (☏ 2290-4100; www.flysansa.com). Sansa is linked with Grupo TACA.

○ Both airlines fly small passenger planes, and you're allocated a baggage allowance of no more than 12kg.

○ Space is limited and demand is high in the dry season, so reserve and pay for tickets in advance.

○ In Costa Rica schedules change constantly and delays are frequent because of inclement weather. You should not arrange a domestic flight that makes a tight connection with an international flight back home.

○ All domestic flights originate and terminate at San José. Destinations reached from San José include Bahía Drake, Barra del Colorado, Golfito, Liberia, Palmar Sur, Playa Nosara, Playa Sámara/Carrillo, Playa Tamarindo, Puerto Jiménez, Quepos, Tambor and Tortuguero.

Climate Change & Travel

Every form of transport that relies on carbon-based fuel generates CO_2, the main cause of human-induced climate change. Modern travel is dependent on aeroplanes, which might use less fuel per person than most cars but travel much greater distances. The altitude at which aircraft emit gases (including CO_2) and particles also contributes to their climate change impact. Many websites offer 'carbon calculators' that allow people to estimate the carbon emissions generated by their journey and, for those who wish to do so, to offset the impact of the greenhouse gases emitted with contributions to portfolios of climate-friendly initiatives throughout the world. Lonely Planet offsets the carbon footprint of all staff and author travel.

Domestic Air Routes

----- High season scheduled flights with Sansa or Nature Air
- - - Some connecting flights with Sansa or Nature Air
• Some airports for light charter planes
Flights subject to change, especially in low season

Charters

○ Travelers on a larger budget or in a larger party should consider chartering a private plane, which is by far the quickest way to travel around the country.

○ It takes under 90 minutes to fly to most destinations, though weather conditions can significantly speed up or delay travel time.

○ The two most reputable charters in the country are Nature Air (p359) and **Alfa Romeo Aero Taxi** (www.alfaromeoair.com). Both can be booked directly through the company, a tour agency or some high-end accommodations.

○ Luggage space on charters is extremely limited.

Bicycle

○ With an increasingly large network of paved secondary roads and heightened awareness of cyclists, Costa Rica is emerging as one of Central America's most comfortable cycle-touring destinations.

○ Mountain bikes and beach cruisers can be rented in towns with a significant tourist presence, for US$6 to US$15 per day. A few companies organize bike tours around Costa Rica.

Boat

○ Ferries cross the Golfo de Nicoya, connecting the central Pacific coast with the southern tip of Península de Nicoya.

○ The **Coonatramar Ferry** (📱 2661-1069; www. coonatramar.com; adult/ child/bicycle/motorcycle/ car US$2/1/4/6/18) links the port of Puntarenas with Playa Naranjo four times daily. The **Ferry Naviera Tambor** (📱 2661-2084; www. navieratambor.com; adult/ child/bicycle/motorcycle/car US$1.65/1/4.50/7/23) travels between Puntarenas and Paquera every two hours, for a bus connection to Montezuma.

- On the Golfo Dulce a daily passenger ferry links Golfito with Puerto Jiménez on the Península de Osa, and a weekday water taxi travels to and from Playa Zancudo. On the other side of the Península de Osa, water taxis connect Bahía Drake with Sierpe.

- On the Caribbean coast there is a bus and boat service that runs several times a day, linking Cariari and Tortuguero, while another links Parismina and Siquirres.

- Boats ply the canals that run along the coast from Moín to Tortuguero, although no regular service exists. A daily water taxi connects Puerto Viejo de Sarapiquí with Trinidad on the Río San Juan. The San Juan is Nicaraguan territory, so take your passport. You can try to arrange boat transportation for Barra del Colorado in any of these towns.

Bus

Local Buses

- Local buses are a cheap and reliable way of getting around Costa Rica. The longest domestic journey out of San José costs less than US$20.

- San José is the transportation center for the country, though there is no central terminal. Bus offices are scattered around the city: some large bus companies have big terminals that sell tickets in advance, while others have little more than a stop – sometimes unmarked.

- Buses can be very crowded but don't usually pass up passengers on account of being too full. Note that there are no buses from Thursday to Saturday before Easter Sunday.

- There are two types of bus: *directo* and *colectivo*. The *directo* buses should go from one destination to the next with few stops; the *colectivos* make more stops and are very slow going.

- Trips longer than four hours usually include a rest stop as buses do not have toilets.

- Space is limited on board, so if you have to check luggage be watchful. Theft from overhead racks is rampant, though it's much less common than in other Central American countries.

- Bus schedules fluctuate wildly, so always confirm the time when you buy your ticket. If you are catching a bus that picks you up somewhere along a road, get to the roadside early.

- For information on departures from San José, pay a visit to the ICT office to pick up the reasonably up-to-date copy of the master bus schedule, which is also available online at www.visitcostarica.com.

Shuttle Buses

The tourist-van shuttle services (aka gringo buses) are an alternative to the standard intercity buses. Shuttles are provided by **Grayline** (☎ 2220-2126; www.grayline-costarica.com) and **Interbus** (☎ 2283-5573; www.interbusonline.com). Both companies run overland transportation from San José to the most popular destinations, as well as directly between other destinations (see the websites for the comprehensive list). These services will pick you up at your hotel, and reservations can be made online, or through local travel agencies and hotel owners.

Car

- Drivers in Costa Rica are required to have a valid driving license from their home country. Many places will also accept an International Driving Permit (IDP), issued by the automobile association in your country of origin. After 90 days, however, you will need to get a Costa Rican driver's license.

- Gasoline (petrol) and diesel are widely available, and 24-hour service stations are along the Interamericana Hwy. At the time of research, fuel prices averaged US$1.25 per liter.

- In more remote areas, fuel will be more expensive and might be sold at the neighborhood *pulpería* (corner store).

- Spare parts may be hard to find, especially for vehicles with sophisticated electronics and emissions-control systems.

Rental & Insurance

- There are car-rental agencies in San José and in popular tourist destinations on the Pacific coast.

- All of the major international car-rental agencies have outlets in Costa Rica, though you can sometimes get better deals from local companies.

- Due to road conditions, it is necessary to invest in a 4WD unless travel is limited only to the Interamericana.

SURVIVAL GUIDE   GETTING AROUND

○ Many agencies will insist on 4WD in the rainy season, when driving through rivers is a matter of course.

○ To rent a car you need a valid driver's license, a major credit card and a passport. The minimum age for car rental is 21 years.

○ Carefully inspect rented cars for minor damage and make sure that any damage is noted on the rental agreement. If your car breaks down, call the rental company. Don't attempt to get the car fixed yourself – most companies won't reimburse expenses without prior authorization.

○ Prices vary considerably, but on average you can expect to pay over US$200 per week for a standard SUV, including *kilometraje libre* (unlimited mileage). Economy cars are much cheaper, as little as US$80 a week. The price of mandatory insurance makes this more expensive, often doubling the rate.

○ Costa Rican insurance is mandatory, even if you have insurance at home. Expect to pay about US$15 to US$25 per day. Many rental companies won't rent you a car without it. The basic insurance that all drivers must buy is from a government monopoly, the Instituto Nacional de Seguros. This insurance does not cover your rental car at all, only damages to other people, their cars, or property. It is legal to drive only with this insurance, but it can be difficult to negotiate with a rental agency to allow you to drive away with only this minimum standard. Full insurance through the rental agency can be up to US$50 a day.

○ The roads in Costa Rica are rough and rugged, meaning that minor accidents or car damage are common.

○ Note that if you pay basic insurance with a gold or platinum credit card, the card company will usually take

responsibility for damages to the car, in which case you can forgo the cost of the full insurance. Make sure you verify this with your credit-card company ahead of time.

○ Most insurance policies do not cover damage caused by flooding or driving through a river, so be aware of the extent of your policy.

○ Rental rates fluctuate wildly, so shop around. Some agencies offer discounts for extended rentals. Note that rental offices at the airport charge a 12% fee in addition to regular rates.

○ Thieves can easily recognize rental cars. Never leave anything in sight in a parked car – not a thing! – and remove all luggage from the trunk overnight. Whenever possible, park the car in a guarded parking lot rather than on the street.

○ Motorcycles (including Harleys) can be rented in San José and Escazú.

Flat-Tire Scam

For years Aeropuerto Internacional Juan Santamaría has suffered from a scam involving sudden flat tires on rental cars. Many readers have told of similar incidents and it is commonly reported, but it continues to happen.

It goes like this: after you pick up a rental car and drive out of the city, the car gets a flat; as you pull over to fix it, the disabled vehicle is approached by a group of locals, ostensibly to help. There is inevitably some confusion with the changing of the tire, and in the commotion you are relieved of your wallet, luggage or other valuables.

This incident has happened enough times to suggest that travelers should be very wary – and aware – if somebody pulls over to help after they get a flat on a recently rented car. Keep your wallet and passport on your person whenever you get out of a car.

Road Conditions & Hazards

○ The quality of roads varies from the quite smoothly paved Interamericana to the barely passable rural back roads. Any can suffer from landslides, sudden flooding and fog.

○ Most roads are single-lane and winding, lacking hard shoulders; others are dirt-and-mud affairs that climb mountains and traverse rivers.

○ Drive defensively and expect a variety of obstructions in the roadway – from cyclists and pedestrians to broken-down cars and cattle. Unsigned speed bumps are placed on

Driving Through Rivers

Driving in Costa Rica will likely necessitate a river crossing at some point. Unfortunately, too many travelers have picked up their off-road skills from watching TV, and every season Ticos (Costa Ricans) get a good chuckle out of the number of dead vehicles they help wayward travelers fish out of waterways.

If you're driving through water, follow the rules below:

o **Only do this in a 4WD** Don't drive through a river in a car. (It may seem ridiculous to have to say this, but it's done all the time.) Getting out of a steep, gravel riverbed requires a 4WD. Besides, car engines flood very easily.

o **Check the depth of the water before driving through** To accommodate an average rental 4WD, the water should be no deeper than above the knee. In a sturdier vehicle (Toyota 4Runner or equivalent), water can be waist deep.

o **The water should be calm** If the river is gushing so that there are white crests on the water, do not try to cross. Not only will the force of the water flood the engine, it could sweep the car away.

o **Drive very, very slowly** The pressure of driving through a river too quickly will send the water right into the engine and will impair the electrical system. Keep steady pressure on the accelerator so that the tailpipe doesn't fill with water, but go slowly.

o **Err on the side of caution** Car-rental agencies in Costa Rica do not insure for water damage, so ruining a car in a river can come at an extremely high cost.

some stretches of road without warning.

o Roads around major tourist areas are adequately marked; all others are not.

o Always ask about road conditions before setting out, especially in the rainy season; a number of roads become impassable in the rainy season.

Road Rules

o There are speed limits of 100km/h or less on all primary roads and 60km/h or less on secondary roads.

o Traffic police use radar, and speed limits are enforced with speeding tickets.

o It's illegal to stop in an intersection or make a right turn on a red light.

o At unmarked intersections, yield to the car on your right.

o Drive on the right. Passing is allowed only on the left.

o If you are driving and see oncoming cars with headlights flashing, it often means that there is a road problem or a radar speed trap ahead. Slow down immediately.

Local Transportation

Bus

Local buses operate chiefly in San José, Puntarenas, San Isidro, Golfito and Puerto Limón, connecting urban and suburban areas. Most local buses pick up passengers on the street and on main roads. For years, these buses were converted from the USA, but they have been slowly upgraded and now many include coach buses.

Taxi

o In San José taxis have meters, called *marías*. Note that it is illegal for a driver not to use the meter. Outside of San José, however, most taxis don't have meters and fares tend to be agreed upon in advance. Bargaining is quite acceptable.

o In rural areas, 4WD jeeps are often used as taxis, and prices vary wildly, though generally speaking a 10-minute ride should cost between US$5 and US$15.

o Taxi drivers are not normally tipped unless they assist with your luggage or have provided above-average service.

Language

Spanish pronunciation is not difficult as most of the sounds are also found in English. You can read our pronunciation guides below as if they were English and you'll be understood just fine. And if you pronounce 'kh' in our guides as a throaty sound and remember to roll the 'r,' you'll even sound like a real Costa Rican.

To enhance your trip with a phrasebook, visit lonelyplanet.com. Lonely Planet iPhone phrasebooks are available through the Apple App store.

BASICS

Hello.
Hola. o·la

How are you?
¿Cómo está? (pol) ko·mo es·ta
¿Cómo estás? (inf) ko·mo es·tas

I'm fine, thanks.
Bien, gracias. byen gra·syas

Excuse me. (to get attention)
Con permiso. kon per·mee·so

Yes./No.
Sí./No. see/no

Thank you.
Gracias. gra·syas

You're welcome./That's fine.
Con mucho gusto. kon moo·cho goo·sto

Goodbye./See you later.
Adiós./Nos vemos. a·dyos/nos ve·mos

Do you speak English?
¿Habla inglés? (pol) a·bla een·gles
¿Hablas inglés? (inf) a·blas een·gles

I don't understand.
No entiendo. no en·tyen·do

How much is this?
¿Cuánto cuesta? kwan·to kwes·ta

Can you reduce the price a little?
¿Podría bajarle el po·dree·a ba·khar·le
el precio? el pre·syo

ACCOMMODATIONS

I'd like to make a booking.
Quisiera reservar kee·sye·ra re·ser·var
una habitación. oo·na a·bee·ta·syon

Do you have a room available?
¿Tiene una habitación? tye·ne oo·na a·bee·ta·syon

How much is it per night?
¿Cuánto es por noche? kwan·to es por no·che

EATING & DRINKING

I'd like ..., please.
Quisiera ..., por favor. kee·sye·ra ... por fa·vor

That was delicious!
¡Estuvo delicioso! es·too·vo de·lee·syo·so

Bring the bill/check, please.
La cuenta, por favor. la kwen·ta por fa·vor

I'm allergic to ...
Soy alérgico/a al ... (m/f) soy a·ler·khee·ko/a al ...

I don't eat ...
No como ... no ko·mo ...
  chicken *pollo* po·yo
  fish *pescado* pes·ka·do
  (red) meat *carne (roja)* kar·ne (ro·kha)

EMERGENCIES

I'm ill.
Estoy enfermo/a. (m/f) es·toy en·fer·mo/a

Help!
¡Socorro! so·ko·ro

Call a doctor!
¡Llame a un doctor! ya·me a oon dok·tor

Call the police!
¡Llame a la policía! ya·me a la po·lee·see·a

DIRECTIONS

Where's a/the ...?
¿Dónde está ...? don·de es·ta ...
  bank
  el banco el ban·ko
  ... embassy
  la embajada de ... la em·ba·kha·da de ...
  market
  el mercado el mer·ka·do
  museum
  el museo el moo·se·o
  restaurant
  un restaurante oon res·tow·ran·te
  toilet
  el baño el ba·nyo
  tourist office
  la oficina de la o·fee·see·na de
  turismo too·rees·mo

Behind the Scenes

Our Readers

Many thanks to the travelers who used the last edition and wrote to us with helpful hints, useful advice and interesting anecdotes: Orsolya Nagy, Ida Slåtto Neerbye, Allan Rudick, Dan Sponseller.

Author Thanks

Wendy Yanagihara

I wish to acknowledge some amazing staff at Lonely Planet with whom I've had the pleasure of working, who have since departed, and who are greatly missed. Catherine, Kathleen and Bruce laid the groundwork for *Costa Rica 11*. Special thanks in Costa Rica go to Corey, Chapu, Bob, Monique and Marcel, Kathleen, rangers Herold and Roger, Yolanda and Manuel. *Abrazos* to Chris for traveling all the way from the Middle East to Central America, and to my superstar support system in Carp.

Acknowledgments

Climate map data adapted from Peel MC, Finlayson BL & McMahon TA (2007) 'Updated World Map of the Köppen-Geiger Climate Classification', *Hydrology and Earth System Sciences*, 11, 163344.

Cover photographs: Front: Cordillera Central, Kevin Schafer/Alamy; Back: Frog, Parque Nacional Tortuguero, Paolo Giocoso/4Corners.

This Book

This 3rd edition of Lonely Planet's *Discover Costa Rica* guidebook was researched and written by Wendy Yanagihara, Gregor Clark and Mara Vorhees. The previous edition was written by Nate Cavalieri, Adam Skolnick and Wendy Yanagihara. This guidebook was commissioned in Lonely Planet's US office and produced by the following:

Destination Editor Brana Vladisavljevic
Coordinating Editor Andrea Dobbin
Product Editor Anne Mason
Senior Cartographer Mark Griffiths
Book Designers Lauren Egan, Mazzy Prinsep
Assisting Book Designers Katherine Marsh, Virginia Moreno, Jessica Rose, Wibowo Rusli
Assisting Editors Judith Bamber, Jenna Myers, Alison Ridgway, Tracy Whitmey
Cover Researcher Naomi Parker
Thanks to Penny Cordner, Ryan Evans, Larissa Frost, Jouve India, Claire Naylor, Karyn Noble, John Taufa, Juan Winata

SEND US YOUR FEEDBACK

Index

INDEX S-W

How to Use This Book

These symbols give you the vital information for each listing:

♩	Telephone Numbers	🛜	Wi-Fi Access	🚌	Bus
⊙	Opening Hours	🏊	Swimming Pool	⛴	Ferry
P	Parking	🥗	Vegetarian Selection	M	Metro
⊖	Nonsmoking	📋	English-Language Menu	S	Subway
❄	Air-Conditioning	👨‍👩‍👧	Family-Friendly	⊖	London Tube
@	Internet Access	🐾	Pet-Friendly	🚊	Tram

Look out for these icons:

FREE No payment required

🌿 A green or sustainable option

Our authors have nominated these places as demonstrating a strong commitment to sustainability – for example by supporting local communities and producers, operating in an environmentally friendly way, or supporting conservation projects.

All reviews are ordered in our authors' preference, starting with their most preferred option. Additionally:

Sights are arranged in the geographic order that we suggest you visit them, and within this order, by author preference.

Eating and Sleeping reviews are ordered by price range (budget, mid-range, top end) and within these ranges, by author preference.

Map Legend

Sights
- 🏖 Beach
- 🛕 Buddhist
- 🏰 Castle
- ✝ Christian
- 🕉 Hindu
- ☪ Islamic
- ✡ Jewish
- ◎ Monument
- 🏛 Museum/Gallery
- ◎ Ruin
- 🍷 Winery/Vineyard
- 🦁 Zoo
- ◎ Other Sight

Activities, Courses & Tours
- 🤿 Diving/Snorkelling
- 🛶 Canoeing/Kayaking
- 🎿 Skiing
- 🏄 Surfing
- 🏊 Swimming/Pool
- 🚶 Walking
- 🏄 Windsurfing
- ◎ Other Activity/Course/Tour

Sleeping
- ◎ Sleeping
- ◎ Camping

Eating
- ◎ Eating

Drinking
- ◎ Drinking
- ◎ Cafe

Entertainment
- ◎ Entertainment

Shopping
- ◎ Shopping

Information
- ◎ Post Office
- ◎ Tourist Information

Transport
- ◎ Airport
- ◎ Border Crossing
- ◎ Bus
- ◎ Cable Car/Funicular
- ◎ Cycling
- ◎ Ferry
- ◎ Monorail
- P Parking
- S S-Bahn
- ◎ Taxi
- ◎ Train/Railway
- ◎ Tram
- ◎ Tube Station
- U U-Bahn
- M Underground Train Station
- • Other Transport

Routes
- Tollway
- Freeway
- Primary
- Secondary
- Tertiary
- Lane
- Unsealed Road
- Plaza/Mall
- Steps
- Tunnel
- Pedestrian Overpass
- Walking Tour
- Walking Tour Detour
- Path

Boundaries
- International
- State/Province
- Disputed
- Regional/Suburb
- Marine Park
- Cliff
- Wall

Population
- ❂ Capital (National)
- ◉ Capital (State/Province)
- ◯ City/Large Town
- ◯ Town/Village

Geographic
- 🏠 Hut/Shelter
- 🔦 Lighthouse
- ◎ Lookout
- ▲ Mountain/Volcano
- ◎ Oasis
- ◎ Park
-)(Pass
- ◎ Picnic Area
- ◎ Waterfall

Hydrography
- River/Creek
- Intermittent River
- Swamp/Mangrove
- Reef
- Canal
- Water
- Dry/Salt/Intermittent Lake
- Glacier

Areas
- Beach/Desert
- Cemetery (Christian)
- Cemetery (Other)
- Park/Forest
- Sportsground
- Sight (Building)
- Top Sight (Building)

Our Story

A beat-up old car, a few dollars in the pocket and a sense of adventure. In 1972 that's all Tony and Maureen Wheeler needed for the trip of a lifetime – across Europe and Asia overland to Australia. It took several months, and at the end – broke but inspired – they sat at their kitchen table writing and stapling together their first travel guide, *Across Asia on the Cheap*. Within a week they'd sold 1500 copies. Lonely Planet was born.

Today, Lonely Planet has offices in Melbourne, London, Oakland and Delhi, with more than 600 staff and writers. We share Tony's belief that 'a great guidebook should do three things: inform, educate and amuse'.

Our Writers

Wendy Yanagihara

Coordinating Author, Central Pacific Coast, Southern Costa Rica & Península de Osa
Wendy Yanagihara first ventured to Costa Rica in 1996. Ten years later, she went on her first research trip to the land of *pura vida* and has been covering it since. She has explored Costa Rica from border to border and coast to coast as well as contributing to over 20 guides for Lonely Planet, including *Japan, Vietnam, Mexico* and *Grand Canyon National Park*. As it tends to do, Costa Rica has helped transform her into a budding birder, better sloth-spotter, still-terrible surfer (who sticks to the bunny breaks) and improviser of California-style *gallo pinto*.

Gregor Clark

San José, Central Valley, Caribbean Coast On his first Costa Rican adventure in 1997, Gregor made a beeline for Corcovado National Park, where he so thoroughly enjoyed hiking and camping that he returned with his fiancée (now wife) the next year. Highlights of researching *Costa Rica 11* included discovering off-the-beaten track destinations such as La Danta Salvaje and Volcan Turrialba Lodge with his nature-loving family, and seeing his first quetzal in the company of daughter Meigan Quetzal Clark. Gregor contributes regularly to Lonely Planet's Latin American and European guides.

Read more about Gregor at:
lonelyplanet.com/thorntree/profiles/gregorclark

Mara Vorhees

Northwestern Costa Rica, Península de Nicoya In 18 years of travel to Costa Rica, Mara has spotted 156 species of birds, all four New-World monkeys, anteaters, sloths and tapirs, a kinkajou and a jaguarundi. None of it, she attests, is quite as wild as her four-year-old twins, who accompanied her while hiking, swimming, rafting, birding and horseback-riding around Costa Rica. Mara has written many guidebooks for Lonely Planet, including *Central America on a Shoestring* and *Belize*. When not spying on sloths, she lives in Somerville, Massachusetts with her husband, two kiddies and two kitties. Follow her adventures online at www.havetwinswilltravel.com.

Published by Lonely Planet Publications Pty Ltd
ABN 36 005 607 983
3rd edition – December 2014
ISBN 978 1 74220 900 5
© Lonely Planet 2014   Photographs © as indicated 2014
10 9 8 7 6 5 4 3 2 1
Printed in China